The Constitution of the United States of America:

Annotated with

The Federalist Papers: Modern English Edition Two

Mary E Webster, editor

Table of Contents

do ordain and establish this.. **84**

Constitution for the United States of America **84**

ARTICLE 1 SECTION 1. All legislative Powers herein granted **95**

shall be vested in a Congress of the United States, which shall consist of a Senate and House of Representatives. **97**

ARTICLE 1 SECTION 2. The House of Representatives shall be composed of Members chosen every second Year... **99**

by the People of the several States, and the Electors in each State shall have the Qualifications requisite for Electors of the most numerous Branch of the State legislature. **103**

No person shall be a Representative who shall not have attained to the Age of twenty five Years, and been seven Years a Citizen of the United States, and who shall not, when elected, be an Inhabitant to that State in which he shall be chosen. **105**

[Representatives and direct Taxes shall be apportioned among the several States which may be included within this Union, according to their respective Numbers, which shall be determined by adding to the whole Number of free Persons, including those bound to Service for a Term of Years, and excluding Indians not taxed, three-fifths of all other persons.] **108**

*changed by Amendment 14, section 2, ratified in 1868: **109**

Representatives shall be apportioned among the several States according to their respective numbers, counting the whole number of persons in each State, excluding Indians not taxed. But when the right to vote at any election for the choice of Electors for President and Vice-President of the United States, Representatives in Congress, the executive and

Legislature thereof; but the Congress may at any time by Law make or alter such Regulations, except as to the Places of Chusing Senators. 140

The Congress shall assemble at least once in every Year, and such Meeting shall be [on the first Monday in December,]** unless they shall by Law appoint a different Day.. 146

Changed by Amendment 20, section 2, ratified in 1933: 146

Section 2. The Congress shall assemble at least once in every year, and such meeting shall begin at noon on the 3d day of January, unless they shall by law appoint a different day. 146

ARTICLE 1 SECTION 5. Each House shall be the Judge of the Elections, Returns and Qualifications of its own Members, and a Majority of each shall constitute a Quorum to do Business; but a smaller Number may adjourn from day to day, and may be authorized to compel the Attendance of absent Members, in such manner, and under such Penalties, as each House may provide.. 148

Each House may determine the Rules of its Proceedings, punish its Members for disorderly Behaviour, and, with the Concurrence of two thirds, expel a member. 148

Each House shall keep a Journal of its Proceedings, and from time to time publish the same, excepting such Parts as may in their Judgment require Secrecy; and the Yeas and Nays of the Members of either House on any question shall, at the desire of one fifth of those Present, be entered on the Journal. 148

Neither House, during the Session of Congress, shall, without the Consent of the other, adjourn for more than three days, nor to any other Place than that in which the two Houses shall be sitting. 148

ARTICLE 1 SECTION 6. The Senators and Representatives shall receive a Compensation for their Services, to be ascertained by Law, and paid out in the Treasury of the United States.. 150

They shall in all Cases, except Treason, Felony and Breach of the Peace, be privileged from Arrest during their Attendance at the Session of their respective Houses, and in going to and returning from the same; and for any Speech or Debate in either House, they shall not be questioned in any other Place.. 150

No Senator or Representative shall, during the Time for which he was elected, be appointed to any civil Office under the Authority of the United States, which shall have been created, or the Emoluments whereof shall have been increased during such time; and no Person holding any Office

[The Electors shall meet in their respective States, and vote by Ballot for two Persons, of whom one at least shall not be an Inhabitant of the same State with themselves. And they shall make a List of all Persons voted for, and of the Number of Votes for each; which List they shall sign and certify, and transmit sealed to the Government of the United States. Directed to the President of the Senate. The President of the Senate shall, in the Presence of the Senate and House of Representatives, open all the Certificates, and the Votes shall then be counted. The Person having the greatest Number of Votes shall be the President, if such Number be a Majority of the whole Number of Electors appointed; and if there be more than one who have such Majority, and have an equal Number of Votes, then the House of Representatives shall immediately chuse by Ballot one of them for President; and if no person have a Majority, then from the five highest on the List the said House shall in like manner chuse the President. But in chusing the President, the Votes shall be taken by States, the Representation from each State having one Vote; a quorum for this Purpose shall consist of a Member or Members from two-thirds of the States, and a Majority of all the States shall be necessary to a Choice. In every Case, after the Choice of the President, the Person having the greatest Number of Votes of the Electors shall be the Vice President. But if there should remain two or more who have equal Votes, the Senate shall chuse from them by Ballot the Vice President.] 253

The Electors shall meet in their respective states, and vote by ballot for President, and Vice President, one of whom, at least, shall not be an inhabitant of the same State with themselves; they shall name in their ballots the person voted for as President, and in distinct ballots the person voted for as Vice-President, and they shall make distinct lists of all persons voted for as President, and of all persons voted for as Vice-President, and of the number of votes for each, which lists they shall sign and certify, and transmit sealed to the seat of the government of the United States, directed to the President of the Senate;--The President of the Senate shall, in the presence of the Senate and House of Representatives, open all the certificates and the votes shall then be counted; The person having the greatest number of votes for President, shall be the President, if such number be a majority of the whole number of Electors appointed; and if no person have such majority, then from the persons having the highest numbers not exceeding three on the list of those voted for as President, the House of Representatives shall choose immediately, by ballot, the President. But in choosing the President, the votes shall be taken by states, the representation from each State having one vote; a quorum for this purpose shall consist of a member or members from two-thirds of the states, and a majority of all the states shall be necessary to a choice. [And if the House of Representatives shall not choose a President whenever the right of choice shall devolve upon them, before the fourth day of March next following, then the Vice-President shall act as President, as in the case of the death or other constitutional disability of the President---]* The person having the greatest number of votes as Vice-President, shall be the Vice-President, if such number be a majority of the whole number of Electors appointed, and if no person have a majority, then from the two highest numbers an the list, the Senate shall choose the Vice-President; a quorum for the purpose shall consist of two-thirds of the whale number of Senators, and a majority of the whale number shall be

ARTICLE 5. The Congress, whenever two-thirds of both Houses shall deem it necessary, shall propose Amendments to this Constitution, or, on the Application of the Legislatures of two thirds of the several States, shall call a Convention for proposing Amendments, which, in either Case, shall be valid to all Intents and Purposes, as Part of this Constitution, when ratified by the Legislatures of three-fourths of the several States, or by Conventions in three fourths thereof, as the one or the other Mode of Ratification may be proposed by the Congress; provided that no Amendment which may be made prior to the Year One thousand eight hundred and eight shall in any manner affect the first and fourth Clauses

Editor's note

       This book uses my second "translation" of the Federalist Papers. <u>The Federalist Papers: Modern English Edition Two</u>, to annotate the United States Constitution. This book is not a substitute for reading the Federalist Papers, either the original or one of my translations.

       I hope that the Papers' comments about specific clauses will entice the reader to want to learn more by reading all the Papers. They give a full overview of the Founding Fathers' vision and hopes for the United States. Their keen insight into psychology-- individual and group behavior--that is needed in the 21st century more than any time in our history.

       I have repeated some paragraphs in the Papers to conform to the structure of the Constitution. The index lists all the Papers and paragraph numbers used in this text. I always put the paragraph numbers in brackets after the Paper number.

       Any errors or omissions in this text are entirely mine. As I find them, I will update the book, an advantage of print-on-demand. I appreciate feedback and can be reached through my website.

                                     Mary E Webster
                                     http://Mary.Webster.org

                                     March 2010

Constitution of the United States of America

Before studying the Constitution, a couple of basic questions need to be asked. Why did the colonies combine to form one country? Prior to the revolution they had been part of a country. Why did they immediately form another country with power over the individual colonies/States?

Why Do We Need a Federal Government?

Number 15 [12]

...Why should we have a government? Because the passions of men won't conform to the dictates of reason and justice without constraint...

Number 23 [3]

The most important reasons for a union and federal government are:
- Defense.
- To keep the peace against both internal turmoil and external attacks.
- To regulate commerce with other nations and between the States.
- To supervise our political and commercial interests with foreign countries.

Number 51 [4]

Government is, after all, the greatest of all reflections on human nature. If men were angels, no government would be necessary. If angels governed men, no controls on government would be necessary. But men govern men. So, security measures are necessary to control the abuses of government.

Six Categories of Federal Power

Having just revolted against a powerful central government, the first worry of the newly liberated citizens was creating the same situation in North America. Unfortunately, as we will see later, the federal powers in the Articles of Confederation were too limited; they didn't fulfill the basic needs, as listed above, of the new country. So the drafters of the new Constitution determined the precise powers the new government would need to fulfill its responsibilities.

Number 41 [5]

1. Security against foreign danger.
2. Regulation of interactions with foreign nations.
3. Maintain harmony and interactions among the States.
4. Miscellaneous objects of general utility.
5. Restraint of the States from certain injurious acts.
6. Provisions giving effectiveness to these powers.

We, the people of the United States,

September 17, 1787

As people of the 21st century we like to think that we are advanced in every area of life. However, the passage of time doesn't guarantee increased knowledge, understanding and happiness. If it did, there would be no illiteracy, poverty, or third-world countries and there would be no reason to study history.

We've been told that studying history is important. But many people--myself included--spend most of their lives avoiding the study of history because it seems irrelevant to our current lives and problems--a waste of valuable time.

On the other hand, we watch Dr. Phil and read self-help books, go to psychiatrists and psychologists, even enjoy learning about criminal profilers. Over the past 50 years we've seen gurus and mega-churches rise in popularity. The war on poverty was both well-funded and a complete failure. Legal abortion hasn't decreased the number of children living in poverty.

As I studied The Federalist Papers I have discovered that memorizing the dates of history's events is not the goal of studying history. It is the human motivations behind the events that are important for us to understand. Every time we forget history, tyranny grows. Every time we ignore history, our freedoms disappear. Every time we think we are just too smart to need to study the lessons of history, we lose bits of ourselves.

American Spirit Unique in History

The United States is unique. But the older it gets, the more of that uniqueness is stripped away. Without a determined effort, the American experiment will soon fail, not through bombs from the Soviet Union or Nazi Germany. It is on the verge of failing not because we, as individuals, don't feel we are unique, but because we refuse to recognize, acknowledge, and allow our fellow citizens their uniqueness. In modern jargon, we are a nation of enablers. In former times we said it more directly: The road to hell is paved with good intentions.

The Federalist Papers predicted the positive influence the United States eventually would have on the world. This is our legacy. As so often happens, much of it has been squandered. But We, the People, can reclaim it with the help of the instructions left by our Founding Fathers.

Number 1 [1]

You are asked to study and consider adopting a new Constitution for the United States of America to replace the current, ineffective federal government. This is a very important decision. Our country's existence depends on it. So does the safety and welfare of its people, communities, and States. We will decide the fate of a nation that is, in many respects, the most interesting in the world.

The people of this country will decide important questions: Can societies establish a good government by careful thought and choice? Or are people destined to be governed only by accident and force? The answers depend on our response to the current crisis. And the wrong decision will be unfortunate for all of mankind.

Number 2 [1-2]

Government is necessary. The people must cede some of their natural rights to the government to give it some powers…

Number 14 [12]

…Americans study and respect opinions of former times and other nations. But, to their glory, they do not suffer from blind devotion for antiquity or custom. They overrule suggestions that go against their good sense, the knowledge of their situation, and the lessons of their experience.

Posterity will be indebted to the American spirit for its many innovations that improve private rights and public happiness. The Revolutionary leaders took unprecedented steps. They established a unique model of government. If they hadn't, the people of the United States might currently be laboring under the weight of some form of government that has crushed the liberties of the rest of mankind.

Happily for America. Happily, we trust, for the whole human race, they pursued a new and more noble course. Their revolution has no parallel in the annals of human society. They designed a great Confederacy. Their successors must improve and perpetuate it. If their works have imperfections, we wonder at how few.

If they erred most in the structure of the Union [Articles of Confederation], this was their most difficult work. Your Constitutional Convention has made a new model. And it is that act on which you are now to deliberate and decide.

Number 15 [12]

Why should we have a government? Because the passions of men won't conform to the dictates of reason and justice without constraint.

Confederation Near Total Collapse

Before studying the United States Constitution, a brief look at the state of the country in 1787 is important. Some people believe our liberty and freedom were safer under the Articles of Confederation. However, a quick review assures us that the country was in dire need of a governmental organization that could both protect the citizens and block overreaching power-grabs by the government.

We, the People of the United States,

Number 51 [4]

There needs to be a way to block a branch of government from getting more power than the constitution gives it. Each branch needs both constitutional tools and personal motives to block encroachments. Ambition must counteract ambition. The personal interests of the man must be connected with the constitutional rights of his office.

Government is, after all, the greatest of all reflections on human nature. If men were angels, no government would be necessary. If angels governed men, no controls on government would be necessary. But men govern men. So, security measures are necessary to control the abuses of government.

In framing a government, the great difficulty lies in this:

first, the government must control the governed, and

second, it must be forced to control itself.

The primary control on the government is its dependency on the people. But experience teaches us that more precautions are necessary.

Number 15 [1-3]

…I next discuss truths that have not been mentioned. This may seem tedious, but this is the most important subject to free people. There's a lot of information, and sophistry has increased the difficulties. I want to both simplify and thoroughly discuss the issues.

I will next discuss why the present Confederation cannot preserve the Union.

Both opponents and supporters of the new Constitution agree this is true. Our national system has significant imperfections. We need to be rescued from impending anarchy.

Facts—not speculation—support this opinion. Even the people whose bad policies have made our dangerous situation even worse reluctantly agree that there are defects in the organization of our federal government. Intelligent friends of the Union point out and regret these defects.

Nation Faces Total Humiliation

We are close to total national humiliation. We have experienced nearly everything that can wound the pride or degrade the character of an independent nation:

We violate our commitments. During the war, we borrowed money from foreigners and our own citizens, but we don't have a plan to repay them.

We are entitled by nature and treaty to navigate the Mississippi, but Spain bans us. This should have been corrected a long time ago. But the Union has no troops, nor treasury, nor government to repel an aggressor. We can't even protest with dignity.

During dangerous times, public credit is absolutely necessary. But we seem to have decided it's impossible.

Commerce is important to our national wealth; ours has totally deteriorated.

Our government is so weak that foreign governments don't need to negotiate with us. Our ambassadors only imitate representatives of a sovereign nation.

A dramatic decrease in land value is a symptom of national distress. The price of improved land is much lower than can be accounted for by the quantity of wasteland on the market. Lack of private and public confidence has depreciated property.

Private credit supports industry. But credit is at its lowest because of insecurity, not a scarcity of money.

Is there any type of national disorder, poverty, and insignificance that does not form a part of the dark list of our public misfortunes? Yet we are blessed with many natural advantages.

Some of the Defects of United States Articles of Confederation

It is tempting to not study the defects in the Articles of Confederation. However, by examining them, we get the first glimpse of the meanings behind the clauses in the Constitution. As The Federalist Papers *remind us many times, experience is our best teacher.*

Number 2 [8-9]

Current Government Hastily Formed

Very early, while their homes were in flames and citizens were bleeding, the people created a federal government. However, there wasn't time for the calm and mature reflections that must precede the formation of a wise and well-balanced government for free people. Therefore, it's not strange that the government has a lot of problems and is unable to serve its purpose.

Being intelligent, the people saw the government's defects. They were attached to the union and loved liberty. They saw that the union was in immediate danger, a danger that would eventually jeopardize their liberty. The people knew that a more wisely framed national government could secure the union and personal liberty. They recently met in Philadelphia to consider this important subject.

Number 15 [5-7, 10, 12, 15]

Amendments Can't Correct Flaws

…The defects and basic flaws of the Confederation must be listed. It cannot be amended but must be completely rebuilt.

Problem: Legislation for States

The basic defect of the Confederation is the principle of legislation for states in their collective capacities rather than for the individuals living in the States.

This principle doesn't apply to all the federal government's powers. However, it is such an important part of our current system that it leaves the Union virtually powerless. For example, the United States can requisition men and money, but it has no authority to directly raise either from individual citizens. In theory, federal resolutions are constitutionally binding on the States; but in practice, they are merely recommendations that the States observe or disregard.

This shows how fickle people are. Some men object to the new Constitution because it doesn't include the principle [legislation for States] that ruined the old, a principle that can only be enforced with the violence of the sword. Courts and judges will do the enforcement under the new Constitution.

...Union authority must extend to the citizens—the only proper objects of government.

We were told that States wouldn't violate federal regulations. Some people said that States would comply because of our common interests. Today, this sounds ludicrous. It betrayed an ignorance of psychology and contradicted the original reason for establishing civil power. Current pronouncements will sound just as wild after we receive more lessons from that best oracle of wisdom, experience.

Why should we have a government? Because the passions of men won't conform to the dictates of reason and justice without constraint. Do groups of men act with more virtue than individuals? Observers of human behavior know that the opposite happens. An individual worries more about his reputation than that of his group, because blame for the detestable action of a group is divided among a number of people. A group of people is often poisoned by faction, pushing it into improper and excessive behavior that would embarrass the individuals.

States Not Supporting Confederation

Under the current Confederation, the thirteen sovereign States must agree to enforce every important resolution and law proposed by the Union. What happened was expected. The measures have not been executed. State delinquencies have grown, stopping the wheels of the national government. Congress is barely able to keep some kind of administration until the States can agree on a functioning replacement for the present shadow of a federal government.

Our current awful situation didn't happen overnight. At first, a few States didn't fulfill the Union's requisitions. When they didn't pay, the least delinquent States were tempted not to pay, feeling that they shouldn't pay proportionately more than other States in the Union. Why should they pay more than their share of the common burden? Each State has successively withdrawn its support. Now the frail and tottering national confederation seems ready to fall on our heads and crush us beneath its ruins.

Number 21 [1-9]

I will now list the most important defects in our system. To decide a safe and satisfactory remedy, we must know the extent and harmfulness of the disease.

No Power to Enforce Federal Laws

The existing Confederation has no sanction—no way to enforce—its laws. Currently, the federal government doesn't have the power to demand obedience or the authority to use force against delinquent members. We might say that the nature of the social compact between the States includes the right to enforce federal laws. But this assumption is contrary to the *States' rights* clause, Article Two, Articles of Confederation: "that each State shall retain every power, jurisdiction, and right, not *expressly* delegated to the United States in Congress assembled." This leaves us two options: either accept the crazy idea that the federal government has no power to enforce federal laws or violate the States' rights clause in Article Two.

The new Constitution has no States' rights clause. It has been severely criticized for this. However, if we don't weaken the States' rights provision, the United States will become the weird spectacle—a government without any constitutional power to enforce its own laws.

No Federal, State Mutual Guaranty

The Articles say nothing about a mutual guaranty of the State governments. A guaranty would be useful and we might suggest that it exists, but it would flagrantly violate the States' rights clause. Although not having a guaranty may endanger the Union, it isn't as dangerous as the federal government not having the constitutional power to enforce federal laws.

Without a guaranty, the Union cannot help fight domestic threats to State constitutions. Usurpations could trample State liberties and the national government could legally do nothing but watch in anger and sorrow. A successful faction could erect a tyranny within a State and the Union could not constitutionally help supporters of the State's constitutional government.

Massachusetts barely survived the recent turmoil. What if someone like Caesar or Cromwell had led the malcontents? If despotism had been established in Massachusetts, how would it have changed liberty in New Hampshire, Rhode Island, Connecticut, or New York?

Some people object to a federal government guaranty. They say that the federal government should not interfere in internal State issues. But they misunderstand the provision. And they want to deprive us of advantages expected from union. A majority of the people could still legally and peacefully reform a State's constitution. The guaranty could only operate when violence was used to force changes.

People Hold Governmental Authority

The people hold the whole power of the government. When disagreements appear, the people will have fewer excuses to use violence. In a representative government, the natural cure for poor administration is changing men. A national guaranty would be used against both tyrannical rulers and community factions.

Taxation by State Quotas

Currently, State contributions to the national treasury are regulated by quotas, which haven't been met. There is no one standard to measure the degrees of national wealth. Land values and population numbers have been suggested as ways to determine each State's quota. But neither truly represents the State's wealth.

For example, let's compare the wealth of the United Netherlands to Russia, Germany, or France. There is no relationship between their wealth and their land value and population. The United Netherlands has the higher wealth; the three other nations have immense land and much larger populations.

We can compare American States in the same way and get a similar result. Compare Virginia with North Carolina, Pennsylvania with Connecticut, or Maryland with New Jersey. Their comparative wealth has little relationship to their lands and populations. Counties within New York State illustrate the same thing. If either land value or population is the criterion, the active wealth of King's County is much greater than that of Montgomery County.

An infinite variety of causes create a nation's wealth. They include location, soil, climate, products, the type of government, the genius of its citizens, knowledge, commerce, arts, and industry. And there are many more causes that are too complex to quantify. These combine to create differences in the relative wealth of different countries. There is no common measure of national wealth. And there is no way to measure a State's ability to pay taxes. Therefore, trying to calculate each State's quota by using a rule based on land or population would be glaringly unequal and extremely oppressive.

Even if federal requisitions could be enforced, the inequality between States' wealth alone would eventually destroy the American Union. Public burdens would be unequally distributed. Some States would be impoverished and oppressed while citizens of others would scarcely notice their small tax burden. Suffering States would secede. The principle of quotas and requisitions creates this evil.

To avoid this problem, the national government must be able to raise its own revenue…

Number 22 [1-7, 14-18]

The existing federal system is unfit to administer the Union and it has several more defects.

No Federal Regulation of Commerce

Currently, the federal government has no power to regulate commerce. But we must have federal regulation of commerce. We haven't been able to have good commercial treaties with other nations. Since the States have been arguing about commerce, no nation will sign a commercial treaty with the United States. They know that individual States could violate the treaty at any time. Besides, they already have every advantage in our markets without giving us any in return except when it is convenient.

In England, Mr. Jenkinson introduced a bill in the British House of Commons to temporarily regulate commerce between our two countries. He declared that earlier bills with similar provisions answered Great Britain's commercial needs. He said that they shouldn't change their policies until the American government became more consistent.

Some States have tried to change Great Britain's commercial policies by limiting or prohibiting some British products. But different States have different restrictions. We won't be able to influence Great Britain's commercial conduct until we have one federal authority and one commercial policy.

Uniform Interstate Commerce Laws

Contrary to the true spirit of the Union, some State regulations hurt the commerce in other States. Without national control, there will be more of these policies and anger between the States will grow, further damaging commerce.

The Encyclopaedia (The article title is "Empire") describes Germany's commercial situation. Each German prince taxes the merchandise that travels through his state. The wide variety of taxes within Germany has put commerce in constant turmoil. And shippers have to stop and pay taxes so many times along the commercial routes that they don't even bother using Germany's navigable rivers.

This description may never completely apply to us. But as each State makes different commercial regulations, citizens of one State will treat citizens of other States no better than foreigners and aliens.

Quotas, Requisitions to Raise Armies

Under the Articles of Confederation, when the federal government needs to raise troops it must requisition quotas from the States. During the recent war, the requisition system made a vigorous and economical defense very difficult. To fill their quotas, States competed against each other, offering enormous rewards. Men who wanted to serve put off enlisting, hoping to get a larger bonus.

The result? During emergencies, enlistments were few, slow, short-term and very expensive. The constantly changing troops ruined discipline and the soldiers who had mustered out threatened public safety. The occasional forced enlistment only worked because of enthusiasm for liberty.

Using State quotas to raise troops doesn't work. The enlistment bonuses hurt the economy. And only some of the States filled their quotas. The States near the heart of the war, influenced by self-preservation, furnished the required number of men. Usually, the States that were not in immediate danger didn't fulfill their quotas. Of course, if a State falls behind paying their money quota, it can be made up. It's impossible to supply delinquent deficiencies of men. However, States probably won't pay for their monetary failures. Whether it is used to raise men or money, the quota system is unequal and unjust.

Problems from States' Equal Suffrage

Currently, each State has an equal vote in the national congress. This is another problem. Every rule of fair representation condemns the principle that gives Rhode Island equal power with Massachusetts or Connecticut or New York. This goes against the basic principle of republican government: the will of the majority should prevail.

Some people may say that each State in the Union is a sovereign and sovereigns are equal. Therefore a majority of the votes of States will be a majority of confederate America. But this logical sleight-of-hand doesn't remove the dictates of justice and common sense. A majority of States can be a small minority of American citizens.[*]

Two thirds of the people will not allow one third to manage their interests. After a while, the larger States will revolt. Giving up majority rights is contrary to the love of power and it sacrifices equality. It is not rational to expect the first nor just to require the second. Since the smaller States depend on union for their safety and welfare, they should readily renounce a pretension that, if not relinquished, would be fatal to that union.

Lack of Federal Supreme Court

The Confederation's worst defect is the lack of a judiciary power. Laws are pointless without courts to interpret and define their true meaning and operation.

---

[*] New Hampshire, Rhode Island, New Jersey, Delaware, Georgia, South Carolina and Maryland are a majority of the whole number of States but they do not contain one third of the people.
    —PUBLIUS

Treaties must be considered as part of the law of the land. Their effect on individuals must, like all laws, be defined by judicial decisions. To have uniform decisions, as a last resort they should be submitted to one supreme tribunal that is created under the same authority that signs the treaties.

If each State has a court of final jurisdiction, there may be as many different final decisions on an issue as there are courts. Men hold a limitless variety of opinions. We often see not only different courts, but also judges of the same court, differing from each other. Contradictory decisions create confusion. To avoid this, all nations have established one court of last resort, authorized to settle a uniform rule of civil justice.

State Courts Will Not Always Agree

This is more important when the laws of the whole country are in danger of being contradicted by the laws of the States or regions. If State or regional courts have the final opinions, a bias based on local views and local regulations would produce contradictions. People might prefer a local law over a federal law. Men in office naturally yield to the authority to which they owe their job.

Currently, thirteen different legislatures and thirteen different supreme courts can interpret or misinterpret every treaty signed by the United States. Therefore, the reputation and peace of the whole country are at the mercy of the prejudices, passions, and interests of each State. Can foreign nations either respect or trust such a government? How long will Americans entrust their honor, happiness, and safety to this unstable foundation?

Amendments Won't Cure Flaws

I have mentioned the Confederation's most significant defects, passing over the imperfections that make its power largely impotent. All unbiased men must realize that the system is radically vicious and unsound. It cannot be cured by amendments. It requires an entire change in its important features and character.

One Congress: Inadequate and Dangerous

Currently, Congress does not have the powers that the federal government needs. The federal government has limited authority. Therefore, a single congress may be proper. But even rational adversaries of the proposed Constitution say that the federal government needs more power. And a single assembly cannot be trusted with the additional powers.

If the new Constitution is not adopted, the country will either fall apart or Congress will be given tyrannical powers. A weak federal government and the schemes of ambitious men who expect to increase their personal power will push the Union towards dissolution. If the country doesn't fall apart, a single "congress" will accumulate all the sovereign powers, creating the tyranny that adversaries of the new Constitution say they don't want.

People Didn't Ratify Articles

The PEOPLE never ratified the Articles of Confederation. Instead, the State legislatures approved it. Now some people are questioning whether it is valid, which has led to the outrageous doctrine of legislative repeal—since it was ratified by the State, the State can repeal it. This is the same as saying that a *party* to a *contract* has a right to revoke that *contract*. As silly as it sounds, some respectable people support the doctrine.

The foundation of our national government must be laid deeper than just the approval of the people's representatives. The American empire should rest on the consent of the people. The streams of national power should flow from that pure, original fountain of all legitimate authority.

Alter/Abolish Constitution

The citizens of the United States relinquish a few rights to give various levels of governments--community, local, state, federal--their power. This is the consistent theme throughout The Federalist Papers. It is appropriate that any study of the United States Constitution start with these reminders.

Number 40 [16]

The people have the right to "abolish or alter their governments as to them shall seem most likely to effect their safety and happiness."*

Number 78 [18]

The people can alter or abolish the constitution if it is not consistent with their happiness. This is the fundamental principle of republican government... The courts could not uphold the unconstitutional law. Until the people have changed or abolished the Constitution, through an authoritative act, it is binding on them collectively and individually. No presumption or knowledge of the people's wishes gives representatives the authority to depart from the Constitution...

Call to Study New Constitution

I never tire of reading Federalist Paper Number 1. The author answers some of the questions I had before starting to study the Papers--answers I never expected to find in the Papers. In December 1994, Federalist Paper Number 1 was the catalyst that led me to study the Papers until today.

Number 1 [all]

You are asked to study and consider adopting a new Constitution for the United States of America to replace the current, ineffective federal government. This is a very important decision. Our country's existence depends on it. So does the safety and welfare of its people, communities, and States. We will decide the fate of a nation that is, in many respects, the most interesting in the world.

The people of this country will decide important questions: Can societies establish a good government by careful thought and choice? Or are people destined to be governed only by accident and force? The answers depend on our response to the current crisis. And the wrong decision will be unfortunate for all of mankind.

Special Interests, Prejudices will Influence Debate

Conscientious patriots understand the importance of deciding whether to adopt the new Constitution. And they know their decision will affect all human societies.

---

* Declaration of Independence--PUBLIUS

We, the People of the United States,

It would be wonderful if we based our decision only on the best interests of our society, unbiased by less noble interests not connected with the public good. Although we may sincerely wish this, it can't be expected. The Constitution affects many special interests and changes many local institutions. Subjects other than its merits will be discussed. The debate will include passions and prejudices unrelated to discovering the truth and meaning of the Constitution.

Politicians May Fear a Loss of Power

Many politicians will oppose the new Constitution. Some politicians are afraid that the Constitution will decrease the power and benefits of their current State offices. Others think that they can have more power if the country is in turmoil or is broken up into several small countries.

Moderation Urged; Remember Good Men Argue on Both Sides of an Issue

However, I don't plan to talk about political motives. I don't know if a person's opposition is due to self-interest or ambition even if their views seem suspicious. Even opponents of the new Constitution may be motivated by upright intentions. And much of the opposition will spring from blameless, if not valid, motivations. Jealousies and fears will lead arguments astray into honest errors in thinking.

A false bias can be created for a variety of good reasons. Wise and good men often argue on both the wrong and right side of society's most important questions. This fact should teach moderation to anyone who thinks they are always in the right in any argument.

There's a further reason for caution. People who support the right side of a question can also have ulterior motives like ambition, avarice, personal animosity, and party opposition.

Moderation is important. The mean spirit that characterizes political parties is awful. In politics, as in religion, it's absurd to try to persuade people with fire and sword. Bad ideas can rarely be defeated by persecution.

Angry and malignant passions will be let loose about this subject, as in all former cases of great national debate. To get supporters, the opponents of the new Constitution will loudly and bitterly condemn it.

People supporting the energetic government proposed by the Constitution will be demonized as liking dictators and hating liberty. When supporters declare that the rights of the people must be very carefully protected, it will be called insincere and an obvious attempt to become popular while hurting the general public.

Dangers to the rights of people usually spring from the head rather than the heart. Enthusiasm for liberty is often infected with narrow-minded bigotry and distrust.

A healthy government is essential to secure liberty. A strong government and liberty can never be separated. Dangerous ambition is more often masked by a zeal for the rights of the people than the zeal for a firm and efficient government. History teaches us that most men who have overturned the liberties of republics began their career by proclaiming their devotion to the people. They gain position by arousing people's prejudices and end as tyrants.

I Support the New Constitution

My fellow citizens, guard against all attempts, from whatever side, to influence you. Your decision on the new Constitution, which is very important to your welfare, should be based on truth.

I'm sure you have noticed that I like the new Constitution. Yes, my countrymen, I admit that after giving it careful thought, I believe it is in your interest to adopt it. I am convinced that this is the safest course for your liberty, your dignity, and your happiness. The new Constitution has my full and unambiguous support.

I don't pretend that I am undecided about ratifying the Constitution. I have decided. And I will tell you why I think it is a good idea. I will try to make my arguments truthful. Everyone who reads them can judge for themselves whether I've succeeded.

I propose to discuss the following subjects in a series of papers:

- Why the union is important to our political life.
- Why the current Confederation can't preserve the union.
- Why we need an energetic federal government.
- How the proposed Constitution conforms to the principles of republican government.
- A comparison of the proposed Constitution to the New York constitution.

How the Constitution will preserve liberty, property and the republican form of government.

As this discussion progresses, I will try to answer objections that arise.

It may seem like everyone agrees that remaining united is important. But some opponents of the new Constitution say thirteen States are too many. They argue that we must break into several separate confederacies.*

The alternative to adoption of the new Constitution is dismemberment of the Union. Therefore, I will examine the advantages of staying united, the probable dangers, and certain evils of dissolution. This will be the subject of my next editorial.

An unfriendly press and political corruption in 1774--some things never change.

Number 2 [11]

Constitution Only a Recommended Plan

This plan is only *recommended*, not imposed. It is neither recommended for *blind* approval nor *blind* rejection. This important subject demands calm and candid consideration. However, a thoughtful examination of the Constitution is more to be wished than expected. Experience teaches us not to be too optimistic. Let's remember what happened in 1774. Americans felt that they were in imminent danger. They formed the Congress of 1774, which made some wise recommendations. However, the press wrote against

---

* The same idea, tracing the arguments to their consequences, is held out in several recent publications against the new Constitution. --PUBLIUS

them. Some people said the advice of that patriotic Congress should be rejected. Many politicians opposed them, putting self-interest before the good of the country. Others were unduly influenced by political allies or saw it as a threat to personal ambitions. However, the majority of Americans saw through the deceit and decided judiciously. Reflecting back, they are happy they did so.

Number 37 [1-2]

Papers Discuss Constitution

We have studied the Confederation's defects. To correct the defects, we need an energetic government as proposed in the new Constitution…

The objective of these papers is to determine the quality of this Constitution and whether it is a good idea to adopt it…

We should study a proposed public policy objectively. Will it advance or block the public good? Unfortunately, because of human nature, people are rarely objective when they discuss public policy. And people actually become less objective as the issues become more important.

The Constitution has important changes and innovations. It touches passions and interests on both sides of the issues. Therefore, many people have not judged its merits objectively. Some people condemned the proposed Constitution before they read it. Other people have an opposite bias, making their opinions unimportant. However, the people predetermined to praise the new Constitution may have purer intentions than those predetermined to condemn it.

Everyone admits our situation is critical and something must be done. Therefore, the person who wants the Constitution might be biased because of these considerations, as well as from sinister motives. On the other hand, the predetermined adversary has no venial motive whatever. The intentions of the first may be upright while also being culpable. The views of the last cannot be upright and must be culpable.

But these papers are not addressed to people in either category. They solicit the attention of people who can objectively judge how to promote the happiness of their country.

Constitutional Convention

Over the years I have talked with people who believe that the 1787 Constitution Convention had no authority to create a new Constitution. They use this belief and jump to the conclusion that the United States Constitution is not the supreme law of the land. However, as the Federalist Papers remind us, until it was ratified, the new Constitution was nothing more than words on paper.

Number 2 [10, 12-end]

Respected Men Framed Constitution

The men at the convention are respected. Many showed their patriotism, virtue, and wisdom during a time that tried the minds and hearts of men.

The convention undertook the difficult task. During a time of peace, they spent many months in cool, uninterrupted, daily discussions. They were neither awed by power nor influenced by any passion except love for their country. They unanimously recommended to the people their plan—the proposed Constitution.

Americans concluded that wise and experienced men composed the 1774 Congress. Each delegate was committed to public liberty and prosperity. It was their duty to recommend only wise measures. And Americans relied on the judgment and integrity of that Congress.

There are even more reasons to respect the judgment and advice of the recent convention. Members of the 1774 Congress have proved that they are patriotic and talented. They continued learning about politics and governments. Some of the most distinguished men from the 1774 Congress brought their accumulated knowledge and experience to this year's Constitutional Convention.

Remaining One Union Important

The prosperity of America depends on its Union. The Constitutional Convention wrote the proposed Constitution to preserve and perpetuate the Union. What are the real motives behind current attempts to depreciate the importance of the Union? Why do some people say that we should break into three or four confederacies?

I believe Americans have always thought right on this subject. Their attachment to the Union is based on great and important reasons, which I will try to explain in some ensuing papers.

The people who want to break up America into several separate confederacies know that if the Constitution is rejected, the Union will be in jeopardy. I sincerely wish that every good citizen realizes that, if the Union is dissolved, America will have reason to exclaim, in the words of the poet: "FAREWELL! A LONG FAREWELL TO ALL MY GREATNESS."

Number 40 [all]

Was Convention Authorized to Draft Constitution?

…Was the convention authorized to create and propose this mixed [with both national and federal features] Constitution?

Call for Constitutional Convention

Why did the States send delegates to the Convention? The meeting in Annapolis in September 1786 and the congressional meeting in February 1787 defined their mission.

The Annapolis meeting in September, 1786, recommended that the States appoint delegates to meet and consider "the situation of the United States; to devise *such further provisions* as shall appear to them necessary to render [make] the Constitution of the federal government *adequate to the exigencies of the Union;* and to report such an act for that purpose to the United States in Congress assembled, as when agreed to by them, and afterwards confirmed by the legislature of every State, will effectually provide for the same."

In February, 1787, Congress recommended: "Whereas there is provision in the Articles of Confederation and perpetual Union for making alterations therein, by the assent of Congress of the United States and the legislatures of the several States; and whereas experience has evinced that there are defects in the present Confederation; as a means to remedy which, several States, and *particularly the State of New York,* by express instructions to their delegates in Congress, have suggested a convention for the purposes expressed in the following resolution; and such convention appearing to be the most probable means of establishing in these States a *firm national government*:

"*Resolved,* —That in the opinion of Congress it is expedient that on the second Monday in May next a convention of delegates, who shall have been appointed by the several States, be held at Philadelphia for the sole and express purpose *of revising the Articles of Confederation,* and reporting to Congress and all the legislatures the *alterations and provisions therein* as shall, when agreed to in Congress and confirmed by the States, render [make] the federal Constitution *adequate to meet the exigencies of government and the preservation of the Union"*

These two acts seem to say:

1) The convention's objective was to establish a firm national government that is adequate for the needs of the government and the preservation of the Union.

2) This goal could be met either by "revising the Articles of Confederation [with] alterations and provisions" (from act of Congress) or by "such further provision as should appear necessary" (Annapolis).

3) To take effect, Congress and the States must agree to the changes.

Convention's Mission Statement

We can summarize the convention's authority: (1) Frame a **national government** that can (2) meet the needs of government and the Union, and (3) change the Articles of Confederation into a form that accomplishes these purposes.

Conflicting Goals: Sacrifice Less Important

To analyze this mission statement, logic and legal axioms have two rules:

First, if possible, every part of the mission statement should have meaning and made to reach some common goal.

Second, if parts of the mission statement conflict, the less important should give way to the more important part. The means should be sacrificed to the goal, rather than the goal to the means.

Change Articles vs. New Constitution

What if the convention felt that they could not form a *national government that meets the Union's needs* [#1 and 2 in paragraph 6 above] . . . by *alterations* of the *Articles of Confederation* [#3 in paragraph 6 above]. Which part of the mission should be pursued and which part should be rejected? Which is more important—forming an adequate government or preserving the Articles of Confederation?

The people who object to the convention's work should answer this question: What was the purpose of government reform? To preserve the Articles? Or to establish an adequate government, even if the Articles have to be sacrificed?

But are these goals irreconcilable? Perhaps the convention did alter the ***Articles of the Confederation*** to form a national and adequate government.

Alteration vs. Transmutation

The convention was authorized to *alter* and add *new provisions* to the **Articles of Confederation**. Therefore, changing the **title** to "**Constitution**" is not an exercise of ungranted power.

Where is the line between authorized and unauthorized changes? What degree of change is an *alteration*? How much change is actually a *transmutation* of the government? The States solemnly appointed a convention with big objectives. They must have expected some *substantial* reforms.

Did the convention change the ***fundamental principles*** of the Confederation**?**

Both the Articles and the proposed Constitution regard the States as independent sovereigns.

Under the Articles of Confederation, the people, not the State legislatures, may elect the delegates to Congress—a trait of a **national** government.

Some opponents say that the national government's power must act on States rather than individuals. Sometimes the new government will act on the States. And sometimes the existing confederation acts on individuals.

Do these fundamental principles require that States must play a role in all taxation? The current Confederation has a direct tax on the post office. And Congress says the power of coinage is a tax.

Besides these examples, one of the convention objectives—and the people expected—that the national government would regulate trade so it would be an immediate source of general revenue. Congress said that federal trade regulations are consistent with the fundamental principles of the Confederacy. And twelve States have already complied with the plan of Congress.

Should the federal government's powers be limited? Beyond this limit, should the States have sovereign and independent jurisdiction? In the new government—as in the old—the national powers are limited. And the States have sovereign, independent jurisdiction over all powers not specifically stated in the Constitution.

The important principles in the proposed Constitution are not new. They expand the principles found in the Articles of Confederation. The Constitution only looks like a new system because the Articles needed so much clarification.

Ratification Process Changed

In one area, the convention departed from their specific commission. *Nine States* need to ratify the Constitution, instead of *all the States.*

Although this could be an objection to the Constitution, it is rarely mentioned. This is probably because it would be absurd to subject the fate of twelve States to the perverseness or corruption of the thirteenth. Therefore, it has received little criticism. I dismiss it without further comment.

Did Duty Override Authority?

…How much did the delegates' feelings of duty to their country supply any lack of regular authority?

We, the People of the United States,

Convention Only Recommends Plan

Up to this point, we have rigorously analyzed the convention's work as if it had the authority to establish a Constitution for the United States. It has held up to scrutiny.

The convention was only authorized to advise and recommend. And the proposed Constitution is nothing more than pieces of paper, unless the people approve it.

Convention Delegates: Considerations

From the convention notes, the delegates seemed deeply concerned about the crisis in their country. Almost with one voice, they created the solemn Constitution to correct the errors that produced this crisis. They all agreed that the proposed reform is necessary to meet the convention's goals.

Citizens throughout this great empire anxiously watched their deliberations. And delegates believed that every external and internal foe of liberty and prosperity of the United States hoped they would fail.

Virginia offered an amendment to the Confederacy, which the delegates studied. The Annapolis convention—with *very few* deputies from a *very few* of the States—had recommended an important change that was not part of their commission; however, the public accepted it and twelve of the thirteen States made the change. And Congress has assumed powers to solve problems, problems far less urgent than those faced by the convention.

Delegates knew that when an established government needs great changes, form must give way to substance. The people have the right to "abolish or alter their governments as to them shall seem most likely to effect their safety and happiness."* Rigidly holding onto a specific form would make this nearly impossible. People don't spontaneously and universally move together towards their objectives. Therefore, some *informal and unauthorized proposals* made by some patriotic, respectable citizens start changes.

The States first united against danger because people believe that they could plan for their safety and happiness. Committees and congresses worked hard, defending the people's rights. *Conventions* established the *State* constitutions. The only people who demanded that existing forms be followed were people who secretly wanted to block delegates from creating the constitutions.

As they wrote the new Constitution, delegates knew that it would be submitted *to the people themselves*. If the people reject the plan, it will be destroyed forever. Likewise, approval by the people overrides any irregularities in its formation.

The delegates might have realized that once trivial objections are settled, the question of whether they exceeded their authority would not be criticized, particularly if their recommendation met the national needs.

Judging the Delegates

What if the convention hadn't created a system that they felt could secure the country's happiness? What if they had coldly decided to disappoint the country's deep hopes and sacrificed substance to form? Their country would have faced the uncertainties

---

* Declaration of Independence--PUBLIUS

of delay and the hazard of events. Let me ask the rational patriot — how would the impartial world judge the convention? How would the friends of mankind and every virtuous citizen judge the conduct and character of this assembly?

If there is a man who wants to condemn the delegates and the convention, how does he plan to punish the twelve States who *usurped power* by sending deputies to the convention? How will he punish Congress, who recommended the appointment of this body? Or punish the State of New York, which first urged and then complied with this unauthorized intervention?

Source of Good Advice Unimportant

To disarm the objectors, let's agree for a moment that the convention was neither authorized by their commission nor justified by circumstances to propose a Constitution for their country. Does it follow that the Constitution, for that reason alone, should be rejected?

If it is lawful to accept good advice from an enemy, shall we refuse advice when our friends offer it? In all cases, the prudent inquiry shouldn't be *from whom* the advice comes but whether the advice is *good*.

Convention Didn't Exceed Authority

Opponents of the proposed Constitution say that the convention exceeded its power. The only change was the ratification process, which is rarely mentioned by the objectors. Otherwise, the charge has no foundation.

And if they did exceed their powers, they were not only justified but also required. They were servants of their country, who used their liberty to fulfill their mission.

And finally, even if they violated both their powers and their duty in proposing a Constitution, it should be ratified, if it seems to meet the goals and promote the happiness of the people of America. We are investigating whether this describes the Constitution.

Constitution Imperfect--Some Criticisms

What we now call The Federalist Papers *were written as newspaper editorials, explaining and supporting ratification of the new Constitution drafted in Philadelphia during the summer of 1787. What has come to be known as the Anti-Federalist Papers were newspaper editorials criticizing the new Constitution. We could say that the criticisms found in the Anti-Federalist Papers were rejected when the States voted to ratify the Constitution. However, the criticisms play an important role in our understanding the correct "interpretation" of the Constitution. The authors of the Federalist Papers used the criticisms to more fully explain their support of ratification.*

Below is only a partial list of the criticisms of the new Constitution. Other criticisms are quoted below the specific topics to which they refer.

Number 16 [11]

…Deadly feuds sometimes spread violence through a whole nation or a large part of it. Discontent with the government would spread the violent feuds. We can't estimate how far the violent feuds would spread. When they happen, they usually become revolutions that dismember an empire. No form of government can always either avoid or control them. It is impossible to guard against events that are impossible to predict. It is stupid to object to a government because it could not perform impossibilities.

Number 37 [2-end]

...these papers...solicit the attention of people who can objectively judge how to promote the happiness of their country.

These people will not magnify the Constitution's faults. They didn't expect a faultless plan. The convention was fallible. They will keep in mind that they, themselves, are only men. They will not assume infallibility as they judge the fallible opinions of others. And they will make allowances for the difficulties the convention faced.

Precedents Show Errors to Avoid

This was a novel under taking. The existing Confederation is founded on fallacious principles. Consequently, we must change both the foundation and the building resting on it.

Other confederacies had the same problems. They show us what not to do but don't point us in the right direction. The Convention could only avoid the errors made by our Confederation and other countries, and provide an amendment process to correct the convention's errors, as future experience exposes them.

Balance Between Stability and Liberty

Combining government energy and stability with liberty and the republican form was difficult. But this was their task.

A government must have energy to protect the country from external and internal danger, and enforce its laws.

A stable government gets respect. It gives the people confidence, a blessing of civil society. Irregular and changing legislation is not particularly evil but the people hate it. People want the uncertainties within the State administrations corrected.

However, it is difficult to combine energy and stability with the principles of liberty. Inherently, republican liberty seems to demand that all power comes from the people. Government officials should depend on the people by having short terms. And the trust should be placed not in a few but a large number of hands.

However, to be stable, government officials must continue in office for a longer time. Frequent elections create a frequent change in men and a frequent change of policies. Energy in government requires both long terms in office and only one person.

Did the convention create the right balance? It will become clearer as we study the Constitution. It was a difficult task.

State v. Federal Authority

Deciding the proper boundary between federal and State authorities was also a complicated task. Scientists and philosophers have tried to classify the abilities of the mind but no one has completed the task. The boundaries between the mental activities of sense, perception, judgment, desire, choice, memory, and imagination elude the subtlest investigations and are a source of controversy.

The boundaries between the various genuses and species in nature are another example of the same truth. Naturalists have not perfectly defined the line separating vegetable life from non-organic matter, or the line separating vegetable and animal life. There is an even greater obscurity between the objects in each category of nature.

Objective boundaries do exist in nature. They are unclear only because we are unable to make perfect observations. When we study man-made organizations, two things make it difficult to define the lines of authority: the subject and the imperfections of the humans who study it.

Political science hasn't been able to define the exact boundaries between the legislative, executive, and judiciary branches of government. Or even the powers of the different legislative houses. These obscure subjects puzzle the greatest political science experts.

Three Sources of Ambiguity

Brilliant legislators and jurists have tried to define the objectives and limits of different laws and courts of justice. This subject has been extensively studied in Great Britain. But the line between the different types of laws—common law, statute law, maritime law, ecclesiastical law, corporate law, and local laws and customs—still isn't clearly defined. The jurisdiction of Great Britain's different courts is frequently discussed, but it still isn't perfectly clear.

New laws are written with the greatest technical skill and passed after long deliberations. Yet they are considered as more or less obscure and equivocal until their meaning is ascertained by a series of discussions and adjudications.

Obscurity comes from (1) the complexity of the subjects, (2) human imperfections, and (3) the medium [i.e. words, sentences] used to convey men's ideas.

Humans use words to express ideas. Clear expression requires well-formed ideas and the appropriate words. But no language has words and phrases for every complex idea. And many words have several meanings. Therefore, the definition of even a precise subject can be inaccurate because words are inaccurate. This unavoidable inaccuracy grows worse as the subject becomes more complex or novel.

When God himself talks to mankind in our language, his meaning—brilliant as it must be—is made dim and doubtful by the cloudy medium through which it is communicated.

There are three sources of vague and incorrect definitions: (1) indistinctness of the subject, (2) the brain's imperfections, and (3) the language's inadequacies. When the constitutional convention worked to define the boundary between federal and State jurisdictions, it must have experienced all three problems.

States Have Conflicting Interests

Additionally, large and small States had conflicting demands. Larger States wanted power matching their superior wealth and importance. Smaller States wanted equality. They had to compromise.

After compromising on the ratio of representation, a fresh struggle probably started. Each State wanted to organize the government and distribute its powers so they got the greatest share of influence.

Every State is divided into districts. Citizens have competing interests and feel local jealousies. Different States have different policies. And the different parts of the United States have competing interests. This variety of interests may have a healthy influence on the administration of the government once it is formed. However, as they wrote the Constitution, they must have experienced many conflicting interests. Features in the Constitution suggest these assumptions. The convention had to sacrifice theoretical perfection to other considerations.

Drafting Constitution

Sitting at home, alone, a person could write a "perfect" constitution. But the constitutional convention felt pressure from all sides; it couldn't be "perfect." It's amazing that so many difficulties were surmounted. The convention's ability to reach agreements was unprecedented. Any honest man must find this amazing. Any pious man must see the finger of that Almighty hand that has so frequently come to our relief at critical times of the revolution.

Opinions Sacrificed

The United Netherlands repeatedly and unsuccessfully tried to reform the ruinous and notorious vices of their constitution. Factions disrupted the councils that tried to reconcile discordant opinions, assuage jealousies, and compromise. They are dark and degraded pictures. They show the infirmities and depravities of the human character. The few scattered instances of cooperation only serve as exceptions to caution us about the general truth.

After studying history, we are led to two important conclusions. First, the convention must have been free from the destructive influence of party animosities—the disease of deliberative bodies that contaminates their proceedings. Second, the delegations composing the convention were either satisfied by the Constitution or they agreed to it because they felt it was important to sacrifice their private opinions and interests to the public good or they feared the consequences of delays or new experiments.

Number 38 [5-9]

United States Constitution Historically Unique

Writing a new Constitution is complicated and difficult. In areas with little historical experience, there will be errors even if the subject is carefully researched. And the errors will not be found until actual trial points them out.

Both logical reasoning and our experience with the Articles of Confederation suggest this. During the ratification of the Articles of Confederation, many objections were made and amendments were suggested. But no one mentioned the great error that actual trial uncovered. Although the objections proved immaterial, some States would have clung to them with dangerous inflexibility if their zeal for their opinions and interests had not been stifled by the more powerful sentiment of self-preservation. Although the enemy was within our country, one State refused to ratify the Articles for several years. She finally complied out of fear of being charged with protracting the public calamities and endangering the outcome of the war.

Medical Allegory

Let's study the case of a person who grows sicker every day. He finally decides that if he waits any longer to get help, he will be in extreme danger. He evaluates the reputations of different physicians, then calls the doctors that he thinks are the best and that are entitled to his confidence. The doctors arrive and carefully examine the patient. The doctors consult. They all agree that the symptoms are critical but that with proper and timely care the patient can actually have improved health. And they all agree on what must be done to produce this happy effect.

As the prescription is written, however, a number of other people arrive. They agree that the patient is in real danger. Then they tell the patient that the prescription will poison him and forbid him, under pain of certain death, to make use of it.

Before he followed the second suggestion, won't the patient demand that the group should agree on some other remedy? If the second group can't agree on a remedy, wouldn't he try the remedy that the first group of doctors unanimously recommended?

Criticisms: Irreconcilable Wide Variety

This patient mirrors America's current situation. She realizes she is sick. She has obtained unanimous advice from men of her own choice. Now other people warn her against following this advice under the pain of fatal consequences.

Does the new group say there is no danger? No.

Do they deny that a speedy and powerful remedy is needed? No.

Do even *two* critics agree on what is wrong with the proposed remedy or the proper substitution? Let them speak for themselves:

One says we should reject the proposed Constitution because it's not a confederation of the States, but a government over individuals.

Another admits it should be a government over individuals, but not to the extent proposed.

A third doesn't object to the government over individuals but wants a bill of rights.

A fourth says a bill of rights is necessary but it should not declare the personal rights of individuals, but the rights reserved to the States.

A fifth believe that a bill of rights would be superfluous, but the Constitution has the fatal power of regulating the times and places of election.

An objector from a large State exclaims loudly against the unreasonable equality in the Senate. An objector from a small State is equally loud against the dangerous inequality in the House of Representatives.

One group is alarmed with the huge expense because a large number of people will be needed to administer the new government. Another group—and even some of the people in the first group at a different time—cry out that Congress is too small and the government would be less objectionable if the number and the expense were doubled.

A patriot in a State, which doesn't import or export, objects to direct taxation. The patriot in an exporting and importing State is dissatisfied because the whole burden of taxes may be thrown on consumption.

One politician says the Constitution promotes a monarchy. Another is equally sure it will end in aristocracy. Another is puzzled over which of these shapes it will ultimately assume but sees clearly it must be one or the other. A fourth fears the opposite: the Constitution is not energetic enough to keep it upright and firm against anarchy.

Another group of adversaries to the Constitution says the legislative, executive, and judiciary are intertwined, which contradicts all the ideas of regular government and all the required precautions in favor of liberty. This is a vague objection with few supporters.

Two people rarely agree on one objection.

One says the Senate should not have to approve presidential appointments. Another says that House of Representatives should also approve appointments. Another person says that giving the President any power is always dangerous.

Some people say that the trial of impeachments by the Senate is wrong: they believe the judiciary should have this power.

Others reply that the judiciary already has too much power.

People who want an executive council can't agree on how it would be formed. Some people want a small council appointed by the House of Representatives. Others think the President should appoint a large council.

If the Critics Wrote a Constitution, They Would Never Agree

Let's look at the situation in a different way. Let's assume the critics of the Constitution are brilliant and they can write a better constitution. Let's further assume the country agrees and a second convention is formed to revise the work of the first.

You've read some of their opinions. And know how hostile they have been towards the Constitutional Convention. Wouldn't their deliberations be full of discord?

If the current, proposed Constitution was ratified and used, not until a better but until this new group of lawgivers agrees on another, wouldn't it have a good chance of becoming immortal?

New Constitution Better than Articles of Confederation

People who object to the new Constitution never talk about the defects in the Articles of Confederation. The Constitution doesn't need to be perfect; it just has to be better than the Articles. No man would refuse to leave a shattered, tottering house for a large, solid building because the latter had no porch, or because some of the rooms might be a little larger or smaller, or the ceiling a little higher or lower than his fancy would have planned them…

Number 41 [4]

Is Federal Power Too Extensive?

Some people say the new Constitution gives the federal government too much power. They rarely consider whether these powers are necessary. Instead, they talk about the inconveniences and how the power might be abused. They may inflame the passions of the unthinking and confirm the prejudice of the misthinking.

But cool and candid people know that even the purest of human blessings are part alloy. The choice must always be made, if not of the lesser evil, at least of the greater, not the perfect, good. All political power may be misapplied and abused. Therefore, whenever power is to be conferred, it must first be decided whether such a power is necessary for the public good. If the Constitution is ratified, we will need an effective guard against the misuse of power.

Number 59 [7]

States as Part of National Government

...The Constitution establishes the organization of the national government. If the Constitutional organization of the national government is exposed to injury from States, it is an evil. But this evil could not be completely avoided. The States, as political units, need to be part of the national government. Therefore, the State legislatures appoint Senators...

Number 65 [11]

Government is Never Perfect

...If no government could be set up until every part of it is perfect, society would soon become an anarchy and the world a desert. Adversaries to the Constitution should prove, not merely that certain provisions are not the best possible, but that the whole plan is bad and very harmful.

Number 82 [1]

A new government can be carefully and wisely created. But there still will be questions. This is especially true when a country's new constitution incorporates a number of distinct sovereignties. This type of compound system needs time to mature and become perfect...

Number 85 [7-8,15]

The friends of the new Constitution have said that it isn't absolutely perfect. Its enemies see this as a small triumph. They ask, "Why should we adopt an imperfect plan? Why not amend it and make it perfect before it is irrevocably established?"

This may be plausible, but it is only plausible. In the first place, they have exaggerated the concessions. They are stated as if they are an admission that the Constitution is very defective. And that it needs some big changes before the rights and the interests of the community can be safely confided to it.

Although the Constitution may not be perfect, it is a good plan. It is the best that the present views and circumstances of the country will permit. And it promises every type of security that a reasonable people can desire.

It is unwise to prolong the dangerous state of our national affairs. We should not expose the Union to the jeopardy of more experiments in the effort to find a perfect plan.

Imperfect men can never create a perfect plan. Group discussions always include errors and prejudices, as well as good sense and wisdom, just like the people in the groups. The agreement that will make thirteen States into a union must be a compromise of many different interests. How can a perfect plan come from such materials?

The people who want to amend the Constitution before it is established must stop if they agree with the following observations of a writer equally solid and ingenious

"To balance a large state or society (says he), whether monarchical or republican, on general laws, is a work of so great difficulty, that no human genius, however comprehensive, is able, by using only reason and reflection, to do it. The judgments of many must unite in the work; Experience must guide their labor; Time must bring it to perfection, and the feeling of inconveniences must correct the mistakes which *inevitably* are seen during their first trials and experiments." .[*]

These wise thoughts contain a lesson of moderation to all the sincere lovers of the Union. They should guard against hazarding anarchy, civil war, a perpetual alienation of the States from each other, and perhaps the military despotism of a victorious demagogue, while they pursue what they can only learn from time and experience. I may lack political fortitude, but I believe that it is dangerous to continue in our present situation.

A nation without a national government is an awful spectacle. The establishment of a Constitution, during peacetime, by the voluntary consent of a whole people, is an extraordinary accomplishment. I look forward to its completion with trembling anxiety.

I can think of no reason to let go of the hold we now have on this arduous enterprise. Seven out of the thirteen States have ratified the Constitution. There is no reason to start over again. I dread the consequences of new attempts because I know that powerful individuals, in this and in other States, are enemies of any national government.

---

[*] Hume's *Essays*, vol. I, page 128: "The Rise of Arts and Sciences."—PUBLIUS

Despite being a short, clearly written document, many people have never read the United States Constitution. For the majority of my life, I was part of that group. In fact, I had been studying The Federalist Papers for several weeks before I read the entire Constitution. I had heard so many arguments about the "meaning" of the Constitution and the need for scholarly and court interpretation that I assumed that it was highly ambiguous.

Even after reading the Constitution (and discovering its clarity), I still didn't appreciate the importance of the Preamble and, most importantly, the first seven words.

There's an original Star Trek episode where a group of people are fighting for freedom against their tyrannical rulers. I first saw the episode in the 1970s when I was worried about the direction of our federal government but knew nothing about our Constitution. I was completely surprised when it was revealed that the freedom fighters' sacred document was the Constitution of the United States. And I really didn't understand why Kirk read the first seven words of the document with such deep reverence.

If I would have found the document at that time in my life, I wouldn't have known its significance. Now I understand that these are some of the most important words ever written:

We, the people of the United States,

Number 84 [8]

This [Preamble] recognizes popular rights And it is more effective than the large number of aphorisms that make up our State bills of rights, which would sound much better in a treatise on ethics than in a constitution of government.

People Source of Government's Power

Number 2 [2]

Government is necessary. The people must cede some of their natural rights to the government to give it some powers.

Number 16 [10]

…Enlightened citizens will know the difference between legal authority and illegal usurpation of authority… The people are the natural guardians of the Constitution.

Number 21 [5]

…The people hold the whole power of the government…

Number 23 [11]

We should not entrust our national interests to a government that doesn't have all the powers a free people *should give to any government*…

Number 26 [2, 11]

The people delegate power to the government.

Schemes to subvert liberty *require time* to develop before taking action… If we assume that this could happen, there should be no more delegated authority. The people should take back the powers already given the government and divide themselves into as many States as there are counties so they can manage their government in person.

Number 28 [7]

If the citizens understand their rights and want to defend them, the ability to stop usurpation increases with the increased size of the state. The people in a large community have a natural strength. And that strength is greater than the artificial strength of the government and more able to stop an attempt to establish a tyranny.

In a confederacy, the people are the masters of their own fate. Since power is usually the rival of power, the national government will always stand ready to check State usurpations. And the States will be in the same position towards the national government.

Whichever side [State or national government] the people support will be the stronger. If their rights are invaded by either, they can use the other as the instrument of redress. The people will cherish the Union, preserving to themselves an advantage that can never be too highly prized!

Number 31 [12]

…In republics, strength is always on the side of the people… We should study the nature and extent of the powers as they are delineated in the Constitution. Everything beyond this must be left to the prudence and firmness of the people. They hold the scales and, it is hoped, they will always take care to preserve the constitutional equilibrium between the federal and the State governments…

Number 33 [6]

If the federal government overreaches its authority and uses its power tyrannically, the people, who created it, must go to the Constitution. They must correct the injury done to the Constitution. To determine if a law is constitutional, we must look at whether the law is based on Constitutional powers.

Number 37 [6]

…republican liberty seems to demand that all power comes from the people.

Number 39 [4]

…We define a republic as a government that gets all its powers—directly or indirectly—from the people… A republican government **must** come from all citizens, not just a favored class. If this is not true, a tyrant or a few tyrannical nobles could say they were creating a republic.

Number 46 [1 ,6]

…The federal and State governments are agents and trustees of the people… The ultimate authority resides in the people alone.

…Both the State and federal governments will depend on the people,

Number 49 [J]

People are the source of all government power. Government gets all its power from the constitution, which gets its power from the people. If government's powers need to be changed or one branch of government encroaches on the authorities of another branch, republican theory says that the people—the original authority—should make the corrections. Therefore, only the people can declare the constitution's true meaning and enforce it.

Number 51 [4, 9, 10]

...The primary control on the government is its dependency on the people...

In a single republic, the people surrender some of their power to a single government... America is a compound republic. The people surrender some power, which is divided between the State and federal governments.

[In] the federal republic of the United States...all authority will come from and depend on the citizens.

Number 53 [2]

...Americans understand that the people create a Constitution. And it is the supreme power. The government cannot alter the Constitution...

Number 78 [13]

This doesn't mean that judicial power is superior to the legislative power. It only means that the power of the people is superior to both.

Number 84 [8, 10]

...The proposed Constitution is founded on the power of the people...a bill of rights doesn't belong in the Constitution. The people surrender nothing. And they keep everything.

A bill of rights is not only unnecessary in the proposed Constitution, but would be dangerous. It would contain exceptions to powers not granted.

in Order to form a more perfect Union,

Number 11 [14]

Union Eliminates European Domination

We should aim for a position of dominance in American affairs.

The world is politically and geographically divided into four parts. Each part has a distinct set of interests. Unhappily for the other three, Europe, using arms and negotiations, by force and fraud, has extended her dominion, to varying degrees, over them all. Africa, Asia and America have successively felt her domination. Europe's superiority has tempted her to crown herself Mistress of the World, considering the rest of mankind as created for her benefit.

Some philosophers say Europeans are physically superior. And they have gravely asserted that all animals, including humans, degenerate in America. They say that even dogs cease to bark after breathing our air for a while.

For too long, facts have supported these European pretensions. We must save the honor of the human race and teach Europe moderation. As a Union, we can do it. Disunion will add another victim to Europe's triumphants.

Let Americans refuse to be European pawns! Let the 13 States, as a Union, erect one great American system that controls all transatlantic force or influence, and dictate how the old and new world will be connected.

States Must Remain United

We return to the fundamental question: Why should the States unite under one federal government? These arguments also explain why President Lincoln fought to re-unify the country.

Number 1 [8]

It may seem like everyone agrees that remaining united is important. But some opponents of the new Constitution say thirteen States are too many. They argue that we must break into several separate confederacies.[*]

The alternative to adoption of the new Constitution is dismemberment of the Union. Therefore, I will examine the advantages of staying united, the probable dangers, and certain evils of dissolution. This will be the subject of my next editorial.

Number 2 [1-7, 14]

Government is necessary. The people must cede some of their natural rights to the government to give it some powers. Will one federal government best serve the people

---

[*] The same idea, tracing the arguments to their consequences, is held out in several recent publications against the new Constitution. --PUBLIUS

of America? Or should they divide themselves into separate confederacies, giving each the powers of a national government?

Dividing America into Several Nations

Until recently, everyone agreed that America should remain united and that our prosperity depends on being one nation. Now some politicians say that looking for safety and happiness in one country is wrong. They want to divide the States into separate confederacies or nations. Before adopting this new idea, citizens should be sure that it is based on sound policy.

America is Geographically United

America is one connected, fertile, wide-spreading country. Providence blessed it with a variety of soils, watered with countless streams to delight and fulfill the needs of its inhabitants. As if to tie it together, navigable water forms a chain around its borders. The noblest rivers in the world form convenient highways for easy communication and transportation of commodities.

American is Culturally United

Providence gave this one connected country to one united people. The people speak the same language and profess the same religion. They believe in the same principles of government and have similar manners and customs. They fought side by side through a long and bloody war, establishing liberty and independence.

This country and this people seem to have been made for each other. It appears like this inheritance was designed by Providence for a band of brethren united by the strongest ties. They should never split into a number of unsocial, jealous, and alien sovereignties.

States Have Acted as One Nation

Until recently, everyone agreed that we should remain united. We have acted as one people. Each individual citizen enjoys the same national rights, privileges, and protection. As a nation we made peace and war. As a nation we formed alliances and made treaties.

Remaining One Union Important

The prosperity of America depends on its Union. The Constitutional Convention wrote the proposed Constitution to preserve and perpetuate the Union. What are the real motives behind current attempts to depreciate the importance of the Union? Why do some people say that we should break into three or four confederacies?

I believe Americans have always thought right on this subject. Their attachment to the Union is based on great and important reasons, which I will try to explain in some ensuing papers.

The people who want to break up America into several separate confederacies know that if the Constitution is rejected, the Union will be in jeopardy. I sincerely wish that every good citizen realizes that, if the Union is dissolved, America will have reason to exclaim, in the words of the poet: "FAREWELL! A LONG FAREWELL TO ALL MY GREATNESS.

Number 3 [1-2]

      People of any country (if, like Americans, they are intelligent and well informed) seldom hold erroneous beliefs about their best interests for many years. This is why Americans feel that the States should remain united with one federal government. And the federal government needs enough power to fulfill its responsibilities.

      The more I study the reasons for this opinion, the more I'm convinced they are valid.

Number 4 [1, 14-end]

      With only one national government, other nations would have fewer *just* causes for wars. And when problems developed, it would settle them more easily than either the State governments or the proposed small confederacies.

Example: Great Britain

      The fleets of Britain have been praised. If we are wise, in time the fleets of America may also be praised. But if Britain's one national government hadn't regulated navigation, making it a place for seamen to learn—if one national government hadn't used national resources and materials to form fleets—their prowess and ability would not be praised.

      Let England have its navigation and fleet—let Scotland have its navigation and fleet—let Wales have its navigation and fleet—let Ireland have its navigation and fleet—let the four parts of the British empire be under four independent governments and they would each dwindle into insignificance.

Divided America More Vulnerable

      Apply these facts to our case. Divide America into thirteen or three or four independent confederacies. What armies could they raise and pay? What fleets could they hope to have? If one was attacked, would the others fly to its aid, spend blood and money in its defense? Or would foreign powers talk the other confederacies into remaining neutral by making false promises of peace? The confederacies would fear threatening their peace and safety for the sake of their neighbors—neighbors they may already envy.

      Although such conduct is not smart, it is natural. The history of Greece and other countries has many examples. And under similar circumstances, it probably would happen again.

Better Defense Decisions

      Let's say neighboring States are willing to help another State or confederacy that has been attacked. How, when, and what shall determine the amount of men and money? Who will command the allied armies? Who will settle terms of peace? Who will settle disputes and make the nations obey the decisions? There would be many difficulties.

      But one government, watching over the interests and directing the powers and resources of the whole, would be free from these tricky questions.

Strong Nation Creates Strong Defense

      Whatever our situation—one national government or several confederacies—foreign nations will know and will act towards us accordingly. If they see an efficient national government with regulated trade, a disciplined army, well-managed resources, good credit, and a free and united people, they will want to be our friends rather than our enemies.

However, if they find our government ineffectual (each State doing right or wrong, as its ruler finds convenient) or split into three or four independent republics or confederacies that probably don't get along—one a British ally, another an ally of France, a third to Spain, and perhaps played off each other by the three—America will be a poor, pitiful figure in their eyes! She'd become a target for their contempt and their outrage.

When a people or family divides, it never fails to be against themselves.

Number 5 [all]

Greatest Threat to American Confederacies: Each Other

Queen Anne wrote to the Scot Parliament on July 1, 1706. She talked about the importance of the *Union* then forming between England and Scotland. She said, "An entire and perfect union will be the solid foundation of lasting peace: It will secure your religion, liberty, and property; remove the animosities amongst yourselves, and the jealousies and differences betwixt our two kingdoms. It must increase your strength, riches and trade; and by this union the whole island, being joined in affection and free from all apprehensions of different interest, will be *enabled to resist all its enemies. . .*"

"We most earnestly recommend to you calmness and unanimity in this great and weighty affair, that the union may be brought to a happy conclusion, being the only *effectual* way to secure our present and future happiness, and disappoint the designs of our and your enemies, who will . . . *use their utmost endeavors to prevent or delay this union.*"

Weak Nation Invites Foreign Danger

When a nation is weak and has many internal disagreements, it invites danger from other nations. Union, strength, and good government protect us. There is a lot to say about this subject.

Disputes Before Britain United

We may learn from the history of Great Britain without paying the price it cost them.

It seems obvious that the island should be only one nation. But for many, many years it was divided into three. They were almost always at war. Policies and jealousies kept them angry, despite their common interest in dealing with continental Europe. They hurt each other more than they helped each other.

Bordering Nations, Disputes Arise

If America divides into three or four nations, the same thing would happen. Instead of being "joined in affection," envy and jealousy would kill all affection. Each confederacy would pursue its own policies, not the general interests of all America. Like most *bordering* nations, they would always be either involved in disputes and war, or live with the constant fear of them.

Confederacies Won't Remain Equal

If created, the three or four American confederacies would not be equal in strength. No human plan can guarantee equality. Geography and local resources will increase power in one confederacy and hurt progress in another. Better policy and good management would raise one government above the rest. This would destroy the relatively equal strength. Good policy, prudence, and foresight would not be uniform among the confederacies.

One confederacy would become more politically important than her neighbors, who would envy and fear her. The other confederacies would do anything to decrease her importance; they would not help her prosper. She would notice the unfriendly feelings, lose confidence in her neighbors, and feel equally unfavorable to them. Distrust creates distrust. Nothing changes goodwill more quickly than jealousies and insinuations, whether expressed or implied.

North Would Become Strongest

The North is generally the region of strength. In time, the most Northern confederacy would be the strongest. Then the southern parts of America would have the same feelings about the northern States as the southern parts of Europe felt towards the *Northern Hive*. And the northerners might be tempted to invade and exploit their luxurious and more delicate southern neighbors.

Confederacies Become Enemies

History shows that American confederacies would not become neighbors. They would neither love nor trust one another. Instead, they would suffer from discord, jealousy, and mutual injuries. We would be in the exact situation some nations wish to see us, which is *threatening only to each other*.

The confederacies would not become allies. They would not unite arms and resources in defense against foreign enemies.

Different Commercial Goals

Britain and Spain are independent states. When did they ever unite their forces against a foreign enemy?

The proposed American confederacies would be *distinct nations*. Each would have commerce with foreign nations, regulated by treaties. And since their products and commodities are different and targeted for different markets, the treaties would be different.

Different commercial concerns create different interests and different political alliances with different foreign nations. The *Southern* confederacy might be at war with an ally of the *Northern* confederacy. Therefore, an alliance between the confederacies would not be easy to form. Or, if formed, it wouldn't be easy to maintain.

Foreign Alliances against Neighbors

In America, as in Europe, neighboring nations, with opposite interests and unfriendly passions, would frequently take different sides.

Because of our distance from Europe, the confederacies would be more fearful of other American confederacies than distant nations. They would use foreign alliances to guard against each other, rather than guard against foreign dangers with alliances between themselves.

Don't forget, it is easier to receive foreign fleets into our ports and foreign armies into our country than it is to persuade or force them to leave. How many conquests did the Romans and other nations make under the guise of allies? What changes did they make in the governments they pretended to protect?

Separation Wouldn't Stop Foreign Influence

Let candid men judge whether dividing America into several independent sovereignties would secure us against the hostilities and improper interference of foreign nations.

Throughout The Federalist Papers, the authors remind us that by studying history we learn psychology. Most importantly, they highlight the negative qualities of people who want to have positions of power. The history of the 20th century proves the accuracy of the warnings.

Number 6 [1-2]

Disunion would expose us to worse dangers than those from foreign nations—the dangers from each other.

Only a dreamer would believe that if the States break apart they wouldn't frequently fight each other. Men are ambitious, vindictive, and greedy. If you expect harmony between neighboring countries, you have ignored both history and psychology.

Number 7 [all]

Potential Reasons for Wars Between Disunited States

Some people condescendingly ask: If the States disunite, what reasons would they have to make war on each other? A full answer is: The same reasons that have started the wars in other nations.

Unfortunately for us, however, the question has a more specific answer. Even under the restraints of a federal constitution, we have felt the effect of the differences between us. We can figure out what would happen if those restraints were removed.

Disputes Over Territory

Arguments over land cause the greatest number of wars between nations. The disunited States would fight over land.

A large amount of land within the United States remains unsettled. If the Union were dissolved, all the States would make claims on the land.

Some land was not granted at the time of the Revolution and remains the subject of serious disagreements. The States that controlled their colonial governments claim them as property; other States say that land rights granted by Britain no longer existed after the founding of the Union.

Great Britain gave up the Western territory in the peace treaty. To settle the disputes over it, Congress had the States give it to the United States. If the Confederacy broke up, States that had given up the property would probably want it back. The other States would insist on a part, arguing that the territory was acquired by joint efforts of the Confederacy.

Even if all the States agreed to share in this common territory, the question of how to divide it would remain. Agreement between the States would be difficult.

Recent Territorial Disputes

We should fear that sometimes war would decide the differences over western territory.

The dispute over Wyoming land reminds us not to expect easy answers. Under the Articles of Confederation, Connecticut and Pennsylvania asked a federal court to decide. The court decided in favor of Pennsylvania. But Connecticut was unhappy. After negotiation, some other land was given to Connecticut. I'm not saying that Connecticut did anything wrong. She thought she deserved the land. States, like people, don't like decisions where they lose something.

When New York and Vermont disagreed, other States got involved. They were afraid that New York would become too powerful. If New York had tried to assert its rights by force, a war between the States might have started.

Some States seemed to want to divide New York into smaller States. New Jersey and Rhode Island supported Vermont's independence; Maryland agreed until it looked like Canada and Vermont were allies. If the States disunited, there could be more disagreements like these.

Commerce Can Create Controversies

Commerce is another source of controversy. Each State or separate confederacy would have a unique commercial policy with different taxes and product incentives. Commerce in this country has always been based on equal privileges. The change would make some States unhappy.

Injuries are caused by legitimate and justifiable acts of independent sovereignties with different interests.

America's enterprising businesses use every opportunity to improve. If trade regulations are made that only benefit one State, the other States probably won't obey them, which would lead to arguments, new regulations aimed at hurting the other States, then wars.

Some States would make commercial laws that make other States involuntarily subservient. The situation of New York, Connecticut, and New Jersey is an example.

New York put a tax on imports from Connecticut and New Jersey. Consumers in the two exporting States pay a large part of these taxes. New York will not voluntarily give up this advantage. How long would Connecticut and New Jersey pay taxes that only benefit New York? Would New York survive with the weight of Connecticut on one side and New Jersey on the other?

Conflict over National Debt

The Union's public debt would also cause conflict between the separate States or confederacies. Both the decision about how much each State should pay and paying the debt would produce anger. Some States either don't know the importance of national credit or they don't want to pay the nation's debt. In other States, the nation owes the citizens more than their State's proportion of the national debt.

States that owe money would procrastinate; citizens that are owed money in other States would become resentful. Arguments and excuses would delay making the decision about how much each State should pay. Foreign nations would demand the money owed to them. And the peace of the States would be in double jeopardy from external invasion and internal quarrels.

Suppose a decision about each State's debt payment was made. It would be difficult for some States to pay and they would want their share lowered. The other States would refuse to have their part of the debt increased. Their refusal would give the complaining States an excuse to withhold their contributions, creating bitter arguments.

Even if the division of the debt payment was equal in principle, some States would not pay for several reasons: lack of resources, financial mismanagement, governmental mismanagement, and the reluctance of men to postpone purchases by using money to pay debts.

Delinquencies, from whatever causes, produce complaints, recriminations, and quarrels. Mutual financial obligations that don't yield an equal benefit disturb the tranquility of nations. It is as true as it is trite: men differ over nothing so quickly as the payment of money.

Conflicts Between State Laws

Laws that violate private contracts and injure citizens of a State are another source of hostility. State codes have often been disgraced. If legislatures are unrestrained by a national government, they will not behave fairly.

For example, Connecticut wanted to retaliate against Rhode Island because of offenses by the Rhode Island legislature. Under other circumstances, a war, not of *paper* but of the sword, would punish breaches of moral obligation and social justice.

Alliances with European Nations

Preceding Papers explained why States or confederacies would probably ally with different foreign nations and how such alliances would hurt the peace of the whole. If America is not connected at all or only by the feeble tie of a league, foreign alliances will gradually entangle it in all the harmful labyrinths of European politics and wars. And the arguments between the American States would be used by nations who are equally the enemies of them all. *Divide et impera* (Divide and command) must be the motto of every nation that either hates or fears us.

Number 8 [all]

Disunited States Threat to Each Other

Let us assume the States disunite and alliances are formed from the wreck of the Union. All neighboring nations face peace and war, friendship and enmity. We would face the same thing.

Armies and Forts Block Invasions

At first, war between the American States would cause more distress than in countries with long military establishments. Although they damage liberty and the economy, the presence of disciplined armies in Europe make sudden conquests difficult.

Fortifications also delay conquests. The nations of Europe are encircled by fortified places. Campaigns against armed forts waste invasion resources. Obstacles occur at every step. Their strength is exhausted. The invader's progress is delayed. Formerly, an invading army got to the heart of a country almost as quickly as news of its approach reached its rulers. Now, a small force of disciplined defensive troops block larger invasions.

In Europe, whole nations are no longer conquered. Instead, towns are taken and returned, battles decide nothing. There is much effort and little acquisition.

Disunited States Will Lead to Conquests, Ruin

In this country, the opposite would happen. The separated States would postpone military spending. There are no forts, leaving State frontiers unguarded. Populous States would easily overrun less populous neighbors. However, conquests would be difficult to keep. Random wars would be followed by PLUNDER and devastation. Our military actions would create disasters for our citizens

Military Bases Destroy Freedom

This is not an exaggeration. But the situation would soon change.

Safety from external danger is the most powerful motivator of national conduct. After a time, even the deep love of liberty will diminish. War destroys life and property, and creates continuous state of danger. For security, even nations that love liberty must build institutions that tend to destroy their civil and political rights. To be safer, they will risk being less free.

Arms Race Between Confederacies

If the Union dissolves, standing armies will be used. Frequent wars and constant fear require a trained military.

The weaker States or confederacies—those with a smaller population and less money—would build a stronger defense, including disciplined standing armies and military fortifications. Their executive branch of government would be strengthened, evolving towards a dictatorship. During war, executive power increases at the expense of legislative authority.

Small nations with less natural strength but vigorous governments and disciplined armies, often triumph over larger nations or nations with greater natural strength.

The other States or confederacies would quickly use military means to get back what they lost. In a little time, the same type of tyrannies that hurt Europe will be established in this country.

This is the way people and nations naturally act.

America Commercial Nation

The ancient republics of Greece frequently fought. Why didn't standing armies spring up? This question has several answers.

Greece was primarily a nation of soldiers. Today, people pursue profits and spend their time and money improving agriculture and commerce. This activity is incompatible with a nation of soldiers. The growth of revenue and industry has completely changed how a nation defends itself. Professional, disciplined armies, rather than citizen armies (militias), are used when there are frequent wars.

Little Interior Defense

When a country is seldom exposed to military invasions, the rulers don't have any excuse to keep armies as large as in a nation that is easily invaded. And armies are rarely used for interior defense, so the people are in no danger of living under military rule. Citizens' rights and freedoms remain strong because there are few military emergencies. The civil state remains strong, not corrupted by the activities of a military state. The community is stronger than the small army.

Since the citizens don't need to be protected by the military and they don't live under oppressive military rule, they neither love nor fear soldiers. The citizens view soldiers as a necessary evil and are ready to resist any attempt to limit their civil rights.

The executive branch of government may use the army to suppress a small faction or an occasional insurrection. But it won't be able to stop a rebellion staged by the united efforts of all the citizens.

Large Military Decreases Civil Rights

In a country always afraid of war, the opposite happens. The government must always be prepared, needing armies large enough for instant defense. The constant need for their protection makes soldiers more important and reduces the citizens' freedoms. The military state becomes elevated above the civil.

Territories are often the theater of war. The inhabitants are subjected to frequent limitations on their rights, weakening their sense of those rights. Gradually, the people begin to consider soldiers not only as their protectors but also as their superiors. The transition to seeing them as masters is not difficult. Once it has happened, however, it's difficult to get the people to effectually resist usurpations.

Britain Doesn't Need Large Army

Great Britain is seldom exposed to internal invasions. Since it is an island and has a powerful navy it doesn't need a large army within the kingdom. It only needs a force large enough to hold invaders at bay until the militia can be raised. Neither national policy nor public opinion has tolerated a lot of domestic troops. And it has been a long time since an internal war has produced a military state.

Britain being an island has helped preserve its liberty, in spite of corruption. If Britain was on the continent, she would need internal military establishments as big as other European powers. She, like them, would probably be a victim of a dictator.

The island might be enslaved from other causes, but not from the small army that is usually kept within Britain.

United States Insulated from Danger

If we're wise enough to preserve the Union, we may enjoy the advantage of an insulated situation for a long time. Europe is a great distance from us. Her neighboring colonies will probably continue having so little strength that they won't be dangerous. Therefore, our security will not require extensive military establishments.

But if we disunite, our liberties would be at risk. We would need armies to defend against the ambition and jealousy of each other.

This concern is solid and weighty. It deserves serious and mature consideration by all men. If they think about it and look at all its consequences, they will give up trivial objections to a Constitution because if the Constitution is rejected, the Union will probably end. The ghosts that flit before the sick imaginations of some opponents of the Constitution would quickly be replaced by more substantial forms of dangers: real, certain, and formidable.

Number 12 [8-9]

Illicit Trade Between States Easy

The closeness of the States, the intersecting rivers, the bays, the ease of communication in every direction, the same language and manners, and similar commercial habits make illicit trade easy. The commercial regulations of each State are frequently evaded.

If the States separated, duties would have to be low to avoid the temptations of illicit trade. European nations guard the land and water avenues into their countries. France uses more than twenty thousand army troops to enforce their commercial regulations against contraband. Yet people still find ways to smuggle goods.

Preventing illicit trade over an inland border is very difficult. If the States disunited, it would be difficult to collect duties. Border patrols would need more powers, powers that are intolerable in a free country.

Number 13 [all]

While discussing tax revenue, it is proper to consider the smaller cost of having one national government. If the States remain united, they will need less total tax revenue. The federal government can apply money saved in one area to another area. And we will support only one national government. If the States divide into several confederacies, each confederacy will have a full national bureaucracy.

Few people have suggested that the States should divide into thirteen unconnected sovereignties. It would be expensive and dangerous. The men who want the States to disunite usually suggest three confederacies: the four Northern States, four Middle States, and five Southern States. A greater number of confederacies is improbable.

Each confederacy would need a government as large as the one in the proposed Constitution. When a nation reaches a certain size, its government needs to be the same size as much larger nations. This cannot be proven, but consider this: each proposed confederacy is approximately the size of the British island, which has a population of eight million. And the British government is probably large enough for a much larger population. Properly organized, civil power can become very large and wide spread. Using subordinate institutions, it can reproduce itself in every part of a great empire.

The government of each confederation of States would be as large as the one proposed in the Constitution.

If the States disunite, they will probably league themselves under two governments.

The four Eastern States (New Hampshire, Massachusetts, Connecticut, and Rhode Island) would unite. New York and New Jersey would probably join them. Penn-

...ylvania would join the Northern group of States because her foreign commerce is similar. For various reasons, the Southern States may not want to encourage shipping, allowing all nations to be both carriers and purchasers of their commodities. Pennsylvania may not want to join the Southern States because of their commercial policies.

No matter what happens, Pennsylvania will be a frontier. She may decide it is safest to have her exposed side turned towards the weaker power of the Southern Confederacy, rather than towards the stronger Northern power. This would give her the best chance to avoid being the Flanders of America.

Whatever Pennsylvania decides, if New Jersey joins the Northern Confederacy, there will be only one confederacy south of that State.

Thirteen States will be able to support a national government better than one-half, or one-third, or any number less than the whole. Yet people object to the Constitution based on its expense. This objection appears to be a mistake.

There are expenses in addition to having several civil bureaucracies. People must be employed to guard the inland borders against illicit trade. Conflicts between the divided States would make military forts necessary. Separation would injure the economy, tranquility, commerce, revenue, and liberty of every part.

Number 14 [all]

We have seen that we need a Union:

- o   to protect us from foreign danger
- o   to keep the peace among ourselves
- o   to guard our commerce and other common interests,
- o   as the only substitute for those military establishments that have subverted the liberties of the Old World.
- o   as the antidote to diseases of faction that have destroyed other popular governments. Alarming symptoms of them have already appeared in ours.

The last objection to discuss is based on the size of the Union. Some people fear that a republic isn't practical in such a large geographic area. Opponents of the new Constitution use this prejudice to invent problems because they can't find solid objections.

Democracy Must be Small

A republic does not have to be limited to a small area. A republic has been confused with a democracy. Opponents have applied democracy theories to a republic.

In a democracy, the people meet and administer the government in person. In a republic, representatives and agents assemble and administer it. Consequently, a democracy must be small. But a republic may be large.

Monarchy vs. Democracy or Republic

This is an unintentional error. Some famous authors influence modern public opinions. Since the authors lived in monarchies, they are biased. They stress the advantages or rationalize the evils of monarchies by comparing them to the vice and defects of a republic. To prove their points, they cite the turbulent democracies of ancient Greece and modern Italy.

The terms "democracy" and "republic" are misused. Observations made about a "democracy" are erroneously transferred to a "republic." One is that a republic must have a small number of people, living within a small territory.

Most ancient popular governments were democracies. Modern Europe developed the great principle of representation. However, it has no example of a completely popular and republican government.

America developed representation as the basis of large republics. It is sad that some people want to block America from adopting the Constitution and showing how well the system works.

Democracy Limits Area, Population

A democracy must be small with a limited population. All citizens must be able to assemble and administer the government.

The natural limit of a republic is the distance from the capital that allows representatives to meet and administer public affairs. Is the United States too big? During the last thirteen years, representatives of the States have been almost continually assembled. The attendance records of members from distant States have been no worse than those from the States in the neighborhood of Congress.

Let's look at the actual dimensions of the Union. According to the peace treaty, the eastern boundary is the Atlantic, the southern is the latitude of 31 degrees, the western is the Mississippi, and the northern is an irregular line running between 42 degrees and 45 degrees. The average north-south distance is 868¾ miles. The average distance between the Atlantic and the Mississippi probably doesn't exceed 750 miles.

Let's compare this size to European countries and we'll see that a republic is practical. Our territory is not much larger than Germany, where representatives continually assemble. Until the national assembly was recently ended in Poland, it was the center of supreme power. Although Great Britain is smaller, representatives from the northern most part of the island travel as far to their national council as required of those from the most remote parts of our Union.

Federal Government: Defined, Limited Jurisdiction

More observations will place the subject in a still better light.

First, the federal government will not have the whole power of making and administering laws. Its jurisdiction is limited to specific objectives. The State and local governments will keep their authority to care for all other concerns. If the new Constitution abolished the State governments, there would be a reason to object. In fact, if they were abolished, self-preservation would force the national government to reinstate them.

Constitution: Union, Adding States

Second, the immediate goal of the federal Constitution is to secure the union of the thirteen original States and adding new States. But how will the territory on our north-western frontier be handled? This is best left to people whose experience, at the time, will make them equal to the task.

Improves Commerce, Communication

Third, national infrastructure improvements will make commerce easier throughout the Union. Roads will be shortened and better maintained. Places for travelers to eat and sleep will increase and improve. River navigation will extend through most of the thirteen States. Communication will become easier. Nature gave our country many rivers; engineers find them easy to connect with canals.

States Benefit from Union's Defense

A fourth and most important consideration is safety.

Almost every State will be a frontier. For general protection, some sacrifices will be required. States furthest from the heart of the Union may receive fewer ordinary benefits from the Union but they share a border with foreign nations. Sometimes they will have the greatest need for the Union's strength and resources. Sending representatives to the capital may be inconvenient. However, it would be harder for them to struggle alone against an invading enemy or carry the full expense of defensive precautions. So, if they get fewer benefits in some respects than less distant States, they will get greater benefits in other respects. Thus, the proper balance will be maintained throughout.

American Spirit Unique in History

I know you will objectively evaluate these observations. You will never automatically allow predictions of catastrophe to drive you into despair, even if they appear formidable.

Affection binds America together. Don't listen to people who say we can no longer live together as members of the same family and guardians of our mutual happiness. Or that we can no longer be citizens of one great, respectable, and flourishing empire. Do not listen to the voice that says the government framed by the Constitution is so unusual that it has no place in even the wildest political theories and that it is impossible to establish.

No, my countrymen, shut your ears against this unhallowed language. Shut your hearts against its poison. Kindred blood flows in the veins of Americans. They shed blood to defend their sacred rights and consecrate their Union. We should be horrified at the idea of their becoming aliens, rivals, enemies.

If we are to shun new concepts, the rashest new concept is the idea that breaking apart will preserve our liberties and promote our happiness.

Why should the idea of a large republic be rejected just because it is a new concept? Americans study and respect opinions of former times and other nations. But, to their glory, they do not suffer from blind devotion for antiquity or custom. They overrule suggestions that go against their good sense, the knowledge of their situation, and the lessons of their experience.

Posterity will be indebted to the American spirit for its many innovations that improve private rights and public happiness. The Revolutionary leaders took unprecedented steps. They established a unique model of government. If they hadn't, the people of the United States might currently be laboring under the weight of some form of government that has crushed the liberties of the rest of mankind.

Happily for America. Happily, we trust, for the whole human race, they pursued a new and more noble course. Their revolution has no parallel in the annals of human society. They designed a great Confederacy. Their successors must improve and perpetuate it. If their works have imperfections, we wonder at how few.

If they erred most in the structure of the Union [Articles of Confederation], this was their most difficult work. Your Constitutional Convention has made a new model. And it is that act on which you are now to deliberate and decide.

Number 15 [1, 8-9]

I have tried to show that remaining united is important to your political safety and happiness. A sacred knot binds the American people. I've showed the dangers if the knot is severed by ambition or avarice, by jealousy or misrepresentation…

Treaties: Very Limited Effectiveness

A treaty creates a league or alliance of nations. Treaties depend on the good faith of the signature nations. Treaties can change or be ignored during peace and war, they can be observed or not observed, as the interests or passions of the signature nations dictate.

Earlier this century, treaties were very popular in Europe. Politicians hoped for benefits that never appeared. Alliances were formed then quickly broken, showing how little reliance should be placed on treaties.

States as Nations: Both Allies, Enemies

If the States become separate nations then form alliances, it would be ruinous. We'd make offensive and defensive alliances, which would change as jealousies and rivalries changed. Foreign nations would promote hostile relationships between the States. And the States would be alternately friends then enemies.

Number 41 [14-15,18,26]

The proposed Constitution is prudent. It keeps the States united. And dangerous military establishments won't be needed. America united—without a single soldier—does a better job of blocking foreign ambition than America disunited with a hundred thousand veterans ready for combat.

Geography and a great navy insulate Great Britain, which has saved its liberties. British rulers have never been able to create a large peacetime military establishment. The distance of the United States from the powerful nations of the world gives us the same security. As long as the States are united, a dangerous peacetime military will not be necessary.

However, the moment the Union breaks apart, things will change. The fears of the weaker States or ambition of the stronger States or Confederacies will set the same example in the New World as Charles VII did in the Old World. Instead of using our advantage as Great Britain has used hers, America would become a copy of the European continent. Standing armies and perpetual taxes would crush liberty.

The fortunes of a disunited America would be more disastrous than those of Europe. The sources of evil in Europe are confined by geography. No superior powers from other parts of the globe will ally with her rival nations, inflaming their mutual animosities. However, internal jealousies and wars would form only part of the problem in

America. Another source of evil is the unique relationship between Europe and this part of the earth.

The consequences of disunion cannot be too strongly or too often stated. Every man who loves peace, every man who loves his country, every man who loves liberty, should always have it before his eyes. He should cherish the Union of America and highly value preserving it.

Union Prevents Multiple Armies

A bad cause seldom fails to betray itself. The opposition to the federal government is an example of this truth. And their most striking blunder is their attempt to enlist the support of people who have sincere concerns about a standing army.

This is an important subject. The Constitution is the best guard against this danger. If the States disunite, each separate State or Confederacy will have a standing army. These armies will endanger properties and liberties more than the size of the military necessary under a united and efficient government. A strong Constitution will preserve the Union and support national defense.

Constitution Copies "Articles"

The objection seems even odder because the language in the Constitution appears to be a copy of the Articles of Confederation. The objective of forming a Union among the States, as described in Article Three, is "their common defense, security of their liberties, and mutual and general welfare." Article eight says: "All charges of war and all other expenses that shall be incurred for the common defense or general welfare, and allowed by the United States in Congress, shall be defrayed out of a common treasury," etc. Similar language again occurs in Article Nine.

If we interpret these articles in the Articles of Confederation by the rules objectors have used on the new Constitution, the existing Congress has the power to legislate about everything. But what if Congress disregarded the specifications that define and limit the general expressions and exercised an unlimited power of providing for the common defense and general welfare? Would the people making the objections have employed the same reasoning in justification of Congress as they now make against the Convention. How difficult it is for error to escape its own condemnation!

Number 45 [2]

Is the Union essential for the security of the American people? Does it protect us from foreign danger? Does it protect us from wars among the States? Does it guard against violent and oppressive factions that threaten liberty and the poisoning effect of military bases? In a word, is the Union essential to the happiness of the American people? The proposed federal powers are needed to meet the Union's objectives. It is preposterous to argue against a federal government by saying it may make the State governments less important.

We fought the American Revolution. We formed the American Confederacy. Thousands of people spilled their precious blood. And we spent the hard-earned money of millions. Did we do this so Americans can enjoy peace, liberty, and safety? Or did we do it for the State governments, so they can have power and sovereignty?

in Order to form a more perfect Union,

Number 59 [10]

Public Interests v. Ambition

Some people say that each State will have federal Representatives. And this will provide some security against the States using federal elections to abuse their power. This argument is somewhat valid.

But it will not provide complete security. There is a difference between the people's interest in public happiness and their local rulers' interest in power. The American people may like the federal government at the same time that some State rulers—supported by strong factions—want power and personal aggrandizement. There is already a conflict in some States between a majority of the people and powerful government officials.

If the nation was divided into several separate confederacies, the chance of this conflict multiplies. It will be a constant temptation to State politicians to increase their own benefits instead of advancing the public welfare.

If the States had exclusive power to regulate national elections, a few men from influential States might destroy the Union. They could use some little dissatisfaction among the people (that they may have promoted) to stop choosing Representatives.

European nations will be jealous of a firm Union with an efficient government. Sometimes foreign powers will try to subvert our government. And they will support internal intrigues. Therefore, when possible, the government's preservation should be guarded by people with an immediate interest in faithful and vigilant performances of the trust.

Number 84 [18]

Most Americans believe that their political happiness depends on staying united in one Union...

Number 85 [3]

If we adopt the Constitution, our republic, our liberty, and our property will be more secure.

Keeping the Union will restrain local factions and insurrections. And it will restrain the ambition of powerful people in single States who could become despots.

Breaking up the Confederacy would invite foreign intrigue. Keeping the Union will limit foreign influence.

If the States disunited, they would find reasons to fight each other. By staying united, fewer military forts and bases will be needed.

It will guarantee a republican form of government in each State.

It will exclude all titles of nobility.

And it will guard against the States repeating acts that have hurt property and credit, planted mutual distrust between citizens, and caused an almost universal decrease of morals.

establish Justice,

establish Justice,

Justice: Goal of Civil Society

Number 51 [10]
　　… Justice is the final goal of civil society and government. It will be pursued until it is obtained or until liberty is lost in the pursuit…

Number 70 [1]
　　Property must be protected against conspiracies that block justice.

Number 78 [18]
　　Independent judges guard both the Constitution and the rights of individuals. People need protection from bad ideas. Bad ideas can come from designing men. Or they can simply spread through the community. As the people get better information, bad ideas quickly go away. However, before they do, the government can make dangerous changes and seriously oppress the minority in the community.

　　The people can alter or abolish the constitution if it is not consistent with their happiness. This is the fundamental principle of republican government. Friends of the proposed Constitution will never agree with its enemies[*] and question that fundamental principle.

　　But let's say a majority of the people don't like a provision in the existing constitution. They tell their representatives. Then the representatives pass an unconstitutional law based on the people's wishes. The courts could not uphold the unconstitutional law. Until the people have changed or abolished the Constitution, through an authoritative act, it is binding on them collectively and individually. No presumption or knowledge of the people's wishes gives representatives the authority to depart from the Constitution. Judges need great fortitude. They must faithfully guard the Constitution after legislative invasions of it are started by the majority voice of the community.

---

[*] *Vide* "Protest of the Minority of the Convention of Pennsylvania," Martin's Speech, etc.—
　　PUBLIUS

insure domestic Tranquility,

Number 85 [3]

...Keeping the Union will restrain local factions and insurrections. And it will restrain the ambition of powerful people in single States who could become despots...

Strong Union Preserves Peace

Number 6 [3]

....Rulers often abuse their public office by using the excuse of doing something good for their citizens to start a war for personal gain or other selfish motives.

Number 7 [8]

...Mutual financial obligations that don't yield an equal benefit disturb the tranquility of nations. It is as true as it is trite: men differ over nothing so quickly as the payment of money.

Number 10 [all]

A well-constructed Union is the best way to control the violence of faction. Faction is a dangerous vice that occurs in popular governments. We welcome a plan that provides a cure for faction without violating the principles of liberty.

Unstable and unjust government agencies and departments kill popular governments. Opponents of the Constitution use this excuse in their most specious arguments.

The American State constitutions improve the popular governing models, both ancient and modern. They were expected to remove the danger, but they don't.

Our most virtuous citizens, men devoted to personal liberty, complain that our governments are too unstable. They say rival parties disregard the public good. An overbearing majority too often make decisions that should be based on justice and the rights of the minority party.

We may wish that these complaints had no foundation, but the evidence shows that they are in some degree true.

The government has been erroneously blamed for some of our problems. However, other causes, alone, don't account for our worst misfortunes. All across the continent, people worry about the nation's debt and they fear of loss of their personal rights. This is largely the effect of distrusting the unjust, factious spirit that is part of our government administration.

Faction Defined: Group Acts Against Community Interests

A faction is a group of citizens, either a majority or minority, whose actions are motivated by a passion or interest adverse to the rights of other citizens or to the permanent and aggregate interests of the community.

48

Faction Cure: Remove Causes or Control Effect

Faction can be cured two ways: remove its causes or control its effects.

Remove Causes

To **remove its causes** either (1) liberty must be destroyed or (2) every citizen must have the same opinions, passions, and interests.

The first remedy is far worse than the disease. Liberty is to faction what air is to fire. Without the nourishment of liberty, faction instantly dies. But abolishing liberty because it nourishes faction is as silly as the wish to annihilate air because it gives fire its destructive energy.

The second cure is as impractical as the first is unwise. Men's abilities are diverse, creating yet another barrier to their agreeing on common interests. As long as a connection between reasoning and self-love exists, opinions and passions will influence each other. And passions will sway opinions.

Property rights originate from the people. But men's abilities are diverse, creating an insurmountable obstacle to equality of acquisitions. Protection of these abilities is government's primary function. Because government protects different and unequal abilities to acquire property, the people end up owning properties of varying value and kind. This diversity of property ownership divides society into groups with different interests and concerns.

Faction: Inherent in Human Nature

Therefore, faction is part of the very nature of man. People have different opinions about religion and government. Ambitious leaders, human passions and diverse interests divide mankind into parties and inflame animosities. People tend to oppress each other, not cooperate for their common good. Frivolous differences become excuses to kindle unfriendly passions and excite violent conflicts.

The most common source of factions is the unequal distribution of property. Property owners and people without property have different interests. Likewise, creditors and debtors.

Civilized nations have property owners, manufacturers, merchants, bankers and many less defined occupations. This creates different groups of people with different views and interests. Regulating these conflicting interests is the principal task of modern legislation. Therefore, factions are a part of the ordinary operations of government.

Legislators: Advocates and Parties to Causes

No man is allowed to be a judge in his own cause. His interest would bias his judgment and probably corrupt his integrity.

For even greater reasons, a group of men are unfit to be both judges and litigants at the same time. Yet legislative acts are basically judicial determinations, not about the rights of individuals, but about the rights of groups of citizens. Yet legislators are both advocates and parties to the causes they determine.

If a proposed law concerns private debts, creditors and debtors are the parties. Justice should balance between them. Yet legislators, who are both creditors and debtors, arc the judges. The most numerous group or, in other words, the most powerful faction will prevail.

Should foreign manufacturers be restricted to support domestic manufacturers? Landowners would say no; manufacturers would say yes. Neither would probably use justice and the public good as their only guide.

Determining the amount of taxes on different types of property requires impartiality. Yet no legislative act has a greater opportunity and temptation for the majority party to trample on the rules of justice. With every dollar they overburden the minority party, they save a dollar in their own pockets.

It is naïve to say that enlightened statesmen will adjust the different interests, making them all subservient to the public good. First, enlightened statesmen will not always be at the helm. Second, we must consider indirect and future effects. These less obvious consequences will rarely prevail over the immediate interest one party may have in disregarding the rights of another or the good of the whole.

Effect of Faction Must Be Controlled

Obviously, the **causes** of faction cannot be removed. Its **effects** must be controlled.

Majority Faction: Downside of Popular Government

If a faction isn't a majority, the majority can defeat its sinister views. The minority faction may clog the government and agitate society, but under the Constitution, it can't carry out its plans and hide its violence.

When a faction is a majority, it can sacrifice public good and the rights of other citizens to their passions and interests.

We want to secure the public good and private rights against the danger of a majority faction. At the same time, we want to preserve the popular government form. Our great task is to rescue the reputation of popular government so that it will be valued and adopted by mankind.

Prevent Majority Faction's Passions or Actions

To control the effects of a majority faction, either (1) the negative passions and interests in a majority faction must be prevented or (2) the majority faction must be unable to carry out plans of oppression.

If desire and opportunity coincide, neither moral nor religious values will control oppressive behavior. Morality doesn't control the injustice and violence of individuals. And its ability to control bad behavior decreases as the number of people involved increases. In other words, as the need for morality increases, its effectiveness decreases.

Pure Democracy: Magnifies Violence of Factions

In a pure democracy, citizens assemble and administer the government in person. Democracy doesn't cure the harm caused by faction. Usually, the majority will feel a common passion. There is nothing to stop the desire to sacrifice the weaker party or obnoxious individual.

Therefore, pure democracies are always turbulent. They don't secure personal or property rights. They have short lives and violent deaths. Some political theorists think that after people become politically equal, their possessions, their opinions, and their passions will also be equal. This doesn't happen.

Republic vs. Pure Democracy

A republic—a government administered by representatives of the people—promises the cure we are seeking. We will examine the differences between a republic and a pure democracy. This will show both the cure and why the Union makes it more effective.

A republic and a democracy differ in two ways: First, in a republic, the citizens elect a small number of governmental delegates. Second, a republic can have more citizens living across a larger country.

Representation refines public views by passing them through the delegates. The representatives' wisdom may see their country's true interests. Their patriotism and love of justice will make them less likely to sacrifice their country. Representatives of the people may do a better job of looking out for the public good than if all the people gathered and spoke for themselves.

On the other hand, the opposite effect may happen. Men with local prejudices or sinister plans may use intrigue or corruption to be elected, and then betray the interests of the people.

Will small or large republics elect better guardians of the public good? For two reasons, large republics do.

Representative/Constituent Ratio

First, in a small republic there still must be enough representatives to guard against the plots of a few. In a large republic, the number must be limited to guard against the confusion of a multitude. The proportion of representatives to their constituents is larger in the small republic. If the proportion of qualified people is the same in a large as a small republic, the large republic will have more options and a greater probability of a good choice.

In a large republic, each representative is chosen by a greater number of citizens. It will be more difficult for unworthy candidates to successfully win through vicious election practices. And with wide voter freedom, elections will more likely center on men who possess the most merit and highest character.

When a representative has too many constituents, it will be difficult for him to know all the local issues. When a representative has too few constituents, his worry about local issues will make him unfit to understand and pursue national issues. The federal Constitution forms a good combination. The national issues are referred to the national government; local issues are referred to State legislatures.

Large Area: Conspiracy Harder

Second, a republic can have more citizens and a larger territory than a democracy. This makes raising a damaging amount of support for a faction more difficult.

A small society has fewer people, parties and interests. In a small community, it is easy for a faction to become a majority and execute oppressive plans.

A large society has a variety of people, parties and interests. It is less likely that a majority will invade the rights of other citizens. Even if a common motive exists, it will insure domestic Tranquility,

be more difficult for those holding it to discover their combined strength and act in unison with each other. When unjust or dishonorable purposes exist, communication is limited by distrust in proportion to the number whose concurrence is necessary.

Union as Control of Effects of Faction

Hence, a republic controls the effects of faction better than a democracy. And a large republic controls it better than a small republic. It may have more enlightened, virtuous representatives who are above local prejudices and schemes of injustice. There will be a greater variety of parties, so one party can't outnumber and oppress the rest. An increased variety of parties increases the Union's security. A large republic has more obstacles to the secret wishes of an unjust majority.

Factious Passions: Effect on Union

Factious leaders may kindle a flame within their States, while not able to spread a conflagration through the other States. A religious sect may degenerate into a political faction in a part of the Confederacy. But the variety of sects dispersed over the entire country secures the national councils against this danger. A rage for paper money, for an abolition of debts, for an equal division of property, or for any other improper or wicked project, will be less able to pervade the whole Union, just like a malady is more likely to taint a specific county or district than an entire State.

Positive Effects of Size, Structure of Government

In the size and proper structure, therefore, we see that our Union cures the most common diseases of republican government. And according to the degree of pride we feel in being a republic, we will cherish and support the character of federalists.

Number 9 [1]

A strong Union will reduce domestic violence and revolts. This preserves the peace and liberty of the States…

Number 16 [7]

If a federal government is supposed to regulate common concerns and preserve tranquility, it must have authority over the citizens.

Number 28 [4]

…Whether we have one government for all the States or several governments, sometimes a force other than the militia may be necessary to keep the peace and maintain the lawful authority against revolts and rebellions.

Number 45 [2]

…Is the Union essential for the security of the American people? Does it protect us from foreign danger? Does it protect us from wars among the States? Does it guard against violent and oppressive factions that threaten liberty and the poisoning effect of military bases? In a word, is the Union essential to the happiness of the American people? The proposed federal powers are needed to meet the Union's objectives. It is preposterous to argue against a federal government by saying it may make the State governments less important.

We fought the American Revolution. We formed the American Confederacy. Thousands of people spilled their precious blood. And we spent the hard-earned money of millions. Did we do this so Americans can enjoy peace, liberty, and safety? Or did we do it for the State governments, so they can have power and sovereignty? The Old World doctrine said that people were made to serve kings, not kings to serve the people. Should we follow the same doctrine—in another shape—in the New World? Should we sacrifice the people's happiness to the States?

No form of government has any intrinsic value. A government's value is judged by how it fulfills the public good and meets the needs of the people. If the Constitution harmed public happiness, I would say: Reject the plan. If the Union hurt public happiness, I would say: Abolish the Union. In a similar manner, when State sovereignty is incompatible with the happiness of the people, every good citizen should cry out: Let the former be sacrificed to the latter.

provide for the common defence,

Number 19 [14]

    ...Poland, a government over local sovereigns, might be noticed. It gives striking proof of the calamities flowing from institutions that are equally unfit for self-government and self-defense. Poland has long been at the mercy of its powerful neighbors who recently, and graciously, disburdened it of one-third of its people and territories.

Number 23 [all]

Federal Responsibilities, Powers, Organization

An energetic Constitution is necessary to preserve the Union.

    Our inquiry covers four topics:

- The reasons for having a federal government.
- The amount of power the federal government needs to fulfill its purposes.
- The people who should control that power.
- The organization of the federal government.

The most important reasons for a union and federal government are:

- Defense.
- To keep the peace against both internal turmoil and external attacks.
- To regulate commerce with other nations and between the States.
- To supervise our political and commercial interests with foreign countries.

Powers Essential for Defense

    To defend the country, the federal government needs the power to raise armies, build and equip fleets, direct army and navy operations and provide support for both. These powers should not be limited *because it is impossible to predict future national emergencies or the size and type of force that may be necessary to solve them.*

    An infinite number of things can endanger the nation's safety. Therefore, constitutional limits on the power to protect the nation are unwise. Defensive power should equal the strength of all possible emergencies.

    This truth carries its own evidence. It rests on universal axioms. The *means* should be proportionate to the *end*; the persons charged with attaining the *end* should possess the *means* for attaining it.

    Should a federal government be entrusted with the common defense? If the answer is yes, the government needs the power to execute that trust. Authority to provide for defense cannot be limited. Any matter essential to the *formation, direction,* or *support* of the NATIONAL FORCES should not be limited.

    The people who wrote the Articles of Confederation apparently understood this principle. But they didn't provide a way to do it. Congress can requisition (demand that each State send a specific amount) men and money and control the army and navy. Congressional requisitions are constitutionally binding on the States; the States have a legal duty to furnish the required supplies. The Articles of Confederation authorized the federal government to command all resources that are necessary for the "common defense and general welfare." The authors of the Articles assumed that the States would be aware of their best interests and duty to the Union and they would fill the federal requisitions.

Direct Authority Over Citizens

However, this was a mistaken assumption. If we really want to give the Union energy and a long life, we must stop making laws that States are supposed to obey. Federal laws must extend to individual citizens. Quotas and requisitions are impractical and unjust. They must be discarded.

The Union should have the power and money to draft troops, support an army, and build and equip a navy in the same way as other governments.

Powers to Fulfill Responsibilities

We need a compound or confederate government instead of a simple, single government. The RESPONSIBILITIES of each branch of power must be determined. And each branch must have enough authority to fulfill its responsibilities.

Should the Union guard the common safety? Are fleets, armies and money necessary? The Union must have the power to pass all laws and regulations that relate to them. The same is true for commerce and every other area under its jurisdiction.

Is the administration of justice between citizens of the same State a responsibility of local government? The local governments must have the authority to fulfill their responsibilities.

It is unwise to not give each part of government the amount of power that it needs to fulfill its duties. And it would put the future national needs in disabled hands.

The federal government is charged with public safety and defense. It will have the most information needed to understand the extent and urgency of threats. Representing the WHOLE, it will want to protect every part. With authority throughout the States, it can establish uniform plans to secure the common safety.

Isn't it illogical to make the federal government responsible for national defense, but leave the *effective* power of providing for defense with the State governments?

The States won't always cooperate. There will be weakness and disorder. Some States will face more of the horrors of war and the intolerable increase of expense that accompanies it. We saw these effects during the revolution.

Proposed Powers = Federal Goals

We should not entrust our NATIONAL INTERESTS to a government that doesn't have all the powers a free people *should give to any government*. The government that is supposed to take care of these interests must have the power to do it.

Adversaries of the Constitution would seem more sincere if they limited their arguments to showing that the people can't trust the internal structure of the proposed government. They shouldn't have wandered into pointless discussions about how much power the national government will have.

provide for the common defence,

The POWERS are not too extensive for the OBJECTIVES of a federal government; or, in other words, for the management of our NATIONAL INTERESTS. And there are no good arguments that show it has excess powers. If the federal government has too much power, then the difficulty stems from the nature of government. If it is unsafe to give the country all of the powers it needs, then we should downsize our ideas and simply form smaller, separate confederacies.

It is absurd to entrust national interests to a government that doesn't have the authority to properly manage them.

I don't believe that anyone can prove that one general system is impractical. This is a large country; only an energetic government can preserve the Union. The people who oppose the proposed Constitution predict that a national system spread across the entire area of the present Confederacy is impractical.

Number 25 [1]

Some people say the States should provide armies, under the direction of the federal government. However, the primary purpose of our combining to form a confederacy under a federal government is defense. If States held the military power, it would oppress some States, be dangerous to all, and harmful to the Confederacy.

Number 26 [2]

The legislature will authorize national defense...

Number 31 [6]

The Union government has a duty to supervise the national defense and secure the public peace against foreign and domestic violence...

Number 34 [4, 5]

...The federal government must provide the national defense. It must protect the nation against foreign war and domestic violence...

...the government must be able guard the community against the ambition or hatred of other nations. If war breaks out in Europe, will we feel some of its fury? Or will another cause or country disturb our tranquility? Peace or war will not always be left to our option. We might be moderate or unambitious but we can't count on the moderation or hope to extinguish the ambition of others.

Number 45 [10]

The federal government's operations will be most extensive and important in times of war and danger. The State governments will be most important in times of peace... as the national defense improves, there will be less danger that the federal government will become more important than the State governments.

Safety, Purpose of Government

Number 3 [3]

Wise and free people have several goals. *Safety* is first...

Number 2 [3]

Until recently, everyone agreed that America should remain united and that our prosperity depends on being one nation. Now some politicians say that looking for safety and happiness in one country is wrong. They want to divide the States into separate confederacies or nations. Before adopting this new idea, citizens should be sure that it is based on sound policy.

Number 15 [1]

I have tried to show that remaining united is important to your political safety and happiness.

Number 25 [2,5]

The territories of Britain, Spain, and the Indian nations do not border specific States. They encircle the Union. To differing degrees, all of the States are in danger. Therefore, the national government and treasury should be responsible for defense.

Some States are exposed to more danger, including New York. If the States had to provide for their own defense, New York would carry the whole burden of her immediate safety and, ultimately, the protection of her neighbors. This would not be fair to New York or safe for other States.

The States who need military posts won't be willing or able to support a military for a long time. Therefore, national security would depend on the stinginess, lack of foresight, or inability of one State.

On the other hand, if a State had the men and money, it would increase its military spending proportionately. If two or three powerful States held the whole military force of the Union, the other States would be alarmed. They would take counter measures. Military establishments, nourished by mutual jealousy, would swell. The State armies would destroy the national authority.

Improper restraints on the national legislature create problems. Some people object to standing armies during peacetime. But how far should the prohibition extend? Will it ban raising armies, as well as, to *keeping them up* in time of tranquility?

A prohibition that only limits keeping armies isn't specific and will not fulfill the purpose intended. Once armies are raised, what does the constitution mean by "keeping them up?" How much time would be a violation? A week, a month, a year? Or may they continue as long as there is a danger?

This means they can be kept up *in time of peace*, if there are threats or impending danger. This is different than the literal meaning of the prohibition. Who will judge that the danger continues? The national government can first raise troops, then keep them as long as the peace or safety of the community is in jeopardy. The provision could be easily ignored.

Number 40 [16]

…The States first united against danger because people believe that they could plan for their safety and happiness. Committees and congresses worked hard, defending the people's rights…

provide for the common defence,

Number 43 [30]

      …Self-preservation is a primary law of nature and God. All political institutions are created to keep people safe and able to pursue happiness. When a political system fails to fulfill those goals, it must be sacrificed…

Number 45 [2]

      … Is the Union essential for the security of the American people? Does it protect us from foreign danger? Does it protect us from wars among the States? Does it guard against violent and oppressive factions that threaten liberty and the poisoning effect of military bases? In a word, is the Union essential to the happiness of the American people? The proposed federal powers are needed to meet the Union's objectives…

      We fought the American Revolution. We formed the American Confederacy. Thousands of people spilled their precious blood. And we spent the hard-earned money of millions. Did we do this so Americans can enjoy peace, liberty, and safety?

Number 54 [8]

      …Government is established to protect both property and people… In the federal Constitution, the same hands protect both property and personal rights. Therefore, some attention ought to be paid to property when choosing those hands.

Number 85 [5]

      …is the Constitution necessary for public safety and prosperity?

Danger from Foreign Nations

Number 14 [1]

We have seen that we need a Union:
      as our **bulwark against foreign danger**

Number 3 [all]

Union Provides Safety Against Foreign Danger

      People of any country (if, like Americans, they are intelligent and well informed) seldom hold erroneous beliefs about their best interests for many years. This is why Americans feel that the States should remain united with one federal government. And the federal government needs enough power to fulfill its responsibilities.

      The more I study the reasons for this opinion, the more I'm convinced they are valid.

Safety: Government's First Objective

      Wise and free people have several goals. *Safety* is first. The desire to be *safe* can mean many things. I will discuss two: safety against dangers from *foreign arms and influence* and dangers arising from domestic causes.

Danger from Foreign Nations

      The first danger is from foreign nations. If we remain one nation, with an efficient national government, we will have the best security against *hostilities* from other nations.

58

Both *real* and *imagined* grievances *provoke* or *invite* wars. Will a *united* America or a *disunited* America find more *just* causes for war? If a united America will find fewer reasons, then if we remain one Union, it will tend to preserve a state of peace with other nations.

Just causes for war include treaty violations and direct violence, attack or invasion. America already has treaties with at least six nations. All, except Prussia, have navies that could injure us. We have extensive commerce with Portugal, Spain, and Britain. Spain and Britain also have neighboring territory.

To stay at peace, America must observe the laws of nations. One national government can do this more easily than either thirteen separate States, or three or four confederacies.

Highly Qualified Men in National Government

When an efficient national government is established, usually the best men in the country will be appointed to manage it. A town or county can place men in State and local offices. However, to recommend men to national offices, a wider reputation for talents and qualifications is necessary. The public will choose from the widest field, never lacking qualified persons. Therefore, the administration, legislation, and judicial decisions of the national government will be more wise and judicious than those of individual States. Consequently, a Union will be *safer* with respect to other nations, as well as *safer* with respect to us.

Standard Treaties, Policies

One national government will always interpret treaties and laws of nations in one way. However, if thirteen States—or three or four confederacies—interpreted the same treaties and laws, they would sometimes come to different conclusions. Different local laws and interests would influence each government. Therefore, it is wise to have one judicial system appointed by and responsible to one national government to decide such questions.

The people governing one or two States may be tempted to swerve from trustworthiness and justice. But local temptations would have little or no influence on the national government, preserving good faith and justice. The peace treaty with Britain is a good example.

Fewer Temptations for National Officials

Individual States have specific interests that cause temptations. The governing party may not be able or willing to stop an injustice or punish the aggressors. Unaffected by local interests, national officials will not be tempted to commit such wrongs themselves. They will try to prevent it. And they will punish its commission by others.

Treaty Violations Lead to Just Causes for War

Both intentional and accidental violations of treaties and laws of nations provide *just* cause for war. They are less likely to happen under one general government than several lesser ones. Therefore, the people are *safer* under one national government.

provide for the common defence,

States Provoke Wars

Direct, unlawful violence also starts wars. Passions and interests of one or two States rather than the whole Union usually cause it. One good national government provides the greatest security against this.

For example, the federal government has never started an Indian war. But the improper conduct of individual States provoked several Indian wars. Those States were either unable or unwilling to stop or punish offenses that led to the slaughter of many innocent people.

Some States border Spanish and British territories. Only bordering States, because of an irritation or sense of injury, would be likely to use violence to start a war with these nations. Regional passions won't sway a wise and prudent national government. And the national government can block the danger.

Cool Heads Will Settle Disputes

A national government will have more power to settle hostilities. It will be more temperate and cool than the offending State. Pride makes both men and States justify their actions and oppose acknowledging or correcting their errors and offenses. Not affected by this pride, the national government will be more moderate. And it will work towards a solution for the threatening difficulties.

Apologies of Strong Nations Accepted

Explanations and compensations from a strong nation are often accepted as satisfactory, when they would be rejected as unsatisfactory if offered by a State or confederacy of little power. In 1685, the state of Genoa offended Louis XIV. He demanded they send their chief magistrate to *France* to ask his pardon and receive his terms. To make peace, they had to obey. Would he have demanded or received the same humiliation from Spain, Britain or any other *powerful* nation?

Number 4 [all]

Strong Union Provides Strong Defense

With only one national government, other nations would have fewer *just* causes for wars. And when problems developed, it would settle them more easily than either the State governments or the proposed small confederacies.

Just and Pretended Reasons for War

To remain safe, America must not give other nations *just* causes for war. *And* it must not get into situations that *invite* hostility. Nations start wars both for legitimate and illegitimate (pretended) reasons.

Kings Start Wars for No Logical Reason

It is a sad fact that nations, in general, will start a war whenever they think they can get something from it. In fact, dictators and kings often start wars when their nation gains nothing. Motives include: a desire for military glory, revenge for personal insults, ambition, and private agreements to promote families or friends. Personal motives lead dictators and kings to start wars that are neither just nor good for the people they govern.

But there are other reasons that both nations and kings use to start wars. And some of them grow out of situations like ours.

International Trade

France, England and America catch and sell fish. But America can sell fish in France and England at a cheaper price than their own fishermen. To try to stop us, their governments pay rewards to their fishermen and tax the American fish.

Our boats also compete with European nations in cargo transport. They don't want to see our transportation business increase because it decreases theirs. It's in their interest to limit our trade, not promote it.

Our trade with China and India has reduced the profits of several nations. We now directly import items that we used to purchase through a monopoly.

Regional Trade

Any nation with territories on or near this continent can't be happy about our commercial growth. Our products are cheap and excellent. Our convenient location gives our hard-working merchants and ships advantages in those territories, to the displeasure of Europe.

Spain doesn't allow our boats on the Mississippi river. Britain doesn't allow our ships on the Saint Lawrence River. And neither permits commercial ships on the other waterways that flow between them and us.

For these—and some other reasons—other nations may become jealous and afraid of us. They will worry about our advancement in union and power, land and sea.

One Government Safer Than Several

Americans know these circumstances may lead to war. As will other reasons, not currently obvious. When there is an opportunity, nations find an excuse to start a war. Therefore, if we remain united under a good national government, we will defensively discourage war instead of *inviting* it. The best defense depends on the government, the arms, and the resources of the country.

The safety of the whole is the interest of the whole. To be safe, we must have a government, either one or many. In this context, will one good government provide more safety than any other number?

One government can use the talents and experience of the very best men. It can have a uniform policy. It can look ahead, create standard policies for the whole nation, and protect the parts.

In drafting treaties, one government will think of both the whole nation and its parts. And when one part is attacked, it can use the resources and power of the whole to defend that part. The army will have one chain of command up to the President. One army is more efficient than thirteen, or three or four independent forces.

Example: Great Britain

Consider the British army. What if the English army obeyed the government of England, the Scot army obeyed the government of Scotland, and the Welsh army obeyed the government of Wales? If invaded, would those three governments (if they agreed at all) operate as effectively against the enemy as the single government of Great Britain?

provide for the common defence,

The fleets of Britain have been praised. If we are wise, in time the fleets of America may also be praised. But if Britain's one national government hadn't regulated navigation, making it a place for seamen to learn—if one national government hadn't used national resources and materials to form fleets—their prowess and ability would not be praised.

Let England have its navigation and fleet—let Scotland have its navigation and fleet—let Wales have its navigation and fleet—let Ireland have its navigation and fleet   let the four parts of the British empire be under four independent governments and they would each dwindle into insignificance.

Divided America More Vulnerable

Apply these facts to our case. Divide America into thirteen or three or four independent confederacies. What armies could they raise and pay? What fleets could they hope to have? If one was attacked, would the others fly to its aid, spend blood and money in its defense? Or would foreign powers talk the other confederacies into remaining neutral by making false promises of peace? The confederacies would fear threatening their peace and safety for the sake of their neighbors—neighbors they may already envy.

Although such conduct is not smart, it is natural. The history of Greece and other countries has many examples. And under similar circumstances, it probably would happen again.

Better Defense Decisions

Let's say neighboring States are willing to help another State or confederacy that has been attacked. How, when, and what shall determine the amount of men and money? Who will command the allied armies? Who will settle terms of peace? Who will settle disputes and make the nations obey the decisions? There would be many difficulties.

But one government, watching over the interests and directing the powers and resources of the whole, would be free from these tricky questions.

Strong Nation Creates Strong Defense

Whatever our situation—one national government or several confederacies—foreign nations will know and will act towards us accordingly. If they see an efficient national government with regulated trade, a disciplined army, well-managed resources, good credit, and a free and united people, they will want to be our friends rather than our enemies.

However, if they find our government ineffectual (each State doing right or wrong, as its ruler finds convenient) or split into three or four independent republics or confederacies that probably don't get along—one a British ally, another an ally of France, a third to Spain, and perhaps played off each other by the three—America will be a poor, pitiful figure in their eyes! She'd become a target for their contempt and their outrage.

When a people or family divides, it never fails to be against themselves.

Number 11 [2, 8, 10-11, 14]

…Some nations have colonies in North America. Those nations worry about our abilities. If we stay united and have the resources to create a powerful navy, we will be a threat to their American colonies.

Disunited, Europe Dominate Commerce

If we disunite, European alliances might be successful. Nations with a powerful navy could dictate the conditions of our political existence…

Commerce Improves Navigation

Commerce will improve our navigation. This resource will help when we build a navy.

A navy. Staying united will support this great national objective. Every institution grows and flourishes in proportion to the amount of resources put towards its formation and support.

It will be easier for the United States to create a navy than any single State or small confederacy. Different areas of the country have different resources. The southern States have naval stores—tar, pitch, and turpentine. Their wood is more solid and lasting. Some southern and middle States have high quality iron. The northern States will supply most of the seamen.

Naval protection of our commerce is important; maritime commerce will help our navy.

Union Eliminates European Domination

We should aim for a position of dominance in American affairs.

The world is politically and geographically divided into four parts. Each part has a distinct set of interests. Unhappily for the other three, Europe, using arms and negotiations, by force and fraud, has extended her dominion, to varying degrees, over them all. Africa, Asia and America have successively felt her domination. Europe's superiority has tempted her to crown herself Mistress of the World, considering the rest of mankind as created for her benefit.

Some philosophers say Europeans are physically superior. And they have gravely asserted that all animals, including humans, degenerate in America. They say that even dogs cease to bark after breathing our air for a while.

For too long, facts have supported these European pretensions. We must save the honor of the human race and teach Europe moderation. As a Union, we can do it. Disunion will add another victim to Europe's triumphants.

Let Americans refuse to be European pawns! Let the 13 States, as a Union, erect one great American system that controls all transatlantic force or influence, and dictate how the old and new world will be connected.

Number 14 [11]

States Benefit from Union's Defense

A fourth and most important consideration is safety.

Almost every State will be a frontier. For general protection, some sacrifices will be required. States furthest from the heart of the Union may receive fewer ordinary benefits from the Union but they share a border with foreign nations. Sometimes they will have the greatest need for the Union's strength and resources. Sending representatives to the capital may be inconvenient. However, it would be harder for them to struggle alone against an invading enemy or carry the full expense of defensive precautions. So, if they get fewer benefits in some respects than less distant States, they will get greater benefits in other respects. Thus, the proper balance will be maintained throughout.

Number 18 [9-10, 18]

Enter as Ally; Stay as Conqueror

When a weak government is not at war, disagreements within the nation bring new dangers from other nations. After the Phocians plowed up consecrated ground at the temple of Apollo, the Amphictyonic council fined the sacrilegious offenders. The Phocians, aided by Athens and Sparta, refused to submit to the decree. On the other side, the Thebans, with some other cities, supported the Amphictyons' authority to avenge the violated god.

Philip of Macedon was invited to help the Thebans. However, he'd secretly started the feud. He gladly seized the opportunity to execute his plans against the liberties of Greece. By his intrigues and bribes, he won over the popular leaders of several cities. Their influence and votes gained his admission into the Amphictyonic council. And by his intrigues and his arms, Philip made himself master of the confederacy.

If Greece had been united by a stricter confederation and fought to stay unified, she never would have worn the chains of Macedon. And she might have been a barrier to Rome.

Faction Caused Problems

When the Achaean cities fell to Macedon, Philip II and his son, Alexander the Great, saved Greece. Their successors followed a different policy. Each city had separate interests and the union was dissolved. Some fell under the tyranny of Macedonian garrisons; others fell to usurpers within Greece.

Before long, shame and oppression awakened their love of liberty. Cities reunited when opportunities to cut off their tyrants were found. Soon the league embraced almost the whole Peloponnesus [southern peninsula of Greece]. Macedon saw its progress but internal dissensions hindered her from stopping it.

All Greece seemed ready to unite in one confederacy until jealousy and envy in Sparta and Athens, over the rising glory of the Achaeans, threw a fatal wrench into the enterprise. The dread of Macedonian power induced the league to court an alliance with the kings of Egypt and Syria who, as successors of Alexander, were rivals of the Macedonian king.

Ambition led Cleomenes, king of Sparta, to make an unprovoked attack on the Achaeans. As an enemy of Macedon, Cleomenes got the Egyptian and Syrian princes to breach their treaty with the league. The Achaeans were reduced to the dilemma of submitting to Cleomenes or requesting the aid of Macedon, its former oppressor.

The Achaeans chose the aid of Macedon. A Macedonian army quickly appeared and took possession of Sparta. Cleomenes was vanquished to Egypt. But the Achaeans soon learned that a victorious and powerful ally is often just another name for a master.

The tyrannies of Philip, the king of Macedon, provoked new alliances among the Greeks. The Achaeans were weakened by internal dissensions and by the revolt of one of its members, Messene, but they joined the Aetolians and Athenians in opposition. But they weren't strong enough and had to resort to the dangerous expedient of help from foreign arms. The Romans were invited and eagerly accepted. Philip was conquered. Macedon was subdued.

The league faced a new crisis. Rome promoted hostilities between its members. Popular leaders manipulated their countrymen. To nourish discord and disorder, Rome suggested members leave the league; Rome appealed to their pride, saying the league violated their sovereignty. This union, the last hope of Greece and the last hope of ancient liberty, was torn into pieces. Such imbecility and distraction reigned that the Roman army easily completed the ruin that their intrigues began. The Achaeans were cut to pieces and Achaia loaded with chains under which it groans at this hour.

Number 41 [5-12]

Six Categories of Federal Power

To judge this subject, we will review the powers given the federal government. The classes of federal power relate to the following issues:

- o Security against foreign danger.
- o Regulation of interactions with foreign nations.
- o Maintain harmony and interactions among the States.
- o Miscellaneous objects of general utility.
- o Restraint of the States from certain injurious acts.
- o Provisions giving effectiveness to these powers.

1. Security Against Foreign Danger

The powers within the *first* class are: declaring war, granting letters of marquee, providing armies and fleets, regulating and using the militia, levying and borrowing money.

Security against foreign danger is a primary objective of civil society. It is an essential objective of the American Union. Therefore, the federal government must have the powers to keep the nation safe.

Declare War

Everyone agrees that the power to declare war is necessary. It doesn't need to be proved. The existing Confederation has this power.

Power to Raise Armies

Is the power to raise armies and equip fleets necessary? This is part of self-defense.

But is an INDEFINITE POWER of raising TROOPS and fleets necessary? Should troops and fleets be maintained in PEACE? This is discussed in another place. The answer seems obvious. How can we limit the U.S. defensive force when the offensive force of other nations cannot be limited? If a federal Constitution could block the ambition of all other nations, then it might prudently limit its own government's defense.

provide for the common defence,

In Peacetime, Military Prevents War

How can readiness for war during peacetime be safely prohibited unless we can also prohibit the preparations of every hostile nation?

Security can only be regulated by the means and danger of attack. It will always be determined by these rules and no others. It is vain to oppose constitutional barriers to self-preservation. If one nation keeps a disciplined army, ready to serve ambition or revenge, the peaceful nations within its reach must take corresponding precautions.

During the 15th century, Charles VII of France created a peacetime army. If the other European nations hadn't built up their defenses, long ago all of Europe would have worn the chains of one king. Now, if every nation except France disbanded its peacetime armies, the same thing might happen. The veteran Roman army was an overmatch for the undisciplined valor of all other nations, making her the mistress of the world.

Number 85 [3]

...Breaking up the Confederacy would invite foreign intrigue. Keeping the Union will limit foreign influence...

promote the general Welfare,

Number 41 [26]

...the language in the Constitution appears to be a copy of the Articles of Confederation. The objective of forming a Union among the States, as described in Article Three, is "their common defense, security of their liberties, and mutual and general welfare." Article eight says: "All charges of war and all other expenses that shall be incurred for the common defense or general welfare, and allowed by the United States in Congress, shall be defrayed out of a common treasury," etc.) Similar language again occurs in Article Nine.

If we interpret these articles in the Articles of Confederation by the rules objectors have used on the new Constitution, the existing Congress has the power to legislate about everything. But what if Congress disregarded the specifications that define and limit the general expressions and exercised an unlimited power of providing for the common defense and general welfare? Would the people making the objections have employed the same reasoning in justification of Congress as they now make against the Convention. How difficult it is for error to escape its own condemnation!

Number 26 [2]

The public firmly believes that greater government energy is essential to the welfare and prosperity of the community.

Number 62 [11]

A good government implies two things. First, it is faithful to government's objective—the happiness of the people. Second, it knows how to reach this objective.

Some governments don't have either of these qualities. Most governments don't have the first. In American governments, too little attention has been paid to the last. The federal Constitution avoids this error. And it provides for the last in a way to increase the security for the first.

Number 10 [6]

Property rights originate from the people. But men's abilities are diverse, creating an insurmountable obstacle to equality of acquisitions. Protection of these abilities is government's primary function.

and secure the Blessings of Liberty...

and secure the Blessings of Liberty to ourselves, and our Posterity,

<u>What Does "Liberty" Mean?</u>

When I started reading the Federalist Papers, I immediately began to wonder if words had the same meaning in September 1787 as in December 1994. Fortunately, my brother had given me <u>Webster's Third New International Dictionary</u>, unabridged, nearly 30 years earlier.

I began looking up words--even words that seemed perfectly clear. The dictionary gave me a thorough understanding of words, how they developed and were used through time.

Here is an example from Paper #1, paragraph #1:

"...are [men] forever destined to depend for their political constitutions* on accident and force."

*constitutions: makeup; composition

My easier-to-read translation in <u>The Federalist Papers: Modern English Edition Two</u> is:

"...are people destined to be governed only by accident and force?"

"Liberty" is part of the foundation of the United States Constitution. "Liberty" makes the United States different than all other countries. This is how Webster's Third International Dictionary defines "liberty":

> **liberty 1 :** the quality or state of being free: **a** (1) : freedom from usu. external restraint or compulsion : the power to do as one pleases (2) : a condition of legal non-restraint of natural powers -- compare PRIVILEGE 1e **b** : exemption from subjection to the will of another claiming ownership or services -- compare BONDAGE, SERFDOM, SLAVERY **c** : freedom from arbitrary or despotic control **d** : the power of choice : freedom from necessity : freedom from compulsion or constraint in the act of willing something **e** (1) : CIVIL LIBERTY (2) : POLITICAL LIBERTY (3) : INDIVIDUAL LIBERTY (4) : PERSONAL LIBERTY

I had been "reading" [I put "reading" in quotes because I wrote a summary of each paragraph before moving on to the next paragraph. It was a very slow process.] Federalist Paper #1 for about two weeks when I got to paragraph 5. I was amazed! The author explained how people like Lenin and Hitler get power. It also explains how some politicians in the United States have been elected, despite their obvious plans to limit liberty.

Number 1 [5-7]

...A healthy government is essential to secure liberty. A strong government and liberty can never be separated. Dangerous ambition is more often masked by a zeal for the rights of the people than the zeal for a firm and efficient government. History teaches us that most men who have overturned the liberties of republics began their career by proclaiming their devotion to the people. They gain position by arousing people's prejudices and end as tyrants.

...after giving it careful thought, I believe it is in your interest to adopt [the Constitution]. I am convinced that this is the safest course for your liberty, your dignity, and your happiness...

I propose to discuss the following subjects in a series of papers: ...How the Constitution will preserve liberty, property and the republican form of government.

Strong Union Secures Liberty

At first glance, it may seem like a "strong Union" and "energetic" government would crush liberty. The Federalist Papers use these terms to describe a federal government with well-defined and limited powers that are necessary to fulfill its responsibilities.

These quotes from The Federalist Papers highlight that much of the analysis of human behavior is missed if only a few Papers are studied.

Number 20 [18]

...A weak constitution ends up being ignored. Then it dissolves either from a lack of power or government officials usurp the powers necessary for the public safety. The usurpation may stop at a healthy point or go forward to a dangerous extreme. Tyranny more frequently grows out of the assumptions unconstitutional power that is needed in an emergency but is not included in a defective constitution, than out of the full exercise of the largest constitutional authorities.

Number 38 [11]

I don't mean, by anything said here, to criticize the current Congress. I know they had to act. They had to overstep their constitutional limits. But doesn't this prove that it is dangerous when a government doesn't have the necessary powers to fulfill its responsibilities? It is continually exposed to the dangers of dissolution or usurpation.

Number 2 [5, 9, 12-13]

...[the people] fought side by side through a long and bloody war, establishing liberty and independence.

Being intelligent, the people saw the government's defects [under the Articles of Confederation]. They were attached to the union and loved liberty. They saw that the union was in immediate danger, a danger that would eventually jeopardize their liberty. The people knew that a more wisely framed national government could secure the union and personal liberty. They recently met in Philadelphia to consider this important subject.

...each delegate [to the Constitutional Convention] was committed to public liberty and prosperity.

and secure the Blessings of Liberty...

Number 5 [1]

Queen Anne wrote to the Scot Parliament on July 1, 1706. She talked about the importance of the *Union* then forming between England and Scotland. She said, "An entire and perfect union will be the solid foundation of lasting peace: It will secure your religion, liberty, and property...

Number 9 [1-2]

A strong Union will reduce domestic violence and revolts. This preserves the peace and liberty of the States...

Number 10 [1, 5]

...Our most virtuous citizens, men devoted to personal liberty, complain that our governments are too unstable.

...Liberty is to faction what air is to fire. Without the nourishment of liberty, faction instantly dies. But abolishing liberty because it nourishes faction is as silly as the wish to annihilate air because it gives fire its destructive energy.

Number 14 [12]

...If we are to shun new concepts, the rashest new concept is the idea that breaking apart will preserve our liberties and promote our happiness.

Why should the idea of a large republic be rejected just because it is a new concept? Americans study and respect opinions of former times and other nations. But, to their glory, they do not suffer from blind devotion for antiquity or custom. They overrule suggestions that go against their good sense, the knowledge of their situation, and the lessons of their experience.

Posterity will be indebted to the American spirit for its many innovations that improve private rights and public happiness. The Revolutionary leaders took unprecedented steps. They established a unique model of government. If they hadn't, the people of the United States might currently be laboring under the weight of some form of government that has crushed the liberties of the rest of mankind.

Happily for America. Happily, we trust, for the whole human race, they pursued a new and more noble course. Their revolution has no parallel in the annals of human society. They designed a great Confederacy. Their successors must improve and perpetuate it. If their works have imperfections, we wonder at how few...

Number 41 [15]

The consequences of disunion cannot be too strongly or too often stated. Every man who loves peace, every man who loves his country, every man who loves liberty, should always have it before his eyes. He should cherish the Union of America and highly value preserving it.

Number 45 [2]

Is the Union essential for the security of the American people? ... Does it guard against violent and oppressive factions that threaten liberty... We fought the American Revolution. We formed the American Confederacy. Thousands of people spilled their precious blood. And we spent the hard-earned money of millions. Did we do this so Americans can enjoy peace, liberty, and safety?...

Number 4/ |5|

... power should be separate to preserve liberty.

Number 50 [10]

...we should never even desire no partisanship, because an extinction of parties implies either a massive threat of danger or an absolute extinction of liberty.

Number 51 [2, 10]

To preserve liberty, government's powers must be separated.

... Justice is the final goal of civil society and government. It will be pursued until it is obtained or until liberty is lost in the pursuit...

Number 57 [13]

If the people of America ever tolerate a law that does not apply to legislators, as well as on the people, the people will be prepared to tolerate anything but liberty.

Number 63 [17]

Liberty can be endangered by the abuses of liberty as well as by the abuses of power. There are many examples of both. And the former, rather than the latter, are apparently most to be feared by the United States.

Number 85 [3]

If we adopt the Constitution, our republic, our liberty, and our property will be more secure.

States Protect Liberty

Number 28 [8]

It is an axiom in our political system that the State governments will, in all situations, provide complete security against invasions of liberty by the national authority.

Usurpation cannot be hidden by pretenses; the people and their representatives will see them. The legislatures can discover the danger in its infancy. They have civil power and the confidence of the people. They can immediately oppose them, using all the resources of the community. The States can unite their forces to protect their liberty.

Armed citizens protect Liberty

Number 29 [7]

...if circumstances ever force the government to form a large army, it will never be a big threat to the liberties of the people. There will be a large body of citizens who are members of the militia. They will be disciplined and trained in the use of arms. They will be ready to defend their own rights and those of their fellow citizens. This is the only substitute for a standing army. And it is the best security against a standing army, if it exists.

and secure the Blessings of Liberty...

Liberty endangered by the new Constitution

Number 61 [1, 3]

If liberty is ever the victim of ambitious national rulers, it can not be blamed on the election provision.

If someone says, "The defects in the State constitutions don't excuse defects in the proposed federal Constitution," I answer, "No one has said that the State constitutions don't secure liberty. But the complaints thrown at the federal Constitution apply to them also."

Therefore, we must assume that these trivial accusations have been created to support a predetermined opposition to the Constitution. They are not logical conclusions from an honest search for the truth.

To people who believe that this is an unforgivable error in the federal Constitution and it is only an innocent omission in the State constitutions, nothing can be said. Or we must ask them, "Why can State representatives resist the lust of power better than federal representatives?"

They should prove that it is easier to subvert the liberties of the entire country than a single State. The country has three million people. Their local governments will support them if they must oppose a tyrannical federal government. 200,000 citizens of a State don't have that advantage.

They should also prove that a strong faction in a single State will be less likely to promote a specific class of electors than the representatives of thirteen States, spread over a vast region, with a diversity of local circumstances, prejudices, and interests.

Number 85 [4]

...Supporters of the new Constitution have been indiscriminately charged with conspiracy against liberty. This charge is wanton and malignant. Everyone who knows it is a lie is angry. The lies keep citizens from hearing the truth...

Liberty endangered by Bill of Rights

Number 84 [10-11]

A bill of rights is not only unnecessary in the proposed Constitution, but would be dangerous. It would contain exceptions to powers not granted. This would give the government a good pretext to claim more powers than were granted. Why declare that things shall not be done when there is no power to do it?

For instance, why say that the liberty of the press shall not be restrained when no power is given to impose restrictions? Such a provision would not confer a regulating power. However, men who want to usurp power could use it to claim that power. They might argue—with some logic—that it is absurd to say there is no authority when the Constitution has a provision against the abuse of that authority. They could say that the provision against restraining the liberty of the press clearly implies that the national government has a power to regulate it.

This is an example of the many handles that would be given to the doctrine of constructive powers by the indulgence of an injudicious zeal for bills of rights.

I cannot help adding a remark or two about liberty of the press.

In the first place, New York's constitution says nothing about it.

In the new, the provisions in other State constitutions amount to nothing. What does it mean that "liberty of the press shall be inviolably preserved"? What is liberty of the press? Who can define it in a way that would not leave wide latitude for evasion?

I believe it is impractical. Whatever any constitution might say, security must depend on public opinion and the spirit of the people and the government.* This is, after all, where we must look for the only basis of all our rights.

Liberty endangered under Articles of Confederation

Number 2 [9]

Being intelligent, the people saw the government's defects (under the Articles of Confederation). They were attached to the union and loved liberty. They saw that the union was in immediate danger, a danger that would eventually jeopardize their liberty. The people knew that a more wisely framed national government could secure the union and personal liberty. They recently met in Philadelphia to consider this important subject.

Number 38 [9]

… The primary objections to the new Constitution lie with tenfold weight against the existing Confederation… Is a bill of rights essential to liberty? The Articles has no bill of rights…

Liberty endangered by aristocracy

Number 48 [4]

The founders of our republic knew that an all-grasping hereditary monarch, supported by a hereditary legislature, jeopardizes liberty. Legislative usurpations lead to the same tyranny as executive usurpations.

Number 84 [5]

The proposed Constitution … prohibits titles of nobility, [which] secures liberty and the republic better than anything in the New York constitution…

---

* The power of taxation has been used to show there is a constitutional power to affect liberty of the press. It is said that high taxes could be the same as a prohibition. Would the statement in the State constitutions in favor of the freedom of the press block the State legislatures from taxing publications? No amount of taxes, however low, would limit the liberty of the press.
Newspapers are taxed in Great Britain. But the British press enjoys great liberty. If any tax can be laid without violating liberty, the amount must depend on legislature, regulated by public opinion. Statements about liberty of the press will not add security. Some State constitutions declare liberty of the press. Yet they can use taxation to limit freedom of the press. The same thing can happen under the proposed Constitution. Saying that the government should be free or that taxes should not be excessive would have the same significance as saying that the liberty of the press should not be restrained.—PUBLIUS

and secure the Blessings of Liberty...

Liberty endangered by bigotry

Number 1 [5]

...People supporting the energetic government proposed by the Constitution will be demonized as liking dictators and hating liberty. When supporters declare that the rights of the people must be very carefully protected, it will be called insincere and an obvious attempt to become popular while hurting the general public.

Dangers to the rights of people usually spring from the head rather than the heart. Enthusiasm for liberty is often infected with narrow-minded bigotry and distrust.

Liberty endangered by civil appointments

Number 55 [9]

...The members of Congress cannot hold any civil offices that were created or the pay increased during their term in Congress. Therefore, no offices can be given to existing members except when vacated by ordinary casualties. And to say this would be enough to purchase the guardians of the people, elected by the people, is to renounce every rule by which events are forecast and substitute an indiscriminate, illogical jealousy.

The sincere friends of liberty, who extravagate this danger, are injuring their own cause. Mankind does have a degree of depravity that requires carefulness and distrust. But human nature also has qualities that justify some esteem and confidence. Republican government assumes that these qualities exist.

Political jealousy influences the opinion of some people. If the way they see human character is accurate, then people are not virtuous enough for self-government. And the only way they can be stopped from destroying each other is to live under a dictator.

Liberty endangered by congress and excessive/mutable laws

Number 26 [11]

Schemes to subvert liberty *require time* to develop before taking action. A large army would be needed to threaten our liberties. The legislature and executive would have to conspire for a long time.

Would this happen? Would every man elected to the national Senate or House of Representatives instantly become a traitor to his constituents and his country? Would not one man be able to see the atrocious conspiracy, or bold or honest enough to tell his constituents of their danger?

Number 48 [5]

... In a representative republic, the chief executive's power and term in office are limited. But legislators assume they have influence over the people and they fearlessly use their power. The people should take precautions against the ambition of the legislature.

Number 52 [5]

To maintain liberty, the government and the people must have a common interest. The House of Representatives needs to both depend on the people and sympathize with their constituents. Frequent elections secure this dependence and sympathy...

Will the temporary, small number of representatives be dangerous to liberty? There will be 65 members for a few years, then 100 or 200 for a few more. Is this number safe for the limited power of legislating for the United States?

To answer no, I would have to change my beliefs about the spirit of the State legislatures and the upright political character of our citizens.

I cannot imagine that Americans will elect—and every second year reelect—65 or 100 men who want to pursue tyranny. And I am unable to believe that any 65-100 elected Representatives will have the desire or ability, in only two years, to betray the solemn trust given to them.

I can't predict the future. But judging from our present circumstances and what may happen in the near future, American liberties will be safe in the number of hands proposed by the federal Constitution.

Number 57 [12-13, 21]
...What stops the House of Representatives from making laws that favor them-selves and a specific class of society? The whole system. The nature of just and constitutional laws. And, above all, the vigilant spirit of the people of America—a spirit which nourishes freedom and, in return, is nourished by it.

If the people of America ever tolerate a law that does not apply to legislators, as well as on the people, the people will be prepared to tolerate anything but liberty.

... The entire State of Connecticut elects the members of one branch of the State legislature. So are the governors of that State, Massachusetts, and New York, and the president of New Hampshire.

Every man can decide whether these methods of choosing State officials tend to elevate traitors and undermine public liberty.

Number 62 [12, 15]
Frequent changes in public councils, however qualified the new members may be, shows why a stable institution in the government is necessary.

Every election changes half the representatives. This turnover creates a change of opinions and a change of legislation. But continual change, even if it is good legislation, is inconsistent with every rule of prudence and every hope of success. Private life verifies this observation. And it becomes more just and more important in national transactions.

The domestic effects of a mutable policy are even worse. It poisons the blessings of liberty itself.

It won't benefit the people that the laws are made by men of their own choice, if the laws are so voluminous that they cannot be read or so incoherent that they cannot be understood. Or if they are repealed or revised before they are promulgated or are changed so frequently that no man who knows what the law is today can guess what it will be tomorrow.

Law is defined to be a rule of action. But how can it be a rule when it is little known and less fixed?

Number 63 [7]
In all governments, the community's objectives should prevail over the objectives of its rulers. And it will prevail in all free governments. However, inappropriate

passions sometimes influence citizens. Ambitious and clever men may mislead them. Then citizens may ask for laws that they will later lament and condemn... The Athenians would have escaped bitter pain if their government had such a safeguard against the tyranny of their own passions. We might not now blame liberty for decreeing, to the same citizens, hemlock on one day and statues on the next.

Number 78 [6]

All federal judges will hold their offices *during good behavior*...In a monarchy, it is a barrier to a king's tyranny. In a republic, it helps block encroachments and oppressions by the legislature. In any government, it is the best way to secure an impartial administration of the laws.

Liberty endangered by disunion

Number 8 [13]

... But if we disunite, our liberties would be at risk. We would need armies to defend against the ambition and jealousy of each other.

Number 9 [1]

A strong Union will reduce domestic violence and revolts. This preserves the peace and liberty of the States.

Horror filled the republics of Greece and Italy. Revolutions produced the extremes of tyranny and anarchy. Short-lived calms were followed by bloody rebellions. People who seem to want a dictator use this historical example as an argument against both the republican form of government and the principles of civil liberty. They say a free government cannot be ordered. And they maliciously attack its supporters.

Fortunately, a few glorious governments were founded on liberty. They disprove the ugly lies. I hope America will be the solid foundation of other governments that are no less magnificent.

Number 13[4]

...Conflicts between the divided States would make military forts necessary. Separation would injure the economy, tranquility, commerce, revenue, and liberty of every part.

Liberty endangered by executive

Number 48 [4-5]

The founders of our republic knew that an all-grasping hereditary monarch, supported by a hereditary legislature, jeopardizes liberty. Legislative usurpations lead to the same tyranny as executive usurpations.

In a monarchy, the executive branch is dangerous to liberty...

Number 70 [1-2, 21-22]

Some people say that a republic cannot have an energetic Executive. People who understand and support this type government must hope that there is no foundation for this idea. If it were true, it would condemn their belief in the principles of good government.

The executive branch of government must have the powers to fulfill its duties. Energy in the executive is an important characteristic of good government.

The community must be protected against foreign attacks. Property must be protected against conspiracies that block justice. And liberty must be protected from the negative effects of ambition, faction, and anarchy.

The republic of Rome often had to give all executive power to a single man with the title of Dictator. He stopped internal conspiracies, led by ambitious and tyrannical people who threatened the government. And he blocked invasions by external enemies who tried to conquer and destroy Rome.

A feeble executive implies a feeble execution of government. A feeble execution is another way to say a bad execution. And a badly executed government is a bad government.

Many State constitutions include a council to the Executive. They have developed from the maxim of republican jealousy, which considers power as safer in the hands of a number of men than of a single man. In this case, I think the disadvantages outweigh this possible advantage.

But I do not think the rule applies to the national executive power. I agree that to be "deep, solid, and ingenious, the executive power is more easily confined when it is one."[*] It is far safer for the people to watch one person. And a plural Executive is more dangerous than friendly to liberty.

The kind of security sought for in a plural EXECUTIVE is unattainable. The number has to be so great that conspiracy is difficult; otherwise conspiracies become a source of danger rather than security.

When power is placed in a small number of men, a talented leader can easily get them to agree to a common enterprise. A small group is easier to abuse and more dangerous when abused, than a single man. One man can be closely watched and more easily suspected.

The Decemvirs of Rome, whose name denotes their number,[**] could more easily usurp power than any one of them, alone.

No one would think of proposing an executive much larger than the Decemvirs. From six to a dozen have been suggested for the number of the council. The largest number isn't too great for an easy conspiracy. America would have more to fear from such a conspiracy than from the ambition of any single individual.

A council to an executive, who is responsible for what he does, clogs his good intentions, becomes accomplices of his bad deeds, and almost always is a cloak to his faults.

Number 71 [7]

A four-year term contributes to the firmness of the Executive. But it is not long enough to justify any alarm for the public liberty.

[*] DeLolme.—PUBLIUS
[**] Ten.—PUBLIUS

and secure the Blessings of Liberty...

Liberty endangered by foreign invaders

Number 25 [7]

  If the constitution prohibits the *raising* of armies in time of peace, the United States would be in the strangest situation ever seen—a nation that cannot prepare for its defense before it was actually invaded. The government couldn't begin drafting men until an enemy was physically within our borders. The nation couldn't prepare for a danger. Our property and liberty would be exposed to foreign invaders. They could capture us because we were afraid that rulers—elected by us and ruling according to our will—might endanger our liberty by abusing the power necessary to defend us.

Liberty endangered by military/militia

Number 8 [2-4]

  [If the States disunited] war between the American States would cause more distress than in countries with long military establishments. Although they damage liberty and the economy, the presence of disciplined armies in Europe make sudden conquests difficult...

  In this country...The separated States would postpone military spending. There are no forts, leaving State frontiers unguarded. Populous States would easily overrun less populous neighbors. However, conquests would be difficult to keep. Random wars would be followed by plunder and devastation. Our military actions would create disasters for our citizens.

  This is not an exaggeration. But the situation would soon change. Safety from external danger is the most powerful motivator of national conduct. After a time, even the deep love of liberty will diminish. War destroys life and property, and creates continuous state of danger. For security, even nations that love liberty must build institutions that tend to destroy their civil and political rights. To be safer, they will risk being less free.

Number 25 [9]

  ... [Pennsylvania's] Bill of Rights says that standing armies are dangerous to liberty and should not be kept up in peacetime. Nevertheless, during this time of peace, Pennsylvania has used disorders in one or two counties as an excuse to raise troops. And the troops will probably remain as long as there is any appearance of danger to the public peace.

Number 26 [2, 4-6, 13]

  The legislature will authorize national defense. Some people want to limit this authority. This idea comes from false beliefs about liberty rather than knowledge.

  For a long time after the Norman Conquest [1066], the English monarch's authority was almost unlimited. Gradually, liberty made inroads into the monarch's power, first by barons and later by the people, until the monarch lost most of his power and importance.

  King Charles II [1661-1685] kept a body of 5,000 troops during peacetime. King James II [1685-1688] increased the number to 30,000. Finally, after the revolution in 1688, Prince William of Orange became king of Great Britain and English liberty triumphanted. The Bill of Rights limited his authority. It said "the raising or keeping a standing army within the Kingdom in time of peace, *unless with the consent of Parliament,* was against the law."

Liberty was at its highest peak in Britain. But the only security against the danger of standing armies was the prohibition against the monarch raising and keeping them.

The revolutionary patriots were well informed. They didn't want to restrain the legislature's discretion. They knew that a certain number of troops are indispensable. National emergencies can't be limited. A power equal to every possible scenario must exist somewhere in the government. By giving the legislature this power, they found the balancing point between precaution and the safety of the community.

From this history, the people of America learned that standing armies in peacetime could endanger liberty. The revolution made us zealous protectors of our liberty. In some cases, our desire to protect our civil rights went further than is practical. Two States tried to restrict legislative authority over military establishments. A monarch's power must be feared. However, the over-reaction by these States extended this fear to the people's representatives. Some States didn't make this error but they have unnecessarily declared that standing armies are not to be kept up in peacetime without the consent of the legislature. There is a similar provision in the English Bill of Rights. But the States don't have the same reason for the provision. Under the State constitutions, only the legislatures have the power to raise armies. So, it was superfluous to declare that it should not be done without the consent of a body, which alone had the power of doing it. The other State constitutions are silent on the subject.

If defense of the community makes it necessary to have an army large enough to threaten its liberty, this is one of those calamities that can't be prevented or cured. No form of government can provide against this.

Number 29 [3, 7, 9, 11]
Standing armies can endanger liberty.
...if circumstances ever force the government to form a large army, it will never be a big threat to the liberties of the people. There will be a large body of citizens who are members of the militia. They will be disciplined and trained in the use of arms. They will be ready to defend their own rights and those of their fellow citizens. This is the only substitute for a standing army. And it is the best security against a standing army, if it exists.

The idea that the militia will endanger liberty is far-fetched. Where are our fears to end if we can't trust our sons, brothers, neighbors, and fellow citizens? We all share the same feelings, sentiments, habits, and interests.

The States have the *sole and exclusive power to appoint officers.* Since they appoint the militia's officers, the States will have the greatest influence over the militia. This should remove our fears about a militia under the federal government.

...First they say a large army will ruin the liberties of the people. Then they say Virginia's militia will be dragged 500 or 600 miles to tame rebels in Massachusetts, and Massachusetts's militia will travel an equal distance to subdue aristocratic Virginians. Do the people who make these wild claims think that their eloquence can convince the people of America that any absurd statement is true?

and secure the Blessings of Liberty...

Number 38 [4]

The Greeks jealously guarded their liberty. To protect their liberty, the citizens of Athens demanded that a minimum of ten generals command an army. And they felt that if a fellow-citizen became famous, it was a danger to their liberties…

Number 41 [13-14. 18]

The liberties of Rome became the final victim of her military triumphs. And Europe has lost the few liberties it once had because of military establishments. Therefore, a standing army is dangerous, even if it is necessary. At its best, a peacetime military is inconvenient. At worst, it may be fatal. Therefore, it deserves extreme caution.

A wise nation doesn't rashly prohibit any resource that may become essential to its safety. At the same time, it will limit a resource that may damage liberties.

The proposed Constitution is prudent. It keeps the States united. And dangerous military establishments won't be needed. America united—without a single soldier—does a better job of blocking foreign ambition than America disunited with a hundred thousand veterans ready for combat.

Geography and a great navy insulate Great Britain, which has saved its liberties. British rulers have never been able to create a large peacetime military establishment. The distance of the United States from the powerful nations of the world gives us the same security. As long as the States are united, a dangerous peacetime military will not be necessary.

However, the moment the Union breaks apart, things will change. The fears of the weaker States or ambition of the stronger States or Confederacies will set the same example in the New World as Charles VII did in the Old World. Instead of using our advantage as Great Britain has used hers, America would become a copy of the European continent. Standing armies and perpetual taxes would crush liberty.

The fortunes of a disunited America would be more disastrous than those of Europe. The sources of evil in Europe are confined by geography. No superior powers from other parts of the globe will ally with her rival nations, inflaming their mutual animosities. However, internal jealousies and wars would form only part of the problem in America. Another source of evil is the unique relationship between Europe and this part of the earth.

… If the States disunite, each separate State or Confederacy will have a standing army. These armies will endanger properties and liberties more than the size of the military necessary under a united and efficient government…

Liberty endangered by presidential term limits

Number 72 [13]

… Let's say a man was excluded from the office [of president] for the rest of his life. A man of irregular ambition would reluctantly leave the office forever, an office where he had acquired a passion for power and preeminence. If he had been fortunate or adroit enough to become a favorite of the people, he might get them to reconsider the effects of term limits. He could show that term limits are an odious and unjustifiable restraint on the people because it takes away their right to give a fresh proof of their attachment to a favorite.

80

We can imagine the people becoming disgusted because they can't reelect a favorite man. Liberty could be in more danger than could be feared from the possibility of continuing in office by the voluntary votes of the community.

Liberty endangered by no separation of powers

Number 47 [2]

There is an important political rule. It says the legislative, executive, and judiciary departments should be separate.

Number 38 [7]

...Another group of adversaries to the Constitution says the legislative, executive, and judiciary are intertwined, which contradicts all the ideas of regular government and all the required precautions in favor of liberty...

Number 47 [2-8]

Some opponents of the Constitution say the Constitution violates the separation of powers rule. They say the separation-of-powers rule is an essential precaution to preserve liberty. And that some parts of the proposed federal government are exposed to the danger of being crushed by the greater power of other parts.

This objection is based on a political truth. A government becomes a tyranny when one person or a group of people holds all of government's powers—legislative, executive, and judiciary. It doesn't matter if the government is a monarchy, dictatorship, or a democratic republic. Therefore, if the new Constitution mixes powers in a way that could lead to one branch taking over the powers of the other branches, it should be rejected.

However, the Constitution does not violate this rule. Opponents are using the rule incorrectly. To understand this important subject, we will look at why the three types of power should be separate to preserve liberty.

The famous Montesquieu is the expert on this rule. And he said the British Constitution mirrors political liberty.

However, the British legislative, executive, and judiciary departments are not totally separate from each other.

The chief executive has some legislative authority. He makes treaties with foreign nations that sometimes have the force of legislative acts. The monarch appoints all judges; and he can petition the two Houses of Parliament to remove them. And if he wants to consult legislators, they can become one of his constitutional councils.

One legislative house is the monarch's constitutional council. It also has judicial power in cases of impeachment and is the supreme court of appeals in all other cases.

Judges often participate in the legislature's discussions, though they cannot vote.

Montesquieu said, "There can be no liberty where the legislative and executive powers are united in the same person, or body of magistrates," and "if the power of judging be not separated from the legislative and executive powers."

He didn't mean that the government's branches should have no *partial agency* in or no *control* over the acts of each other. His words and examples make his meaning clear. If one person or one group holds all the power of two branches of government, the basic principles of a free constitution are subverted. For example, this would be true if the British king, the sole executive, also held all the legislative power. Or if the king acted as the country's supreme court. Or if the entire legislature was also the supreme court or held all executive authority.

The king cannot make law, though he can veto laws. He doesn't personally administer justice, though he appoints the judges.

The judges have no executive power, though the executive chooses them. And judges don't make laws, although they can advise legislative councils.

The entire legislature doesn't act as a court, but it can remove a judge from office, and one house has the judicial power of final appeal. The entire legislature, again, has no executive powers, though one house acts as the supreme executive magistracy. And the other house, after an impeachment vote, can try and condemn all the subordinate officers in the executive department.

Montesquieu's reasons for the separation rule clarify his meaning.

"When the legislative and executive powers are united in the same person or body," says he, "there can be no liberty, because apprehensions may arise lest *the same* monarch or senate *enact* tyrannical laws then *execute* them in a tyrannical manner."

And: "Were the power of judging joined with the legislative, the life and liberty of the subject would be exposed to arbitrary control, for *the judge* would then be *the legislator*. Were it joined to the executive power, *the judge* might behave with all the violence of *an oppressor*."

Some of the reasons are more fully explained in other places. But even these brief comments establish the meaning of the rule.

Number 51 [2]

To preserve liberty, government's powers must be separated.

Number 78 [8]

The courts of justice might oppress a single person. However, if the judiciary is separate from the legislature and the executive branches, it will not be dangerous to the general liberty of the people. "There is no liberty, if the power of judging is not separated from the legislative and executive powers."[*]

Liberty has nothing to fear from the judiciary alone. But if the judiciary unites with either of the other branches, liberty will be in danger. If the judiciary had to depend on the other branches, we would see the negative effects.

Liberty endangered by slavery

Number 54 [4]

The slave is forced to labor for a master. The master can sell him. His liberty is limited. And his body is forced to do what another person tells him to do. For these reasons, the slave may not seem human. He may seem more like a farm animal, which is defined as property.

---

[*] *Spirit of Laws,* Vol. I, page 181.

Liberty endangered by States

Number 17 [2]

It is always easier for State governments to gradually take over the national powers, than for the national government to take over State powers. If the State governments are honest and wise, they will usually have more influence over the people. Therefore, federal constitutions are always weak. They must be carefully structured to give them all the power that is compatible with the principles of liberty.

Number 21 [4]

Without a guaranty, the Union cannot help fight domestic threats to State constitutions. Usurpations could trample State liberties and the national government could legally do nothing but watch in anger and sorrow. A successful faction could erect a tyranny within a State and the Union could not constitutionally help supporters of the State's constitutional government.

Massachusetts barely survived the recent turmoil. What if someone like Caesar or Cromwell had led the malcontents? If despotism had been established in Massachusetts, how would it have changed liberty in New Hampshire, Rhode Island, Connecticut, or New York?

Number 25 [3]

State and federal governments are rivals because all governments love power. In a dispute between the federal government and a State, people will probably support their local government. If the State had military forces, it would be tempted to challenge and subvert the constitutional authority of the Union.

The people's liberty would be less safe. An army is a dangerous weapon of power; it is better if the targets of envy control it. History proves that people are in the most danger when a group or individual they least suspect have the ability to injure their rights.

Constitution for the United States of America

do ordain and establish this

Number 40 [15]

...the proposed Constitution is nothing more than pieces of paper, unless the people approve it.

Constitution for the United States of America

Number 16 [10]

...Enlightened citizens will know the difference between legal authority and illegal usurpation of authority... The people are the natural guardians of the Constitution.

Number 17 [2]

...federal constitutions are always weak. They must be carefully structured to give them all the power that is compatible with the principles of liberty.

Number 32 [5]

Interpreting Constitution

In some cases, joint jurisdiction is necessary. It results from dividing sovereign power. All authorities, except those the States explicitly relinquished to the Union, remain fully with the States. This is the clear meaning of the proposed Constitution. The Constitution has negative clauses prohibiting the States from exercising the authorities that are exclusively the Union's.

Article one, section ten contains such provisions. This clearly shows the convention's intentions. And it furnishes a rule for interpreting the Constitution—within the Constitution—that justifies my position and refutes every hypothesis to the contrary.

Number 51 [4]

...Government is, after all, the greatest of all reflections on human nature. If men were angels, no government would be necessary. If angels governed men, no controls on government would be necessary. But men govern men. So, security measures are necessary to control the abuses of government.

In framing a government, the great difficulty lies in this:
first, the government must control the governed, and second, it must be forced to control itself.

Number 53 [2]

... Americans understand that the people create a Constitution. And it is the supreme power. The government cannot alter the Constitution. On the other hand, the government makes laws and the government can change them. Other countries don't seem to understand this distinction...

I love watching shows like "Engineering an Empire," showing ancient engineering feats. To my untrained mind, ancient artists and architects seemed to understand "advanced" techniques. A vast, unsupported dome in Rome is breathtaking. As is the perfectly proportioned columns of the Parthenon and the perfectly sloped aqueducts. However, as I watch, I can't help but wonder why further technological advances didn't continue until the 18th century. There is only one answer: The United States of America. And The United States of America has only succeeded technologically because the Constitution establishes a confederate republic.

Republican Form of Government

Interestingly, the Constitution never says that the United States is a republic (or democracy), although it does guarantee that the State governments will have the republican form. The Federalist Papers assume that the citizens of the United States have agreed that they must have a republic. Two questions come to mind: What are the characteristics of a republic? Why did Americans think it was the best form of government?

Number 9 [all]

Constitution Refines "Confederate Republic" Form

A strong Union will reduce domestic violence and revolts. This preserves the peace and liberty of the States.

Horror filled the republics of Greece and Italy. Revolutions produced the extremes of tyranny and anarchy. Short-lived calms were followed by bloody rebellions. People who seem to want a dictator use this historical example as an argument against both the republican form of government and the principles of civil liberty. They say a free government cannot be ordered. And they maliciously attack its supporters.

Fortunately, a few glorious governments were founded on liberty. They disprove the ugly lies. I hope America will be the solid foundation of other governments that are no less magnificent.

Republican Government Improved

Like most sciences, the science of politics has improved. We now understand important principles that ancient governments either didn't know about or didn't understand. We know that government's power needs to be divided into several separate parts or branches with legislative balances and checks. Judges need lifetime appointments and can only be removed for bad behavior. And the people elect legislative representation. These principles save the good parts of republican government and reduce its flaws.

Another improvement is enlarging the size, both of the country and the number of States in a confederacy. We will now study the latter. The country's size will be examined later.

Republic Doesn't Need to be Small

A confederacy guards the peace of states. It can suppress internal faction and increase external security.

Opponents of the Constitution claim that Montesquieu said that a republican government requires a small territory. But they have overlooked other things he said. And they don't see the consequence of their argument.

When Montesquieu recommends a small area for republics, he's referring to a size much smaller than almost every one of our States. If we adopt this view of Montesquieu's ideas, we would have to either become a monarchy or split ourselves into an infinity of little, jealous, clashing nations. And we would become the miserable objects of universal pity or contempt.

Some opponents of the Constitution take Montesquieu's idea and then suggest that the large states should be divided. Doing this would create a lot of political offices. Men who have no qualifications to hold office—beyond their narrow scope of personal intrigue—could have political positions. But it could never promote the greatness or happiness of the American people.

Montesquieu's theory only refers to the SIZE of the largest MEMBERS of the Union. It does not argue against them being joined under one confederate government.

Montesquieu: Confederate Republic

Montesquieu doesn't oppose a Union of the States. He says that a CONFEDERATE REPUBLIC is suitable. It combines the advantages of a monarchy with republicanism.

In the *Sprit of Laws*, book 9, he says mankind probably would have always lived under a monarch or dictator. Then a constitution was developed that incorporated the internal advantages of a republic and the external force of a monarchy, that is, a CONFEDERATE REPUBLIC.

In a confederate republic, he continues, several *States* agree to become members of a large *one*. It can add new States until it is powerful enough to provide security for the entire nation. This kind of republic can withstand external force and internal corruption.

He explains that if one man attempted usurping supreme authority, he wouldn't have equal influence in all the States. If he had too much influence in one, it would alarm the rest. If he subdued a part, the rest would oppose and overpower him.

A popular rebellion in one State would be stopped by the others. If abuses creep into one part, he argues, the other parts can reform it. The State may be destroyed on one side and not on the other. The confederacy can be dissolved and the States remain sovereign. Since the government is composed of small republics, it has internal happiness. And it has the advantage of a large monarchy in external situations.

Union Represses Domestic Faction

This should explain how Montesquieu's writing supports our proposed Union. He also writes about how a Union tends to repress domestic faction and rebellion.

Confederate Republic Form

Some people say that a confederacy has limited authority. They say it only has authority over the member States in their collective capacities [legislation for States], without reaching the individual citizens. They think the national government should not be involved with any part of internal administration and that the States have equal suffrage.

This is an arbitrary definition. Neither principle nor experience support it. Historically, many confederate governments had these characteristics, but there have been many exceptions. There is no absolute rule on the subject. On the other hand, where such strict limitations [legislation for States rather than individuals] have been tried, disorder and stupid consequences followed.

We define a *confederate republic* as "an assemblage of societies" or an association of two or more States into one nation. The extent and objects of federal authority are discretionary. The member States can remain separate, constitutionally existing for local purposes. They can even subordinate their authority to the authority of the union. It will be a confederacy.

The proposed Constitution doesn't abolish the State governments. It makes them part of the national government with direct representation in the Senate. They will have certain exclusive and important sovereign powers. This corresponds with the idea of a federal government.

The Lycian confederacy had 23 CITIES or republics. The largest had *three* votes in the COMMON COUNCIL, the middle *two*, and the smallest *one*. The COMMON COUNCIL appointed judges and executives of the CITIES. This was invasive control of the CITIES. If local jurisdictions have any exclusive authority, it should be the appointment of their own officers. Yet Montesquieu says, "Were I to give a model of an excellent Confederate Republic, it would be that of Lycia."

Therefore, we see that Montesquieu did not strictly limit the authority of confederacies as some erroneously suggest.

Number 14 [all]

Republic: Best for American People

We have seen that we need a Union:
- to protect us from foreign danger,
- to keep the peace among ourselves,
- to guard our commerce and other common interests,
- as the only substitute for those military establishments that have subverted the liberties of the Old World,
- as the antidote to diseases of faction that have destroyed other popular governments. Alarming symptoms of them have already appeared in ours.

The last objection to discuss is based on the size of the Union. Some people fear that a republic isn't practical in such a large geographic area. Opponents of the new Constitution use this prejudice to invent problems because they can't find solid objections.

Democracy Must be Small

A republic does not have to be limited to a small area. A republic has been confused with a democracy. Opponents have applied democracy theories to a republic.

In a democracy, the people meet and administer the government in person. In a republic, representatives and agents assemble and administer it. Consequently, a democracy must be small. But a republic may be large.

Monarchy vs. Democracy or Republic

This is an unintentional error. Some famous authors influence modern public opinions. Since the authors lived in monarchies, they are biased. They stress the advantages or rationalize the evils of monarchies by comparing them to the vice and defects of a republic. To prove their points, they cite the turbulent democracies of ancient Greece and modern Italy.

The terms "democracy" and "republic" are misused. Observations made about a "democracy" are erroneously transferred to a "republic." One is that a republic must have a small number of people, living within a small territory.

Most ancient popular governments were democracies. Modern Europe developed the great principle of representation. However, it has no example of a completely popular and republican government.

America developed representation as the basis of large republics. It is sad that some people want to block America from adopting the Constitution and showing how well the system works.

Democracy Limits Area, Population

A democracy must be small with a limited population. All citizens must be able to assemble and administer the government.

The natural limit of a republic is the distance from the capital that allows representatives to meet and administer public affairs. Is the United States too big? During the last thirteen years, representatives of the States have been almost continually assembled. The attendance records of members from distant States have been no worse than those from the States in the neighborhood of Congress.

Let's look at the actual dimensions of the Union. According to the peace treaty, the eastern boundary is the Atlantic, the southern is the latitude of 31 degrees, the western is the Mississippi, and the northern is an irregular line running between 42 degrees and 45 degrees. The average north-south distance is 868¾ miles. The average distance between the Atlantic and the Mississippi probably doesn't exceed 750 miles.

Let's compare this size to European countries and we'll see that a republic is practical. Our territory is not much larger than Germany, where representatives continually assemble. Until the national assembly was recently ended in Poland, it was the center of supreme power. Although Great Britain is smaller, representatives from the northern most part of the island travel as far to their national council as required of those from the most remote parts of our Union.

Federal Government: Defined, Limited Jurisdiction

More observations will place the subject in a still better light.

First, the federal government will not have the whole power of making and administering laws. Its jurisdiction is limited to specific objectives. The State and local governments will keep their authority to care for all other concerns. If the new Constitution abolished the State governments, there would be a reason to object. In fact, if they were abolished, self-preservation would force the national government to reinstate them.

Constitution: Union, Adding States

Second, the immediate goal of the federal Constitution is to secure the union of the thirteen original States and adding new States. But how will the territory on our northwestern frontier be handled? This is best left to people whose experience, at the time, will make them equal to the task.

Improves Commerce, Communication

Third, national infrastructure improvements will make commerce easier throughout the Union. Roads will be shortened and better maintained. Places for travelers to eat and sleep will increase and improve. River navigation will extend through most of the thirteen States. Communication will become easier. Nature gave our country many rivers; engineers find them easy to connect with canals.

States Benefit from Union's Defense

A fourth and most important consideration is safety.

Almost every State will be a frontier. For general protection, some sacrifices will be required. States furthest from the heart of the Union may receive fewer ordinary benefits from the Union but they share a border with foreign nations. Sometimes they will have the greatest need for the Union's strength and resources. Sending representatives to the capital may be inconvenient. However, it would be harder for them to struggle alone against an invading enemy or carry the full expense of defensive precautions. So, if they get fewer benefits in some respects than less distant States, they will get greater benefits in other respects. Thus, the proper balance will be maintained throughout.

American Spirit Unique in History

I know you will objectively evaluate these observations. You will never automatically allow predictions of catastrophe to drive you into despair, even if they appear formidable.

Affection binds America together. Don't listen to people who say we can no longer live together as members of the same family and guardians of our mutual happiness. Or that we can no longer be citizens of one great, respectable, and flourishing empire. Do not listen to the voice that says the government framed by the Constitution is so unusual that it has no place in even the wildest political theories and that it is impossible to establish.

No, my countrymen, shut your ears against this unhallowed language. Shut your hearts against its poison. Kindred blood flows in the veins of Americans. They shed blood to defend their sacred rights and consecrate their Union. We should be horrified at the idea of their becoming aliens, rivals, enemies.

If we are to shun new concepts, the rashest new concept is the idea that breaking apart will preserve our liberties and promote our happiness.

Why should the idea of a large republic be rejected just because it is a new concept? Americans study and respect opinions of former times and other nations. But, to their glory, they do not suffer from blind devotion for antiquity or custom. They overrule suggestions that go against their good sense, the knowledge of their situation, and the lessons of their experience.

Posterity will be indebted to the American spirit for its many innovations that improve private rights and public happiness. The Revolutionary leaders took unprecedented steps. They established a unique model of government. If they hadn't, the people of the United States might currently be laboring under the weight of some form of government that has crushed the liberties of the rest of mankind.

Happily for America. Happily, we trust, for the whole human race, they pursued a new and more noble course. Their revolution has no parallel in the annals of human society. They designed a great Confederacy. Their successors must improve and perpetuate it. If their works have imperfections, we wonder at how few.

If they erred most in the structure of the Union [Articles of Confederation], this was their most difficult work. Your Constitutional Convention has made a new model. And it is that act on which you are now to deliberate and decide.

Number 39 [all]

Is Proposed Government a Republic?

...We will now study the proposed Constitution

Is the proposed government a republic? The American people want a republic. Everyone who loves freedom wants self-government. We fought the Revolution to attempt this political experiment. Therefore, we cannot defend the proposed Constitution—and must abandon it—if it does not create a republic.

What are the unique characteristics of a republic? We call several countries "republics," but they are not:

In Holland, none of its supreme authority comes from the people. In Venice, hereditary nobles exercise the absolute power over the people. Poland has a bad mixture of aristocracy and monarchy. England has one republican branch plus an aristocracy and a monarch.

The term "republic" is often inaccurately used in political discussions.

Republic = All Power from People

We define a republic as a government that gets all its powers—directly or indirectly—from the people. The people elect some of a republic's administrators, who appoint other officials. And government officials remain in office either for a limited term or during good behavior.

A republican government *must* come from all citizens, not just a favored class. If this is not true, a tyrant or a few tyrannical nobles could say they were creating a republic.

It is *enough* that the people appoint government officials either directly or indirectly. And government officials stay in office for a specific term or during good behavior. The people indirectly appoint many State officers. The governors and most State legislators have a specific term in office. Most State judges have lifetime appointments, during good behavior.

Constitution: Republic Form

The Constitution follows the republican form. The people elect the House of Representatives and indirectly appoint the Senate. The people indirectly elect the President. As in the States, even the judges and other officers of the Union will be the choice, though a remote choice, of the people.

The term in office also follows the republican form. Representatives serve two years. Senators serve six years. The President's term in office is four years. And he is impeachable at any time during his time in office. Judges have a lifetime appointment and can be impeached and removed from office. Congress will create laws to regulate the term in office for other ministers and administers.

The Constitution prohibits titles of nobility and guarantees the republican form of government.

Convention's Authority, Objective

Opponents of the Constitution say, "But it was not enough that the Convention followed the republican form. They should have kept the *federal* form; the Union should be a *confederacy* of sovereign States. Instead, they have created a *national* government; the Union will become a *consolidation* of the States." And they ask, "What authority did the Convention have to make this change?"

Analyzing Convention's Work

We will study this objection and (1) determine if the proposed government is federal or national, (2) ask if the convention was authorized to propose such a government, and (3) determine whether the delegates' duty to their country replaced their lack of regular authority.

Character of Proposed Government

We will determine the real character of the government through studying:
- the **foundation** on which the government is to be established,
- the **sources** of its ordinary powers,
- the **operation** of those powers,
- the **extent** of the government's powers,
- and the **authority** to make future changes in the government.

Foundation: Ratification: Federal Form

The Constitution's **foundation** refers to the ratification process. It could have been set up several ways. If ratification required that a *majority* of the people of the entire nation accept the Constitution, then ratification would be a *national* act. However, this is not how the Constitution will be ratified. Nor will a *majority* of the States make the decision.

Instead, the people of each State will vote to ratify the Constitution. They will be acting as citizens of independent States, not as citizens of one nation. And the States must *unanimously* ratify the Constitution. The people—not the legislature—must accept the Constitution.

91

As they vote to ratify the Constitution, each State is a sovereign body. Each State will act independently and be bound only by its own voluntary act. In its **foundation**, the new government will be *federal*, not *national*.

Power Source: Both Federal, National

Next we'll look at the **source** of the ordinary powers of government. [Do the people (national) or the States (federal) elect/appoint the nation's officials?]

The people will elect the House of Representatives and will be represented proportionately. In this, the government is *national*, not *federal*.

The Senate, on the other hand, will derive its powers from the States as equal societies. In this, the government is *federal*, not *national*.

The executive power will come from a compound source. The States, as political units, will elect the President. The number of votes each State gets is based on a compound ratio. Each State has the same number of votes as their number of members in the US Congress: an equal number (two Senators) and a proportional number (number of Representatives). If no one wins that election, the national House of Representatives will pick the President; each State will have one vote, making the States distinct, equal political bodies.

As to its **source of powers**, the government structure appears mixed. It has as many *federal* as *national* features.

Government Operation: National Form

Opponents of the proposed Constitution say that a *federal* government operates on the political bodies [States] within the Confederacy and a *national* government operates on the nation's individual citizens. Using this criterion, the Constitution falls under a *national*, not *federal*, character. However, when there is a controversy between States, States will be viewed in their collective, political capacities only.

The government's operation most resembles a *national* government.

Extent of Powers: Federal Form

The **extent of** the proposed governments' **powers** has the *federal* form.

A *national* government has authority over individual citizens with an indefinite supremacy over all persons, things, and issues that can be objects of lawful government. A *federal* government vests some supremacy in the united body and some in the local legislatures.

A *national* legislature can control, direct, or abolish local authority at any time. In a *federal* system, local governments have areas of supreme power. The areas of local authority are no more subject to the federal authority than the federal authority is subject to State and local governments.

In the **extent of its powers**, the proposed government is not *national*. Federal jurisdiction extends to specific objectives only. The States will have a total sovereignty over all other issues.

The Supreme Court will ultimately decide boundary disputes between two jurisdictions. The federal government will establish the Supreme Court. But this doesn't change the principle. Such a tribunal is essential to prevent armed conflict between States and dissolution of the Union. Few people would argue against the national government creating the Supreme Court.

Amending: Federal, National Features

The Constitution's **amendment** process is neither totally *national* nor totally *federal.*

If it was totally *national*, a *majority* of the people of the Union could vote to ratify the Constitution. And a majority of people could alter or abolish the Union's government at any time.

On the other hand, if it were totally *federal*, every State in the Union would have to agree to constitutional amendments.

The amendment process in the Constitution doesn't follow either principle. By requiring more than a majority of *States,* not *citizens*, it has a *federal* character. By requiring less than the total number of States agree, it is less *federal* and more *national*.

Neither Strictly National nor Federal

Therefore, the proposed Constitution is not completely *national* or *federal*, but a composition of both:
- Its **foundation** is *federal*.
- Its **source** of governmental powers is part *federal* and part *national*.
- In the **operation** of these powers, it is *national*.
- In the **extent** of these powers, it is *federal*.
- And the **amendment** process is both *federal* and *national.*

ARTICLE 1 SECTION 1. All legislative Powers herein granted

I am continually amazed at the preciseness of the United States Constitution. Currently, the federal legislature seems to want to regulate every part of our lives. Yet the Constitution tells us what the legislature's powers are, starting with the very first sentence of the Constitution: All legislative Powers herein granted...

Number 48 [2, 4-13, 15, 16]

...power has an encroaching nature and must be stopped from overstepping its authority...

...Legislative usurpations lead to the same tyranny as executive usurpations.

In a monarchy, the executive branch is dangerous to liberty.

In a democracy, all the citizens gather to exercise the legislative functions. However, this huge number of people cannot regularly meet to discuss and make laws. Therefore, the executive can easily declare an emergency and assume tyrannical powers.

In a representative republic, the chief executive's power and term in office are limited. But legislators assume they have influence over the people and they fearlessly use their power. The people should take precautions against the ambition of the legislature.

Legislative Limits Imprecise

The legislative branch has many constitutional powers with imprecise limits. It can surreptitiously encroach on the other branches.

Executive power is better defined and less extensive. The judiciary is even more limited. People could immediately see and stop usurpation attempts by the executive or judiciary.

Nor is this all. The legislature both imposes taxes and sets the wages of the executive and judiciary branches. Therefore, all government officials are dependent on the legislature, making legislative encroachments even easier.

State Legislatures Usurping Power

Every State has an example of legislative power encroachments. I will give examples from two States.

The first example is Virginia. Its constitution says that the three government branches should not be intermixed. Mr. Jefferson is the governor.

In *Notes on the State of Virginia*, page 195, Mr. Jefferson says that all of government's powers—legislative, executive, judiciary—revert to the legislative body. In a despotic government, the same people hold all of the government's powers. Having a group of people hold all the power is no better than if a single person holds it. One hundred and seventy-three despots are as oppressive as one. For proof, look at the republic of Venice.

It is no consolation that we elect the representatives. We did not fight for an *elective despotism*. We fought for a government founded on free principles with powers divided and balanced among the government branches so that no one branch can use powers beyond their legal limits without being effectually checked by the others.

"For this reason, the convention that organized [Virginia's] government made the legislative, executive, and judiciary separate and distinct, so that no person should exercise the powers of more than one of them at the same time. *But no barrier was provided between these several powers*. The judiciary and executive branches were left dependent on the legislative for their subsistence in office, and some of them for their continuance in it. If, therefore, the legislature assumes executive and judiciary powers, no opposition is likely to be made; nor, if made, can be effectual because" they can create "acts of Assembly", which the other branches must okay. The legislature has often "*decided rights* which should have been left to *judiciary controversy*, and *the direction of the executive, during the whole time of their session, is becoming habitual and familiar.*"

The Council of Censors in Pennsylvania assembled in 1783 and 1784 "to inquire whether the constitution had been preserved inviolate in every part; and whether the legislative and executive branches of government had performed their duty as guardians of the people, or assumed to themselves, or exercised, other or greater powers than they are entitled to by the constitution."

The council compared the actual legislative and executive acts with the constitutional powers of these branches. Most of the council agreed that the legislature flagrantly violated the constitution in a variety of important instances:

As a precaution, the Pennsylvania constitution requires that all bills of a public nature be previously printed for the people to consider. Yet many laws were passed without public notification.

The constitutional trial by jury has been violated and powers not delegated by the constitution have been assumed.

Executive powers have been usurped.

The Pennsylvania constitution requires that the salaries of judges must be fixed, but the legislature has occasionally changed them. And the legislature has frequently heard and judged cases belonging to the judiciary.

It appears that Pennsylvania's executive branch has also violated the constitution...

Pennsylvania's executive council has more members than the other States, so it's similar to a legislative assembly. And a council doesn't feel the same restraint as an individual, who is personally responsible for his acts. Members get confidence from each other and are influenced by each other so that unauthorized measures are more easily tried than where the executive branch is administered by a single hand or a few hands.

Words, Alone, Don't Block Tyranny

Defining the limits of each branch in the Constitution is not enough. Encroachments can lead to a tyrannical concentration of all the powers of government in the same hands.

Number 50 [2, 3, 8]

I am examining ways to *enforce* the Constitution and keep the branches of power within their limits… If a legislature is determined to achieve an unconstitutional objective, they will not stop because their conduct might be censored in ten, fifteen, or twenty years.

When the Pennsylvania Council of Censors met in 1783 and 1784, one objective was to ask if "the constitution had been violated, and whether the legislative and executive branches had encroached on each other."

The Council's constitutional decisions, whether right or wrong, have not influenced the legislature. In one case, the current legislature denied the opinions of the council and actually prevailed.

shall be vested in a Congress of the United States, which shall consist of a Senate and House of Representatives.

Number 22 [17]

Currently, Congress does not have the powers that the federal government needs. The federal government has limited authority. Therefore, a single congress may be proper. But even rational adversaries of the proposed Constitution say that the federal government needs more power. And a single assembly cannot be trusted with the additional powers…

Number 47 [3]

…A government becomes a tyranny when one person or a group of people holds all of government's powers—legislative, executive, and judiciary. It doesn't matter if the government is a monarchy, dictatorship, or a democratic republic…

Number 51 [1, 6]

The Constitution divides government power among three branches. The government must be designed so that the three branches—executive, legislative, and judiciary—can keep each other in their proper places…

But it is impossible to give each branch of government an equal power of self-defense. In a republic, the legislature always has the most power. To counteract this, (1) the legislature is divided into two houses, (2) the houses are elected in different ways, and (3) they have different constitutional powers.

The legislative houses are as little connected as their duties and dependence on society will allow. And more blocks to dangerous encroachments may be necessary.

The strength of the legislative power requires that it be divided…

Under Articles of Confederation

Number 22 [7-9]

Currently, each State has an equal vote in the national congress. This is another problem. Every rule of fair representation condemns the principle that gives Rhode Island equal power with Massachusetts or Connecticut or New York. This goes against the basic principle of republican government: the will of the majority should prevail.

Some people may say that each State in the Union is a sovereign and sovereigns are equal. Therefore a majority of the votes of States will be a majority of confederate

America. But this logical sleight-of-hand doesn't remove the dictates of justice and common sense. A majority of States can be a small minority of American citizens.[*]

Two thirds of the people will not allow one third to manage their interests. After a while, the larger States will revolt. Giving up majority rights is contrary to the love of power and it sacrifices equality. It is not rational to expect the first, nor just to require the second. Since the smaller States depend on union for their safety and welfare, they should readily renounce a pretension that, if not relinquished, would be fatal to that union.

It may be proposed that two-thirds of the States (9) must consent to pass important resolutions. But an equal vote between States of unequal dimensions and populations is improper. Besides, nine States can have less than a majority of the people.[*] A bare majority might still decide significant issues. Additionally, the number of States will probably increase and there is no provision for increasing the ratio of votes.

2/3 Majority = Minority Control

But this is not all. A two-thirds majority may look like a solution. In reality it makes the problem worse. When more than a majority is needed to make a decision, the minority gets a negative over the majority. It subordinates the feelings of the majority to the minority. Because a few States have been absent from our current Congress, a single VOTE—one-sixtieth part of the union—has frequently stopped all business.

A two-thirds majority is supposed to provide security. In practice, it does the opposite. It becomes nearly impossible to administer the government. And it substitutes the desires or schemes of a tiny or corrupt group of politicians for the decisions of a majority.

During national emergencies, the government needs to be strong and it must often take an action. Public business must, one way or another, go forward. If a stubborn minority is in control, to accomplish anything, the majority must accept the decisions of the minority. Delays, negotiations, and intrigue would hurt the public good. Sometimes compromises won't be possible and the legislature will be unable to act. This would create a government that is weak and sometimes bordering on anarchy.

New Congress Less Expensive

Number 84 [22-23]

...both the Senate and the House of Representatives will need to be in session for only part of the year. We may suppose about a fourth for the latter and a third, or perhaps half, for the former. The extra business of treaties and appointments may make the Senate sessions longer. Until the House of Representatives is increased greatly beyond its present number, there will be a large saving of expense from the difference between the constant session of the present and the temporary session of the future Congress.

---

[*] New Hampshire, Rhode Island, New Jersey, Delaware, Georgia, South Carolina and Maryland are a majority of the whole number of States but they do not contain one third of the people. —PUBLIUS

[*] Add New York and Connecticut to the foregoing seven and they will be less than a majority. — PUBLIUS

Henceforth, State legislatures will attend only to the affairs of their specific States. They will not have to sit nearly as long as they have done until now. The shorter sessions of the State legislatures may be a saving equivalent to any additional expense from adopting the new system.

ARTICLE 1 SECTION 2. The House of Representatives shall be composed of Members chosen every second Year

Number 41 [17]

...In Great Britain, the House of Commons has seven-year terms. A small proportion of the people elect a great proportion of the members. The representatives corrupt the voters; the Crown corrupts the representatives. The representative body has the power to make appropriations to the army for any period of time beyond one year.

The House of Representatives will be elected freely by all citizens every second year. Military appropriations are limited to two years. Shouldn't we be suspicious of people who pretend that our representatives can't be trusted?

Number 52 [4-5, 8-9]

The representatives' term is two years. We will consider two questions: (1) Will biennial elections be safe? (2) Are biennial elections necessary?

To maintain liberty, the government and the people must have a common interest. The House of Representatives needs to both depend on the people and sympathize with their constituents. Frequent elections secure this dependence and sympathy. But it is impossible to figure out how frequent the elections need to be. Let us consult experience, the guide that should always be followed whenever it can be found.

The example of the States, when British colonies, is well known. At least one house of each State legislature follows the principle of representation. But the election periods varied from one to seven years.

Let's look at how the people's representatives behaved before the Revolution. Does their behavior give us any reason to think that biennial elections are dangerous to liberty? The fact that we were able to fight a revolution for independence proves that some liberty existed. This was as true for the colonies that had elections every seven years as well as those with annual elections.

Virginia was the first colony to resist the parliamentary usurpations of Great Britain. And it was the first to pass the resolution of independence. At the time, Virginia held elections every seven years. This proves that biennial elections will not endanger liberty.

Three things will strengthen the conclusions from these examples:

First, the federal House of Representatives will have only part of the supreme legislative authority. It is an important rule that, excluding all other circumstances, the greater the power, the shorter ought to be its duration. And conversely, the smaller the power, the more safely may its duration be lengthened.

Second, in addition to being dependent on the people, the House of Representatives will be watched and controlled by the State legislatures.

Third, we cannot compare the ability of the more permanent branches of the federal government to seduce, if they want to, the House of Representatives from their duty to the people, and the ability of the Senate to influence the House of Representatives. Therefore, with less power to abuse, the federal representatives will be less tempted on one side and doubly watched on the other.

Number 53 [all]

Some people say, "Where annual elections end, tyranny begins." Although clichés develop for a reason, people often use them for cases to which they do not apply. For proof, look at the case before us.

What was the original reason for this cliché? Of course, there is no scientific connection between how many times the earth goes around the sun and how long a man can remain virtuous and not be tempted by power.

Fortunately, liberty is not limited to any single amount of time. Under different circumstances, different lengths of time are appropriate. If it was important, elections could be held daily, weekly, monthly, or annually. But in some circumstances less frequent elections are needed.

The largest house of each State legislature has a variety of term lengths: six months in Connecticut and Rhode Island, two years in South Carolina, and yearly in the other States. But it would be hard to show that Connecticut or Rhode Island is better governed or enjoys more liberty than South Carolina.

I found only one reason for this cliché and it does not apply to our case. Americans understand that the people create a Constitution. And it is the supreme power. The government cannot alter the Constitution. On the other hand, the government makes laws and the government can change them. Other countries don't seem to understand this distinction.

When the legislature has supreme power, the legislature can change government's structure. British citizens discuss political liberties, civil liberties, and constitutional rights. But Parliament's authority is supreme. Several times, Parliament has passed laws that fundamentally change the government, specifically, the election period. On the last occasion, they replaced three-year terms with seven-year terms. The people elected them to a three-year term but they stayed in office seven years.

Free governments have frequent elections. Parliament's actions alarmed the voters. The voters wanted to find a way to secure their liberty against this danger. The United States has a Constitution. Other nations don't have this security. Other security was sought. The length of time between elections became the way to measure the danger of changes. The simplest length of time was a year. Hence, the annual-election doctrine became a barrier against the gradual changes of an unlimited government. And the approach of tyranny was measured by how far away from annual elections.

But the Constitution will limit our federal government. Annual elections will not be needed. Constitutionally mandated biennial elections will keep the liberties of the

American people more secure than annual elections in other nations. Those nations can change the length of time between elections by simply passing a law.

Several reasons show that biennial elections are necessary and useful.

A competent legislator has good intentions, sound judgment, and some knowledge of legislative subjects. He gets some knowledge in private life. Another part can only be completely learned while serving as a legislator. Therefore, the length of service should be somewhat proportional to how much the legislator must know to adequately serve.

In most States, the larger legislative house has annual elections. A federal congressman has more to learn than a State congressman. Is two years long enough to learn the increased information? Can a federal congressman learn the greater knowledge needed for federal legislation in two years?

A State legislator needs to know existing laws, which are uniform throughout the State. Most citizens understand the general affairs of the State. State issues are not very diversified and everyone studies and discusses them.

Understanding national issues is different. The laws vary in every State. The country is large with diverse responsibilities. They are difficult to learn outside the federal capitol, where representatives of the entire nation bring knowledge of them.

All federal legislators need to know something about State issues and laws. To write national regulations for foreign trade, legislators need to know something about the commerce, ports, and regulations of the different States. To regulate trade between States, they need to know about their different situations. To fairly impose and effectively collect taxes, they need to know the laws and situations in the different States. To write national militia regulations, they need to know the issues that make the States different from each other.

Trade, taxes, and the militia are the important subjects of federal legislation. Federal representatives need a lot of information on these and other subjects.

Starting the new government and creating the first federal code will be a difficult task. Improvements will become easier and fewer every year. New members can learn from what the federal government has done before. Citizens will discuss the Union's affairs. As commerce between the States increases, so will knowledge of State affairs. And the different State laws will become more similar.

But even with these changes, federal legislation will always be more difficult than the legislative business of a single State. Therefore, the longer term is justified.

A federal representative also needs to understand foreign affairs, including commercial treaties and policies of the United States and other nations. He should have some knowledge of the law of nations. The House of Representatives will not directly participate in foreign negotiations. However, the different areas of public affairs are connected. And they will sometimes demand legislative sanction and cooperation.

A man may learn some of these things in his private life. But some things can only be learned from public sources of information. And the majority will be learned during the period of actual service in the legislature.

Other considerations are less important, but are worth mentioning.

If terms are only one year, some qualified men will not serve because of the travel distance. Although the existing Congress is elected annually, most members are automatically reelected by the State legislatures. But Representatives will be elected by the people.

As happens in all such assemblies, a few members will have superior talents, be reelected and become members of long standing. They will be masters of public business. The more new members, the less information the assembly will have. And they will be more likely to fall into the snares laid for them. This is true for both the House and the Senate.

If elections are held every year, there wouldn't be enough time to investigate spurious elections. If election results need to be annulled, there wouldn't be enough time for the annulment to take effect. If an election is won, even if won illegally, the irregular member will hold his seat long enough time to fulfill his goals. This would encourage election fraud, particularly in the more distant States.

Each house judges the legality of member elections and qualifications. And even if the process is simplified and faster, a great part of a year would go by before an illegitimate member could be removed from his seat. The fear of being unseated would do little to stop unfair and fraudulent elections.

Biennial elections will be useful for handling public affairs and safe to the liberty.

Number 55 [4, 7]

Remember the discussion about biennial elections. The limited powers of the House justify less frequent elections than the public safety might otherwise require...

I cannot imagine that Americans will elect—and every second year reelect—65 or 100 men who want to pursue tyranny. And I am unable to believe that any 65-100 elected Representatives will have the desire or ability, in only two years, to betray the solemn trust given to them.

Number 57 [11]

... bi-annual elections to the House of Representatives will remind members of their dependence on the people.

Before they have time to forget how they got the power of their high office, they will be forced to think about the next election, when their actions will be reviewed. They will be reminded that they will become a common citizen if they haven't faithfully discharged their trust and truly deserve to be reelected.

by the People of the several States, and the Electors in each State shall have the Qualifications requisite for Electors of the most numerous Branch of the State legislature.

Number 10 [18-19]

In a large republic, each representative is chosen by a greater number of citizens. It will be more difficult for unworthy candidates to successfully win through vicious election practices. And with wide voter freedom, elections will more likely center on men who possess the most merit and highest character.

When a representative has too many constituents, it will be difficult for him to know all the local issues. When a representative has too few constituents, his worry about local issues will make him unfit to understand and pursue national issues. The federal Constitution forms a good combination. The national issues are referred to the national government; local issues are referred to State legislatures.

Number 22 [13]

In a republic, people are elected to important offices and have great power...

Number 39 [5, 12]

The Constitution follows the republican form. The people elect the House of Representatives... and will be represented proportionately.

Number 44 [26]

... Federal officials will not be agents of State constitutions. However, State officials will be essential agents of the federal Constitution... State officers will probably conduct the election of the House of Representatives, according to the laws of the States.

Number 45 [7]

Even though the people elect the House of Representatives, the State legislators will influence their decision.

Number 52 [2]

In each State, the citizens who are qualified to vote for the State legislature will vote for members of the House of Representatives. Voting is a basic right of republican government. The Constitution defines and guarantees this right. The federal House of Representatives should depend on the people, not the State governments.

It would have been difficult for the convention to establish one rule for the entire country. And some of the States would have been dissatisfied. Therefore, the Constitution has the best solution. It satisfies every State, using the rule established by the State itself. The United States will be safe because, even though the State governments make the rule, it is base on the State constitutions and the State governments cannot change it. And the people will not change this part of the State constitutions to lose the rights secured to them by the federal Constitution.

Number 54 [7, 9]

...each State decides who can vote for Representatives. Different States may have different voter qualifications. Some people in every State will not be allowed to vote... the Constitution doesn't require that all States have the same suffrage policy...

...Wealthy States, unlike wealthy individuals, don't influence each other. Although a wealthy citizen has only one vote, his wealth frequently influences other voters towards his choice. Through this invisible channel, property rights are conveyed into public representation...

Number 57 [5, 14-17]

Who will elect the federal Representatives? Not the rich more than the poor. Not the educated more than the ignorant. Not the haughty heirs of famous names more than the humble sons of obscurity without a family fortune. The people of the United States will vote. They will be the same people who elect representatives to the State legislatures.

...What should we say to men who profess a love for republican government, yet boldly impeach the fundamental principle of it? What should we say about men who pretend to support the right and ability of the people to choose their own rulers, yet maintain voters will only elect people who will immediately betray the trust given to them?

What if someone reads this objection but doesn't read the Constitution, which defines how representatives will be chosen? He would conclude that only people owning a large amount of property could vote. Or that only special families or wealthy people could vote. If nothing else, he would think that the election method in the federal Constitution is quite different from the State constitutions.

However, there are no property, family, or wealth qualifications for voters. The only difference between the States and federal Constitutions is the number of people who elect representatives. 5,000 or 6,000 citizens will elect each United States Representative. In the States, 500 or 600 citizens elect representatives. Does this difference mean that the State governments are good and the federal government is not? Let's examine this point.

Is this conclusion *logical*? No. Five or six thousand citizens can choose as capable a representative as 500 or 600 citizens. And the larger group is not more easily corrupted than the smaller. Logic says that it will be easier to find a fit Representative in the larger group. And it will be harder for ambitious or rich people to corrupt the election.

Is the *consequence* from this doctrine admissible? If we say that only 500 or 600 citizens can vote, shouldn't we take away the peoples' right to choose public servants whenever the administration of the government does not require as many of them as will amount to one for that number of citizens?

Number 60 [3, 11]

...each part [of the federal government] will be elected in a different way. The House of Representatives will be elected directly by the people...

...The only way rich people could take over control is if there were property qualifications for either voters or nominees. But the national government doesn't have this power. It can only regulate the times, the places, and the manner of elections. The qualifications of voters or nominees are defined in the Constitution and Congress can't change them.

No person shall be a Representative who shall not have attained to the Age of twenty five Years, and been seven Years a Citizen of the United States, and who shall not, when elected, be an Inhabitant to that State in which he shall be chosen.

Number 52 [3]

This defines the qualifications of Representatives:

A Representative of the United States must be 25 years old, must be a citizen of the United States for seven years, at the time of his election he must be an inhabitant of the State he is to represent, and while serving as a Representative, he must hold no other office under the United States.

These are reasonable qualifications. Good people of every description may become Representatives, whether native or adoptive, young or old, and without regard to poverty, wealth, or religion.

Number 60 [11]

…The only way rich people could take over control is if there were property qualifications for either voters or nominees. But the national government doesn't have this power…

Number 62 [2]

A Senator must be at least thirty years old and a citizen for nine years. A Representative must be 25 years old and a citizen for 7 years.

Probable Characteristics of Representatives

Number 10 [16]

Representation refines public views by passing them through the delegates. The representatives' wisdom may see their country's true interests. Their patriotism and love of justice will make them less likely to sacrifice their country. Representatives of the people may do a better job of looking out for the public good than if all the people gathered and spoke for themselves.

On the other hand, the opposite effect may happen. Men with local prejudices or sinister plans may use intrigue or corruption to be elected, and then betray the interests of the people.

Number 35 [6-11]

The idea that every class of people have representatives from their class is a Utopian fantasy. Unless the Constitution expressly says that each occupation should send one or more members, it will never happen.

Mechanics and manufacturers will probably vote for merchants rather than persons in their own professions. Mechanics and manufactures furnish the materials of commerce. The merchant is their natural patron and friend. They may feel confident in their own good sense but they know that the merchant can more effectively promote their interests. They know that their life experiences haven't given them the skills needed in a legislative assembly. The merchants' influence, status, and talents can better oppose attitudes unfriendly to the manufacturing and trading interests in public councils. Artisans and manufacturers will usually vote for merchants or the people who merchants recommend. So merchants are the natural representatives of all of these classes of people.

With regard to the learned professions, little need be said. They truly form no distinct interest in society. According to their situation and talents, they will be indiscriminately the objects of the confidence and choice of each other and of other parts of the community.

Lastly, the landed interest. This group includes the wealthiest landlord down to the poorest tenant. Their political views, particularly in relation to taxes, are perfectly united. Property taxes affect the owner of millions of acres as well as the owner of a single acre. Every landholder will want to keep the taxes on land as low as possible. And common interests always create bonds of sympathy.

But even if the rich landholder and the small farmer had different interests, why would we think that the rich landholder would stand a better chance of being elected to the national legislature than the farmer? In fact, small landowners prevail in the New York senate and assembly. Where voters' qualifications are the same, their votes will go to men in whom they have the most confidence, whether they happen to have large fortunes, moderate property, or no property at all.

Some people say that every class of citizen should have a member of their class in the representative body, so that their feelings and interests are better understood and attended to. However, if the people are free to vote for anyone, this will never happen. In open and free elections, the representative body will be composed mostly of landlords, merchants, and learned professions.

Won't the interests and feelings of the different classes of citizens be understood by men in these professions? The landlord will understand and promote the interests of property owners. Since he owns property, he will probably resist every attempt to prejudice or encumber it.

The interests of the merchant are tied to the interests of mechanic and manufacturer. The merchant will understand their interests and, as far as proper, promote them.

The learned professionals will be neutral towards the rivalships between different branches of industry. They will be impartial arbiters between them. And they will be ready to promote either, as it seems to promote the general interests of the society.

Wise administrators pay attention to the current feelings or desires in the different parts of society. A candidate depends on the votes of his fellow citizens to continue his public job. He will learn their dispositions and inclinations. And they will influence his conduct to a proper degree. The representative feels dependent on the citizens. He knows that he will be judged by the laws he approves.

Taxation policy requires extensive information and a thorough knowledge of political economic principles. Anyone who understands these principles will not want oppressive taxes nor will they want to sacrifice any group of citizens to get more tax revenue.

The most productive system of obtaining governmental revenue will always be the least burdensome. In order to tax judiciously, the person with the power to tax should understand the general characteristics, habits, and thinking of the people, and the country's resources. Let every thinking citizen judge for himself who has the required qualifications.

Number 36 [1-2]

The previous paper explained why representatives will usually be property own-ers, merchants, and members of the learned professions. They will represent all the com-munity's different interests and views.

There will be exceptions to this rule. Occasionally, people will rise above the disadvantages of their situation and their merit will be recognized by society. The door should be equally open to all. To the credit of human nature, such people will be in both the federal and State legislatures.

Mechanics, manufacturers, and labor can be great rivals. But to have representa-tives of every occupation, the legislature would be too big to have wise deliberations. I refuse to continue discussing this rather vague objection.

Number 53 [4, 5, 9]

A competent legislator has good intentions, sound judgment, and some know-ledge of legislative subjects. He gets some knowledge in private life. Another part can only be completely learned while serving as a legislator…A federal congressman has more to learn than a State congressman…

…Most citizens understand the general affairs of the State. State issues are not very diversified and everyone studies and discusses them.

Understanding national issues is different. The laws vary in every State. The country is large with diverse responsibilities. They are difficult to learn outside the federal capitol, where representatives of the entire nation bring knowledge of them.

All federal legislators need to know something about State issues and laws…

As happens in all such assemblies, a few members will have superior talents, be reelected and become members of long standing. They will be masters of public business. The more new members, the less information the assembly will have. And they will be more likely to fall into the snares laid for them. This is true for both the House and the Senate.

Number 57 [3, 6-10]

The first goal of every political constitution is finding men to rule who have the wisdom to understand and the virtue to pursue society's common good. Next, it needs a way to keep them virtuous while they are in office.

Republican governments elect rulers. Many things help to prevent their degene-racy. The most effective is limiting their term in office. Because they have to face reelec-tion, they will feel responsible to the people.

Who will be elected? The candidate will be a citizen whose merit recommends him to the esteem and confidence of his country. There are no qualifications of wealth, birth, religious faith, or civil profession.

Several things assure us that the Representatives will be faithful to their constitu-ents.

First. Their fellow citizen will choose them. They will have some good quali-ties, including an understanding of their obligations as an elected official.

Second. When they begin to serve, they will have at least a temporary affection for their constituents. When citizens honor a person, he responds positively. This guaran-tees some grateful and benevolent returns.

People often discuss ingratitude. And it does happen too frequently, both in public and private life. But the extreme anger the discussion of ingratitude inspires proves that most people feel grateful.

Third, the representative is also tied to his constituents for selfish reasons. Being an elected official flatters his pride and vanity. A large number of men advance politically because of their influence with the people. And they have more to gain from preserving the voters' favor, than from working to change the government in a way that subverts the people's authority.

Number 60 [3]

...People in different parts of the Union have different behaviors and habits. Representatives will bring a wide range of feelings to the national government. As they work closely together, they will begin to think more alike. But physical and moral causes may nourish their different propensities and inclinations...

Objections to Probable Characteristics of Representatives

Number 57 [1-4]

The *third* charge against the House of Representative is that members will come from the upper class of citizens, who have little in common with the mass of the people. And their ambition will sacrifice the many to the benefit of the few.

This objection to the Constitution suggests an oligarchy will develop. And it strikes at the root of republican government.

The first goal of every political constitution is finding men to rule who have the wisdom to understand and the virtue to pursue society's common good. Next, it needs a way to keep them virtuous while they are in office.

Republican governments elect rulers. Many things help to prevent their degeneracy. The most effective is limiting their term in office. Because they have to face reelection, they will feel responsible to the people.

What in the Constitution about the House of Representatives violates the principles of republican government? How does it favor the election of an upper class of people?
Isn't the opposite true? Doesn't the Constitution strictly follow republican principles? Isn't it impartial to the rights of every class and description of citizens?

Number 62 [10]

Most members of the House of Representatives will be men with jobs in the private sector. They will have a short term in office with no reason to devote their time while serving as Representatives to the study of laws and all the interests of their country.

[Representatives and direct Taxes shall be apportioned among the several States which may be included within this Union, according to their respective Numbers, which shall be determined by adding to the whole Number of free Persons, including those bound to Service for a Term of Years, and excluding Indians not taxed, three-fifths of all other persons.]

*changed by Amendment 14, section 2, ratified in 1868:

Representatives shall be apportioned among the several States according to their respective numbers, counting the whole number of persons in each State, excluding Indians not taxed. But when the right to vote at any election for the choice of Electors for President and Vice-President of the United States, Representatives in Congress, the executive and judicial officers of a State, or the members of the Legislature thereof, is denied to any of the male inhabitants of such State, being twenty-one of age, and citizens of the United States, or in any way abridged, except for participation in rebellion, or other crime, the basis of representation therein shall be reduced in the proportion which the number of such male citizens shall bear to the whole number of male citizens twenty-one years of age in such State.

Number 54 [11]

In one respect, using one rule to calculate representation and taxation will have a very good effect. To a large degree, the accuracy of the federal census will depend on the disposition, if not on the cooperation, of the States. It is important that the States feel as little bias as possible to increase or reduce their numbers.

If the census was only used to determine proportional representation, the States would want to exaggerate their population. If the census was only used to determine proportional taxation, States would want a smaller number. By using the census to determine both, the States will have opposite interests, which will control and balance each other, and produce an impartial census.

Number 55 [1-3]

The number of members in the House of Representatives is an interesting topic. Some respected people argue against it. They say:

1) Such a small number of Representatives is unsafe.

2) With such a large number of constituents, Representatives will not know enough about the local circumstances.

3) Representatives will be from the upper class of citizens. They will not understand the feelings of the mass of the people and will aim at a permanent elevation of the few on the depression of the many.

4) As the population increases, the number of representatives will become more disproportionate. And it will be difficult to increase the number of representatives.

Constituent/Legislator Ratios

There is no formula to determine the correct size for a representative legislature. The State legislatures have many different representatives-to-population ratios.
Delaware has the smallest legislature. Its largest branch has 21 representatives.
Massachusetts, the largest State legislature, has 300-400 members. With nearly the same size population, Pennsylvania's legislature is 1/5 the size of Massachusetts with a representative for every 4 or 5,000 constituents.

New York's population is to that of South Carolina as 6:5, but it has about 1/3 the number of representatives.

There is also a great difference between Georgia and Delaware or Rhode Island. In Rhode Island, the proportion is 1:1,000. In Georgia, the proportion may be 1:10 voters, far exceeding the proportion in any other State.

Ratio Changes with Population

Very large and very small populations should have different representative to constituent ratios. If the Virginia ratio was the same as Rhode Island, Virginia would have 400-500 representatives. And 20 years from now, 1,000. And if Pennsylvania's ratio was used in Delaware, Delaware would have 7-8 representatives.

Political decisions cannot be based on arithmetic. Sixty men might be more trusted with power than six. But that doesn't mean 600 men would be even safer. And 6,000 men reverses the whole reasoning.

The number needs to be large enough for open discussion and to guard against conspiracies. But the number can be too large, creating confusion and an intolerant mob. In all very large assemblies, passion always over-takes reasoning. Even if every Athenian citizen had been a Socrates, every Athenian assembly would still have been a mob.

Number 21 [11]

… Direct taxes principally relate to land and buildings, and they may be appropriate for the rule of apportionment. Either the land value or the number of people may serve as a standard. Agriculture and population density are co-related. For taxation, numbers are usually preferred because of their simplicity and certainty.

Land valuation is a herculean task. In a country only partly settled and constantly being improved, the difficulties make it nearly impossible. And the expense of an accurate valuation is a major objection.

There are no natural limits to direct taxes. Therefore the establishment of a fixed rule, compatible with its purpose, might be a better idea than leaving the discretion unbound.

Number 22 [7-13]

Currently, each State has an equal vote in the national congress. This is another problem. Every rule of fair representation condemns the principle that gives Rhode Island equal power with Massachusetts or Connecticut or New York. This goes against the basic principle of republican government: the will of the majority should prevail.

Some people may say that each State in the Union is a sovereign and sovereigns are equal. Therefore a majority of the votes of States will be a majority of confederate America. But this logical sleight-of-hand doesn't remove the dictates of justice and common sense. A majority of States can be a small minority of American citizens.[*]

---

[*] New Hampshire, Rhode Island, New Jersey, Delaware, Georgia, South Carolina and Maryland are a majority of the whole number of States but they do not contain one third of the people.
    –PUBLIUS

Two thirds of the people will not allow one third to manage their interests. After a while, the larger States will revolt. Giving up majority rights is contrary to the love of power and it sacrifices equality. It is not rational to expect the first, nor just to require the second. Since the smaller States depend on union for their safety and welfare, they should readily renounce a pretension that, if not relinquished, would be fatal to that union.

It may be proposed that two-thirds of the States (9) must consent to pass important resolutions. But an equal vote between States of unequal dimensions and populations is improper. Besides, nine States can have less than a majority of the people.** A bare majority might still decide significant issues. Additionally, the number of States will probably increase and there is no provision for increasing the ratio of votes.

But this is not all. A two-thirds majority may look like a solution. In reality it makes the problem worse. When more than a majority is needed to make a decision, the minority gets a negative over the majority. It subordinates the feelings of the majority to the minority. Because a few States have been absent from our current Congress, a single vote—one-sixtieth part of the union—has frequently stopped all business.

A two-thirds majority is supposed to provide security. In practice, it does the opposite. It becomes nearly impossible to administer the government. And it substitutes the desires or schemes of a tiny or corrupt group of politicians for the decisions of a majority.

During national emergencies, the government needs to be strong and it must often take an action. Public business must, one way or another, go forward. If a stubborn minority is in control, to accomplish anything, the majority must accept the decisions of the minority. Delays, negotiations, and intrigue would hurt the public good. Sometimes compromises won't be possible and the legislature will be unable to act. This would create a government that is weak and sometimes bordering on anarchy.

If a two-third majority is required, both foreign corruption and domestic faction will be easier. If a large number is needed to pass a national act, nothing improper is likely *to be done*. However, good legislation may be prevented and bad things might happen because the Congress is unable to act.

For instance, suppose a foreign ally wants a war with a third nation but we want a peace treaty. It would be easier for our ally to use bribes or threats to tie the hands of our government from making peace if a vote of two-thirds were required rather than a simple majority. In the first case, a smaller number (34%) would need to be corrupted; in the latter, a greater number (51%). By the same principle, a foreign power at war with us could stop our congress from functioning and embarrass us.

We may also suffer commercial inconveniences. We might have a commerce treaty with a nation, who could easily block a treaty with her trade competitor, even though it would be beneficial to us.

These evils are not imaginary. A weak side to republics is that foreign corruption is easy. A king or dictator often sacrifices his subjects to his ambition but it is difficult for a foreign power to make a bribe large enough for him to sacrifice his state.

** Add New York and Connecticut to the foregoing seven and they will be less than a majority. – PUBLIUS

In a republic, people are elected to important offices and have great power. They may be offered bribes that only the most virtuous can refuse. Other officials may be more motivated by ambition or personal interests than their obligations to duty.

History has many horrible examples of foreign corruption in republican governments: It helped ruin the ancient republics. Neighboring nations have bought the officials of the United Provinces. And France and England alternately bought officials in Sweden.

Number 36 [6, 9]

Internal taxes may be either *direct* or *indirect* taxes. Objections based on a "lack of local knowledge" have been made against both types of internal taxes…

Remember, the national legislature will not decide how much the people of each State must pay. That will be determined by each State's population, as described in Article one, Section two.

Number 38 [7]

An objector from a small State is equally loud against the dangerous **inequality** in the **House of Representatives.**

Number 83 [14]

Trial by jury cannot influence the legislature, which decides the *amount* of taxes, the *objects* of taxation, and the tax apportionment *rule*.

Number Representatives/Direct Taxes: Same Rule

Number 54 [1-10]

The States use the same rule for direct taxes and appointing Representatives.

Proportional representation should be based on State populations. The Constitution also uses population to determine each State's tax obligation. Using a State's population for both is based on two different principles.

In the case of the House of Representatives, proportional representation refers to the personal rights of the people.

In the case of taxes, it is proportional wealth. It is not an exact measure of wealth. In fact, it is very imperfect. However, it is the least objectionable method. And Americans recently agreed to use this method, so the convention selected it.

Some people want slaves counted for taxation but not counted for proportional representation. They argue that slaves are considered property, not persons; therefore, they should be counted for taxation. But they should not be counted when determining representation, which is determined by a census of persons. This seems to be the objection. I will state the opposite side of the argument.

A Southern friend might say, "We agree representation relates more to persons and taxation more to property. But we deny that slaves are only property and in no way persons. They have both qualities. Our laws consider them, in some ways, persons and, in other ways, property.

"The slave is forced to labor for a master. The master can sell him. His liberty is limited. And his body is forced to do what another person tells him to do. For these reasons, the slave may not seem human. He may seem more like a farm animal, which is defined as property.

"However, the slave is protected against violence, even by his master. And if the slave hurts another person, he can be punished. Therefore, the law considers the slave a member of society, not an animal. He is seen as a moral person, not as a mere article of property.

"The federal Constitution, therefore, correctly looks at slaves as both persons and property. Non-slave States don't want to include slaves in the census. But the pretexts of laws, alone, have made Negroes property. And if laws restored the rights that have been taken away, the Negroes could not be refused an equal share of representation.

"We can look at this question in another way. Numbers measure wealth and taxation. And numbers measure representation. What if the convention had excluded slaves from the population when calculating representation, then inserted them to calculate taxes? Would the Southern States agree to a system that considered their slaves, in some degree, as men when the burden of tax is imposed, but refused to consider them in the same way when the advantage of representation is conferred?

"Some people reproach the Southern States for the barbarous policy of considering part of their human brethren as property. Now the same people say the federal government should consider this unfortunate race more completely in the unnatural light of property than the very laws they complain about.

"They may argue that, in the States with slaves, slaves are not included in computing the state representation. They neither vote nor increase the votes of their masters. If the Constitution didn't use them to compute representation, it would follow State laws.

"One fact voids this objection. The number of representatives from each State is determined by a rule in the federal Constitution, based on population. However, each State decides who can vote for Representatives. Different States may have different voter qualifications. Some people in every State will not be allowed to vote. But they will be included in the federal census that determines the number of representatives. Southern States might argue that the Constitution doesn't require that all States have the same suffrage policy. Therefore, the full number of slaves should be included in the census, because other States count people who do not have all the rights of citizens.

"However, the southern States have waived a strict adherence to this principle. They want equal moderation on the other side. Let slaves be considered a specific case and the Constitutional compromise adopted. Slaves are people debased by servitude below the equal level of free people; the Constitution regards the *slave* as divested of 2/5 of the *man*.

"There is a better defense of this article of the Constitution. So far, we have assumed that representation relates only to persons and not to property. But is this valid?

"Government is established to protect both property and people. Therefore, government represents both property and people. In several States, one branch of government guards property and is elected by people most interested in this governmental objective.

"In the federal Constitution, the same hands protect both property and personal rights. Therefore, some attention ought to be paid to property when choosing those hands.

"There is another reason federal representation should be somewhat proportional to the comparative wealth of the States. Wealthy States, unlike wealthy individuals, don't influence each other. Although a wealthy citizen has only one vote, his wealth frequently influences other voters towards his choice. Through this invisible channel, property rights are conveyed into public representation.

"A State doesn't have this kind of influence over other States. The richest State will probably never influence the choice of a single representative in any other State. And the representatives of large, rich States will have no advantage in the federal legislature over the representatives of other States, except the advantage resulting from their superior number. Therefore, if their superior wealth entitles them to any advantage, they should get it through a larger share of representation.

"The new Constitution is very different from the existing Confederation and other confederacies where federal resolutions must be approved by the states before becoming laws. In those confederacies, each state has an equal vote in the federal councils. However, they have an unequal influence, depending on the subject of the resolutions.

"Under the proposed Constitution, the federal laws will take effect without the agreement of the individual States. They will depend only on the majority of votes in the federal legislature. Therefore, each vote, whether from a large or small State, or a State more or less wealthy or powerful, will have equal weight and efficacy. Any influence will come from the personal character of a representative rather than whether he comes from a wealthy district."

This is how an advocate for the Southern interests might discuss this subject. And although it may appear to be a little strained in some points, I believe it shows that the Constitution's rule for representation works.

The actual Enumeration shall be made within three Years after the first Meeting of the Congress of the United States, and within every subsequent Term of ten Years, in such Manner as they shall by Law direct. The number of Representatives shall not exceed one for every thirty Thousand, but each State shall have at Least one Representative;

Number 36 [9]

The population will be determined by a census.

Number 55 [6]

When the government begins, the number will be 65. A census will be taken within three years. Then the number may increase to one for every 30,000 inhabitants. A new census is to be taken every ten years. The House may continue to grow under the above limitation.

The first census will probably increase the number of representatives to at least 100. Using a 3/5 proportion for Negroes, the population will be three million, if it isn't already.

After 25 years, the number of representatives will probably be 200. In 50 years, 400. This should end fears that it is too small.

The number of representatives will increase from time to time. If the Constitution did not provide for this increase, the objection would be legitimate.

Number 58 [4]

A census of inhabitants will be taken every ten years. The census has two objectives: First, to periodically adjust the ratio of representatives to inhabitants; the exception is that each State will have at least one representative. Second, to increase the number of representatives, but the whole number will not exceed one for every 30,000 inhabitants...

and until such enumeration shall be made, the State of New Hampshire shall be entitled to choose three, Massachusetts eight, Rhode Island and Providence Plantations one, Connecticut five, New York six, New Jersey four, Pennsylvania eight, Delaware one, Maryland six, Virginia ten, North Carolina five, South Carolina five, and Georgia three.

Objections to Number of Representatives

Number 35 [5]

Critics of the Constitution often say that the House of Representatives is too small. They say more members are needed to represent all different classes of citizens, the interests of every part of the community, and to produce sympathy between the representative body and its constituents. This is a specious and seducing argument. And it is impractical and unnecessary to accomplish the goal it supposedly supports.

Number 58 [1-14]

I will examine one more charge against the House of Representatives. It has been said that the number of members will not grow as population growth may demand.

If true, this would be an important objection. However, it is like most objections against the Constitution. It is either the result of limited information about the subject or a jealousy that produces an irrational hatred towards all things.

One. The number of Representatives stated in the Constitution is temporary, for only three years.

A census of inhabitants will be taken every ten years. The census has two objectives: First, to periodically adjust the ratio of representatives to inhabitants; the exception is that each State will have at least one representative. Second, to increase the number of representatives, but the whole number will not exceed one for every 30,000 inhabitants.

Some State constitutions have no regulations on this subject. Others are very similar to the federal Constitution. And the highest security in any of them is only a suggestion.

Two. The States have increased their representatives as the populations increased. When the citizens requested an increase, the representatives have agreed.

Three. Both the people and their representatives will carefully watch the growth in the number of federal Representatives.

The House of Representatives represents the citizens; the Senate represents the States. Consequently, in the House of Representatives, the larger States will have the most weight. The Senate favors the smaller States. We can assume that large States will want to increase the number of Representatives from their States and their influence will predominate.

The four largest States will have a majority of the votes in the House of Representatives. Therefore, if the nine smaller States oppose adding members, the four large States can overrule the opposition. Normally, rivalries and prejudices might prevent the

States from agreeing to an issue. But they would join together to support their common interest and desire to uphold the equity and principals of the Constitution.

It may be argued that the Senate might block efforts to increase the number of Representatives. Since the Senate's agreement is necessary, it could defeat the just, constitutional actions of the House. This problem worries the jealous friends of a large representation. Fortunately, it is an illusion. It vanishes on close inspection.

The House and Senate will have equal authority on all legislative subjects except money bills—the House originates all money bills. However, the House will have more members. When the more powerful/larger States follow the will of a majority of the people, they will support the House of Representatives. And the House will have an advantage over the Senate.

Logic and the Constitution make the House of Representatives even stronger. And opponents to increasing the size of the House will be fighting against the force of all these strong forces.

Senate Also Influenced By State Size

The States range in size from small to large. Several medium size States, are closer in size to the large than the small States. Therefore, those Sates will probably not oppose the larger States' just and legitimate claims. Therefore, it is not certain that a majority of votes, even in the Senate, would block the growth in the number of Representatives.

Also, the Senators from new States may agree to increase the House of Representatives. The population in the new States will increase rapidly. They will want frequent reapportionments to reflect their increased population.

The large States will have the most power in the House of Representatives. They will want both reapportionments and increased membership in the House. And the Senators from all the fastest growing States will fight for increasing House membership because of their States' interest in reapportionment. For these reasons, alone, there should be no fear that the House will not increase in size. However, the larger States will have another, constitutional remedy to increase the size.

The House of Representatives, alone, proposes the bills that provide the government with the supplies it needs. They hold the purse. This is a very important power. Britain has the monarchy, the House of Lords [run by the aristocracy], and the House of Commons, [the representative body of the people]. Because it controls the money, the House of Commons has slowly increased its activity and importance. It is now the most powerful branch of British government.

Power over the purse is the best weapon any constitution can give the people's representatives. It can correct every problem and promote the people's wishes.

Won't the House of Representatives want to maintain the proper functions of the government? Will the House allow the Senate to determine its existence or reputation? Or if there was a trial of firmness between the two houses of Congress, would not either one be as likely as the other to yield first?

These are not difficult questions. When a small, visible group of people with long terms in office hold power, each person feels more personally responsible to fulfill their duties. Senators represent the dignity of their country in the eyes of other nations.

They will be very sensitive to the possibility of public danger or dishonorable stagnation in public affairs.

The British House of Commons has more power than the other branches of the government when money bills are discussed. If the monarchy and House of Lords became absolutely inflexible, the government would have been thrown into confusion. However, this has never happened.

The federal Senate and President will never be able to completely resist the House. And the House will be supported by constitutional and patriotic principles.

Some people might want to temporarily lower the number of representatives to save money. This subject could have been used as an objection to the Constitution. And under the present circumstances, it might be difficult to have as many people in the federal government as the people will probably elect.

I must add one observation, however, because it is very important. The larger the number of members in any assembly or legislature, the fewer the number of men who will, in fact, direct their proceedings. This is the result of several factors.

First, as the number of people in an assembly grows, the rule of passion over reason also grows.

Second, as the size of a group grows, so does the proportion of members with limited information and less ability. A few eloquent leaders can sway people with these personality types. In the ancient republics, where the whole population assembled in person, a single orator or an artful statesman generally ruled as if he was a king or dictator.

Third, on the same principle, the bigger a representative assembly becomes, the more it will take on the problems that accompany collective meetings of the people. Ignorance will be the dupe of cunning. Passion the slave of sophistry and declamation.

People may think that the bigger the assembly, the stronger the barrier against government by the few. However, this is a big mistake. Experience shows the opposite. *After an assembly is large enough to secure safety, to understand local information, and to be sympathetic to society*, every additional representative will defeat this purpose. The government may look more democratic, but it will actually be more oligarchic. The assembly will be larger, but fewer people—often in secret—will direct its actions.

When vacancies happen in the Representation from any State, the Executive Authority thereof shall issue Writs of Election to fill such Vacancies.

The House of Representatives shall chuse their Speaker and other Officers;

and shall have the sole Power of Impeachment.

Number 47 [6-7]

[In Great Britain] one legislative house is the monarch's constitutional council. It also has judicial power in cases of impeachment and is the supreme court of appeals in all other cases...The entire legislature doesn't act as a court, but it can remove a judge from office, and one house has the judicial power of final appeal. The entire legislature, again, has no executive powers, though one house acts as the supreme executive magistracy. And the other house, after an impeachment vote, can try and condemn all the subordinate officers in the executive department.

Number 65 [5]

If one house of the legislature starts the inquiry by impeaching the official, shouldn't the other house be part of the inquiry?

The convention used the British model. The House of Commons prefers the impeachment; the House of Lords decides it.

Several State constitutions follow the example. Those States and Great Britain see impeachment as a bridle in the hands of the legislature on the people in the executive branch of government. Isn't this the proper view?

Number 66 [2, 7]

…Impeachment powers are divided between the two houses of the legislature. The House accuses and the Senate judges. Therefore, the same persons are not both accusers and judges. This guards against the danger of prosecution from a majority faction in either house…

It [House of Representatives] will institute impeachments.

Number 79 [4]

To assure that judges will act responsibly, they can be impeached by the House of Representatives…

ARTICLE 1 SECTION 3. Senate of the United States

<u>The Reasons a Senate is Needed</u>

Number 62 [7-10, 12-end]

...we will look at the purposes of the Senate. What problems would the republic have if it didn't have a Senate?

First. Administrators of the republic may forget their obligations to the people and betray their important trust. A senate as a second house of legislature is a good check on the government. It doubles the people's security. Two separate bodies will have to agree to schemes of usurpation or perfidy. Without it, one corrupt body would be enough.

There are clear principles for this precaution. Sinister conspiracies are less probable as the difference between the geniuses of the two legislative bodies grows. Therefore, making them as different as possible, within the principles of republican government, is prudent.

Second. All single, large assemblies tend to give in to sudden, violent passions; they can be seduced by factious leaders into extreme and harmful resolutions. Therefore, a Senate is necessary.

Numerous examples on this subject could be cited. But no one will contradict this point. A body formed to correct this problem should be, itself, free from it. Consequently, it should be smaller with longer terms in office to make it more stable.

Third. Senators will be familiar with the objectives and principles of legislation... If the House was the only legislative assembly, it would make a variety of important errors.

Many of America's present embarrassments can be charged on the blunders of our governments. These blunders have come from the heads rather than the hearts of most of the authors of them.

Indeed, acts that repeal, explain, and amend laws fill and disgrace our huge codes. They are monuments to a lack of wisdom. Each legislative session discredits the preceding session. A Senate will be very helpful.

Fourth. Frequent changes in public councils, however qualified the new members may be, shows why a stable institution in the government is necessary.

Every election changes half the representatives. This turnover creates a change of opinions and a change of legislation. But continual change, even if it is good legislation, is inconsistent with every rule of prudence and every hope of success. Private life verifies this observation. And it becomes more just and more important in national transactions.

A history of the harmful effects of a mutable government would fill a volume. I will list a few, each of which is a source of others.

A mutable government forfeits the respect and confidence of other nations, and all the advantages connected with national character.

All prudent people know that a person who frequently changes his plans or lives his life without any plan at all will quickly fall victim to his own unsteadiness and folly. His friendly neighbors may pity him, but all will decline to connect their fortunes with his. And more than a few people will seize the opportunity to make their fortunes out of his.

One nation is to another as one individual is to another, with one sad difference. Nations have fewer benevolent emotions than people. They feel fewer restraints from taking advantage of each other. Every nation that shows a lack of wisdom and stability may expect every possible loss to the more systematic policy of their wiser neighbors.

Unfortunately, the best example is America. She is ridiculed by her enemies. And she is prey to every nation that wants to speculate about her changing councils and embarrassed affairs.

The domestic effects of a mutable policy are even worse. It poisons the blessings of liberty itself.

It won't benefit the people that the laws are made by men of their own choice, if the laws are so voluminous that they cannot be read or so incoherent that they cannot be understood. Or if they are repealed or revised before they are promulgated or are changed so frequently that no man who knows what the law is today can guess what it will be to-morrow.

Law is defined to be a rule of action. But how can it be a rule when it is little known and less fixed?

There is another effect of having laws that are not stable. It gives the few perceptive, enterprising, and wealthy citizens an advantage over the industrious and uninformed mass of people.

Every new regulation about commerce or revenue or that affects property value is a new opportunity to those people who watch the change and can predict its consequences. They don't create this opportunity. It is created by the toils and cares of the great body of their fellow citizens. When this happens, it may truthfully be said that laws are made for the *few*, not for the *many*.

An unstable government also hurts the economy. When people don't know what actions the government might take, projects where success and profit may depend on the existing laws continuing will be discouraged.

What prudent merchant will jeopardize his fortunes in a new area of commerce when he doesn't know if his plans may be made unlawful before they can be executed? What farmer or manufacturer will commit himself to a specific cultivation or project when he can't be sure that his preparations and investment will not make him a victim to an inconstant government?

In a word, if an improvement or praiseworthy enterprise needs the protection or security of a consistent national policy, it will not be pursued.

But the worst effect is that the people will feel less attachment and reverence to the government. No government will be respected without being truly respectable. And it will not be respectable if it doesn't have some order and stability.

Number 63 [1-9, 12, 15-17, 21]

A *fifth* aim is national reputation. The government needs a stable part. Without it, our policies will change frequently and we will loose the respect of foreign nations.

And the national government will not be sensitive to the opinion of the world, which is necessary to obtain its respect and confidence.

The judgment of other nations is important for two reasons:

1) Independent of the merits of any specific plan or measure, it is desirable that other nations see it as coming from a wise and honorable policy.

2) In doubtful cases, particularly when some strong passion or momentary concern warps the national government, the opinion of the impartial world may be the best guide.

How has America's poor reputation with foreign nations hurt us? And how many errors would she have avoided, if she had first looked at how her policies appeared to unbiased observers?

A large legislature that has members with only a short term in office cannot create a good national reputation. In a small legislature, each member shares the praise and blame for laws. And when a legislator has a long term in office, his pride becomes part of the reputation and prosperity of the community.

Representatives in Rhode Island serve for six months. When they discussed grossly unjust laws, the opinion of foreign nations or the other States probably had little effect. What if a second, stable legislative body had to agree to the laws? Its members would want national respect. This would have prevented the calamities under which the people now live.

Sixth aim: Less frequent elections increase the government's responsibility to the people. This comment may seem both new and paradoxical. However, it is true and important.

Responsibility must be **reasonable** and **effective**.

To be **reasonable**, it must be limited to objects within the power of the responsible party.

To be **effective**, constituents must be able to see and judge the operations of that power.

There are two types of legislation. Some legislation takes immediate effect. Other legislation is part of a chain of measures that have a gradual and, perhaps, unobserved operation.

The latter type of legislation is important to the welfare of every country. A legislature with a short term can provide only one or two links in a chain of measures. But they cannot be held responsible for the final result. This is the same as a building project that takes six years. A carpenter employed for one year is not responsible for the final result.

When a legislature is elected every year and is working towards a long-term goal, the people don't know how to judge the influence of each annual assembly. And in a very large legislature, it is also hard to make each representative feel personally responsible.

The remedy is a second legislative body. The members should have long enough terms to meet objectives that require constant attention and a series of measures. They can be responsible for meeting those objectives.

Sometimes a Senate protects the people from their own errors and delusions.

In all governments, the community's objectives should prevail over the objectives of its rulers. And it will prevail in all free governments.

However, inappropriate passions sometimes influence citizens. Ambitious and clever men may mislead them. Then citizens may ask for laws that they will later lament and condemn.

If a second, temperate legislative body made up of respectable citizens must agree to the laws, it could block misguided laws. It can stop the blow planned by the people against themselves until reason, justice, and truth can be restored to the public mind.

The Athenians would have escaped bitter pain if their government had such a safeguard against the tyranny of their own passions. We might not now blame liberty for decreeing, to the same citizens, hemlock on one day and statues on the next.

Someone might say that when people are spread over a large area they cannot, like the crowded inhabitants of a city, be infected by violent passions or conspire to pursue unjust measures. This is important. In a former paper, I explained that this is one of the important advantages of a confederated republic.

However, this advantage doesn't mean that other precautions are unnecessary. The large area will exempt Americans from some of the dangers seen in smaller republics. But it also means that we will live for a longer time under the influence of the misrepresentations.

History shows us no long-lived republic without a senate. Sparta and Rome had a senate for life. The senate in Carthage is less known. It probably also had a senate for life. It certainly had some quality that made it an anchor against popular fluctuations. A smaller council, drawn out of the senate, was both appointed for life and filled up vacancies itself.

We should not imitate these examples. They are repugnant to the American spirit. However, when we compare them to other short-lived and turbulent ancient republics, they prove that an institution that blends stability and liberty is necessary.

The American government is different from other ancient and modern popular governments. When comparing governments, we must be very careful. But after noting their differences, their similarities make these examples worth our attention.

A senate corrects some of the defects caused by a large legislature. The people can never willfully betray their own interests, but their representatives may betray them. The danger is greater when one group of men has the whole legislative trust. There is less danger when two dissimilar groups must agree to every public act.

…The senate of Carthage, whatever its power or term in office, appears to have been *elected* by the people. Similar examples might be found in most, if not all, the popular governments of antiquity.

These arguments support having a Senate. However, jealous opponents of the Constitution will disagree. They will probably say that a senate that is not elected directly by the people and with six-year terms will slowly become powerful. And it will eventually turn into a tyrannical aristocracy.

Liberty can be endangered by the abuses of liberty as well as by the abuses of power. There are many examples of both. And the former, rather than the latter, are apparently most to be feared by the United States.

Before transforming into a tyrannical aristocracy, the Senate must first corrupt itself. Next it must corrupt the State legislatures. It must then corrupt the House of Representatives. And, finally, corrupt the people at large.

The Senate must be corrupted first before it can try to establish a tyranny. To do this, it must corrupt the State legislatures; if not corrupted, the States would elect new members to the Senate, changing the whole body.

If the House of Representatives wasn't corrupted, it would inevitably defeat the attempt.

And without corrupting the people, new representatives would quickly restore all things to their perfect order.

Can any man seriously believe that the proposed Senate can achieve the objectives of lawless ambition through all these obstructions?

…[Historical examples] show that the federal Senate will never be able to transform itself, by gradual usurpations, into an independent, aristocratic body.

Additionally, we believe that if the Senate does evolve into an aristocratic body—for a reason that we can't predict—the House of Representatives with the people on their side will restore the Constitution to its original form and principles. Against the force of the people's representatives, the only way the Senate will be able to maintain even its constitutional authority will be enlightened policy and an attachment to the public good. Then the Senate will regain the affections and support of the entire population.

shall be composed of two Senators from each State,

Number 9 [16]

… The proposed Constitution doesn't abolish the State governments. It makes them part of the national government with direct representation in the Senate…

Equal Representation Favors Small States/Supports State Sovereignty

Number 38 [7]

… An objector from a large State exclaims loudly against the unreasonable **equality** in the **Senate**…

Number 39 [12]

The Senate, on the other hand, will derive its powers from the States as equal societies. In this, the government is *federal,* not *national.*

Number 43 [26]

…equality in the Senate, is probably a safeguard to the remaining sovereignty of the States, which have equal representation in one branch of the legislature. The States that worried about equality probably insisted on it…

Number 58 [6]

The Senate favors the smaller States.

Number 59 [8]

…no State is entitled to more than two senators…

Number 62 [4-6]

Equal representation in the Senate doesn't need much discussion. It is a compromise between the opposite demands of the large and small States.

When **people** join to become one nation, every district should have a *proportional* share in the government.

When sovereign **states** form a league, the states, however unequal in size, should have an *equal* share in common councils.

If these principles are true, in a compound republic, with characteristics of both a national and a federal government, that government should have a mixture of proportional and equal representation.

We don't need to evaluate this part of the Constitution. Everyone agrees that it is the result "of a spirit of amity, and the mutual deference and concession that our special political situation made indispensable."

The United States needs a government with the powers necessary to meet its objectives. The smaller States won't agree to a government that favors the large States. Therefore, the large States can either accept the proposed government or one that is more objectionable. Let's look at why it may be a good idea to not have proportional representation in the Senate.

Equal votes in the Senate constitutionally preserve the sovereignty that remains in the States. Both large and small States want to guard against an improper consolidation of the States into one simple republic. Therefore, the large States should accept this equality.

Equality in the Senate also helps block improper legislative acts. No law or resolution will pass without a majority of the people [House of Representatives] and then a majority of the States [Senate] agreeing to it.

This check on legislation can be both injurious and beneficial. Small States will need this defense when they have interests that are different from those of the large States and those interests might be exposed to danger. The larger States will always have more power over supplies than the small States. Therefore, the larger States will always be able to defeat unreasonable laws proposed by small States.

The ease and excess of law-making are the diseases to which our governments are most liable. This part of the Constitution may be more convenient in practice than it appears in contemplation.

[chosen by the legislature thereof,]

changed by Amendment 17, ratified in 1913:

The Senate of the United States shall be composed of two Senators from each State, elected by the people thereof, for six years; and each Senator shall have one vote. The electors in each State shall have the qualifications requisite for electors of the most numerous branch of the State legislatures...

This amendment shall not be so construed as to affect the election or term of any Senator chosen before it becomes valid as part of the Constitution.

Number 27 [2]

... Usually the elected State legislators will carefully select national Senators. This method promises great knowledge and information in the national Senate. It is less likely that faction will taint the national Senate. And they will have fewer prejudices...

Number 39 [5]

...[The people will] indirectly appoint the Senate.

Number 44 [26]

...The election of the President and Senate will depend on the State legislatures...

Number 45 [7]

... The State legislatures will elect federal Senators...

Number 59 [6]

If State legislatures had total power to regulate federal elections, the national Senate might be in danger. By not appointing Senators, State legislatures could give a fatal blow to the Union. The national Senate depends on the States...

Number 60 [3,4,8]

...The Senate [will be elected] by the State legislatures... Representatives, Senators and the President are chosen in very different ways...

The national government will be limited to regulating the "time and manner" of elections. This can't influence the choice of Senators. Entire State legislatures can't be influenced by this regulation. This fact, alone, should satisfy us that the feared discrimination would never be attempted...

When a country is mostly farmers and has equal representation, farm interests will usually predominate in the government. As long as farm interests prevail in State legislatures, they will also prevail in the national Senate. The Senate will usually be a copy of the majorities in the State legislatures. Therefore, we can't assume that farmers will be sacrificed to the benefit of merchants in the federal Senate.

People who strongly support State power cannot believe that outside influences will sway State legislatures from their duty...

Number 62 [3]

There is no need to discuss the appointment of senators by the State legislatures. Public opinion seems to want this method of appointment. It has two advantages. The State government plays a role in the forming the federal government. And it secures the States' authority and links the two systems.

Number 64 [3-4]

...the State legislatures appoint the senators. This system has a great advantage over direct elections by the people. Party zeal has a great influence in direct elections. It can take advantage of indifference, ignorance, and the hopes and fears of the unwary and uninterested people. And men are often elected by a small proportion of the electors.

Electors will choose the President. State legislatures will appoint the senators. They will usually be enlightened and respectable citizens. We can presume that they will vote for able and virtuous men, who have the people's confidence.

The Constitution supports this objective. The President must be at least 35 and Senators 30 years old. The people will have time to judge the candidates. Sometimes a candidate can briefly appear brilliant and patriotic, misleading and dazzling the public. But the electors and legislators will not be deceived.

The electors will have extensive and accurate information about men and their characters. Their appointments should be made with discretion and discernment.

Number 66 [12]

... the Senate, a body carefully selected by each State legislature...

Number 67 [10]

...The State legislatures appoint Senators...

for six years;

Number 39 [5]

... Senators serve six years...

Number 59 [8]

... Senators will serve for six years...

Number 62 [12,14,15,17,18]

Fourth. Frequent changes in public councils, however qualified the new members may be, shows why a stable institution in the government is necessary.

Every election changes half the representatives. This turnover creates a change of opinions and a change of legislation. But continual change, even if it is good legislation, is inconsistent with every rule of prudence and every hope of success. Private life verifies this observation. And it becomes more just and more important in national transactions.

A mutable government forfeits the respect and confidence of other nations, and all the advantages connected with national character.

All prudent people know that a person who frequently changes his plans or lives his life without any plan at all will quickly fall victim to his own unsteadiness and folly. His friendly neighbors may pity him, but all will decline to connect their fortunes with his. And more than a few people will seize the opportunity to make their fortunes out of his.

One nation is to another as one individual is to another, with one sad difference. Nations have fewer benevolent emotions than people. They feel fewer restraints from taking advantage of each other. Every nation that shows a lack of wisdom and stability may expect every possible loss to the more systematic policy of their wiser neighbors.

Unfortunately, the best example is America. She is ridiculed by her enemies. And she is prey to every nation that wants to speculate about her changing councils and embarrassed affairs.

The domestic effects of a mutable policy are even worse. It poisons the blessings of liberty itself.

It won't benefit the people that the laws are made by men of their own choice, if the laws are so voluminous that they cannot be read or so incoherent that they cannot be understood. Or if they are repealed or revised before they are promulgated or are changed so frequently that no man who knows what the law is today can guess what it will be tomorrow.

Law is defined to be a rule of action. But how can it be a rule when it is little known and less fixed?

An unstable government also hurts the economy. When people don't know what actions the government might take, projects where success and profit may depend on the existing laws continuing will be discouraged.

What prudent merchant will jeopardize his fortunes in a new area of commerce when he doesn't know if his plans may be made unlawful before they can be executed? What farmer or manufacturer will commit himself to a specific cultivation or project when he can't be sure that his preparations and investment will not make him a victim to an inconstant government?

In a word, if an improvement or praiseworthy enterprise needs the protection or security of a consistent national policy, it will not be pursued.

But the worst effect is that the people will feel less attachment and reverence to the government. No government will be respected without being truly respectable. And it will not be respectable if it doesn't have some order and stability.

Number 63 [3-6]

A large legislature that has members with only a short term in office cannot create a good national reputation. In a small legislature, each member shares the praise and blame for laws. And when a legislator has a long term in office, his pride becomes part of the reputation and prosperity of the community…

Less frequent elections increase the government's responsibility to the people. This comment may seem both new and paradoxical. However, it is true and important.

… There are two types of legislation. Some legislation takes immediate effect. Other legislation is part of a chain of measures that have a gradual and, perhaps, unobserved operation. The latter type of legislation is important to the welfare of every country. A legislature with a short term can provide only one or two links in a chain of measures. But they cannot be held responsible for the final result.

The remedy is a second legislative body. The members should have long enough terms to meet objectives that require constant attention and a series of measures. They can be responsible for meeting those objectives.

Number 64 [5]

    ...Some people want the House of Representatives to make treaties. However, House membership changes too quickly. Two years is not long enough for Representatives to study all the issues required to make treaties. Therefore, the convention wisely gave the Senate the power to make treaties.

    Senators will have six-year terms. Able and honest Senators will be in office long enough to understand national concerns and create a system to manage them. While in office, they can increase their political information. Their total experience will benefit their country...

and each Senator shall have one vote.

Number 75 [7]

    In the proposed Senate, members will vote individually.

Immediately after they shall be assembled in Consequence of the first Election, they shall be divided as equally as may be into three Classes. The Seats of the Senators of the first Class shall be vacated at the Expiration of the second Year, of the second Class, at the Expiration of the fourth Year, and of the third Class, at the Expiration of the sixth Year, so that one third may be chosen every second Year;

Number 59 [8]

    ...Their terms will rotate. Elections for a third of the Senate seats will be held every two years...

Number 64 [5]

    ...The Constitution has another good feature. If the entire Senate was elected every six years, all great affairs could be totally transferred to new men. By leaving a lot of the members in place, uniformity and order, and the succession of official information, will be preserved.

[and if Vacancies happen by Resignation, or otherwise, during the Recess of the Legislature of any State, the Executive thereof may make temporary Appointments until the next Meeting of the Legislature, which shall then fill such Vacancies.]*

changed by Amendment 17, ratified in 1913:

When vacancies happen in the representation of any State in the Senate, the executive authority of such State shall issue writs of election to fill such vacancies: *Provided*, That the Legislature of any State may empower the executive thereof to make temporary appointments until the people fill the vacancies by election as the legislature may direct.

Number 67 [6-11]

[Opponents of the Constitution] have had the nerve to say that the President of the United States will have a power that the proposed Constitution *expressly* gives to the State Executives. I'm talking about the power to fill Senate vacancies.

This has been argued by a writer who (whatever may be his real merit) has often been applauded by his party. He has built a series of observations. Each is based on this false, unfounded suggestion. Let him now see the evidence. And let him, if he is able, justify the shameful outrage he has offered to the dictates of truth and the rule of fair dealing.

Article 2, section 2, clause 2 gives the President of the United States the power "to nominate, and by and with the advice and consent of the Senate, to appoint ambassadors, other public ministers, and consuls, judges of the Supreme Court, and all other *officers* of the United States whose appointments are *not* in the Constitution *otherwise provided for,* and *which shall be established by law.*"

Opponents use the next sentence to say the President has a power that the Constitution does not give him. It says, "The President shall have power to fill up all *vacancies,* that may happen *during the recess of the Senate,* by granting commissions which shall *expire at the end of their next session.*"

The obvious meaning of the clauses shows that the deduction is not even plausible.

The first clause provides a way to appoint officers, "whose appointments are *not otherwise provided for* in the Constitution, and which *shall be established by law.*" Based on this clause, the President cannot appoint senators. The appointment of Senators is *otherwise provided for* in the Constitution and are *established by the Constitution.* The appointment of Senators is a Constitutional power and cannot be changed by law.

President Never Appoints Senators

Clearly, the second clause does not include the power to fill vacancies in the Senate, for the following reasons.

First. The relationship of the clauses shows that the second clause is only a supplement to the first clause. Since the President and Senate *jointly* make appointments, without the second clause, appointments could only be made while the Senate is in session. However, vacancies might happen *in their recess.* These offices may need to be filled without delay. The second clause authorizes the President, *by himself,* to make temporary appointments "during the recess of the Senate, by granting commissions which shall expire at the end of their next session."

Second. The *vacancies* mentioned in the second clause refer to the "officers" described in the preceding clause. This excludes members of the Senate.

Third. The power is to operate "during the recess of the Senate" and the appointments will last until "to the end of the next session." These phrases further clarify the provision. If it included senators, the clause would have referred to the State legislatures, not the national Senate. The State legislatures appoint Senators. If the clause referred to Senate vacancies, it would mention the recess of State legislatures. And the temporary senators would stay in office until the next session of the State legislature, instead of making it expire at the end of the next session of the national Senate. The clause mentions only the national Senate. Therefore, the clause must be talking about vacancies in offices to which the President and Senate, jointly, make permanent appointments.

Lastly. Article 1, section 3, clauses 1 and 2 destroys all doubt and misconceptions. The former provides that "the Senate of the United States shall be composed of two Senators from each State, chosen *by the legislature thereof* for six years." And the latter directs that "if vacancies in that body should happen by resignation or otherwise, *during the recess of the legislature of* any state, the Executive thereof may make temporary appointments until the *next meeting of the legislature,* which shall then fill such vacancies."

The State Executives will fill vacancies in the Senate by temporary appointments. The President will not have the power to fill vacancies in the national Senate. This proves that the opponents' arguments are deceptive. The deception is obvious. And it is too atrocious to be excused by hypocrisy.

Example Proof of Misrepresentations

This misrepresentation proves the inexcusable cunning used by opponents of the Constitution. They want to prevent a fair, impartial judgment based on the real merits of the Constitution. I ask any honest opponent of the new Constitution: Does language give us severe enough denouncements for this shameless attempt to defraud the citizens of America?

No person shall be a Senator who shall not have attained to the Age of thirty Years, and been nine Years a Citizen of the United States, and who shall not, when elected, be an Inhabitant of that State for which he shall be chosen.

Number 60 [11]

...The qualifications of voters or nominees are defined in the Constitution and Congress can't change them.

Number 62[2]

A Senator must be at least thirty years old and a citizen for nine years. A Representative must be 25 years old and a citizen for 7 years.

A Senator needs more knowledge and a stable character. The Senator should be old enough to have these advantages.

Senators are involved with foreign policy. They should be weaned from attitudes and habits resulting from a foreign birth and education. Nine years is a good compromise. Adopted citizens, who may have talents and earned public confidence, are not totally excluded. But they can't immediately become Senators, which might create a channel for foreign influence in the national council.

Number 64 [4]

… State legislatures will appoint the senators. They will usually be enlightened and respectable citizens. We can presume that they will vote for able and virtuous men, who have the people's confidence.

The Constitution supports this objective. The President must be at least 35 and Senators 30 years old. The people will have time to judge the candidates. Sometimes a candidate can briefly appear brilliant and patriotic, misleading and dazzling the public. But the electors and legislators will not be deceived.

Probable attributes of Senators

Number 3[8]

When an efficient national government is established, usually the best men in the country will be appointed to manage it. A town or county can place men in State and local offices. However, to recommend men to national offices, a wider reputation for talents and qualifications is necessary. The public will choose from the widest field, never lacking qualified persons. Therefore, the administration, legislation, and judicial decisions of the national government will be more wise and judicious than those of individual States.

Number 27 [2]

Usually the elected State legislators will carefully select national Senators. This method promises great knowledge and information in the national Senate. It is less likely that faction will taint the national Senate. And they will have fewer prejudices.

Number 64 [3-4,14-15]

…Qualified men should make treaties, in the manner most conducive to the public good…

…State legislatures will appoint the senators. They will usually be enlightened and respectable citizens. We can presume that they will vote for able and virtuous men, who have the people's confidence.

The problem of corruption is not imaginable. Anyone who thinks that the President and two-thirds of the Senate will ever be capable of such unworthy conduct, must either have been very unfortunate in his interactions with the world or has a heart very susceptible to such impressions.

The idea is too gross and too invidious to be entertained. But if it should ever happen, the treaty so obtained from us would, like all other fraudulent contracts, be null and void by the law of nations.

It is difficult to imagine how their responsibility could be increased. The influences of honor, oaths, reputations, conscience, love of country, and family affections and attachments afford security for their fidelity. The Constitution has been careful that they shall be men of talents and integrity. We believe that the treaties they make will be as advantageous as could be made, all circumstances considered.

And so far as the fear of punishment and disgrace can operate, the motive for good behavior is supplied by the article on the subject of impeachments.

The Vice President of the United States shall be President of the Senate, but shall have no Vote, unless they be equally divided.

Number 68 [10]

The appointment of a second person as Vice President has been objected to as superfluous, if not mischievous. Some people have suggested that the Senate elect a Senator to fill the office.

But two reasons seem to justify the convention's decision. First, so that the Senate will never have a tie vote, the President of the Senate should have only a casting vote. If a Senator from any State was taken from his seat and made President of the Senate, his home State would lose a vote in the Senate.

Second, the Vice President may occasionally become President. So, all the reasons that recommend the way the President is elected, apply to the election of the Vice President.

This objection could be made against the constitution of New York. We have a Lieutenant-Governor, who is chosen by the people at large. He presides in the senate. And New York's Lieutenant-Governor becomes Governor under the same circumstances that would authorize the Vice President to exercise the authorities and discharge the duties of the President.

Number 75 [7]

… When we include the President of the Senate, we will have more security against an improper use of the power to make treaties under the new Constitution than under the Confederation…

The Senate shall choose their other Officers, and also a President *pro tempore*, in the absence of the Vice President, or when he shall exercise the office of President of the United States.

The Senate shall have the sole Power to try all Impeachments.

Number 38 [7]

… Some people say that the **trial of impeachments** by the Senate is wrong: they believe the judiciary should have this power…

Number 47 [7]

…The entire legislature doesn't act as a court, but it can remove a judge from office, and one house has the judicial power of final appeal. The entire legislature, again, has no executive powers, though one house acts as the supreme executive magistracy. And the other house, after an impeachment vote, can try and condemn all the subordinate officers in the executive department.

Number 65 [all]

The Constitution gives the Senate two more powers:

(1) The Senate participates with the executive in the appointment to offices.
(2) The Senate acts as a court for the trial of impeachments.

Since the executive branch makes appointments, appointments will be discussed when we examine that branch. We will now study the judicial character of the Senate.

An elected government needs a court for the trial of impeachments. The court will judge the misconduct of public men. It will judge abuses or violations of public trust. The offenses are called POLITICAL because they usually relate to injuries done to society. Therefore, the prosecution of them will usually bring out the passions of the whole community. Citizens will feel either friendly or hostile to the accused, depending on preexisting factions or political parties. All their anger and interests will line up on one side or on the other. Because of this, there will always be the danger that the stronger party will make the decision. The decision may not be an objective decision about innocence or guilt.

Every public official worries about his political reputation. In an elected government, it is difficult to place trust correctly. The most conspicuous government officials will often be the leaders or the tools of the most cunning or the biggest faction. They probably will not be able to impartially judge impeached officials.

The Constitutional Convention thought that the Senate was the best place to place this important trust. If you understand the intrinsic difficulty of the problem, you will not hastily condemn this decision. Let's look at why they chose the Senate.

What is an impeachment court? It is a NATIONAL INQUEST into the conduct of public men. The proper inquisitors are the representatives of the nation.

If one house of the legislature starts the inquiry by impeaching the official, shouldn't the other house be part of the inquiry?

The convention used the British model. The House of Commons prefers the impeachment; the House of Lords decides it.

Several State constitutions follow the example. Those States and Great Britain see impeachment as a bridle in the hands of the legislature on the people in the executive branch of government. Isn't this the proper view?

The Senate is dignified and independent. What other group of people would feel *enough confidence* to not be awed and influenced? What other group could feel impartial towards both the accused *individual* and the *representatives of the people—the House of Representatives*—his accuser?

Does the Supreme Court fit this description? Some Supreme Court justices will probably not have the courage needed for such a difficult task. Sometimes the impeachment court will not convict the person who has been accused by the people's representatives. Supreme Court justices probably will not have the authority needed for the people to accept their decision.

A deficiency in courage would be fatal to the accused; a deficiency in credibility would be dangerous to the public tranquility. These problems could only be avoided, if at all, by making the Supreme Court so large that it would be very expensive.

An impeachment trial requires a very large court. In common cases, the discretion of courts is limited in favor of personal security. There can never be strict rules for impeachment trials. There can never be a specific list of prosecutable offenses. Nor can there be strict rules for how the judges will construe the offenses. There will be no jury. The judges will pronounce the sentence of the law. A court of impeachments has the awful discretion to doom to honor or infamy the most trusted and distinguished people of the community. Therefore, the responsibility must not be held by a small number of persons.

For these reasons, alone, the Supreme Court should not be an impeachment court.

Another consideration strengthens this conclusion. If an impeached official is found guilty, his punishment is perpetual ostracism from the esteem, confidence, honors, and emoluments of his country. But he can also be prosecuted and punished in the ordinary course of law. Would it be proper for the same judges, who had already found him guilty, judge the case where the accused life and fortune could be forfeited?

Wouldn't an error in the first trial be carried over to the second? Wouldn't the strong bias of the first decision overrule the influence of any new information that might change the second? Those who know anything about human nature will say "yes." If the same people judge both cases, the accused would lose the double security intended by a double trial.

When an official is impeached and found guilty, his punishment is dismissal from his current office and disqualification from future offices. If the same judges preside in both trials, the loss of life and property would often be virtually included with this punishment.

Requiring a jury at the second trial might cancel the danger. But judges frequently influence juries. Juries are sometimes encouraged to find verdicts that the judge wants. Who would be willing to stake his life and his estate on the verdict of a jury acting under the authority of judges who have already decided he is guilty?

Would uniting the Supreme Court with the Senate to form the court of impeachment improve the plan? This union would have several advantages. But they would be overbalanced by the important disadvantage caused by having the same judges preside in the double prosecution of the accused.

The Constitution makes the chief justice of the Supreme Court the president of the court of impeachment. This will have some of the benefits of uniting the Supreme Court and the Senate. At the same time, the inconveniences of combining the entire Supreme Court with the Senate will be substantially avoided. This was, perhaps, the prudent compromise.

Also, if the Constitution gave the power to try impeachments to the Supreme Court, it would have increased the authority of the judiciary. This would have given opponents another pretext to talk against the judiciary.

Should the court for the trial of impeachments be composed of persons who are completely distinct from the other departments of the government? There are strong arguments in favor and against such a plan.

One objection is that it would increase the complexity of the political machine. It would add a new department to the government with little usefulness.

But there are objections that are more important. This type of court would be very expensive and/or very inconvenient. It would have permanent officers based in the capitol, officers that have to be paid. Or it would be made up of specific officers of the State governments who would be called upon whenever an impeachment was actually pending. It isn't easy to imagine any other way it could be organized.

Since it would be a large court, anyone who compares the amount of things that the public wants with the ability of the government to pay for them will reject the first plan.

The second plan will receive only cautious support after the following problems are seriously considered. It will be difficult for men who live throughout the nation to gather together. This would delay decision and injure an innocent person. However, the delay could be an advantage to a guilty person, with its opportunities for intrigue and corruption. And, in some cases, the delay could hurt the government. A designing majority in the House of Representatives could impeach a faithful official, stopping him from performing his duties and exposing him to persecution. This suggestion may seem harsh and it might rarely happen. But we should never forget that the demon of faction will sometimes affect all numerous bodies of men.

But even if there is a better way to set up the court for the trial of impeachments, this is not a reason to reject the entire Constitution. If no government could be set up until every part of it is perfect, society would soon become an anarchy and the world a desert. Adversaries to the Constitution should prove, not merely that certain provisions are not the best possible, but that the whole plan is bad and very harmful.

Objections to Senate as Impeachment Court

Number 66 [all]

There are several objections to the way the court for the trial of impeachments is setup in the Constitution. We will review them.

The *first* objection: It violates the separation of powers maxim because the Senate will have both legislative and judicial authority.

Our discussion of the separation of powers showed that the powers can be partially mixed for special purposes. Sometimes a small mixing of powers is proper and necessary. Each branch of government needs to be able to defend itself against the other branches. The president can use the veto to block legislative encroachments on the executive. Impeachment powers give the legislature a check on executive encroachments.

Impeachment powers are divided between the two houses of the legislature. The House accuses and the Senate judges. Therefore, the same persons are not both accusers and judges. This guards against the danger of prosecution from a majority faction in either house. Two-thirds of the Senate is needed to find a person guilty, providing security to the innocent.

The same men that admire New York's constitution oppose this part of the proposed Constitution, using the separation of powers argument. The New York constitution combines the Senate and the Supreme Court for an impeachment court; it is also the highest court in the State in all civil and criminal cases. New York's Supreme Court is small. In fact, New York's judicial authority resides in its Senate.

If the proposed Constitution violates the separation of powers rule, how much worse is the constitution of New York?[*]

Second objection: If the Senate is the impeachment court, it will have too much power. And it will be too much like an aristocracy.

The Senate will have concurrent authority with the Executive in forming treaties and appointing to offices. The objectors say that if it is also the court for the trial of impeachments, Senators will have too much influence.

---

[*] In the New Jersey constitution, also, the final judiciary authority is in a branch of the legislature. In New Hampshire, Massachusetts, Pennsylvania, and South Carolina, one branch of the legislature is the court for the trial of impeachments.—PUBLIUS

135

This is an imprecise objection. Therefore, a precise answer is difficult. How can we measure if the Senate has too much, too little, or the proper degree of influence? Won't it be safer and simpler to dismiss vague arguments? Shouldn't we examine each power then decide which branch should have it.

The power to make treaties is justified by the reasons stated in a former paper and in others to come. Future papers will explain why joining the Senate with the Executive in the power of appointing to offices is a good idea. And Paper #65 showed that this is the most practical way to form an impeachment court.

If these statements are true, than we shouldn't worry about the Senate having "too much" influence.

The comments about the senators' term in office also refute this worry. The House of Representatives, elected by the people, will have more influence than any other part of the government.

And the Constitution gives the House several important powers that counterbalance the Senate's additional authorities.

It originates money bills. And it will(9a)   institute impeachments. Isn't this a complete counterbalance to judging them?

Sometimes, no presidential candidate will get a majority of electors. The House will decide those elections. This could be a source of influence for that body. As an influence, this will outweigh all the Senate's powers.

A *third* objection to the Senate as an impeachment court is based on the Senate's role in the appointments to office. Since the Senate participates in an appointment, it is imagined that the Senate would be too indulgent when judging the office holder's conduct.

This objection would condemn a practice seen in all the State governments, if not in all governments. I'm talking about the practice of making people who hold offices during pleasure dependent on the pleasure of those who appoint them. The objectors seem to be saying that when political appointees misbehave, the people who appointed them will protect them from punishment.

However, the people who make appointments will feel responsible for the fitness and ability of the people they appoint. They will want a respectable administration of affairs. And they will want to remove anyone whose conduct proves them unworthy of the trust. This is a basically sound presumption.

The Senate only approves executive choices. This will not blind them to such extraordinary evidence of guilt that the Representatives of the nation accuse him.

The Senate will probably not feel a favorable bias towards an impeached official who was appointed by the President. If further arguments are necessary, let's look at the Senate's role in appointments.

The President will *nominate* and, with the advice and consent of the Senate, *appoint*. Of course, the Senate will have no part in the *choice*. The Senate may defeat one person that the President has chosen, but they cannot *choose*. The Senate can only ratify or reject the choice of the President.

The Senate might prefer someone else, but confirm the appointment because it has no grounds to oppose him. And what if the Senate didn't approve the nomination? It would have no way of knowing who the next nominee would be. It might not even be a person who—in their estimation—was more meritorious than the one rejected.

Thus, the majority of the Senate would not be more biased towards the appointee than appearances of merit might inspire and the lack of proof will destroy.

A *fourth* objection comes from the Senate's union with the Executive in making treaties. The objectors say that when a corrupt or perfidious treaty is made, the Senators would have to judge themselves. If they conspired with the Executive to betray the interests of the nation in a ruinous treaty, would they get the punishment they deserved if they were the impeachment court? Would they find themselves guilty of the accusation brought against them for the treachery?

This is the most earnest and reasonable objection against this part of the Constitution. But it rests on an erroneous foundation.

The Constitution provides security against corruption and treachery when forming treaties. This security comes from the numbers and characters of the people who are to make them. Both the President and two-thirds of the Senate, a body carefully selected by each State legislature, must approve treaties. This assures fidelity in forming treaties.

When writing the Constitution, the convention might have included a punishment for the President if he doesn't follow the Senate's instructions or doesn't act with integrity during treaty negotiations. They might also have suggested how a few of the leading individuals in the Senate might be punished, if they used their influence in the Senate for foreign corruption. But the convention could not suggest impeaching and punishing two-thirds of the Senate, if the Senate agreed to an improper treaty.

The Constitution does not include a method for punishing a majority of the Senate or the House for passing a very harmful or unconstitutional law. I don't believe any government has ever done this.

How could a majority in the House of Representatives impeach themselves? This idea is no better than two thirds of the Senate putting themselves on trial. If the House of Representatives can pass an unjust and tyrannical law and not be punished, why should more than two thirds of the Senate be punished for approving an injurious treaty with a foreign power?

The Senate and House of Representatives need to feel free and independent to discuss issues. The members must be exempt from punishment for acts done in a collective capacity. Society's security depends on the care taken to put the trust in proper hands, people who want to execute it with fidelity. It should be as difficult as possible for them to conspire in any interest opposite to that of the public good.

If the Executive misbehaves by perverting the instructions or contravening the views of the Senate, the Senate will want to punish the abuser and defend their authority. For this, we can count on their pride, if not their virtue.

What will happen if leading Senators influence the majority into measures the community doesn't like? If corruption can be proved, the psychology of human nature says that the other Senators will want to divert the public resentment from themselves. They will sacrifice the authors of their mismanagement and disgrace.

Number 79 [4]

To assure that judges will act responsibly, they can be impeached by the House of Representatives and tried by the Senate…

Number 81 [3, 9]

...Some men object to the Senate acting as the impeachment court, saying it improperly mixes powers. Now the same men seem to want to give the ultimate decision of all causes, in the whole or in a part, to the Senate.

...[there is an] important constitutional check on the judiciary. One part of the legislative body can impeach judges and the other tries them.

When sitting for that Purpose, they shall be on Oath or Affirmation. When the President of the United States is tried, the Chief Justice shall preside:

Number 65 [9]

... The Constitution makes the chief justice of the Supreme Court the president of the court of impeachment. This will have some of the benefits of uniting the Supreme Court and the Senate. At the same time, the inconveniences of combining the entire Supreme Court with the Senate will be substantially avoided. This was, perhaps, the prudent compromise...

And no Person shall be convicted without the Concurrence of two thirds of the Members present.

Number 66 [2]

...Two-thirds of the Senate is needed to find a person guilty, providing security to the innocent.

Judgment in Cases of Impeachment shall not extend further than to removal from Office, and disqualification to hold and enjoy any Office of honor, Trust or Profit under the United States: but the Party convicted shall, nevertheless, be liable and subject to Indictment, Trial, Judgment and Punishment, according to Law.

Number 65 [7,8]

...A court of impeachments has the awful discretion to doom to honor or infamy the most trusted and distinguished people of the community...

...If an impeached official is found guilty, his punishment is perpetual ostracism from the esteem, confidence, honors, and emoluments of his country. But he can also be prosecuted and punished in the ordinary course of law... When an official is impeached and found guilty, his punishment is dismissal from his current office and disqualification from future offices...

Number 69 [4]

The President can be impeached, tried, and if convicted of treason, bribery, or other high crimes or misdemeanors, removed from office. Afterwards he can be prosecuted and punished in the ordinary course of law...

Number 70 [15]

...There are two types of responsibility: moral and legal. Irresponsibility leads to censure and to punishment. Censure is the more important, especially in an elective office.

An irresponsible man in public office will more often act in a way that makes him unworthy of trust than in a way that makes him subject to legal punishment…

Article 1 SECTION 4. The Times, Places and Manner of holding Elections for Senators and Representatives, shall be prescribed in each State by the Legislature thereof; but the Congress may at any time by Law make or alter such Regulations, except as to the Places of Chusing Senators.

Number 38 [7]

>...[Others believe that] the Constitution has the fatal power of regulating the times and places of election...

Congress Can Regulate Federal Elections

Number 59 [all]

The Constitution authorizes Congress to regulate elections. It says: "The times, places, and manner of holding elections for Senators and Representatives shall be prescribed in each State by the legislature thereof; but the Congress may at any time by law make or alter such regulations, except as to the places of choosing Senators."

Many people criticize this provision. Some critics condemn the whole Constitution. Other critics have fewer objections. One gentleman agrees with every other part of the Constitution, but objects to this clause.

However, it is the easiest clause in the Constitution to defend. It is proper because *every government should have the ability and means to preserve itself.*

The convention followed this rule. Every logical person will agree with the convention. And he will disapprove of every deviation from it. If the government cannot protect itself, it could become weak and, in the future, may turn into anarchy.

The Constitution cannot have an election law that applies to every possible future situation.   There must be a flexible power over elections. There are three ways to modify this power: completely by the national legislature, or completely by the State legislatures, or primarily by the States and ultimately by the national. The convention chose the last way.

Initially, local governments will regulate federal elections. This will usually be both convenient and satisfactory. But the national legislature may intervene when it feels it is necessary for its safety.

If the States had complete power to regulate national elections, the Union's existence would be entirely at their mercy. At any time, they could end the nation by not having an election. There would be no one to administer the national government.

It is pointless to say that this probably would not happen. Saying something is constitutionally possible but there is no risk of it happening, is an unanswerable objection. And there is no reason for taking that risk.

The conclusion that the federal government will abuse its power is based on jealousy. It is as easy for a local government to abuse power as a national government.

Therefore, it is just as fair to assume that the State governments will abuse their power as the national government. And it is more logical to trust the Union with the care of its own existence, than to give that care to State governments.

Suppose the Constitution gave the national government the power to regulate State elections. Everyone would condemn it. It should be a State, not federal, power. And the federal government could use it to destroy the State governments.

It is just as clear that the existence of the national government should not be left to the States. As far as possible, each government should be able to preserve itself.

If State legislatures had total power to regulate federal elections, the national Senate might be in danger. By not appointing Senators, State legislatures could give a fatal blow to the Union. The national Senate depends on the States.

Each State has an interest in maintaining its representation in the national councils. It could be argued that this would provide complete security against an abuse of the trust.

Although it sounds good, this argument is not valid. If the State legislatures refused to appoint Senators, the national government might be destroyed. But just because the States have the power to not appoint Senators, it does not mean that they should also have the power to not elect Representatives. The States can do more harm with the power to regulate congressional elections than with their power to appoint Senators. And there is no counter-balancing reason for taking the risk.

The Constitution establishes the organization of the national government. If the Constitutional organization of the national government is exposed to injury from States, it is an evil. But this evil could not be completely avoided. The States, as political units, need to be part of the national government. Therefore, the State legislatures appoint Senators.

Under the federal principle, the States need to be included in the national government. And it gives the State governments a safeguard. Although it is inconvenient, States need to appoint Senators. However, we cannot infer from this that the States should control all federal elections when it is not necessary or when it doesn't fulfill a greater good.

There is a greater risk to the national government if the States control the elections of Representatives than from their power to appoint Senators.

Senators will serve for six years. Their terms will rotate. Elections for a third of the Senate seats will be held every two years. And no State is entitled to more than two senators. A Senate quorum will be sixteen members. Therefore, even if a few States stopped appointing senators, the Senate would not disappear and it could keep functioning. And we have nothing to fear from a widespread, permanent conspiracy of the States.

Sinister plots by leaders in a few State legislatures might start a conspiracy. To be permanent, it would require support by the general population. However, it will probably never happen. If a widespread conspiracy does develop, it will probably be because the national government becomes inept at advancing the people's happiness. And if this happens, no good citizen will want it to continue.

But members of the federal House of Representatives will be elected every two years. If the State legislatures had exclusive power to regulate these elections and if the leaders of a few important States conspired to prevent an election, every election would create a crisis that could result in the Union dissolving.

Some people say that each State will have federal Representatives. And this will provide some security against the States using federal elections to abuse their power. This argument is somewhat valid.

But it will not provide complete security. There is a difference between the people's interest in public happiness and their local rulers' interest in power. The American people may like the federal government at the same time that some State rulers—supported by strong factions—want power and personal aggrandizement. There is already a conflict in some States between a majority of the people and powerful government officials.

If the nation was divided into several separate confederacies, the chance of this conflict multiplies. It will be a constant temptation to State politicians to increase their own benefits instead of advancing the public welfare.

If the States had exclusive power to regulate national elections, a few men from influential States might destroy the Union. They could use some little dissatisfaction among the people (that they may have promoted) to stop choosing Representatives.

European nations will be jealous of a firm Union with an efficient government. Sometimes foreign powers will try to subvert our government. And they will support internal intrigues. Therefore, when possible, the government's preservation should be guarded by people with an immediate interest in faithful and vigilant performances of the trust.

Dangers of Union Regulating Its Own Elections

Number 60 [all]

Giving State legislatures total control over federal elections would be dangerous. What are the dangers from the Union regulating its own elections?

No State would ever be excluded from its share in representation. In this respect, the interest of all would be the security of all.

But some people say that the federal government might use the power to regulate the "time and manner" of elections to make sure people from a favorite class will be elected. They say that the national government could exclude some voters by locating polling places in areas that are difficult for some voters to reach. Of all the unbelievable ideas, this seems to be the most unbelievable.

It's impossible to imagine that such dangerous men would ever be part of the national government. However, if men who wanted to create an aristocracy held national offices, they would act more directly than just making polling places difficult to get to.

Such an attempt is improbable because the State governments would immediately revolt.

During turbulent and factious times, a majority might deny a specific group of people the fundamental right of freedom—suffrage. However, if the government tried to take away the voting rights of the great mass of people, the people would revolt.

Let's look at a few facts that will wipe out all fears on the subject. Each part of the national government will be structured differently and will behave differently. The different branches will block election conspiracies.

People in different parts of the Union have different behaviors and habits. Representatives will bring a wide range of feelings to the national government. As they work closely together, they will begin to think more alike. But physical and moral causes may nourish their different propensities and inclinations.

But here is the main reason that the parts of the federal government will probably not conspire to control who is elected: each part will be elected in a different way. The House of Representatives will be elected directly by the people. The Senate by the State legislatures. The president by electors who are chosen for that purpose by the people.

Representatives, Senators and the President are chosen in very different ways. Therefore, they probably won't have a reason to prefer one specific class of electors.

The national government will be limited to regulating the "time and manner" of elections. This can't influence the choice of Senators. Entire State legislatures can't be influenced by this regulation. This fact, alone, should satisfy us that the feared discrimination would never be attempted.

What could induce the Senate to concur in a preference in which it would not share? Or what would be the purpose if it could be established in one federal legislative house but not the other? In this case, the composition of one would counteract the other.

We can never assume the House would agree with Senate appointments, unless we can also assume that the State legislatures will cooperate. If we assume that the State legislatures can be corrupted, then it doesn't matter where the power in the question is placed—whether in their hands or in the Union.

What would be the objective of this unpredictable favoritism in national councils? Who would be discriminated against? Would it be different industries, different kinds of property or different amounts of property? Will property owners, merchants, or manufacturers be favored?

Or, to talk like the opponents of the Constitution, will it encourage the elevation of the "wealthy and the well-born" to the exclusion and debasement of all the rest of society?

If favoritism is shown, I assume the competition will be between property owners and merchants. And it is more likely either would have excessive influence in local rather than national councils.

To various degrees, the States are addicted to agriculture and commerce. In most, if not all, agriculture is predominant. However, commerce is very important in a few States and it has a lot of influence in most of them.

Agriculture and commerce will also influence the national legislature. And there will be a wider variety of interests than found in any single State. Therefore, the national legislature will be less likely to be partial to either interest than in a single State.

When a country is mostly farmers and has equal representation, farm interests will usually predominate in the government. As long as farm interests prevail in State legislatures, they will also prevail in the national Senate. The Senate will usually be a copy of the majorities in the State legislatures. Therefore, we can't assume that farmers will be sacrificed to the benefit of merchants in the federal Senate.

People who strongly support State power cannot believe that outside influences will sway State legislatures from their duty. The same situation will have the same effect on the federal House of Representatives. An improper bias in favor of merchants isn't expected.

Will the national government have an opposite bias? Will federal officials tend to become a monopoly of property owners? Such a bias probably won't worry people who would be immediately injured by it. So an elaborate answer isn't needed.

First, for reasons stated elsewhere, citizens are more likely to favor State rather than Union councils.

Second, there won't be a temptation to violate the Constitution in favor of property owners because that group will have as much influence and power as it will want.

And third, commerce is very important to both public prosperity and revenue to government. Merchants understand managing business. And if they were excluded, it would wound the national government. Commerce is so important that Congress will not make merchants angry. As public needs become apparent, Congress will need their help.

Critics talk about another kind of favoritism. They warn us about "wealthy and the well-born" politicians. I will briefly discuss the probability that specific industries and property owners will be preferred.

Critics say that "wealthy and well-born" politicians will be raised to a status above their fellow citizens. However, first critics claim this is the natural consequence of having a small representative body. Then they say it is the result of not allowing citizens to vote.

But where can an election be held to create a preference? Are "the wealthy and the well-born," confined to specific geographic locations in the States? Have they, by some miraculous instinct or foresight, set apart in each State a common place of residence? Are they only in towns or cities? Or are they scattered over the face of the country as avarice or chance has cast their lot or that of their ancestors? The latter is the case, as every intelligent man knows. Therefore, the policy of confining the places of election to specific districts would subvert its aim.

The only way rich people could take over control is if there were property qualifications for either voters or nominees. But the national government doesn't have this power. Its can only regulate the *times*, the *places*, and the *manner* of elections. The qualifications of voters or nominees are defined in the Constitution and Congress can't change them.

However, let's assume, for argument's sake, that selfish interests prevail. Let's also assume that the national rulers overcame all the scruples arising from a sense of duty or fear of the experiment. It still couldn't be carried out without the help of a military force large enough to subdue the resistance of the population. We've already discussed that raising a big enough force is improbable. But let's pretend that such a force exists and the national government has it. What would happen?

If the rulers wanted to invade the rights of the community and had the ability to do it, would they amuse themselves with the ridiculous task of changing election laws to secure that a favorite class of men be elected?

Wouldn't they do something to immediately gain personal power? Wouldn't they boldly take power with one act of usurpation, rather than trust to precarious expedients that might end in their dismissal, disgrace, and ruin? Wouldn't they fear that citizens would travel great distances to election places, overthrow their tyrants and substitute men who would want to avenge the violated majesty of the people?

Regulation of Federal Congressional Elections

Number 61 [all]

Some critics of the election provision in the Constitution agree that it is proper, but needs one addition. They want it to say that all elections should be in the counties where the voters live to protect against an abuse of the power.

This would be harmless. If it quieted fears, it might be desirable. But it would give little security against the feared danger. And an impartial examiner will never consider the lack of it as a serious objection to the Constitution.

If liberty is ever the victim of ambitious national rulers, it can not be blamed on the election provision.

The State constitutions have provisions about State elections. If we study them, it will remove any negative feelings about this clause in the federal Constitution. I will limit myself to the example of New York.

The New York constitution says members of the Assembly are elected in the *counties,* and members of the State Senate are elected in the State districts. Currently, there are four Senate districts. Each district has two to six counties. Obviously, New York could defeat the voting rights of her citizens by limiting the places where people can vote.

Suppose the city of Albany was the only place to vote in its county and district. The people who live in Albany would quickly become the only electors of both the Senate and Assembly for that county and district. Would the voters who live in the remote areas travel to Albany to vote for State officials quicker than they would travel to New York City to vote for members of the federal House of Representatives?

Voting is a privilege. Yet people seem indifferent about voting. We have seen that when the voting place is at an *inconvenient distance* from the voter, it doesn't matter whether the distance is 20 miles or 20,000 miles. Therefore, objections to the federal power of regulating elections also apply to the same power in the New York constitution. It is impossible to find one satisfactory and condemn the other.

If we look at most State constitutions, we'll come to the same conclusion.

If someone says, "The defects in the State constitutions don't excuse defects in the proposed federal Constitution," I answer, "No one has said that the State constitutions don't secure liberty. But the complaints thrown at the federal Constitution apply to them also."

Therefore, we must assume that these trivial accusations have been created to support a predetermined opposition to the Constitution. They are not logical conclusions from an honest search for the truth.

To people who believe that this is an unforgivable error in the federal Constitution and it is only an innocent omission in the State constitutions, nothing can be said. Or we must ask them, "Why can State representatives resist the lust of power better than federal representatives?"

They should prove that it is easier to subvert the liberties of the entire country than a single State. The country has three million people. Their local governments will support them if they must oppose a tyrannical federal government. 200,000 citizens of a State don't have that advantage.

They should also prove that a strong faction in a single State will be less likely to promote a specific class of electors than the representatives of thirteen States, spread over a vast region, with a diversity of local circumstances, prejudices, and interests.

I have shown that the election clause is theoretically proper. It would be dangerous to place the power elsewhere. And putting it in the proposed Constitution is safe. The federal elections clause also has an advantage that could not have been as effectively gotten in any other way.

I'm talking about a uniform time for the election of federal Representatives. This uniformity may prove important to the public welfare. It can be a security against continuing an unhealthy spirit in the body and a cure for the diseases of faction.

If each State could choose its own time for elections, there could be as many different times as there are months in the year. Currently, States hold elections at different times between March and November. If the House elections are held at different times, it would never be totally dissolved and remade. If an improper spirit took over the House of Representatives, as new members joined, they would probably be infected by the improper spirit. The mass would be likely hold onto the improper spirit and gradually assimilate new members into itself. The older members will have an influence that few new members would have enough willpower to resist.

The entire House of Representatives will be dissolved every two years. This means there will be less danger to liberty than a shorter term with gradual changes.

Uniform election times for Senators seem no less required. The legislature can assemble at a specific time each year.

Why couldn't an election time be in the Constitution? The zealous adversaries of the federal Constitution in New York are, in general, zealous admirers of our New York State constitution. We could ask them, why wasn't an election time put in the State constitution?

The best answer is that it is safe for the legislature to decide. If a time had been fixed in the Constitution, once implemented it might have been found less convenient than some other time.

The same answer applies to the federal Constitution. The possible danger of a gradual change is speculative. Therefore, it would not have been a good idea to establish a time for elections in the Constitution. It would have deprived States of the convenience of having State and national elections at the same time.

The Congress shall assemble at least once in every Year, and such Meeting shall be [on the first Monday in December,] unless they shall by Law appoint a different Day.**

Changed by Amendment 20, section 2, ratified in 1933:

Section 2. The Congress shall assemble at least once in every year, and such meeting shall begin at noon on the 3d day of January, unless they shall by law appoint a different day.

Number 10 [13]

In a pure democracy, citizens assemble and administer the government in person…

Number 14 [2]

...In a republic, representatives and agents assemble and administer it...

Number 58 [14]

...In the ancient republics, the whole body of people assembled in person...

ARTICLE 1 SECTION 5. Each House shall be the Judge of the Elections, Returns and Qualifications of its own Members, and a Majority of each shall constitute a Quorum to do Business; but a smaller Number may adjourn from day to day, and may be authorized to compel the Attendance of absent Members, in such manner, and under such Penalties, as each House may provide.

Number 53 [10]

>… Each house judges the legality of member elections and qualifications…

Number 58 [15]

>This is a good place to discuss how many members are needed for legislative business. It has been said that a quorum should be more than a majority. And in particular cases more than a majority should be required for a decision.

>This precaution may have some advantages. It might be an additional shield against some special interests. And it could be another obstacle to hasty and partial measures. But these considerations are outweighed by the inconveniences on the opposite side.

>Whenever justice or the general good might require new laws or active measures, a quorum of more than a majority would reverse the fundamental principle of free government. The majority would no longer rule. The power would be transferred to the minority.

>If a super majority was limited to specific cases, an interested minority might take advantage of it. They could protect themselves from equitable sacrifices or, in emergencies, to extort unreasonable indulgences.

>Lastly, it would facilitate and foster a bad practice that goes against all principles of good government. This would lead more directly to public tumult and the ruin of popular government—secessions.

Number 59 [8]

>…A Senate quorum will be sixteen members…

Each House may determine the Rules of its Proceedings, punish its Members for disorderly Behaviour, and, with the Concurrence of two thirds, expel a member.

Each House shall keep a Journal of its Proceedings, and from time to time publish the same, excepting such Parts as may in their Judgment require Secrecy; and the Yeas and Nays of the Members of either House on any question shall, at the desire of one fifth of those Present, be entered on the Journal.

Neither House, during the Session of Congress, shall, without the Consent of the other, adjourn for more than three days, nor to

any other Place than that in which the two Houses shall be sitting.

Number 69 [6]

…"the President may, on extraordinary occasions, convene both houses of the legislature, or either of them, and, in case of disagreement between them *with respect to the time of adjournment*, to adjourn them to such time as he shall think proper;" … The President can only adjourn Congress in the single case of disagreement about the time of adjournment…

Number 77 [9]

… powers of the Executive include:… adjourning [both houses of Congress] when they cannot themselves agree on the time of adjournment…

ARTICLE 1 SECTION 6. The Senators and Representatives shall receive a Compensation for their Services, to be ascertained by Law, and paid out in the Treasury of the United States.

Number 51 [3]

...members of each branch should depend—as little as possible—on other branches for their pay...

They shall in all Cases, except Treason, Felony and Breach of the Peace, be privileged from Arrest during their Attendance at the Session of their respective Houses, and in going to and returning from the same; and for any Speech or Debate in either House, they shall not be questioned in any other Place.

No Senator or Representative shall, during the Time for which he was elected, be appointed to any civil Office under the Authority of the United States, which shall have been created, or the Emoluments whereof shall have been increased during such time; and no Person holding any Office under the United States, shall be a Member of either House during his Continuance in Office.

Number 55 [9]

Should we fear the other branches of the federal government? How could the President or the Senate corrupt Representatives? Their salary will not be enough to be used to corrupt them, except if they are already corrupt. Their private fortunes, as American citizens, cannot be sources of danger. The only way they can corrupt Representatives will be through giving out government appointments. Is this where suspicion arises? Sometimes we are told that the President will use this source to corrupt the Senate. Now the fidelity of the other House is to be the victim.

Such a disloyal conspiracy by government officials is improbable. Officials will stand on as different foundations as republican principles will allow. And they will be accountable to the society they govern.

Fortunately, the Constitution has another safeguard. (P liberty endangered by civil appointments The members of Congress cannot hold any civil offices that were created or the pay increased during their term in Congress. Therefore, no offices can be given to existing members except when vacated by ordinary casualties...

ARTICLE 1 SECTION 7. All Bills for raising Revenue shall originate in the House of Representatives; but the Senate may propose or concur with Amendments as on other Bills.

Number 58 [8, 12]

The House and Senate will have equal authority on all legislative subjects except money bills—the House originates all money bills. However, the House will have more members.   When the more powerful/larger States follow the will of a majority of the people, they will support the House of Representatives. And the House will have an advantage over the Senate.

…The House of Representatives, alone, proposes the bills that provide the government with the supplies it needs. They hold the purse. This is a very important power. Britain has the monarchy, the House of Lords (run by the aristocracy), and the House of Commons, (the representative body of the people). Because it controls the money, the House of Commons has slowly increased its activity and importance. It is now the most powerful branch of British government.

Power over the purse is the best weapon any constitution can give the people's representatives. It can correct every problem and promote the people's wishes.

Number 66 [7]

And the Constitution gives the House several important powers that counterbalance the Senate's additional authorities. It originates money bills…

Every Bill which shall have passed the House of Representatives and the Senate, shall, before it becomes a Law, be presented to the President of the United States; If he approve he shall sign it, but if not he shall return it, with his Objections to that House in which it shall have originated, who shall enter the Objections at large on their Journal, and proceed to reconsider it. If after such reconsideration two thirds of that House shall agree to pass the Bill, it shall be sent, together with the Objections, to the other House, by which it shall likewise be reconsidered, and if approved by two thirds of that House, it shall become a Law. But in all Cases the Votes of both Houses shall be determined by Yeas and Nays, and the Names of the Persons voting for and against the Bill shall be entered on the Journal of each House respectively.

Number 51 [6]

…The executive is weak and may need strengthening. The executive should have the power to veto legislation. But veto power, alone, may not be enough. It might be dangerously abused or might not be used when it is needed.

Number 66 [2]

...Each branch of government needs to be able to defend itself against the other branches. The president can use the veto to block legislative encroachments on the executive.

Number 69 [5]

The President will have the power to return a bill that has passed the two houses of Congress for reconsideration. If the bill is later passed by two thirds in both the Senate and House, it will become law.

The king of Great Britain has an absolute negative on the acts of the two houses of Parliament. Although the power hasn't been used for a long time, it still exists. In fact, the only reason it hasn't been used is because the king has used his influence rather than his authority. If the monarch used his authority to permanently veto laws passed by Parliament, there would be some degree of agitation in the nation. Instead, he has learned to gain a majority in one of the two houses of Parliament.

The qualified negative of the President is very different than the king's absolute negative. However, it matches the authority of the Council of Revision of New York, of which the governor is a member. In this respect, the power of the President exceeds that of the governor of New York. The President will have, himself, what the governor shares with the chancellor and judges. But it is the same power as the governor of Massachusetts. This article seems to have been copied from the Massachusetts constitution.

Number 73 [4-end]

The first power is the qualified negative [veto] of the President on the acts or resolutions of the two houses of the legislature. He will have the power to return bills to congress with his objections. The bills will only become law if two-thirds of each house of the legislature ratifies them.

I've discussed how the legislative branch of government tends to intrude on the rights and absorb the powers of the other branches. And words on paper are not enough to maintain the boundaries. The Constitution must provide a way for each branch to defend itself.

The Executive needs either an absolute or qualified negative [veto] on legislative acts. Without the veto power, the President could not defend himself against Congress. The legislature could pass a series of resolutions which take away the President's powers. Or it could vote to take away all the President's powers. Congress could quickly hold both the legislative and executive powers.

Even if the legislative body never wanted to invade the rights of the Executive, no branch of government should be left to the mercy of another branch. Each branch should have a constitutional way to defend itself.

But the veto has another use. It shields the Executive and is another security against improper laws. It is a check on the legislature. It guards the community against the effects of faction, haste, or any impulse unfriendly to the public good that could influence a majority of congress.

Some people say a presidential veto is not proper because it assumes that one man has more virtue and wisdom than a group of men. If this was true, it would be improper to give the executive any type of control over the legislative body.

When examined, this observation will be seen as specious. The veto power isn't proper because the Executive has superior wisdom or virtue. The veto is proper because the legislature won't be infallible. The love of power may sometimes cause the legislature to encroach on other branches of the government. A faction may pervert its deliberation. Passions may hurry it into passing laws that it would condemn after careful reflection.

The primary reason to give the Executive the veto is to enable him to defend himself.

The secondary reason is to decrease the possibility that bad laws, passed through haste or on purpose, will take effect. The more often a law or regulation is examined by different types of people, the less the danger of errors. Errors can happen from a lack of deliberation or from the corruption of some common passion. The same dangerous views will probably not infect all parts of the government at the same moment and about same subject.

The power of preventing bad laws includes the power to prevent good ones. It can be used for both purposes. But this objection will not be very important to anyone who knows that mutable laws hurt the character of our governments. Every power that restrains the excess of law making is more likely to do good than harm, because it favors greater stability in legislation. Preventing bad laws will make up for defeating a few good laws.

Nor is this all. In a free government, the legislature has superior weight and influence. In a trial of strength with the legislature, the Executive can lose some of its authority. This gives security that the veto will be used with   great caution. The Executive is more likely to be charged with not using the veto often enough than using it too frequently.

The British king has sovereign powers and great influence. But he doesn't like to veto resolutions passed by the two houses of Parliament. Instead, he uses his influence to stop bills he doesn't like as they work their way through Parliament. He doesn't want to risk the displeasure of the nation by opposing the will of the legislative body.

The king only uses his veto when it is absolutely proper or necessary. All informed men in that kingdom will agree that this remark is truthful. It has been a very long time since he has used the veto.

If the powerful British king has scruples about using this power, a President of the United States will be even more cautious. A President has the executive authority for only four years.

Clearly, there is greater danger that the President will not use the veto when it in necessary than using it too often. Indeed, an argument against its usefulness has been drawn from this very source. Some people have said that it is a power odious in appearance, useless in practice. But just because a power may be rarely used, doesn't mean it would never be used.

The veto power is chiefly designed to stop an attack on the constitutional rights of the Executive. It is also designed to be used when the public good is clearly sacrificed. In these cases, a man with some firmness would use this constitutional defense. He will be responsible and do his duty. When he sees an attack on the Executive, he will want to secure the power of his office. If the public good is being sacrificed, he will act because his constituents, who would normally agree with the legislative body, would probably support the veto. I speak now of a President with only a normal amount of courage. There

153

are men who, under any circumstances, will have the courage to do their duty at every hazard.

But the convention chose a qualified veto. The executive might use this type of veto more often than an absolute veto. The qualified veto will only take effect if a large part of the legislative body agrees with him.

A man might be afraid to defeat a law by his single veto. But he might not hesitate to return it for reconsideration by congress if it would only be rejected if more than one-third of each house agrees with his objections. He would be encouraged. His opposition would prevail only if it was supported by a very large part of congress. Public opinion would support his conduct.

An absolute negative appears harsher than the stating of objections to be approved or disapproved by those to whom they are addressed. The less it might offend, the more apt it is to be used. For this reason, in practice it may be more effective than an absolute negative. It is hoped that improper views will not often govern two-thirds of both branches of the legislature at the same time, in spite of the counterbalancing weight of the Executive. At any rate, it is less probable than that such views would taint the resolutions and conduct of a bare majority.

The executive veto will often have an unperceived, though strong, operation. When men are pursuing unjustifiable goals and they know that obstructions may come from a person they cannot control, the possibility of opposition often restrains them from doing what they would eagerly rush into, if no such external controls were feared.

The qualified negative in New York is vested in a council, consisting of the governor with the chancellor and judges of the Supreme Court, or any two of them. It has been used, frequently with success. Its usefulness has become apparent. People who were opponents of it when the constitution was being written have become admirers.[*]

When forming this part of the Constitution, the convention followed the Massachusetts' constitution rather than New York's.

There are two probable reasons for this preference. One is that judges, who are interpreters of the law, might be improperly biased because they have a previous opinion. The other is that judges are often associated with the Executive, so they might be too vested in the political views of that executive. Eventually, the executive and judiciary branches might become dangerously close.

Judges cannot be too separate from every other avocation than that of expounding the laws. It is very dangerous to place them in a situation where they could be either corrupted or influenced by the Executive.

If any Bill shall not be returned by the President within ten Days (Sundays excepted) after it shall have been presented to him, the Same shall be a Law, in like Manner as if he had signed it, unless the Congress by their Adjournment prevent its Return, in which Case it shall not be a Law.

---

[*] Mr. Abraham Yate, an opponent of the Constitution, is of this number.—PUBLIUS

Every Order, Resolution, or Vote to which the Concurrence of the Senate and House of Representatives may be necessary (except on a question of Adjournment) shall be presented to the President of the United States; and before the same shall take Effect, shall be approved by him, or being disapproved by him, shall be repassed by two thirds of the Senate and House of Representatives, according to the Rules and Limitations prescribed in the Case of a Bill.

Number 51 [6]

...The strength of the legislative power requires that it be divided. The executive is weak and may need strengthening. The executive should have the power to veto legislation. But veto power, alone, may not be enough. It might be dangerously abused or might not be used when it is needed...

Number 66 [2]

...Our discussion of the separation of powers showed that the powers can be partially mixed for special purposes. Sometimes a small mixing of powers is proper and necessary. Each branch of government needs to be able to defend itself against the other branches. The president can use the veto to block legislative encroachments on the executive. Impeachment powers give the legislature a check on executive encroachments...

Number 73 [4]

The first executive power is the qualified negative [veto] of the President on the acts or resolutions of the two houses of the legislature. He will have the power to return bills to congress with his objections. The bills will only become law if two-thirds of each house of the legislature ratifies them.

I've discussed how the legislative branch of government tends to intrude on the rights and absorb the powers of the other branches. And words on paper are not enough to maintain the boundaries. The Constitution must provide a way for each branch to defend itself.

The Executive needs either an absolute or qualified negative [veto] on legislative acts. Without the veto power, the President could not defend himself against Congress. The legislature could pass a series of resolutions which take away the President's powers. Or it could vote to take away all the President's powers. Congress could quickly hold both the legislative and executive powers.

Even if the legislative body never wanted to invade the rights of the Executive, no branch of government should be left to the mercy of another branch. Each branch should have a constitutional way to defend itself.

The Executive needs either an absolute or qualified negative [veto] on legislative acts. Without the veto power, the President could not defend himself against Congress. The legislature could pass a series of resolutions which take away the President's powers. Or it could vote to take away all the President's powers. Congress could quickly hold both the legislative and executive powers.

Even if the legislative body never wanted to invade the rights of the Executive, no branch of government should be left to the mercy of another branch. Each branch should have a constitutional way to defend itself.

Veto Defends against Bad Laws

But the veto has another use. It shields the Executive and is another security against improper laws. It is a check on the legislature. It guards the community against the effects of faction, haste, or any impulse unfriendly to the public good that could influence a majority of congress.

Critics: Improper Control over Legislature

Some people say a presidential veto is not proper because it assumes that one man has more virtue and wisdom than a group of men. If this was true, it would be improper to give the executive any type of control over the legislative body.

Closely Examine Laws Passed in Haste

When examined, this observation will be seen as specious. The veto power isn't proper because the Executive has superior wisdom or virtue. The veto is proper because the legislature won't be infallible. The love of power may sometimes cause the legislature to encroach on other branches of the government. A faction may pervert its deliberation. Passions may hurry it into passing laws that it would condemn after careful reflection.

The primary reason to give the Executive the veto is to enable him to defend himself.

The secondary reason is to decrease the possibility that bad laws, passed through haste or on purpose, will take effect. The more often a law or regulation is examined by different types of people, the less the danger of errors. Errors can happen from a lack of deliberation or from the corruption of some common passion. The same dangerous views will probably not infect all parts of the government at the same moment and about same subject.

Restraint on Excess Law-making

The power of preventing bad laws includes the power to prevent good ones. It can be used for both purposes. But this objection will not be very important to anyone who knows that mutable laws hurt the character of our governments. Every power that restrains the excess of law making is more likely to do good than harm, because it favors greater stability in legislation. Preventing bad laws will make up for defeating a few good laws.

Veto Rarely Used against People's Will

Nor is this all. In a free government, the legislature has superior weight and influence. In a trial of strength with the legislature, the Executive can lose some of its authority. This gives security that the veto will be used with great caution. The Executive is more likely to be charged with not using the veto often enough than using it too frequently.

The British king has sovereign powers and great influence. But he doesn't like to veto resolutions passed by the two houses of Parliament. Instead, he uses his influence to stop bills he doesn't like as they work their way through Parliament. He doesn't want to risk the displeasure of the nation by opposing the will of the legislative body.

The king only uses his veto when it is absolutely proper or necessary. All informed men in that kingdom will agree that this remark is truthful. It has been a very long time since he has used the veto.

Cautious Use of Veto Power

If the powerful British king has scruples about using this power, a President of the United States will be even more cautious. A President has the executive authority for only four years.

Rare, But Used When Needed

Clearly, there is greater danger that the President will not use the veto when it in necessary than using it too often. Indeed, an argument against its usefulness has been drawn from this very source. Some people have said that it is a power odious in appearance, useless in practice. But just because a power may be rarely used, doesn't mean it would never be used.

The veto power is chiefly designed to stop an attack on the constitutional rights of the Executive. It is also designed to be used when the public good is clearly sacrificed. In these cases, a man with some firmness would use this constitutional defense. He will be responsible and do his duty. When he sees an attack on the Executive, he will want to secure the power of his office. If the public good is being sacrificed, he will act because his constituents, who would normally agree with the legislative body, would probably support the veto. I speak now of a President with only a normal amount of courage. There are men who, under any circumstances, will have the courage to do their duty at every hazard.

Qualified Veto, Legislature Concurrence

But the convention chose a qualified veto. The executive might use this type of veto more often than an absolute veto. The qualified veto will only take effect if a large part of the legislative body agrees with him.

A man might be afraid to defeat a law by his single veto. But he might not hesitate to return it for reconsideration by congress if it would only be rejected if more than one-third of each house agrees with his objections. He would be encouraged. His opposition would prevail only if it was supported by a very large part of congress. Public opinion would support his conduct.

An absolute negative appears harsher than the stating of objections to be approved or disapproved by those to whom they are addressed. The less it might offend, the more apt it is to be used. For this reason, in practice it may be more effective than an absolute negative. It is hoped that improper views will not often govern two-thirds of both branches of the legislature at the same time, in spite of the counterbalancing weight of the Executive. At any rate, it is less probable than that such views would taint the resolutions and conduct of a bare majority.

The executive veto will often have an unperceived, though strong, operation. When men are pursuing unjustifiable goals and they know that obstructions may come from a person they cannot control, the possibility of opposition often restrains them from doing what they would eagerly rush into, if no such external controls were feared.

New York's Veto Successful

The qualified negative in New York is vested in a council, consisting of the governor with the chancellor and judges of the Supreme Court, or any two of them. It has been used, frequently with success. Its usefulness has become apparent. People who were opponents of it when the constitution was being written have become admirers.[*]

Maintaining Independent Judiciary

When forming this part of the Constitution, the convention followed the Massachusetts' constitution rather than New York's.

There are two probable reasons for this preference. One is that judges, who are interpreters of the law, might be improperly biased because they have a previous opinion. The other is that judges are often associated with the Executive, so they might be too vested in the political views of that executive. Eventually, the executive and judiciary branches might become dangerously close.

Judges cannot be too separate from every other avocation than that of expounding the laws. It is very dangerous to place them in a situation where they could be either corrupted or influenced by the Executive.

---

[*] Mr. Abraham Yate, an opponent of the Constitution, is of this number.—PUBLIUS

ARTICLE 1 SECTION 8. The Congress shall have Power To lay and collect Taxes,

"...taxation is the government's most important authority..." Number 33 [4]

Six Federalist Papers are devoted to the subject of taxation. And that doesn't count the Papers that explain why the method of collecting revenue for the federal government under the Articles of Confederation didn't work.

Number 6 [13]

The provinces of Holland, until overwhelmed by debt and taxes, led and participated in European wars.

Number 10 [8]

…Determining the amount of taxes on different types of property requires impartiality. Yet no legislative act has a greater opportunity and temptation for the majority party to trample on the rules of justice. With every dollar they overburden the minority party, they save a dollar in their own pockets.

Number 12 [3, 4, 12]

A country's ability to pay taxes is related to the quantity and turnover of money in circulation. Commerce contributes to these objectives, making payment of taxes easier…

In America, direct taxation is impractical. Despite new tax laws and new collection methods, the States' treasuries remain empty. When trade decreases, money becomes scarce. Extensive tax collections have been impossible. And the State legislatures have learned the folly of attempting them.

A nation needs revenue to exist. Without taxes, it must give up its independence and sink into the degraded condition of a province. Therefore, revenue is necessary.

In this country, if commerce isn't taxed, land must be. The people are largely opposed to internal taxation. With agriculture almost the only employment in the States, there are few objects for excise taxes and collections would be limited. Personal property is difficult to trace, so large tax contributions can only be achieved through consumption taxes. In populous cities, people would probably have to pay oppressive personal taxes and little benefit would go to the State. Outside these cities, most assets escape the eye and hand of the tax collector.

Nevertheless, funds must be gathered to pay the government's expenses. When they can't be obtained from any other source, landowners must carry the majority of the burden.

On the other hand, unless all tax sources are available when needed for government finances, the community won't have the money to remain respectable and secure. So we won't even have the consolation of a full treasury to make up for the oppression of farmers. Public and private distress will be equal. And everyone will deplore the foolishness that led to disunion.

Number 30 [1-2, 5-6, 8, 10]

The federal government should have the ability to support the national army... And the Union must raise revenue for other reasons. It must pay the national government's employees, current and future debts, and other appropriate expenses. Therefore, the government must have the power of taxation.

Government needs money to fulfill its duties. Therefore, the power to raise money, as far as community resources will permit, is an essential part of every constitution.

Two evils result if a government doesn't have enough money. Either the people will be plundered, as a substitute for legitimate taxation, or the government will sink into a fatal atrophy and perish.

...The national government must be able to raise revenues by taxation, as authorized in every well-ordered constitution. It will rescue us from the inconveniences and embarrassments resulting from limited money in the public treasury.

Opponents of the new Constitution agree. But they say the State governments should have exclusive power to collect *internal* taxes. They want the federal government to use *external* taxation—duties on imported articles.

Power Proportionate to Objective

Prohibiting the federal government from using internal taxation violates the maxim of good sense and sound policy. Every power ought to be in proportion to its objective. Commercial imports will never provide enough revenue for the Union's present and future needs. It is important to public justice and public credit that we pay the current foreign and domestic debt. And everyone agrees that some federal agencies are necessary. Import duties alone would never even meet the federal government's current needs. We cannot know its future needs. Therefore, they can't be limited. It must have the unlimited power to provide for them.

I believe history proves that, the necessities of a nation, in every stage of its existence, will be found at least equal to its resources.

During a modern war, even the wealthiest nations need large loans. For a country as poor as ours, loans are necessities. But who would lend to a government that has no reliable method of raising repayment funds? The loans it could get would be the same that loan sharks commonly lend to bankrupt and fraudulent debtors—very small with an enormous interest rate.

If the national government had the authority to raise money through new taxes, it could borrow as much as it might require. Both Americans and foreigners could confidently lend to it...

Number 31 [5-8]

Power Must Equal Responsibility

Government is created to accomplish specific objectives. It should have every power required to fully accomplish its objectives and fulfill its responsibilities. The only control should be regard for the public good and the will of the people.

National Defense Can't Be Limited

The Union government has a duty to supervise the national defense and secure the public peace against foreign and domestic violence. Only two things can limit defense: the needs of the nation and the resources of the community.

Revenue is essential. The government must have the power to get this revenue. State requisitions don't work. The federal government must have the unlimited power of ordinary taxation.

Number 35 [1-4]

If the national government is restricted and can only tax a few specific objects, those objects would carry too much of the public burden. This creates two evils: the industries that create and sell those objects would be oppressed, and States and citizens involved with that industry would be responsible for an unequal part of the tax burden.

Some people argue that the federal taxation power should be limited to import duties. If import taxes were the federal government's only source of revenue, it would frequently want to increase these taxes, which would be injurious. Some people think that import taxes can never be too high because high import taxes discourage extravagant consumption, produce a favorable balance of trade, and promote domestic manufactures. But all extremes cause harm.

Very high taxes on imported articles would increase smuggling. Smuggling hurts honest traders and merchants. And it decreases tax revenue.

High duties also tend to give people who manufacture goods within the country a premature market monopoly. Import taxes creates higher price. Domestic manufactures will be able to charge higher prices than in an open market.

High import taxes can force industry out of its more natural channels into less advantageous areas.

They also oppress merchants that sell imported goods. The merchant, especially in a country with small commercial capital, often must keep prices down to promote sales. To do this, the seller can't raise his price to cover the entire cost of the duty. This reduces or eliminates the merchant's profits and can eat into his business capital.

Usually, the consumer pays the tax duties. Therefore, duties on imports should go into the national treasury rather than be used exclusively by the importing States. But it is not fair that duties should form the only national fund.

When the merchant pays duties, they become an additional tax on the importing State, whose citizens, as consumers, pay the duties. They would produce an inequality among the States that would increase as duties increased.

If import duties were the only source of national revenues, non-manufacturing States would have an unequal tax burden. Citizens in manufacturing States will buy fewer imported articles than non-manufacturing States. Excise taxes would be needed to increase the manufacturing States' contribution to the public treasury. And specific manufactures would be targeted.

The citizens of New York who want to limit the Union to external taxation may not understand the importance of this subject. New York is an importing State. Since New York has a small population in a large territory, the growth of manufacturing will be slow. New York would suffer if the Union were limited to only commercial taxes.

Increased Tax Rate Doesn't Increase Revenue

These are some of the reasons for limiting import duties. As mentioned in another paper, there is another reason: if we want the government to be able to collect tax revenue, import taxes must be limited. And import taxes would be limited as long as the government has other resources. But if other taxation avenues were closed, when the government needed more revenue it would increase import taxes and try other experiments like adding penalties. For a while tax revenues would increase—until people found ways to elude the new taxes. Government officials would get the false impression that raising taxes also raises the amount of money going into the federal treasury. This false impression would take a long time to correct. Necessity, especially in politics, often occasions false hopes, false reasoning, and a system of measures correspondingly erroneous.

Number 36 [3-16]

It has been said that a national power of internal taxation will never be successful for two reasons: 1. There isn't enough knowledge of local circumstances. 2. The revenue laws of the Union and specific States will conflict.

The federal government will have the information. State legislatures learn about a specific county from citizens of that county. The national legislature will get similar information from the representatives of each State.

When discussing taxation, does "local" knowledge mean being topographically familiar with every mountain, river, stream, highway, and road in each State? No. It means a general understanding of its situation and resources, the state of its agriculture, commerce, manufacturers, the nature of its products and consumption, the amount and kinds of wealth, property, and industry.

Small Committees Prepare Tax Plans

In nations, a small group of men usually prepare taxation plans. The sovereign or legislature then turns the plans into laws.

Inquisitive, enlightened statesmen are best qualified to make a judicious selection of the proper objects of taxation. This is the type of "local" knowledge required for taxation.

Local Knowledge Affects Indirect, Direct Taxes

Internal taxes may be either *direct* or *indirect* taxes. Objections based on a "lack of local knowledge" have been made against both types of internal taxes.

When the federal government considers whether it should tax an article, it will look at the nature of the article. [i.e. home heating oil will be used more in northern States than southern States] Well-informed men, especially merchants, will supply more information. [i.e. perhaps an article is more expensive in some States because of shipping costs] If an article is already taxed by a State, the federal government shouldn't add another tax. Understanding an article's different situation in different States is easy.

Does the objection apply to direct taxes on real property, houses or land? No.

Land taxes are determined either by *actual* valuations or *occasional* assessments. In either case, local knowledge is only needed in the execution of the duty by commissioners or assessors. The law can only prescribe the manner the persons will be elected or appointed, fix their numbers and qualifications, and outline their powers and duties.

Either the national legislature or a State legislature can regulate the general principles. Local details must be referred to those who execute the plan.

State Collection System May Be Used

This can be further simplified. Each State's method of laying and collecting tax can be adopted and employed by the federal government.

Taxes Uniform Throughout Nation

Remember, the national legislature will not decide how much the people of each State must pay. That will be determined by each State's population, as described in Article one, Section two. The population will be determined by a census. Therefore, the national government can't be partial or oppressive to some States. It would be difficult to abuse the taxation power. There is also a provision that "all duties, imposts, and excises shall be uniform throughout the United States."

State Requisitions Still Possible

Remember, if internal taxation by the Union is really inconvenient, the federal government may stop using it and use State requisitions instead. It has been asked, why not just omit the ambiguous power and rely on State requisitions?

Two answers may be given: First, if it works, internal taxation will be more effective. Second, if the Union returns to using State requisitions, the constitutional power of direct taxation will have a strong influence. When the States know that the Union can go directly to the people, they will be motivated to fulfill their requisitions.

Federal, States Tax Differently

Legally, Union and State revenue laws cannot interfere with each other. However, Union and State policies do sometimes conflict. A solution will be to not tax those objects that the other side is already taxing. The federal and State governments can't *control* each other. Therefore, each will have an interest in this reciprocal forbearance. And when the current State debts are paid off, their expenses will decrease and the possibility of interference will almost vanish. A small land-tax will fulfill State needs.

Fears about Internal Taxation

The power of internal taxation has raised many fears: double sets of revenue officers, double taxation, and odious, oppressive poll taxes.

Double Sets of Revenue Officers

There won't be double sets of officers in two cases: The first is when the Union has exclusive right to impose the tax, for instance, duties on imports. And second, when the object to be taxed hasn't fallen under a State regulation or provision.

In other cases, the United States probably will either not tax objects the local government taxes or will use State officers and State regulations for collecting the additional tax. This will save collection expense and avoid problems with the State governments and the people.

The predicted evils do not necessarily result from the plan.

States Influences Nation

If a spirit of influence should infest the national councils, State officers could be employed, attaching them to the Union through their compensation. State influence would flow towards the national government, instead of federal influence flowing to the States.

Federal or State, Total Taxes Same

The answer to the worry about double taxation is plain. The wants of the Union are to be supplied in one way or another. If fulfilled by the federal government, the State government will not do them. The quantity of taxes paid by the community must be the same in either case.

If the federal government supplies the provision, it can use commercial taxes. The federal government can improve this revenue source better than the States, making other taxes less necessary.

There is another advantage. If there is a problem with internal taxation, the federal government will be careful about what it taxes. The national tax policy will make the rich pay as much as is practical and diminish the taxes paid by the more numerous, poorer people. It is fortunate when the government's interest in self-preservation coincides with a proper distribution of public burdens and tends to guard the least wealthy part of the community from oppression!

Poll Taxes Bad, May Be Needed

I strongly disapprove of poll taxes. Although they have been used in New England, States that have always promoted citizens' rights, I would hate to see the national government use them.

However, just because there is a power to use them, will they actually be used? Every State in the Union has the power to impose poll taxes. Yet several States have never used them. Are the State governments tyrannies because they have this power? If they are not, how can a similar power justify such a charge against the national government? Or be used as an obstacle to adopting of the Constitution? I hate poll taxes but emergencies are possible. The government should have the option of using them.

This country has few objects that can be used as sources of revenue. This is a reason for not limiting the discretion of the national councils. Nothing exempts this part of the globe from the calamities that have befallen other parts of it. I am averse to everything that disarms the government of a single weapon that might be employed for defense and security.

Number 38 [7]

A patriot in a State, which doesn't import or export, objects to **direct taxation.** The patriot in an exporting and importing State is dissatisfied because the whole burden of **taxes** may be thrown **on consumption**.

Number 41 [22-23]

The power to levy taxes and borrow money—the financial support for national defense—has also been examined. The extent and form in the Constitution is necessary.

Some people believe that the power of federal taxation should be limited to external taxation—taxes on articles imported from other countries. Of course, this will always be a valuable source of revenue. For a long time, in fact, it must be the primary source. And at this moment, it is essential.

However, import tax revenue will vary as the amount and the kind of imports vary. And these variations won't correspond with the growth of our population, which is the general measure of how much money the government will need. As long as agriculture continues to be the only field of labor, as the population increases, the importation of manufactured goods will increase. As the population grows, American manufacturers will employ hands not needed for agriculture and imported manufactured goods will decrease. Eventually, manufacturers may import raw materials that will be made into articles for exportation. As raw material importation overtakes the importation of finished goods, the government will want to encourage imports, not discourage them with import taxes. A good government should remember these cycles and be able to handle them.

The proposed Constitution defines the federal government's taxation power. It says: "The Congress shall have the power to lay and collect taxes, duties, imposts, and excises, to pay the debts, and provide for the common defense and general welfare of the United States." [Article 1, Section 8] Some people have attacked the language that defines the taxation power, saying it amounts to an unlimited license to use any and every power that may be alleged to be necessary for the common defense or general welfare.

Stooping to such a misconstruction proves how far these writers will reach to find objections to the Constitution.

Number 48 [6]
...The legislature both imposes taxes and sets the wages of the executive and judiciary branches. Therefore, all government officials are dependent on the legislature, making legislative encroachments even easier.

Number 53 [5]
To fairly impose and effectively collect taxes, [federal legislators] need to know the laws and situations in the different States... Trade, taxes, and the militia are the important subjects of federal legislation. Federal representatives need a lot of information on these and other subjects.

Number 54 [1-10] (See page 112)

Number 83 [13-16]
It is said that trial by jury is a safeguard against oppressive taxation. This idea deserves to be studied.

Trial by jury cannot influence the legislature, which decides the *amount* of taxes, the *objects* of taxation, and the tax apportionment *rule*. Therefore, trial by jury can only influence how taxes are collected and the conduct of the revenue officers.

In New York, trial by jury is rarely used for tax collection. Taxes are usually levied by the summary proceeding of distress and sale. And everyone agrees that this is essential to the efficacy of the revenue laws. The delay of a trial to recover the taxes imposed on individuals would not fulfill public needs. And it would often cost more than the original tax.

Revenue officers who abuse public authority or extort citizens commit criminal offenses against the government. Trial by jury in criminal cases will give complete security. Officers can be indicted and punished.

Number 84 [footnote 3]

The power of taxation has been used to show there is a constitutional power to affect liberty of the press. It is said that high taxes could be the same as a prohibition. Would the statement in the State constitutions in favor of the freedom of the press block the State legislatures from taxing publications? No amount of taxes, however low, would limit the liberty of the press.

Newspapers are taxed in Great Britain. But the British press enjoys great liberty. If any tax can be laid without violating liberty, the amount must depend on legislature, regulated by public opinion. Statements about liberty of the press will not add security. Some State constitutions declare liberty of the press. Yet they can use taxation to limit freedom of the press. The same thing can happen under the proposed Constitution. Saying that the government should be free or that taxes should not be excessive would have the same significance as saying that the liberty of the press should not be restrained.

Union, States Concurrent Taxation Jurisdiction

Number 31 [10]

The opponents [of the taxation clause] seem to be saying: "Just because the financial needs of the Union may not be limited, doesn't mean its power to tax ought to be unlimited. Local governments require revenue. And local governments are as important to the people's happiness as the national government. But if the *national government* has an unlimited power to tax, in time the *States* would probably not be able to raise revenues. The States would be at the mercy of the national legislature.

"Union laws will be the supreme law of the land and the Union will have the power to pass all the laws that may be necessary to execute its constitutional duties. Therefore, the national government might abolish State taxes on the pretense that they interfere with national taxes. Eventually, all tax resources may become a federal monopoly, excluding and destroying the State governments."

Number 32 [1, 3-4]

Giving the Union the power to tax will not create the dangerous consequences feared by the State governments. Several things will block the oppressive use of taxation: the people's good sense, the danger of resentments from the States, and the need for local governments to fulfill local objectives.

The States need an independent authority to raise revenues that the federal government can't control. With the sole exception of taxes on imports and exports, under the Constitution the States keep that authority. If the national government tries to control State taxation, it would be a violent assumption of power that is not in the proposed Constitution.

The federal government and the individual States have concurrent and coequal authority to impose taxes on all articles other than exports and imports.

The clause does not give the Union *exclusive* power. And no clause prohibits States from the power to tax. On the contrary, the State ban on taxing imports and exports implies that the States have the power to tax. And it also implies that State authority remains undiminished. In all cases not restricted, the States would have a concurrent power of taxation with the Union.

The clause that bans State import and export taxes is called a negative pregnant—that is, a *negation* of one thing and an *affirmation* of another. States **cannot** impose taxes on imports and exports and **can** impose them on all other articles. It is sophistry to argue that it excludes States *absolutely* from duties and allows them to lay other taxes *subject to the control* of the national legislature.

Union, States May Tax Same Objects

If a State taxes a specific article, it may be *inexpedient* for the Union to tax the same article. But another tax isn't unconstitutional. The size of the tax is a question of prudence, but there is no direct contradiction of power. National and State tax policies may sometimes conflict. One or the other may need to change their policy. However, an inconvenience in the exercise of powers does not imply a constitutional ban of a preexisting right of sovereignty.

Number 33 [3, 4, 8]

...Article One, Section 8 says, "Congress shall have power to lay and collect taxes." Therefore, it is a legislative power. In other words, a power to make **necessary and proper** laws about taxes.

...the power to lay and collect taxes includes all laws *necessary* and *proper* to execute that power...

...a United States tax law would be supreme in its nature and couldn't be legally opposed or controlled. However, a federal law abolishing or preventing collection of State taxes (unless on imports and exports) would not be the supreme law of the land. It would be a usurpation of power not granted by the Constitution.

If the State and federal governments taxed the same object and collection became difficult, this would be inconvenient for both. Neither has superior power. The federal government, the State government, or both using their power in a disadvantageous way would cause the problem. Presumably, the federal and State governments would cooperate and change their tax policies until they were more convenient.

The States will be able to raise revenue from any kind of taxation, except duties on imports and exports. The federal government will not have the authority to control States' taxes...

Number 34 [all]

Under the proposed Constitution, the States and the Union will have coequal taxing authority, except duties on imports. The majority of community resources will be available to the States. The States will have many taxation methods but will be responsible for only a small share of the public expenses. Therefore, they will have sufficient resources.

Existence Trumps Theory

Some people have said that this shared authority cannot exist. This is a theoretical argument that is contrary to fact and reality. Arguments that show something *ought not to exist* should be completely rejected when evidence proves that it does exist.

For example, the Roman republic had two legislatures, which had different opposite interests: the patrician and the plebian. Each had the power to *annul* or *repeal* the acts of the other. People may try to prove that having two contradictory authorities won't work. But if a Roman citizen tried to disprove their existence, he would have been called insane.

In the Roman legislature that was called the comitta centuriata, only people who had a specific amount of property could vote and the patrician interest was superior. In the conittia tribuia, all citizens could vote, so the plebcian interest predominated. These two legislatures coexisted for ages and Rome was a great republic.

Coequal Authority Less Contradictory

The coequal taxation authority is not as contradictory as the Roman example. Neither side can annul the acts of the other. And soon the States' needs will be very limited. Until then, the United States will probably not tax the objects that States want to tax.

Union Revenue Needs Unlimited

What expenses will the federal and State governments have? Federal expenses are unlimited and State expenses are limited.

We must look into the remote future. A civil government's constitution tries to combine existing needs with probable future needs. We cannot infer from an estimate of immediate needs, the extent of power it is proper to give the national government. It is unsafe to limit the national government's capacity to provide for future emergencies. The federal government must provide the national defense. It must protect the nation against foreign war and domestic violence. We cannot predict the possibility of internal attacks. We must be able to defend our commerce. And we must be able to support a navy and pay for naval wars

Revenue Needed for Defense

Even if we agree to try the novel and absurd political experiment of tying the hands of government from offensive war, the government must be able guard the community against the ambition or hatred of other nations. If war breaks out in Europe, will we feel some of its fury? Or will another cause or country disturb our tranquility? Peace or war will not always be left to our option. We might be moderate or unambitious but we can't count on the moderation or hope to extinguish the ambition of others. History shows us that the fiery and destructive passions of war are more powerful motivators of human behavior than the mild and beneficent sentiments of peace. Modeling our political systems on speculations of lasting tranquility is to depend on the weaker springs of the human character.

Defense Largest Expense

What are the chief sources of expense in every government? Wars and rebellions. We must guard against these two mortal diseases of society.

The expenses for domestic police, the legislative, executive, and judicial branches of government, and the encouragement of agriculture and manufacturing (in other words, almost all State expenditures), are insignificant when compared with the expense for national defense.

England: Defense vs. Executive

In the kingdom of Great Britain, only 7% of the nation's annual expenses support the ostentatious monarchy. The other 93% goes to national defense.

Someone could say that we can't compare the possible expenses of a republic with the expense of supporting a monarchy. But consider this—Britain is a wealthy kingdom with an extravagant monarchy. Our frugal republic will have a modest executive branch. If we balance a proper deduction from one side against what ought to be deducted from the other, the proportion may still stand.

Union vs. States Revenue Needs

If we look at the large debt from a single war, we see that there will always be an immense disproportion between federal and State expenditures. Currently, several States have excessive debts because of the war. But if the proposed system is adopted, this cannot happen again. After these debts are paid, State governments will only need revenue to support their civil lists.

Future Revenue Needs Unlimitable

In framing a government for both the present and the future, we should figure out how much the offices and departments will cost. The State governments will need an annual sum of about 200,000 pounds. But the Union's requirements cannot be limited, even in imagination. Why should State and local governments be given an exclusive source of revenue for any sum beyond 200,000 pounds? If the States are given sources of tax revenue that the Union is excluded from using, funding sources that are needed for national defense will be given to local governments that have no just or proper use for them.

Current State Debts/Future Needs

Suppose the convention had tried to distribute revenue sources between the Union and the States in *proportion* to their needs. What amount would not be too little or too much for the States—too little for their present needs, too much for their future needs?

Let's say the federal government was limited to external taxation (taxes on imports) and only the States and local government could use internal taxes. 66% of the country's resources would be available to States to pay 5-10% of its expenses. The federal government would have 33% of the country's resources to pay from 90-95% of its expenses.

What if we give the States an exclusive power of taxing houses and lands? There would still be a great disproportion between the *means* and the *end*. The States would possess 33% of the country's resources to supply, at most, 10% of its wants.

If the States had a revenue source that was only large enough to meet the futures needs of the State, they would not be able to raise enough money to pay their current debts. The Union would have to make a provision for this purpose.

Concurrent Tax Jurisdiction

Therefore, a concurrent jurisdiction for taxation was the only admissible substitute for an entire subordination, in respect to taxation, of State authority to that of the Union. Separating objects of taxation would have sacrificed the great interests of the Union to the power of the individual States. A few other points about this important subject of taxation deserve further consideration.

Defects in Articles of Confederation, State quotas, requisitions

Number 7 [8]

Suppose a decision about each State's debt payment was made. It would be difficult for some States to pay and they would want their share lowered. The other States would refuse to have their part of the debt increased. Their refusal would give the complaining States an excuse to withhold their contributions, creating bitter arguments.

Even if the division of the debt payment was equal in principle, some States would not pay for several reasons: lack of resources, financial mismanagement, governmental mismanagement, and the reluctance of men to postpone purchases by using money to pay debts.

Delinquencies, from whatever causes, produce complaints, recriminations, and quarrels. Mutual financial obligations that don't yield an equal benefit disturb the tranquility of nations. It is as true as it is trite: men differ over nothing so quickly as the payment of money.

Number 15 [6, 12, 15]

The basic defect of the Confederation is the principle of legislation for states in their collective capacities rather than for the individuals living in the States.

This principle doesn't apply to all the federal government's powers. However, it is such an important part of our current system that it leaves the Union virtually powerless. For example, the United States can requisition men and money, but it has no authority to directly raise either from individual citizens. In theory, federal resolutions are constitutionally binding on the States; but in practice, they are merely recommendations that the States observe or disregard.

We were told that States wouldn't violate federal regulations. Some people said that States would comply because of our common interests. Today, this sounds ludicrous. It betrayed an ignorance of psychology and contradicted the original reason for establishing civil power. Current pronouncements will sound just as wild after we receive more lessons from that best oracle of wisdom, experience.

Why should we have a government? Because the passions of men won't conform to the dictates of reason and justice without constraint. Do groups of men act with more virtue than individuals? Observers of human behavior know that the opposite happens. An individual worries more about his reputation than that of his group, because blame for the detestable action of a group is divided among a number of people. A group of people is often poisoned by faction, pushing it into improper and excessive behavior that would embarrass the individuals.

Under the current Confederation, the thirteen sovereign States must agree to enforce every important resolution and law proposed by the Union. What happened was expected. The measures have not been executed. State delinquencies have grown, stopping the wheels of the national government. Congress is barely able to keep some kind of administration until the States can agree on a functioning replacement for the present shadow of a federal government.

Our current awful situation didn't happen overnight. At first, a few States didn't fulfill the Union's requisitions. When they didn't pay, the least delinquent States were tempted not to pay, feeling that they shouldn't pay proportionately more than other States in the Union. Why should they pay more than their share of the common burden? Each State has successively withdrawn its support. Now the frail and tottering national confederation seems ready to fall on our heads and crush us beneath its ruins.

Number 19 [7, 10-11]

[German example] Germany has a history of wars. The emperor and the states fight. The weak are oppressed. Foreign nations have invaded and developed conspiracies. The states ignored requisitions for money and men. Either the requisitions were not enforced or they were enforced by the military, which killed the innocent and the guilty. It's a history of stupidity, confusion, and misery.

Germany's small, peacetime army was poorly maintained, badly paid, and infected with local prejudices. Maintaining order and dispensing justice was impossible. The empire was divided into nine or ten circles (states). The military enforced laws against delinquent and disobedient states.

This demonstrates the flaws of their constitution. Each state has the deformities of this political monster. They either fail to do their duties or are forced with all the devastation of civil war. Sometimes whole states default, increasing the problems they were established to remedy.

Number 20 [4, 14-16, 22]

In the United Netherlands…the States-General can … determine tax quotas, and demand contributions. However, all the provinces and cities must agree.

Each province is supposed to pay contributions, but inland provinces have little commerce and cannot pay an equal quota. The provinces that are able to pay must pay, and then use any method to get money from the other provinces. More than once, money was collected at bayonet point. This is an awful solution when one member of a confederacy is much stronger than the rest. And this solution won't work in a confederacy composed of several members of equal strength, resources, and defenses.

A tax system administered by the federal government was conceived. It also failed.

Number 21 [6-11]

Currently, State contributions to the national treasury are regulated by quotas, which haven't been met. There is no one standard to measure the degrees of national wealth. Land values and population numbers have been suggested as ways to determine each State's quota. But neither truly represents the State's wealth.

For example, let's compare the wealth of the United Netherlands to Russia, Germany, or France. There is no relationship between their wealth and their land value and population. The United Netherlands has the higher wealth; the three other nations have immense land and much larger populations.

We can compare American States in the same way and get a similar result. Compare Virginia with North Carolina, Pennsylvania with Connecticut, or Maryland with

New Jersey. Their comparative wealth has little relationship to their lands and populations. Counties within New York State illustrate the same thing. If either land value or population is the criterion, the active wealth of King's County is much greater than that of Montgomery County.

An infinite variety of causes create a nation's wealth. They include location, soil, climate, products, the type of government, the genius of its citizens, knowledge, commerce, arts, and industry. And there are many more causes that are too complex to quantify. These combine to create differences in the relative wealth of different countries. There is no common measure of national wealth. And there is no way to measure a State's ability to pay taxes. Therefore, trying to calculate each State's quota by using a rule based on land or population would be glaringly unequal and extremely oppressive.

Even if federal requisitions could be enforced, the inequality between States' wealth alone would eventually destroy the American Union. Public burdens would be unequally distributed. Some States would be impoverished and oppressed while citizens of others would scarcely notice their small tax burden. Suffering States would secede. The principle of quotas and requisitions creates this evil.

To avoid this problem, the national government must be able to raise its own revenue.

Like fluid, taxes on articles of consumption will, in time, find their level with the means of paying them. To a degree, each citizen's contribution will be his own option, determined by his resources. The rich may be extravagant. The poor can be frugal. And private oppression may be avoided by judiciously selecting the objects to be taxed. If inequalities arise in some States from duties on specific objects, these probably will be counterbalanced by proportional inequalities in other States from duties on other objects. In time, an equilibrium, as far as it is attainable in so complicated a subject, will be established everywhere. Or, if inequalities continue to exist, they will not be as odious as those that come from using quotas.

Consumption taxes tend to block excess taxation. They prescribe their own limit. If they are too high, they defeat their purpose—increasing government's revenue.

When applied to taxation policy, it is true that "in political arithmetic, 2 and 2 do not always make 4." If duties are too high, people make fewer purchases, less tax is collected, and the government's revenue is less than if taxes were confined within proper and moderate bounds. This forms a complete barrier against any significant oppression of citizens by taxes of this kind. And it naturally limits the power of the imposing authority.

For a long time, most of the government's revenue must be raised by indirect taxes.

Direct taxes principally relate to land and buildings, and they may be appropriate for the rule of apportionment. Either the land value or the number of people may serve as a standard. Agriculture and population density are co-related. For taxation, numbers are usually preferred because of their simplicity and certainty.

Land valuation is a herculean task. In a country only partly settled and constantly being improved, the difficulties make it nearly impossible. And the expense of an accurate valuation is a major objection.

There are no natural limits to direct taxes. Therefore the establishment of a fixed rule, compatible with its purpose, might be a better idea than leaving the discretion unbound.

Number 23 [6-8]

Should a federal government be entrusted with the common defense? If the answer is yes, the government needs the power to execute that trust. Authority to provide for defense cannot be limited. Any matter essential to the *formation, direction,* or *support* of the national forces should not be limited.

The people who wrote the Articles of Confederation apparently understood this principle. But they didn't provide a way to do it. Congress can requisition (demand that each State send a specific amount) men and money and control the army and navy. Congressional requisitions are constitutionally binding on the States; the States have a legal duty to furnish the required supplies. The Articles of Confederation authorized the federal government to command all resources that are necessary for the "common defense and general welfare." The authors of the Articles assumed that the States would be aware of their best interests and duty to the Union and they would fill the federal requisitions.

However, this was a mistaken assumption. If we really want to give the Union energy and a long life, we must stop making laws that States are supposed to obey. Federal laws must extend to individual citizens. Quotas and requisitions are impractical and unjust. They must be discarded.

The Union should have the power and money to draft troops, support an army, and build and equip a navy in the same way as other governments.

Number 30 [3-5, 7-8]

The emperor of Turkey [Ottoman Empire] has no right to impose a new tax. Consequently, the local governors [bashaws] pillage the people without mercy, squeezing from them the money the emperor needs to satisfy his needs and those of the state.

The American Union has gradually decayed for the same reason. In both countries, if they could legally tax, it would promote the people's happiness.

Under the Articles of Confederation, the United States was supposed to have unlimited power to provide for the financial needs of the Union. But the system of requisitions hasn't worked. Congress asks the States for money [requisitions the States] to administer the United States. The States have no right to question whether the demand is appropriate. The States' only discretion is how to furnish the money demanded.

Different Papers have explained the consequences of the requisition system. Because of this system, we have embarrassed ourselves and helped our enemies feel triumphant.

The illogical system of quotas and requisitions must be changed. The national government must be able to raise revenues by taxation, as authorized in every well-ordered constitution. It will rescue us from the inconveniences and embarrassments resulting from limited money in the public treasury.

Some people say that State requisitions will make up the money the federal government will need. This shows why federal revenue can't be raised through import taxes alone. It acknowledges that deficiencies will occur. And whenever requisitions are used, it will make the Union weak, create conflict between the federal government and the States, and between the States.

In the future, will the States fulfill their requisitions any better than they do now? If less is required from the States, they will be proportionately less able to answer the demand. At some point, the States would say: this is the limit of where public happiness will be promoted by supplying the government money and everything beyond this point is unworthy of our care or anxiety.

How can a government, half supplied and always in need, provide for the security, advance the prosperity, or support the reputation of the nation? How can it possess energy or stability, dignity or credit, confidence at home or respect from other nations? How will it avoid sacrificing commitments to immediate necessity? How can it undertake large plans for pubic good?

Let's look at what will happen during our next war. Let's assume, for argument's sake, that import duties will be enough to pay our debt and fund the peacetime federal government. Then a war breaks out. We can't depend on State requisitions. The federal government would have to take appropriated funds from their proper objects to defend the States.

During a modern war, even the wealthiest nations need large loans. For a country as poor as ours, loans are necessities. But who would lend to a government that has no reliable method of raising repayment funds? The loans it could get would be the same that loan sharks commonly lend to bankrupt and fraudulent debtors—very small with an enormous interest rate.

Number 31 [7-8]

Revenue is essential. The government must have the power to get this revenue. State requisitions don't work. The federal government must have the unlimited power of ordinary taxation.

Number 36 [10]

Remember, if internal taxation by the Union is really inconvenient, the federal government may stop using it and use State requisitions instead. It has been asked, why not just omit the ambiguous power and rely on State requisitions?

Two answers may be given: First, if it works, internal taxation will be more effective. Second, if the Union returns to using State requisitions, the constitutional power of direct taxation will have a strong influence. When the States know that the Union can go directly to the people, they will be motivated to fulfill their requisitions.

Number 38 [9-10]

People who object to the new Constitution never talk about the defects in the Articles of Confederation. The Constitution doesn't need to be perfect; it just has to be better than the Articles. No man would refuse to leave a shattered, tottering house for a large, solid building because the latter had no porch, or because some of the rooms might be a little larger or smaller, or the ceiling a little higher or lower than his fancy would have planned them. The primary objections to the new Constitution lie with tenfold weight against the existing Confederation.

Is it dangerous for the federal government to have an **indefinite power to raise money**? The present Congress can requisition any amount of money from the States and the States are constitutionally bound to furnish it...

I will be told: The Confederation's powers may appear dangerous. But they are harmless because Congress is dependent on the States to use them. However large the Confederation's total power may appear to be, it is lifeless.

Then I say: we can charge the Confederation with the greater folly of declaring that certain federal powers are necessary and, at the same time, making them worthless. And if the Union is to continue under the Articles of Confederation, effective powers must either be granted to, or assumed by, the existing Congress.

But this is not all. The Confederation has already greatly increased its power. All the dangers from a defectively constructed national government seem to be realized.

The Western territory is a mine of vast wealth to the United States. It won't produce any regular revenue for public expenses for some time to come. But eventually, under proper management, it will help discharge the domestic public debt and furnish, for a certain period, liberal tributes to the federal treasury. Therefore, a rich, fertile territory, equal in size to the inhabited area of the United States, will soon become part of the nation. Congress has assumed its administration, formed new States, erected temporary governments, appointed officers for them, and prescribed the condition by which the States will be admitted into the Confederacy. All this has been done without the least constitutional authority. Yet no blame has been whispered; no alarm has been sounded.

Under the Articles of Confederation, a great and independent fund of revenue is passing into the hands of a single body of men [Congress]. The same group can raise troops to an indefinite number, and appropriate money to support them for an indefinite period of time. Yet some of the same men who have watched and advocated for this system have objected to the new system using the arguments presented here. Shouldn't they urge the adoption of the new Constitution as necessary to guard the Union against future powers and resources of a body constructed like the existing Congress?

Number 45 [11]

The new Constitution adds few NEW POWERS to the Union. Instead, it invigorates its ORIGINAL POWERS... The taxation method is changed. Currently, Congress may REQUIRE MONEY from the States for the common defense and general welfare. Under the Constitution, the future Congress will require the same amount from individual citizens. And the citizens will be no more bound than the States have been to pay their taxes.

If the States had paid or could have been forced to pay with as peaceable a means as may be used with success towards a single person, the State governments would have kept their constitutional powers and not consolidated. To maintain that this would have happened is the same as saying that State governments cannot exist within any system that accomplishes the essential purposes of the Union.

Number 84 [23]

...Up until now, the business of the United States has occupied the State legislatures as well as Congress. Congress has made requisitions that the State legislatures have had to fulfill. Therefore, the State legislative sessions have been much longer than necessary for the local business of the States. Much of their time is employed in matters that relate to the United States...

Duties, Imposts, and Excises,

Number 12 [5-end]

...most of Britain's national revenue comes from indirect taxes, imposts and excises like import duties.

Clearly, America must depend on revenue from import duties for a long time...

We must adopt a government that will improve and extend our valuable resources. Without a doubt, a general Union is the best system. As this helps commerce, State revenues will increase. A Union simplifies regulations and makes collecting duties easier. All States would charge the same amount of duties. And the government would increase the rate without prejudice to trade.

... If the States separated, duties would have to be low to avoid the temptations of illicit trade...Preventing illicit trade over an inland border is very difficult. If the States disunited, it would be difficult to collect duties. Border patrols would need more powers, powers that are intolerable in a free country.

Most of our foreign commercial transactions are only on one side—the atlantic coast. If the States remain united, there would be only one side to guard... Normal vigilance would prevent most tax evasion. At a small expense, a few armed vessels could be stationed at our ports. And since the national government is interested in preventing violations everywhere, each State would tend to cooperate and make them effective.

One national government could have higher duties on imports than separate States or partial confederacies. Until now, I believe duties have averaged about 3%. In France, they are estimated to be 15% and in Britain, the proportion is still greater.

This country could triple import duties. Under federal regulation, alcohol could be heavily taxed, increasing the government's revenue. The United States imports about four million gallons. A shilling per gallon would produce 200,000 pounds. Alcohol would easily bear this rate. However, if the tax decreased alcohol consumption, it would be equally favorable, favorable to agriculture, the economy, the morals, and the health of society. There is, perhaps, no national extravagance like alcohol.

What will happen if we can't fully use import duties? A nation needs revenue to exist. Without taxes, it must give up its independence and sink into the degraded condition of a province. Therefore, revenue is necessary.

In this country, if commerce isn't taxed, land must be. The people are largely opposed to internal taxation. With agriculture almost the only employment in the States, there are few objects for excise taxes and collections would be limited. Personal property is difficult to trace, so large tax contributions can only be achieved through consumption taxes. In populous cities, people would probably have to pay oppressive personal taxes and little benefit would go to the State. Outside these cities, most assets escape the eye and hand of the tax collector.

Nevertheless, funds must be gathered to pay the government's expenses. When they can't be obtained from any other source, landowners must carry the majority of the burden.

On the other hand, unless all tax sources are available when needed for government finances, the community won't have the money to remain respectable and secure. So we won't even have the consolation of a full treasury to make up for the oppression of farmers. Public and private distress will be equal. And everyone will deplore the foolishness that led to disunion.

Number 30 [6, 7]

Opponents of the new Constitution … say the State governments should have exclusive power to collect *internal* taxes. They want the federal government to use *external* taxation—duties on imported articles…

Import duties alone would never even meet the federal government's current needs. We cannot know its future needs…

federal revenue can't be raised through import taxes alone.

Number 35 [2-4]

Some people argue that the federal taxation power should be limited to import duties. If import taxes were the federal government's only source of revenue, it would frequently want to increase these taxes, which would be injurious. Some people think that import taxes can never be too high because high import taxes discourage extravagant consumption, produce a favorable balance of trade, and promote domestic manufactures. But all extremes cause harm.

Very high taxes on imported articles would increase smuggling. Smuggling hurts honest traders and merchants. And it decreases tax revenue.

High duties also tend to give people who manufacture goods within the country a premature market monopoly. Import taxes creates higher price. Domestic manufactures will be able to charge higher prices than in an open market.

High import taxes can force industry out of its more natural channels into less advantageous areas.

They also oppress merchants that sell imported goods. The merchant, especially in a country with small commercial capital, often must keep prices down to promote sales. To do this, the seller can't raise his price to cover the entire cost of the duty. This reduces or eliminates the merchant's profits and can eat into his business capital.

Usually, the consumer pays the tax duties. Therefore, duties on imports should go into the national treasury rather than be used exclusively by the importing States. But it is not fair that duties should form the only national fund.

When the merchant pays duties, they become an additional tax on the importing State, whose citizens, as consumers, pay the duties. They would produce an inequality among the States that would increase as duties increased.

If import duties were the only source of national revenues, non-manufacturing States would have an unequal tax burden. Citizens in manufacturing States will buy fewer imported articles than non-manufacturing States. Excise taxes would be needed to increase the manufacturing States' contribution to the public treasury. And specific manufactures would be targeted.

The citizens of New York who want to limit the Union to external taxation may not understand the importance of this subject. New York is an importing State. Since New York has a small population in a large territory, the growth of manufacturing will be slow. New York would suffer if the Union were limited to only commercial taxes.

These are some of the reasons for limiting import duties. As mentioned in another paper, there is another reason: if we want the government to be able to collect tax revenue, import taxes must be limited. And import taxes would be limited as long as the government has other resources. But if other taxation avenues were closed, when the government needed more revenue it would increase import taxes and try other experiments like adding penalties. For a while tax revenues would increase—until people found ways to elude the new taxes. Government officials would get the false impression that raising taxes also raises the amount of money going into the federal treasury. This false impression would take a long time to correct. Necessity, especially in politics, often occasions false hopes, false reasoning, and a system of measures correspondingly erroneous.

Number 36 [13]

...the Union has exclusive right to impose ... duties on imports...

Number 41 [22]

Some people believe that the power of federal taxation should be limited to external taxation—taxes on articles imported from other countries. Of course, this will always be a valuable source of revenue. For a long time, in fact, it must be the primary source. And at this moment, it is essential.

However, import tax revenue will vary as the amount and the kind of imports vary. And these variations won't correspond with the growth of our population, which is the general measure of how much money the government will need. As long as agriculture continues to be the only field of labor, as the population increases, the importation of manufactured goods will increase. As the population grows, American manufacturers will employ hands not needed for agriculture and imported manufactured goods will decrease. Eventually, manufacturers may import raw materials that will be made into articles for exportation. As raw material importation overtakes the importation of finished goods, the government will want to encourage imports, not discourage them with import taxes. A good government should remember these cycles and be able to handle them.

Number 56 [6]

Duties on commerce will be the primary form of taxation.

to pay the Debts

Number 10 [1]

...All across the continent, people worry about the nation's debt and they fear of loss of their personal rights...

Number 15 [3]

We are close to total national humiliation. We have experienced nearly everything that can wound the pride or degrade the character of an independent nation:

We violate our commitments. During the war, we borrowed money from foreigners and our own citizens, but we don't have a plan to repay them.

Number 29 [11]

Exaggerations about the militia are examples: ...that we plan to pay our debts to France and Holland with militiamen instead of money.

Number 30 [1, 6, 8, 10]

And the Union must raise revenue for other reasons [including] and future debts,

It is important to public justice and public credit that we pay the current foreign and domestic debt.

Let's assume, for argument's sake, that import duties will be enough to pay our debt and fund the peacetime federal government. Then a war breaks out... During a modern war, even the wealthiest nations need large loans. For a country as poor as ours, loans are necessities. But who would lend to a government that has no reliable method of raising repayment funds? The loans it could get would be the same that loan sharks commonly lend to bankrupt and fraudulent debtors—very small with an enormous interest rate.

If the national government had the authority to raise money through new taxes, it could borrow as much as it might require. Both Americans and foreigners could confidently lend to it.

Number 34 [8]

If we look at the large debt from a single war, we see that there will always be an immense disproportion between federal and State expenditures. Currently, several States have excessive debts because of the war. But if the proposed system is adopted, this cannot happen again. After these debts are paid, State governments will only need revenue to support their civil lists.

Number 38 [9,10]

...The present Congress can...borrow both abroad and at home...

The Western territory... eventually, under proper management, it will help discharge the domestic public debt...

Number 41 [6]

The powers within the *first* class are: ...borrowing money.

Number 43 [22-24]

"All debts contracted and engagements entered into, before the adoption of this Constitution, shall be as valid against the United States under this Constitution, as under the Confederation." [Article 6]

This statement may have been put into the Constitution to satisfy foreign creditors of the United States. Some creditors might worry that a change in our political system has the magical effect of dissolving our moral obligations.

One criticism of the Constitution is that the money owed to the United States should be included, as well as the country's debts. And in the spirit that usually characterizes little critics, the omission has been magnified into a plot against national rights. Most people know that, by their nature, debts are reciprocal. If they are valid on one side, they are valid on the other side. The article is a declaration. By establishing the principle in one case, it applies to every case.

Potential Reasons for Wars Between Disunited States

Number 6 [13]

Holland, until overwhelmed by debt and taxes, led and participated in European wars.

Number 7 [7-8]

The Union's public debt would also cause conflict between the separate States or confederacies. Both the decision about how much each State should pay and paying the debt would produce anger. Some States either don't know the importance of national credit or they don't want to pay the nation's debt. In other States, the nation owes the citizens more than their State's proportion of the national debt.

States that owe money would procrastinate; citizens that are owed money in other States would become resentful. Arguments and excuses would delay making the decision about how much each State should pay. Foreign nations would demand the money owed to them. And the peace of the States would be in double jeopardy from external invasion and internal quarrels.

Suppose a decision about each State's debt payment was made. It would be difficult for some States to pay and they would want their share lowered. The other States would refuse to have their part of the debt increased. Their refusal would give the complaining States an excuse to withhold their contributions, creating bitter arguments.

Even if the division of the debt payment was equal in principle, some States would not pay for several reasons: lack of resources, financial mismanagement, governmental mismanagement, and the reluctance of men to postpone purchases by using money to pay debts.

Delinquencies, from whatever causes, produce complaints, recriminations, and quarrels. Mutual financial obligations that don't yield an equal benefit disturb the tranquility of nations. It is as true as it is trite: men differ over nothing so quickly as the payment of money.

and provide for the common Defence

I will not repeat the quotes that are listed in the Preamble about defense. Be sure to read those quotes to fully understand the important subject of defense. Safety is the first goal of government.

Number 24 [all]

There has been only one specific objection to the federal government creating and directing the national military: the Constitution does not ban standing armies during times of peace.

No logical argument supports this objection. And this is not how most Americans feel. Nor is it the practice of other free nations. Some people want to limit the legislature's authority to establish national military bases.

Armies Not Mandatory

Current newspaper articles give the impression that either the Constitution says that standing armies should be kept up in time of peace or it gives the president the whole power of raising troops without any legislative control.

Only Legislature Can Raise Army

However, neither provision is in the Constitution. The *legislature*, not the *president*, has the power to raise armies. And the legislature's power is limited. Money to support an army can only be appropriated for two years. This precaution becomes security against keeping troops when they are unnecessary.

States Allow Peacetime Armies

Do all the State constitutions prohibit standing armies in peacetime? Only *two* State constitutions prohibit them. The other eleven either say nothing on the subject or allow the legislature to authorize their existence.[*]

No Ban of Peacetime Armies

Are the opponents of the Constitution deliberately lying? Is there a logical reason for the outcry? Do the Articles of Confederation explicitly prohibit a peacetime military?

After a careful study of the Articles of Confederation, his astonishment would increase. It doesn't prohibit a peacetime military. The Articles restrict the authority of States on this subject but there is no restraint on the United States.

A rational man would start believing that a sinister opposition is lying. Why else would they harshly criticize a part of the Constitution that reflects the feelings of America as seen in the Articles of Confederation and State constitutions? The proposed Constitution even has a new, powerful guard that is not in any of the State constitutions.

He would sigh at the weakness of human nature. The opposition seems to want to mislead the people by alarming their passions rather than convince them with arguments addressed to their reason.

Ban Wouldn't Be Observed

Putting a clause in the Constitution that prohibits the legislature from establishing a peacetime military would be improper. And even if society demands it, it probably would not be observed.

Europe, Indians Potential Dangers

Although an ocean separates the United States from Europe, we should not be over-confident of our security. British and Spanish settlements surround us. These two powers own the West India Islands, which creates a common interest. The savage tribes on our Western frontier are our enemies, and England and Spain's allies because they have the most to fear from us and the most to hope from them.

Improved navigation has improved communication. Many distant nations seem like neighbors. Britain and Spain are maritime powers in Europe. A future agreement between them seems probable. The family compacts between France and Spain are be-

---

[*] This is taken from the printed collection of State constitutions. Pennsylvania and North Carolina constitutions say: "As standing armies in time of peace are dangerous to liberty, they ought not to be kept up." This is a caution not a prohibition. New Hampshire, Massachusetts, Delaware, and Maryland each have a clause in their bills of rights, to this effect: "Standing armies are dangerous to liberty, and ought not to be raised or kept up without the consent of the legislature," which admits that the legislature has the authority. New York has no bill of rights and her constitution says nothing about the matter. The other States have no bill of rights and their constitutions are silent. I am told, however, that one or two States have bills of rights that are not in this collection and they recognize the legislative authority in this respect. –Publius

coming weaker every day. We must not be over confident, thinking we are entirely out of the reach of danger.

Protection Needed on Borders

Since before the Revolution, small military forts on our Western frontier have been necessary. They are indispensable, if only for protection against the plundering of the Indians. Occasionally, the forts must get more military personnel either militia or federal army soldiers.

Using militia members is impractical and dangerous. Citizens would eventually refuse to leave their jobs and families to perform the most disagreeable duty in times of peace. Even if they could be forced, frequently calling up the militia would be expensive. And losing the commercial and farm labor force would injure both the public and private citizens.

A permanent army paid by the government amounts to a standing army in peace-time–a small one, indeed, but no less real for being small. A constitutional prohibition to a standing army is improper. The legislature should decide when an army is needed.

Border Needs Will Increase

As our strength increases, Britain and Spain will increase their military strength around us. If we don't want to be defenseless, we will need to increase our frontier garrisons as our Western settlements increase. Some military posts will serve large districts of territory. Some posts will also be important to trade with the Indian nations. Leaving them vulnerable to seizure by such powerful neighbors would be imprudent.

Navy will Replace Some Garrisons

We must form a navy. It is necessary for our commerce and safety along our Atlantic coast. We will need forts and soldiers to defend our dockyards and arsenals. A powerful navy can protect its dockyards without additional soldiers. Until our navy is fully established, moderate garrisons will be an indispensable security against destructive attacks on arsenals and dockyards, and sometimes the fleet itself.

Number 25 [all]

Some people say the States should provide armies, under the direction of the federal government. However, the primary purpose of our combining to form a confederacy under a federal government is defense. If States held the military power, it would oppress some States, be dangerous to all, and harmful to the Confederacy.

Danger of Making Defense State Duty

The territories of Britain, Spain, and the Indian nations do not border specific States. They encircle the Union. To differing degrees, all of the States are in danger. Therefore, the national government and treasury should be responsible for defense.

Some States are exposed to more danger, including New York. If the States had to provide for their own defense, New York would carry the whole burden of her immediate safety and, ultimately, the protection of her neighbors. This would not be fair to New York or safe for other States.

The States who need military posts won't be willing or able to support a military for a long time. Therefore, national security would depend on the stinginess, lack of foresight, or inability of one State.

On the other hand, if a State had the men and money, it would increase its military spending proportionately. If two or three powerful States held the whole military force of the Union, the other States would be alarmed. They would take counter measures. Military establishments, nourished by mutual jealousy, would swell. The State armies would destroy the national authority.

State Military a Danger to Liberty

State and federal governments are rivals because all governments love power. In a dispute between the federal government and a State, people will probably support their local government. If the State had military forces, it would be tempted to challenge and subvert the constitutional authority of the Union.

The people's liberty would be less safe. An army is a dangerous weapon of power; it is better if the targets of envy control it. History proves that people are in the most danger when a group or individual they least suspect have the ability to injure their rights.

State Military Would Be Dangerous

Separate State military forces are dangerous to the Union. Under the Articles of Confederation, Congress must approve State ships or troops. Both federal and State governments cannot have armies.

Can't Enforce Peace Military Ban

Improper restraints on the national legislature create problems. Some people object to standing armies during peacetime. But how far should the prohibition extend? Will it ban raising armies, as well as, to *keeping them up* in time of tranquility?

A prohibition that only limits keeping armies isn't specific and will not fulfill the purpose intended. Once armies are raised, what does the constitution mean by "keeping them up?" How much time would be a violation? A week, a month, a year? Or may they continue as long as there is a danger?

This means they can be kept up *in time of peace*, if there are threats or impending danger. This is different than the literal meaning of the prohibition. Who will judge that the danger continues? The national government can first raise troops, then keep them as long as the peace or safety of the community is in jeopardy. The provision could be easily ignored.

Excuses to Fortify Military

Some people want a constitutional ban of peacetime armies. They believe it would stop executive and legislature conspiracies to use the military to take over the government. However, even if the constitution banned peacetime armies, the conspirators could claim there is an approaching danger! Indian hostilities would always be an excuse. Or they could provoke a foreign power into looking like a threat, and then appease it with concessions. If such a conspiracy happened, the army could be raised—using any pretext—and used in the usurpation scheme.

Peacetime Army Ban, Union Defenseless

If the constitution prohibits the *raising* of armies in time of peace, the United States would be in the strangest situation ever seen—a nation that cannot prepare for its defense before it was actually invaded. The government couldn't begin drafting men until an enemy was physically within our borders. The nation couldn't prepare for a danger. Our property and liberty would be exposed to foreign invaders. They could capture us because we were afraid that rulers—elected by us and ruling according to our will—might endanger our liberty by abusing the power necessary to defend us.

Militia Insufficient National Defense

Depending on the country's militia—armed citizens—to defend the nation nearly lost us our independence. And it cost our country millions that could have been saved. The militia can't be our only defense. We must have a regular, disciplined army to defend against other disciplined armies.

The militia's valor during the recent war erected eternal monuments to their fame. But the bravest of them know that they could not have established the liberty of their country alone. Like most things, war is a science that is perfected by diligence, perseverance, time, and practice.

Penn, Mass Peacetime Military

All distorted policies defeat themselves because they don't follow the way people behave. Pennsylvania is a current example. Its Bill of Rights says that standing armies are dangerous to liberty and should not be kept up in peacetime. Nevertheless, during this time of peace, Pennsylvania has used disorders in one or two counties as an excuse to raise troops. And the troops will probably remain as long as there is any appearance of danger to the public peace.

Massachusetts is another example. Under the Articles, States are supposed to get Congressional approval before raising troops. Massachusetts didn't wait for that approval. It raised troops to put down a domestic rebellion. And it keeps a corps to prevent a revival of the revolt. This is instructive. Every government has similar problems and might need the military for internal security. Therefore, legislative discretion to raise and keep armies should not be controlled.

The Massachusetts example teaches us that States do not respect the rights of a weak government. And it teaches us that when there is a choice between written provisions and public necessity, public necessity wins.

Ignoring Laws Weakens Government

It was a basic maxim of the ancient Lacedaemonian commonwealth that no one could serve as their navy's commander-in-chief twice. Lysander had served, and then stepped down. However, after an ally was defeated at sea by the Athenians, Athens demanded that Lysander command the combined fleets. The Lacedaemonians wanted to fulfill their ally's wish and also obey their own law. They gave Lysander the power of the naval commander-in-chief but called him a sub-commander-in-chief.

I could give many examples confirming this truth. Nations ignore rules and maxims that, in their very nature, run counter to the necessities of society.

Wise politicians don't want to create constitutional restrictions that might need to be ignored. Every time a constitution is disobeyed, even if necessary, decreases the reverence that rulers should maintain towards it. And it creates a precedent for other breaches when a necessity does not exist or is less urgent.

Number 26 [2-end]

Balancing Liberty, Public Safety

The legislature will authorize national defense. Some people want to limit this authority. This idea comes from false beliefs about liberty rather than knowledge.

Pennsylvania and North Carolina have tried to limit the legislature's power to authorize armed forces. The other States refuse to consider it. The people delegate power to the government. Therefore, the people must place their confidence in that government. It is better to take the chance that their confidence will be abused than endanger the public safety with impractical limits on the legislature's authority. Unlike the opponents of the proposed Constitution, the majority of Americans agree that the legislature must have full authority to authorize military forces.

We can safely correct the imbalances in our governmental system. But opponents of the Constitution want more dangerous imbalances. If the principles they support became accepted, the people of this country would be utterly unfit for any type of government whatever. But Americans are too intelligent to be persuaded into anarchy. The public firmly believes that greater government energy is essential to the welfare and prosperity of the community.

Origin of No Peacetime Military

Where did the idea of excluding military establishments during peacetime start? Probably England, the country of origin of most Americans.

For a long time after the Norman Conquest [1066], the English monarch's authority was almost unlimited. Gradually, liberty made inroads into the monarch's power, first by barons and later by the people, until the monarch lost most of his power and importance.

King Charles II [1661-1685] kept a body of 5,000 troops during peacetime. King James II [1685-1688] increased the number to 30,000. Finally, after the revolution in 1688, Prince William of Orange became king of Great Britain and English liberty triumphanted. The Bill of Rights limited his authority. It said "the raising or keeping a standing army within the Kingdom in time of peace, *unless with the consent of Parliament*, was against the law."

Power Must Equal Possible Emergencies

Liberty was at its highest peak in Britain. But the only security against the danger of standing armies was the prohibition against the monarch raising and keeping them.

The revolutionary patriots were well informed. They didn't want to restrain the legislature's discretion. They knew that a certain number of troops are indispensable. National emergencies can't be limited. A power equal to every possible scenario must exist somewhere in the government. By giving the legislature this power, they found the balancing point between precaution and the safety of the community.

States: Legislatures Raise Military

From this history, the people of America learned that standing armies in peacetime could endanger liberty. The revolution made us zealous protectors of our liberty. In some cases, our desire to protect our civil rights went further than is practical. Two States tried to restrict legislative authority over military establishments. A monarch's power must be feared. However, the over-reaction by these States extended this fear to the people's representatives. Some States didn't make this error but they have unnecessarily declared that standing armies are not to be kept up in peacetime without the consent of the legislature. There is a similar provision in the English Bill of Rights. But the States don't have the same reason for the provision. Under the State constitutions, only the legislatures have the power to raise armies. So, it was superfluous to declare that it should not be done without the consent of a body, which alone had the power of doing it. The other State constitutions are silent on the subject.

No State Prohibits Military in Peacetime

Two State constitutions seem to prohibit the military. However, they say an army *ought not* be kept up, not that armies *shall not be* kept up in time of peace. This ambiguity seems to result from the conflict between totally excluding them and the belief that an absolute exclusion would be unsafe.

When a situation arises, the legislature will interpret the clause as only an admonition and yield to the real or imagined needs of the State. Pennsylvania is an example. The provision is useless if the legislature can just ignore it whenever they want to.

Ban v. 2-Year Appropriations

Some people want to ban all military during times of peace. The proposed Constitution limits military appropriations to a two-year period. A peacetime military ban tries to do too much and will not be obeyed; a two-year appropriation provides for emergencies and will be a powerful remedy.

Politicians, States Guard Against Abuse

At least once in every two years the United States legislature will be *forced* to decide whether to keep a military force and declare their position by a formal, public vote. They cannot give the president unlimited funds for an army.

A partisan spirit infects all political bodies. Funding a military force will always be a favorite topic to denounce. As often as the question arises, the opposition party will publicly argue about it. If the majority party wants to appropriate more money than seems proper to support the military for two years, the community will be warned and be able to take measures to guard against it.

People will debate the issue. State legislatures will jealously guard the citizens' rights against encroachments from the federal government. If national rulers act improperly, they will sound the alarm. State legislatures will be the voice and, if necessary, the arm of the people's discontent.

Subvert Liberty: Executive, Legislative Collusion

Schemes to subvert liberty *require time* to develop before taking action. A large army would be needed to threaten our liberties. The legislature and executive would have to conspire for a long time.

Would this happen? Would every man elected to the national Senate or House of Representatives instantly become a traitor to his constituents and his country? Would not one man be able to see the atrocious conspiracy, or bold or honest enough to tell his constituents of their danger?

If we assume that this could happen, there should be no more delegated authority. The people should take back the powers already given the government and divide themselves into as many States as there are counties so they can manage their government in person.

Military Expansion in Peace

Concealing such a conspiracy for long would be impractical. People would see a fast growing army during peacetime. Following the discovery, the people would quickly destroy the project and its sponsors.

Reason Needed to Build Military Force

Some people say limiting military appropriations to the period of two years won't be safe. They say that once the president has a large enough military to force the people into submission, it would also be large enough to get supplies without help from the legislature.

But what pretense could the President use to build a big military force in peacetime? If it was created in response to a domestic insurrection or foreign war, it can't be called a peacetime military buildup. Military forces should be raised to stop a rebellion or resist an invasion. If defense of the community makes it necessary to have an army large enough to threaten its liberty, this is one of those calamities that can't be prevented or cured. No form of government can provide against this.) It might even happen in a simple league, if the allies need to form an army for common defense.

Military Expands If States Separate

However, this evil is infinitely less likely to happen to us if we are united than if we are disunited. It is hard to imagine dangers formidable enough to attack the whole nation, demanding a force large enough to place our liberties in jeopardy, especially when we remember that the militia should always be counted on as a valuable and powerful addition to the military. But in a state of disunion, the contrary of this supposition would be almost unavoidable.

and general Welfare of the United States;

Number 23 [7]

...The Articles of Confederation authorized the federal government to command all resources that are necessary for the "common defense and general welfare." The authors of the Articles assumed that the States would be aware of their best interests and duty to the Union and they would fill the federal requisitions.

Number 41 [23-end]

...Some people have attacked the language that defines the taxation power, saying it amounts to an unlimited license to use any and every power that may be alleged to be necessary for the common defense or general welfare.

Stooping to such a misconstruction proves how far these writers will reach to find objections to the Constitution.

If "to raise money for the general welfare" was the only definition of Congressional powers in the Constitution, the critics might have a reason for the objection. However, the specific congressional powers are listed after the general phrase. Nothing is more natural than to first use a general phrase and then to explain and qualify it by a recital of particulars.

The objection seems even odder because the language in the Constitution appears to be a copy of the Articles of Confederation. The objective of forming a Union among the States, as described in Article Three, is "their common defense, security of their liberties, and mutual and general welfare." Article eight says: "All charges of war and all other expenses that shall be incurred for the common defense or general welfare, and allowed by the United States in Congress, shall be defrayed out of a common treasury," etc. Similar language again occurs in Article Nine.

If we interpret these articles in the Articles of Confederation by the rules objectors have used on the new Constitution, the existing Congress has the power to legislate about everything. But what if Congress disregarded the specifications that define and limit the general expressions and exercised an unlimited power of providing for the common defense and general welfare? Would the people making the objections have employed the same reasoning in justification of Congress as they now make against the Convention. How difficult it is for error to escape its own condemnation!

Number 45 [2]

A government's value is judged by how it fulfills the public good and meets the needs of the people. If the Constitution harmed public happiness, I would say: Reject the plan. If the Union hurt public happiness, I would say: Abolish the Union.

Number 45 [11]

...Currently, Congress may REQUIRE MONEY from the States for the common defense and general welfare. Under the Constitution, the future Congress will require the same amount from individual citizens...

but all Duties, Imposts, and Excises shall be uniform throughout the United States;

Number 36 [9]

...the national government can't be partial or oppressive to some States. It would be difficult to abuse the taxation power. There is also a provision that "all duties, imposts, and excises shall be uniform throughout the United States."

To borrow money on the credit of the United States;

Number 12 [3]

…Germany is fertile, cultivated and populous. And it has the best gold and silver mines in Europe. But the monarch's revenues are limited because the country doesn't support commerce. Several times he's been compelled to borrow money from other nations. And he is unable, using his own resources, to sustain a long war.

Number 30 [10]

If the national government had the authority to raise money through new taxes, it could borrow as much as it might require. Both Americans and foreigners could confidently lend to it…

Number 38 [9]

… It can borrow both abroad and at home.

Number 41 [22]

The power to levy taxes and borrow money—the financial support for national defense—has also been examined. The extent and form in the Constitution is necessary…

To regulate Commerce

Number 6 [8,14,16-17]

Despite history, some dreamers—or men who want to increase their personal power—make the false claim that if the States disunite, they will always be peaceful. They say republics are naturally peaceful. They claim that commerce softens men, extinguishing the hot emotions that so often start wars. They say commercial republics will not waste themselves in ruinous wars with each other, but will promote peaceful relationships.

Britain has been commercial for a long time. And one branch of the national legislature—the House of Commons—represent the people. Nevertheless, few nations have been in more wars, frequently started by the people.

The desire to protect or increase trade has influenced the wars of England and France.

A recent war between Britain and Spain started because British merchants were trading illegally with the Spanish Main. The Spaniards cruelly retaliated against British citizens. After a while, both the innocent and guilty were punished. English merchants complained, spreading the desire for violence through the nation, the House of Commons, and the ministry. Letters of reprisal were granted and war started. Consequently, the alliances formed only 20 years before, with hopes of long-term peace, were overthrown.

Number 11 [1] (see all of **Number 11** page 194)

Everyone who has considered the subject, believes that staying united is important to our commerce. The benefits apply to both trade with foreign countries and trade among the States.

Number 23 [9]

We need a compound or confederate government instead of a simple, single government. The responsibilities of each branch of power must be determined. And each branch must have enough authority to fulfill its responsibilities... The same is true for commerce and every other area under its jurisdiction.

Number 34 [4]

We must be able to defend our commerce.

Union Promotes Revenue/National Wealth

Number 11 [8-9]

If we disunite, European alliances might be successful. Nations with a powerful navy could dictate the conditions of our political existence.

They'd want to carry our products and prevent us from becoming their shipper. They'd probably form alliances, destroy our navigation, and confine us to passive commerce. We would have to accept the first price for our commodities. Our profits would be snatched from us to enrich our enemies and persecutors would get our profits. American merchants and navigators have an unequaled spirit of enterprise and an inexhaustible mine of national wealth. It would be stifled and lost. Poverty and disgrace would spread across a country that could have been the envy of the world.

Our Union has some very important trade rights, especially the fisheries and the navigation of Western lakes and the Mississippi. If the Union dissolved, the future of these rights would come into question. Spain's attitude towards the Mississippi needs no comment. France and Britain view our fisheries as important to their navigation. Since we can undersell those nations in their own markets, they would ban our dangerous competition.

Number 12 [all]

Staying united will promote American prosperity and wealth.

Commerce produces the most national wealth. Therefore, it's an important political concern.

The desire to make money, the object of human avarice and enterprise, energizes industry. The hard-working merchant, farmer, mechanic, and manufacturer look forward to this reward for their work.

Farmers and merchants used to be rivals but now their interests are interwoven. Commerce increases land values, improves the movement of agricultural products, stimulates the cultivation of land, and increases the quantity of money in a State. Therefore, commerce helps agriculture, and agriculture creates many commercial products. It's astonishing that some people didn't agree with this simple truth. Jealousy can lead men astray from the plainest truths.

A country's ability to pay taxes is related to the quantity and turnover of money in circulation. Commerce contributes to these objectives, making payment of taxes easier.

Germany is fertile, cultivated and populous. And it has the best gold and silver mines in Europe. But the monarch's revenues are limited because the country doesn't support commerce. Several times he's been compelled to borrow money from other nations. And he is unable, using his own resources, to sustain a long war.

In America, direct taxation is impractical. Despite new tax laws and new collection methods, the States' treasuries remain empty. When trade decreases, money becomes scarce. Extensive tax collections have been impossible. And the State legislatures have learned the folly of attempting them.

Similar situations happen in other countries. In Britain, a rich nation, direct taxes are easier to collect. And the vigorous British government makes it more practical than in America. Yet most of Britain's national revenue comes from indirect taxes, imposts and excises like import duties.

Clearly, America must depend on revenue from import duties for a long time. The people find excise taxes intrusive and dictatorial. Farmers will pay only very limited taxes on their houses and lands. Personal property is such an invisible asset, it can be taxed only through the imperceptible agency of taxes on consumption.

We must adopt a government that will improve and extend our valuable resources. Without a doubt, a general Union is the best system. As this helps commerce, State revenues will increase. A Union simplifies regulations and makes collecting duties easier. All States would charge the same amount of duties. And the government would increase the rate without prejudice to trade.

The closeness of the States, the intersecting rivers, the bays, the ease of communication in every direction, the same language and manners, and similar commercial habits make illicit trade easy. The commercial regulations of each State are frequently evaded.

If the States separated, duties would have to be low to avoid the temptations of illicit trade. European nations guard the land and water avenues into their countries. France uses more than twenty thousand army troops to enforce their commercial regulations against contraband. Yet people still find ways to smuggle goods.

Preventing illicit trade over an inland border is very difficult. If the States disunited, it would be difficult to collect duties. Border patrols would need more powers, powers that are intolerable in a free country.

Most of our foreign commercial transactions are only on one side—the atlantic coast. If the States remain united, there would be only one side to guard. When vessels filled with valuable cargoes arrive from foreign countries, they would rarely choose the danger of unloading prior to coming into port. They would fear the dangers of both the coastal waters and being discovered by government officials. Normal vigilance would prevent most tax evasion. At a small expense, a few armed vessels could be stationed at our ports. And since the national government is interested in preventing violations everywhere, each State would tend to cooperate and make them effective.

In this respect, too, the Union has an advantage over separated States. The United States are a great distance from Europe and all other places with extensive foreign trade. If the States became separate nations, international shipping time would be reduced to a few hours or overnight, as between France and Britain. This would eliminate our natural security against direct contraband with foreign countries. Contraband could easily and safely travel through one State to another. The difference between direct importation and indirect, through a neighboring State in small parcels, is obvious.

One national government could have higher duties on imports than separate States or partial confederacies. Until now, I believe duties have averaged about 3%. In France, they are estimated to be 15% and in Britain, the proportion is still greater.

This country could triple import duties. Under federal regulation, alcohol could be heavily taxed, increasing the government's revenue. The United States imports about four million gallons. A shilling per gallon would produce 200,000 pounds. Alcohol would easily bear this rate. However, if the tax decreased alcohol consumption, it would be equally favorable, favorable to agriculture, the economy, the morals, and the health of society. There is, perhaps, no national extravagance like alcohol.

What will happen if we can't fully use import duties? A nation needs revenue to exist. Without taxes, it must give up its independence and sink into the degraded condition of a province. Therefore, revenue is necessary.

In this country, if commerce isn't taxed, land must be. The people are largely opposed to internal taxation. With agriculture almost the only employment in the States, there are few objects for excise taxes and collections would be limited. Personal property is difficult to trace, so large tax contributions can only be achieved through consumption taxes. In populous cities, people would probably have to pay oppressive personal taxes and little benefit would go to the State. Outside these cities, most assets escape the eye and hand of the tax collector.

Nevertheless, funds must be gathered to pay the government's expenses. When they can't be obtained from any other source, landowners must carry the majority of the burden.

On the other hand, unless all tax sources are available when needed for government finances, the community won't have the money to remain respectable and secure. So we won't even have the consolation of a full treasury to make up for the oppression of farmers. Public and private distress will be equal. And everyone will deplore the foolishness that led to disunion.

Number 14 [1]

We have seen that we need a Union: … to guard our commerce…

Number 15 [3]

…Commerce is important to our national wealth; ours has totally deteriorated…

Number 17 [1]

…People who want power are interested in commerce, finance, negotiation, and war. And the national government should have all these powers…

Number 21 [6-7]

There is no one standard to measure the degrees of national wealth. Land values and population numbers have been suggested as ways to determine each State's quota. But neither truly represents the State's wealth.

For example, let's compare the wealth of the United Netherlands to Russia, Germany, or France. There is no relationship between their wealth and their land value and population. The United Netherlands has the higher wealth; the three other nations have immense land and much larger populations.

We can compare American States in the same way and get a similar result. Compare Virginia with North Carolina, Pennsylvania with Connecticut, or Maryland with New Jersey. Their comparative wealth has little relationship to their lands and populations. Counties within New York State illustrate the same thing. If either land value or population is the criterion, the active wealth of King's County is much greater than that of Montgomery County.

An infinite variety of causes create a nation's wealth. They include location, soil, climate, products, the type of government, the genius of its citizens, knowledge, commerce, arts, and industry. And there are many more causes that are too complex to quantify. These combine to create differences in the relative wealth of different countries. There is no common measure of national wealth. And there is no way to measure a State's ability to pay taxes. Therefore, trying to calculate each State's quota by using a rule based on land or population would be glaringly unequal and extremely oppressive.

Number 22 [2]

Currently, the federal government has no power to regulate commerce. But we must have federal regulation of commerce.

Number 23 [3]

…The most important reasons for a union and federal government are:

- Defense.
- To keep the peace against both internal turmoil and external attacks.
- To regulate commerce with other nations and between the States.
- To supervise our political and commercial interests with foreign countries.

Number 42 [11]

…one of the convention objectives—and the people expected—that the national government would regulate trade so it would be an immediate source of general revenue. Congress said that federal trade regulations are consistent with the fundamental principles of the Confederacy…

Number 45 [11]

The regulation of commerce is a new power. But few people seem to oppose it.

Number 60 [9]

…commerce is very important to both public prosperity and revenue to government… Commerce is so important that Congress will not make merchants angry. As public needs become apparent, Congress will need their help.

Number 62 [16-17]

There is another effect of having laws that are not stable. It gives the few perceptive, enterprising, and wealthy citizens an advantage over the industrious and uninformed mass of people.

Every new regulation about commerce or revenue or that affects property value is a new opportunity to those people who watch the change and can predict its consequences. They don't create this opportunity. It is created by the toils and cares of the great body of their fellow citizens. When this happens, it may truthfully be said that laws are made for the *few*, not for the *many*.

An unstable government also hurts the economy.) When people don't know what actions the government might take, projects where success and profit may depend on the existing laws continuing will be discouraged.

What prudent merchant will jeopardize his fortunes in a new area of commerce when he doesn't know if his plans may be made unlawful before they can be executed? What farmer or manufacturer will commit himself to a specific cultivation or project when he can't be sure that his preparations and investment will not make him a victim to an inconstant government?

In a word, if an improvement or praiseworthy enterprise needs the protection or security of a consistent national policy, it will not be pursued.

Number 64 [6]

Trade and navigation regulations should be cautiously formed and steadily pursued. Both treaties and laws should support trade and navigation. Conformity should be carefully maintained. This is supported by making the Senate agree to both treaties and laws.

Defects in Articles of Confederation, commerce

Number 22 [1-4]

The existing federal system is unfit to administer the Union and it has several more defects.

Currently, the federal government has no power to regulate commerce. But we must have federal regulation of commerce. We haven't been able to have good commercial treaties with other nations. Since the States have been arguing about commerce, no nation will sign a commercial treaty with the United States. They know that individual States could violate the treaty at any time. Besides, they already have every advantage in our markets without giving us any in return except when it is convenient.

In England, Mr. Jenkinson introduced a bill in the British House of Commons to temporarily regulate commerce between our two countries. He declared that earlier bills with similar provisions answered Great Britain's commercial needs. He said that they shouldn't change their policies until the American government became more consistent.

Some States have tried to change Great Britain's commercial policies by limiting or prohibiting some British products. But different States have different restrictions. We won't be able to influence Great Britain's commercial conduct until we have one federal authority and one commercial policy.

Contrary to the true spirit of the Union, some State regulations hurt the commerce in other States. Without national control, there will be more of these policies and anger between the States will grow, further damaging commerce.

The Encyclopaedia[1] ("Empire") describes Germany's commercial situation. Each German prince taxes the merchandise that travels through his state. The wide variety of taxes within Germany has put commerce in constant turmoil. And shippers have to stop and pay taxes so many times along the commercial routes that they don't even bother using Germany's navigable rivers.

This description may never completely apply to us. But as each State makes different commercial regulations, citizens of one State will treat citizens of other States no better than foreigners and aliens.

Number 42 [11-13]

The existing Confederacy doesn't have the power to regulate commerce between the States. Without this provision, the power to regulate foreign commerce is pointless.

---

[1] The article title is "Empire."

Some noncommercial States must import and export through other States. If they could, States would charge import and export taxes on merchandise and material passing through their State. This would create animosities and probably end in violence.

Commercial States' desire to collect indirect taxes from their uncommercial neighbors must seem both unfair and politically inexpedient. It would be a poor political decision. Resentment and self-interest would make the people who have to pay the State duties find longer routes without the added taxes for their trade. However, as a State makes the decision to tax goods that travel through it, the people who want immediate revenue will drown out the people who rationally argue that it is a bad political decision. The mild voice of reason, pleading the cause of a larger interest, is drowned out by the clamors of impatient avarice for immediate and immoderate gain.

The experience in other countries shows that the federal government needs to be able to regulate trade between the States.

In Switzerland, each canton [state] must allow merchandise passage through its jurisdiction into other cantons without additional tolls.

A law in Germany forbids the princes and states from charging tolls or customs on bridges, rivers, or passages without the consent of the emperor and the diet [legislature]. However, this law, like many others in the Germany, hasn't been followed, producing the problems predicted here.

In the Union of the Netherlands, states must get permission to charge imposts that are disadvantageous to neighboring states.

The provision in the Articles of Confederation for regulating commerce with the Indian tribes is obscure and contradictory. It says that the federal power to regulate trade is limited to Indians who are not members of any State, without violating the rights of any State within its own borders. But federal councils haven't determined which Indians are members of a State and which are not. And how can an external authority regulate trade with Indians, who live in a State but are not members of the State, without intruding on the internal rights of a State?

In several areas, the Articles of Confederation tries to do impossible things. One is giving the Union partial sovereignty while giving the States complete sovereignty.

This subverts a mathematical axiom: it takes away a part, yet lets the whole remain.

with foreign Nations

Number 3 [6]

Just causes for war include treaty violations and direct violence, attack or invasion. America already has treaties with at least six nations. All, except Prussia, have navies that could injure us. We have extensive commerce with Portugal, Spain, and Britain. Spain and Britain also have neighboring territory.

Number 4 [4-9]

France, England and America catch and sell fish. But America can sell fish in France and England at a cheaper price than their own fishermen. To try to stop us, their governments pay rewards to their fishermen and tax the American fish.

Our boats also compete with European nations in cargo transport. They don't want to see our transportation business increase because it decreases theirs. It's in their interest to limit our trade, not promote it.

Our trade with China and India has reduced the profits of several nations. We now directly import items that we used to purchase through a monopoly.

Any nation with territories on or near this continent can't be happy about our commercial growth. Our products are cheap and excellent. Our convenient location gives our hard-working merchants and ships advantages in those territories, to the displeasure of Europe.

Spain doesn't allow our boats on the Mississippi river. Britain doesn't allow our ships on the Saint Lawrence River. And neither permits commercial ships on the other waterways that flow between them and us.

For these—and some other reasons—other nations may become jealous and afraid of us. They will worry about our advancement in union and power, land and sea.

Number 5 [10]

...Different commercial concerns create different interests and different political alliances with different foreign nations...

Number 6 [9-14, 17]

...Commerce only changes the objects of war. The love of wealth is as strong a passion as power and glory. Commercial motives have started as many wars as the desire for territory.

Athens and Carthage were commercial republics, yet they often fought wars. Sparta, another republic, was little more than an army camp. And the Roman republic never got tired of war and conquest.

More recently, Venice was in several wars of ambition. Finally, Pope Julius II founded the League of Cambray that defeated Venice.

Holland, until overwhelmed by debt and taxes, led and participated in European wars. They fought England for control of the sea. And they were opponents of Louis XIV.

Britain has been commercial for a long time. And one branch of the national legislature—the House of Commons—represent the people. Nevertheless, few nations have been in more wars, frequently started by the people.

A recent war between Britain and Spain started because British merchants were trading illegally with the Spanish Main. The Spaniards cruelly retaliated against British citizens. After a while, both the innocent and guilty were punished. English merchants complained, spreading the desire for violence through the nation, the House of Commons, and the ministry. Letters of reprisal were granted and war started. Consequently, the alliances formed only 20 years before, with hopes of long-term peace, were overthrown.

Number 10 [8]

...Should foreign manufacturers be restricted to support domestic manufacturers? Landowners would say no; manufacturers would say yes. Neither would probably use justice and the public good as their only guide...

Number 64 [3]

The power to make treaties is important. It relates to war, peace, and commerce.

Number 69 [11]
> The President of the United States... cannot regulate the commerce...

Benefits of Strong Union to American Commerce

Number 11 [all]

Everyone who has considered the subject, believes that staying united is important to our commerce. The benefits apply to both trade with foreign countries and trade among the States.

America's adventurous commercial spirit worries several naval powers in Europe. They worry that we will cut into their shipping trade, which supports their naval strength.

Some nations have colonies in North America. Those nations worry about our abilities. If we stay united and have the resources to create a powerful navy, we will be a threat to their American colonies.

Europe will encourage disagreements between States. This could deprive us of an ACTIVE COMMERCE in our own ships. Therefore, we could not interfere in European navigation; Europe would get the major profits from our trade and keep us from being a dangerously powerful nation. We would probably be able to trace Europe's policy of limiting our commerce to its governments.

If we remain united, we can counteract policies that hurt our prosperity. National regulations may force foreign countries to bid against each other for our markets. Our market of three million people—with a fast growing population of farmers—is important to any manufacturing nation. Our trade and shipping will be very different if we use our own ships rather than be forced to use the ships of another country to bring products to and from America.

For example: We currently have no commerce treaty with Great Britain. Suppose the American government could exclude Great Britain from all our ports. How would this affect her politics? Couldn't we negotiate valuable commercial rights from her?

Some people say that prohibitions would not change our trade with Britain because she could use the Dutch to continue trading with us. Holland would buy and transport British goods to our markets. But British navigation would be seriously hurt and the Dutch would get the primary profits. Paying for freight would reduce Britain's profit. The British circuitous supply line would encourage competition among other nations, increasing the price of British commodities in our markets.

This would hurt Britain. And since Britain trades with America and the West India Islands, Britain would relax her present system.

A federal navy would influence European commerce. If the Union continues, it will create a navy. It might not be a great navy but it could change the outcome of a struggle if it allied with either side of a conflict, especially in the West Indies. A few ships, helping either side, could decide the fate of a campaign that had halted trade. We could bargain for commercial privileges and sell supplies. We could become the arbiter of Europe in America.

But if we disunite, the rivalries between us will produce a stalemate, frustrating our great natural advantages. Warring nations will meddle with our commerce. They'll plunder our property. Neutrality is respected only when defended by adequate power; a weak nation forfeits even the privilege of being neutral.

European alliances could restrain our growth. However, if we have a strong national government, they would be less successful. Europe would be less likely to make the alliances. We would create an active commerce, extensive navigation, and a flourishing navy.

If we disunite, European alliances might be successful. Nations with a powerful navy could dictate the conditions of our political existence.

They'd want to carry our products and prevent us from becoming their shipper. They'd probably form alliances, destroy our navigation, and confine us to passive commerce. We would have to accept the first price for our commodities. Our profits would be snatched from us to enrich our enemies and persecutors would get our profits. American merchants and navigators have an unequaled spirit of enterprise and an inexhaustible mine of national wealth. It would be stifled and lost. Poverty and disgrace would spread across a country that could have been the envy of the world.

Our Union has some very important trade rights, especially the fisheries and the navigation of Western lakes and the Mississippi. If the Union dissolved, the future of these rights would come into question. Spain's attitude towards the Mississippi needs no comment. France and Britain view our fisheries as important to their navigation. Since we can undersell those nations in their own markets, they would ban our dangerous competition.

Commerce will improve our navigation. This resource will help when we build a navy.

A navy. Staying united will support this great national objective. Every institution grows and flourishes in proportion to the amount of resources put towards its formation and support.

It will be easier for the United States to create a navy than any single State or small confederacy. Different areas of the country have different resources. The southern States have naval stores—tar, pitch, and turpentine. Their wood is more solid and lasting. Some southern and middle States have high quality iron. The northern States will supply most of the seamen.

Naval protection of our commerce is important; maritime commerce will help our navy.

Unrestrained commerce between the States will advance trade. The free circulation of commodities will replenish the veins of commerce. The States will have a diversity of products. When the staple of one State fails from a bad harvest, it can get the staple of another.

Both the variety and value of export products contribute to an active foreign commerce. Trade competitions and market fluctuations are a part of foreign commerce. Our commerce will be more profitable if we have a large variety of products of a given value than a small number of the same value. Some products may be in great demand at certain periods and unwanted at others. But if there were a variety of products, rarely would they all be unwanted.

Speculative traders understand that this analysis is valid. The total commerce of the United States would be better than that of 13 separate States or several small confederacies.

Some people may argue that whether the States are united or disunited, interstate commerce would achieve the same ends. But disunity would hurt commerce. Unified commercial and political interests can only be achieved through a unified government.

We should aim for a position of dominance in American affairs.

The world is politically and geographically divided into four parts. Each part has a distinct set of interests. Unhappily for the other three, Europe, using arms and negotiations, by force and fraud, has extended her dominion, to varying degrees, over them all. Africa, Asia and America have successively felt her domination. Europe's superiority has tempted her to crown herself Mistress of the World, considering the rest of mankind as created for her benefit.

Some philosophers say Europeans are physically superior. And they have gravely asserted that all animals, including humans, degenerate in America. They say that even dogs cease to bark after breathing our air for a while.

For too long, facts have supported these European pretensions. We must save the honor of the human race and teach Europe moderation. As a Union, we can do it. Disunion will add another victim to Europe's triumphants.

Let Americans refuse to be European pawns! Let the 13 States, as a Union, erect one great American system that controls all transatlantic force or influence, and dictate how the old and new world will be connected.

Number 12 [10]

Most of our foreign commercial transactions are only on one side—the atlantic coast. If the States remain united, there would be only one side to guard. When vessels filled with valuable cargoes arrive from foreign countries, they would rarely choose the danger of unloading prior to coming into port. They would fear the dangers of both the coastal waters and being discovered by government officials. Normal vigilance would prevent most tax evasion. At a small expense, a few armed vessels could be stationed at our ports. And since the national government is interested in preventing violations everywhere, each State would tend to cooperate and make them effective.

In this respect, too, the Union has an advantage over separated States. The United States are a great distance from Europe and all other places with extensive foreign trade. If the States became separate nations, international shipping time would be reduced to a few hours or overnight, as between France and Britain. This would eliminate our natural security against direct contraband with foreign countries. Contraband could easily and safely travel through one State to another. The difference between direct importation and indirect, through a neighboring State in small parcels, is obvious.

Number 22 [2-3]

Currently, the federal government has no power to regulate commerce. But we must have federal regulation of commerce.) We haven't been able to have good commercial treaties with other nations. Since the States have been arguing about commerce, no nation will sign a commercial treaty with the United States. They know that individual States could violate the treaty at any time. Besides, they already have every advantage in our markets without giving us any in return except when it is convenient.

In England, Mr. Jenkinson introduced a bill in the British House of Commons to temporarily regulate commerce between our two countries. He declared that earlier bills with similar provisions answered Great Britain's commercial needs. He said that they shouldn't change their policies until the American government became more consistent.[*]

Some States have tried to change Great Britain's commercial policies by limiting or prohibiting some British products. But different States have different restrictions. We won't be able to influence Great Britain's commercial conduct until we have one federal authority and one commercial policy.

Number 23 [3]

...The most important reasons for a union and federal government are:

* Defense.
* To keep the peace against both internal turmoil and external attacks.
* To regulate commerce with other nations and between the States.
* To supervise our political and commercial interests with foreign countries.

Number 41 [22]

...Some people believe that the power of federal taxation should be limited to external taxation—taxes on articles imported from other countries. Of course, this will always be a valuable source of revenue. For a long time, in fact, it must be the primary source. And at this moment, it is essential.

However, import tax revenue will vary as the amount and the kind of imports vary. And these variations won't correspond with the growth of our population, which is the general measure of how much money the government will need. As long as agriculture continues to be the only field of labor, as the population increases, the importation of manufactured goods will increase. As the population grows, American manufacturers will employ hands not needed for agriculture and imported manufactured goods will decrease. Eventually, manufacturers may import raw materials that will be made into articles for exportation. As raw material importation overtakes the importation of finished goods, the government will want to encourage imports, not discourage them with import taxes. A good government should remember these cycles and be able to handle them

Number 42 [1]

The federal government's *second* class of powers regulates how the country deals with foreign nations. The federal government will:

o   make treaties
o   send and receive ambassadors, ministers, and consuls
o   define and punish piracies, felonies on the high seas and against the law of nations
o   regulate foreign commerce (after 1808, it may prohibit the importation of slaves; until then, it will charge a duty of ten dollars per head to discourage such importations)

We have already discussed why the regulation of foreign commerce is a federal responsibility.

---

[*] As nearly as I can recollect, this was the sense of his speech on introducing the bill. –PUBLIUS

Number 43 [9]
...Federal powers will be largely external: war, peace, negotiation, and foreign commerce. (Taxation will be the primary federal power over foreign commerce.)...

Number 53 [5]
...All federal legislators need to know something about State issues and laws. To write national regulations for foreign trade, legislators need to know something about the commerce, ports, and regulations of the different States...

A federal representative also needs to understand foreign affairs, including commercial treaties and policies of the United States and other nations. He should have some knowledge of the law of nations. The House of Representatives will not directly participate in foreign negotiations. However, the different areas of public affairs are connected. And they will sometimes demand legislative sanction and cooperation...

Number 69 [7]
...The king of Great Britain is the only representative of the nation in all foreign transactions. On his own, he can make treaties of peace, commerce, alliances, and of every other description...

and among the several States,

Number 7 [5-6]
[If the States separated] Commerce is another source of controversy. Each State or separate confederacy would have a unique commercial policy with different taxes and product incentives. Commerce in this country has always been based on equal privileges. The change would make some States unhappy.

Injuries are caused by legitimate and justifiable acts of independent sovereignties with different interests.

America's enterprising businesses use every opportunity to improve. If trade regulations are made that only benefit one State, the other States probably won't obey them, which would lead to arguments, new regulations aimed at hurting the other States, then wars.

Some States would make commercial laws that make other States involuntarily subservient. The situation of New York, Connecticut, and New Jersey is an example.

New York put a tax on imports from Connecticut and New Jersey. Consumers in the two exporting States pay a large part of these taxes. New York will not voluntarily give up this advantage. How long would Connecticut and New Jersey pay taxes that only benefit New York? Would New York survive with the weight of Connecticut on one side and New Jersey on the other?

Number 11 [all] see previous section, page 190

Number 12 [8-9]
The closeness of the States, the intersecting rivers, the bays, the ease of communication in every direction, the same language and manners, and similar commercial habits make illicit trade easy. The commercial regulations of each State are frequently evaded.

If the States separated, duties would have to be low to avoid the temptations of illicit trade. European nations guard the land and water avenues into their countries.

France uses more than twenty thousand army troops to enforce their commercial regulations against contraband. Yet people still find ways to smuggle goods.

Preventing illicit trade over an inland border is very difficult. If the States disunited, it would be difficult to collect duties. Border patrols would need more powers, powers that are intolerable in a free country.

Number 14 [10]

...national infrastructure improvements will make commerce easier throughout the Union. Roads will be shortened and better maintained. Places for travelers to eat and sleep will increase and improve. River navigation will extend through most of the thirteen States. Communication will become easier. Nature gave our country many rivers; engineers find them easy to connect with canals.

Number 22 [2, 4]

Currently, the federal government has no power to regulate commerce. But we must have federal regulation of commerce. We haven't been able to have good commercial treaties with other nations. Since the States have been arguing about commerce, no nation will sign a commercial treaty with the United States...

Contrary to the true spirit of the Union, some State regulations hurt the commerce in other States. Without national control, there will be more of these policies and anger between the States will grow, further damaging commerce.

The Encyclopaedia* ("Empire") describes Germany's commercial situation. Each German prince taxes the merchandise that travels through his state. The wide variety of taxes within Germany has put commerce in constant turmoil. And shippers have to stop and pay taxes so many times along the commercial routes that they don't even bother using Germany's navigable rivers.

This description may never completely apply to us. But as each State makes different commercial regulations, citizens of one State will treat citizens of other States no better than foreigners and aliens.

Number 23 [3]

The most important reasons for a union and federal government are:... To regulate commerce with other nations and between the States.

Number 42 [9-12, 18, 20]

The *third* class of [federal] powers provide for harmony among the States.

...I will confine myself to a brief review of the remaining powers... regulate commerce among the States...

The existing Confederacy doesn't have the power to regulate commerce between the States. Without this provision, the power to regulate foreign commerce is pointless.

Some noncommercial States must import and export through other States. If they could, States would charge import and export taxes on merchandise and material passing through their State. This would create animosities and probably end in violence.

---

* The article title is "Empire."

Commercial States' desire to collect indirect taxes from their uncommercial neighbors must seem both unfair and politically inexpedient. It would be a poor political decision. Resentment and self-interest would make the people who have to pay the State duties find longer routes without the added taxes for their trade. However, as a State makes the decision to tax goods that travel through it, the people who want immediate revenue will drown out the people who rationally argue that it is a bad political decision. The mild voice of reason, pleading the cause of a larger interest, is drowned out by the clamors of impatient avarice for immediate and immoderate gain.

The experience in other countries shows that the federal government needs to be able to regulate trade between the States.

In Switzerland, each canton [state] must allow merchandise passage through its jurisdiction into other cantons without additional tolls.

A law in Germany forbids the princes and states from charging tolls or customs on bridges, rivers, or passages without the consent of the emperor and the diet [legislature]. However, this law, like many others in the Germany, hasn't been followed, producing the problems predicted here.

In the Union of the Netherlands, states must get permission to charge imposts that are disadvantageous to neighboring states.

The power to establish uniform bankruptcy laws is closely connected with the regulation of commerce. It will prevent many frauds, where people or property may go into different States. Its importance will probably not be questioned.

The power of establishing post-roads is a harmless power and if managed well it may produce a great public convenience, helping interstate commerce.

Number 44 [8]

The federal government should regulate trade. The States may charge a reasonable inspection fee but the federal government can block any abuse of this discretion.

The remaining items in this clause are either obvious or have been previously discussed. Nothing else needs to be said about them.

Number 53 [5, 6]

…To regulate trade between States, [federal legislators] need to know about their different situations…

… As commerce between the States increases, so will knowledge of State affairs. And the different State laws will become more similar…

Number 56 [4-6]

Commerce, taxation, and the militia are the areas of federal legislation that require local knowledge.

The proper regulation of commerce requires a lot of information. However, only a few federal representatives need to know the State commercial laws and situations.

Duties on commerce will be the primary form of taxation…

Number 60 [7]

To various degrees, the States are addicted to agriculture and commerce. In most, if not all, agriculture is predominant. However, commerce is very important in a few States and it has a lot of influence in most of them.

Agriculture and commerce will also influence the national legislature. And there will be a wider variety of interests than found in any single State. Therefore, the national legislature will be less likely to be partial to either interest than in a single State.

and with the Indian Tribes;

Number 24 [12]

...we will need to increase our frontier garrisons as our Western settlements increase. Some military posts will serve large districts of territory. Some posts will also be important to trade with the Indian nations...

Number 42 [10, 13]

... I will confine myself to a brief review of the remaining powers under this third description. They are: to regulate commerce among the States and the Indian tribes...

The provision in the Articles of Confederation for regulating commerce with the Indian tribes is obscure and contradictory. It says that the federal power to regulate trade is limited to Indians who are not members of any State, without violating the rights of any State within its own borders. But federal councils haven't determined which Indians are members of a State and which are not. And how can an external authority regulate trade with Indians, who live in a State but are not members of the State, without intruding on the internal rights of a State?...

To establish an uniform Rule of Naturalization,

Number 32 [2]

...Congress will "establish a uniform rule of naturalization throughout the United States." This must be an exclusive power because if each State had power to prescribe a distinct rule, there could not be a uniform rule.

Number 42 [10, 17]

...make a uniform rule of naturalization...

Our current naturalization rules are confusing. The fourth Article of the Confederacy declares "that the *free inhabitants* of each of these States, paupers, vagabonds, and fugitives from justice excepted, shall be entitled to all privileges and immunities of *free citizens* in the several States; and *the people* of each State shall, in every other, enjoy all the privileges of trade and commerce," etc.

Why were the terms *free inhabitants* used in one part, *free citizens* in another, and *people* in another? And the meaning of the phrase "all the privileges of trade and commerce" is not clear.

It also seems to say that when people defined as *free inhabitants* of one State— but who are not citizens of that State—travel to a different State, they have all the privileges of *free citizens*. In other words, they may have greater privileges than in their home State. If the term "inhabitants" was changed to "citizens," the difficulty would only be diminished, not removed. Each State would retain the very improper power to naturalize aliens in every other State.

For example, let's say that in one State a short-term resident has all criteria for citizenship but another State requires more qualifications. An alien, therefore, only has to first reside in the former to elude the greater qualifications in the latter. Thus, preposterously, the law of the first State is dominant to the law of the second, within the jurisdiction of the second State.

We have escaped embarrassment on this subject only by good luck. Several States prohibit resident aliens from both the rights of citizenship and the privileges of residence. What would have happened if such persons had become citizens under the laws of another State, then demanded their rights to both residency and citizenship within the State that prohibit it? The consequences would probably have been very serious.

The new Constitution corrects this problem. The federal government will establish a uniform rule of naturalization throughout the United States.

and uniform Laws on the subject of Bankruptcies throughout the United States;

Number 42 [10, 18]
...uniform laws of bankruptcy...
The power to establish uniform bankruptcy laws is closely connected with the regulation of commerce. It will prevent many frauds, where people or property may go into different States. Its importance will probably not be questioned.

To coin Money, regulate the Value thereof, and of foreign Coin, and fix the Standard of Weights and Measures;

Number 18 [14]
The [ancient Greece] cities had the same laws and customs, the same weights and measures, and the same money. But it's uncertain whether this was a federal decree. The only mandate was that cities have the same laws and usages.

Number 19 [4, 16]
... [the German legislature] regulates coins...
... [the Swiss States] have...no common coin...

Number 40 [11]
... Congress says the power of coinage is a tax...

Number 42 [10, 14-15, 16]
... [the federal government will have the power] to coin and regulate the value of money...,... fix the standard of weights and measures
The federal government will coin money, regulate its value, and regulate the value of foreign coin. The Articles of Confederation doesn't mention the regulation of foreign currency. Currently, Congress only regulates the value of coin *struck* by its own authority or the States. If the different States valued foreign currency differently, uniformity in the *value* of the currency might be destroyed.

The federal government determines the value of currency and public securities. Therefore, it should have the authority to punish counterfeiters.

The regulation of weight and measures is transferred from the Articles of Confederation and is based on similar reasons as the power of regulating coin.

Number 44 [2, 4-5]

"No State shall ... coin money..."

The States cannot coin money. The federal government regulates the alloy and value of coins. Allowing States to manufacture coins has created two problems: many expensive mints and a diversity of shape, size, and weight of coins. State mints prevented the inconvenience of transporting gold and silver to the central mint. Establishing local mints under the national authority can solve this problem.

Prohibiting State bills of credit [paper money] is just and promotes public prosperity. Since the peace, paper money has eroded the confidence so necessary between man and man, in public councils, in industry, and in the republican government. It has become an enormous debt that the issuing States will not be able to pay off for a long time.

States are denied the power to regulate coin for good reasons. For the same reasons, they should not create paper money. If every State could regulate the value of its coin, every State could have a different currency, hurting interstate commerce. If a State retroactively changed the relative value of its money, it would injure the citizens of other States, kindling animosities among the States themselves. The citizens of foreign nations might also suffer, discrediting and embroiling the Union by the indiscretion of a single State could discredit the entire Union.

Number 69 [11]

The [president of the United States] can prescribe no rules concerning the commerce or currency of the nation; the [monarch of Great Britain] is in several respects the arbiter of commerce, can ... regulate weights and measures,... coin money, can authorize or prohibit the circulation of foreign coin.

Number 80 [3, 13]

...the States, in the new Constitution, are prohibited from doing several things...issuing paper money is an example...

... Constitution restricts the authority of the State legislatures. They are not to emit paper money...

To provide for the Punishment of counterfeiting the Securities and current Coin of the United States;

Number 42 [10, 15]

...[the federal government will have the power] to punish counterfeiting coins and securities of the United States ...

The federal government determines the value of currency and public securities. Therefore, it should have the authority to punish counterfeiters.

To establish Post Offices and post Roads;

Number 14 [10]

...national infrastructure improvements will make commerce easier throughout the Union. Roads will be shortened and better maintained...

Number 42 [10, 20]

...[the federal government's] remaining powers [includes establishing] post offices and post roads.

The power of establishing post-roads is a harmless power and if managed well it may produce a great public convenience, helping interstate commerce.

To promote the Progress of Science and useful Arts, by securing for limited Times to Authors and Inventors the exclusive Right to their respective Writings and Discoveries;

Number 43 [2-3]

A power "to promote the progress of science and useful arts by securing for limited times to authors and inventors the exclusive right to their writings and discoveries."

This is a useful power. In Great Britain, the copyright of authors is a right of common law. The right to benefit from their inventions seems to belong to inventors. In both cases, the public good coincides with the claims of individuals. The States cannot effectively provide for either of these cases.

To constitute Tribunals inferior to the supreme Court;

Number 81 [10-14]

I trust that these points have removed the objections to an independent Supreme Court. I will now show that the power of creating inferior courts is proper. *And I will show the relationship between these and the Supreme Court.

With inferior federal courts, every case of federal jurisdiction will not need to go to the Supreme Court. The national government can *authorize* inferior courts in each State or district. Those courts can decide matters of national jurisdiction within their limits.

Could State courts fill this role? This has several answers.

Even if the State courts are competent to handle federal cases, this constitutional power is necessary. Before the State courts could try federal cases, the national legislature would have to give them jurisdiction over causes arising out of the national Constitution. Congress might give the State courts the power to decide federal cases. That action would perhaps fulfill the requirement "to constitute tribunals."

But should the Constitution say that State courts should be used? There are good reasons why it shouldn't.

Local attitudes and opinions may disqualify local courts from hearing federal cases.

And the structures of some of the State judiciary systems are improper channels of the Union's judicial authority.

---

* Some people claim this power abolishes all the county courts in the States, which are often called inferior courts. But the Constitution says: to constitute "tribunals INFERIOR TO THE SUPREME COURT." This means that local courts, subordinate to the Supreme Court, can be created either in States or larger districts. It is ridiculous to say it abolishes county courts. –PUBLIUS

Some State judges hold their offices during pleasure or from year to year. They will not be independent enough to objectively execute national laws. If the United States Constitution said that State courts must be the first court to hear federal cases, the door for appeals would need to be as wide as possible. Appeals should be easy or difficult in proportion to the grounds of confidence in or distrust of the subordinate tribunals. I believe the appellate jurisdiction, as defined by the Constitution, is proper. However, anything that allows *unlimited* appeals is a source of inconvenience.

The United States might be divided into four, five or six districts. Each district could have a federal court instead of putting one in every State. The district court judges, with the help of State judges, may hold circuits to try cases in their district. Justice can be administered with ease and dispatch. And appeals may be safely limited.

This plan appears to me the best that could be adopted. The power of creating inferior courts should be in the Constitution.

The Constitution gives Congress the power to create inferior federal courts. Without this power, the Constitution would be defective.

To define and punish Piracies and Felonies committed on the high Seas, and Offenses against the Law of Nations;

Number 3 [9, 12]

One national government will always interpret treaties and laws of nations in one way. However, if thirteen States—or three or four confederacies—interpreted the same treaties and laws, they would sometimes come to different conclusions. Different local laws and interests would influence each government. Therefore, it is wise to have one judicial system appointed by and responsible to one national government to decide such questions.

Both intentional and accidental violations of treaties and laws of nations provide *just* cause for war. They are less likely to happen under one general government than several lesser ones. Therefore, the people are *safer* under one national government.

Number 42 [1, 5]

...The national government will... define and punish piracies and felonies committed on the high seas and against the law of nations,...

Another improvement is the national government's power to define and punish piracies and felonies committed on the high seas, and offenses against the law of nations.

The Articles do not mention the law of nations. Consequently, actions by one State could draw the entire Confederation into problems with foreign nations.

On the subject of piracies and felonies, the Articles only creates courts to try these offenses. The definition of "piracies" might be left to the law of nations, even though most municipal codes define them.

A definition of "felonies on the high seas" is required. The term "felony" has many definitions. The common law and statute law of England give it various meanings. And no two States define it in the same way. For uniformity, therefore, the power to define "felonies" is absolutely necessary and proper.

Number 53 [7]

A federal representative also needs to understand foreign affairs, including commercial treaties and policies of the United States and other nations. He should have some knowledge of the law of nations...

Number 64 [14]

The problem of corruption is not imaginable. Anyone who thinks that the President and two-thirds of the Senate will ever be capable of such unworthy conduct, must either have been very unfortunate in his interactions with the world or has a heart very susceptible to such impressions.

The idea is too gross and too invidious to be entertained. But if it should ever happen, the treaty so obtained from us would, like all other fraudulent contracts, be null and void by the law of nations.

Number 80 [2, 6, 10]

The judicial authority of the Union should extend to several types of cases: ...

4. Cases involving the peace of the confederacy, whether they relate to the relationship between the United States and foreign nations or between the States themselves.

5. Cases that originate on the high seas and are of admiralty or maritime jurisdiction;

The fourth type rests on the idea that the peace of the whole should never depend on a part. The Union will answer to foreign powers for the conduct of its States. And the responsibility for an injury should always be accompanied with the ability to prevent it.

If a citizen of another country is denied justice or is wrongfully convicted, it can become a **just cause for war** [Number 3]. Therefore, the federal judiciary should have jurisdiction in all cases concerning the citizens of other countries. This is essential to both public faith and tranquility.

Treaties and the laws of nations may seem different than municipal laws. Treaties and the laws of nations may seem proper for federal jurisdiction and municipal laws for State jurisdiction. However, let's say a foreign citizen gets an unjust sentence solely because of the location in our country where he is tried. If the unjust sentence is not corrected, his native country could see it as an aggression. It could also be seen as a violation of a treaty stipulation or the general laws of nations.

And it would be very difficult, if not impossible, to decide if a case falls under federal or municipal jurisdiction. Many cases in which foreigners are parties involve national questions. It is safer and faster to refer them to national courts.

There will be little criticism of the fifth type. Even the most bigoted idolizers of State authority say the national courts have jurisdiction of maritime causes. These are often based on the laws of nations and often affect the rights of foreigners. They relate to the public peace. Under the present Confederation, the federal courts determine the most important cases.

Number 83 [23]

But this is not the greatest objection. I believe that trial by jury is not appropriate for all cases. This is particularly true in cases that concern the public peace with foreign nations. Those cases usually involve the laws of nations...

To declare War, grant Letters of Marque and Reprisal, and make Rules concerning Captures on Land and Water;

Number 41[6, 8]

The powers within the *first* class [Security against foreign danger] are: declaring war and granting letters of marque...

Everyone agrees that the power to declare war is necessary. It doesn't need to be proved. The existing Confederation has this power.

Number 44[2, 3]

"No State shall...grant letters of marquee..."

...Under the Articles, States could grant letters of marque after war is declared. In the new Constitution, they must be obtained from the federal government. Uniformity in foreign policy justifies this change. The States are responsible to the nation; the nation is responsible for the conduct of every State.

Number 69 [6, 11]

...The British king has far more power. He can declare war, and he can raise and regulate fleets and armies. Under the proposed Constitution, Congress will have this authority...

...[the British monarch has] the authority of declaring war...

To raise and support Armies, but no Appropriation of Money to that Use shall be for a longer Term than two Years;

Number 4 [15]

...Divide America into thirteen or three or four independent confederacies. What armies could they raise and pay? What fleets could they hope to have...

Number 8 [6]

Small nations with less natural strength but vigorous governments and disciplined armies, often triumph over larger nations or nations with greater natural strength...

Number 19 [16]

[The Swiss States] have ... no common armies even in war ...

Number 20 [4]

The States-General [The Netherlands] can ... raise armies and equip fleets...

Number 23 [4]

To defend the country, the federal government needs the power to raise armies...

Number 25 [5-8]

Improper restraints on the national legislature create problems. Some people object to standing armies during peacetime. But how far should the prohibition extend? Will it ban raising armies, as well as, to keeping them up in time of tranquility?

A prohibition that only limits keeping armies isn't specific and will not fulfill the purpose intended. Once armies are raised, what does the constitution mean by "keeping them up?" How much time would be a violation? A week, a month, a year? Or may they continue as long as there is a danger?

This means they can be kept up *in time of peace*, if there are threats or impending danger. This is different than the literal meaning of the prohibition. Who will judge that the danger continues? The national government can first raise troops, then keep them as long as the peace or safety of the community is in jeopardy. The provision could be easily ignored.

Some people want a constitutional ban of peacetime armies. They believe it would stop executive and legislature conspiracies to use the military to take over the government. However, even if the constitution banned peacetime armies, the conspirators could claim there is an approaching danger! Indian hostilities would always be an excuse. Or they could provoke a foreign power into looking like a threat, and then appease it with concessions. If such a conspiracy happened, the army could be raised—using any pretext—and used in the usurpation scheme.

If the constitution prohibits the *raising* of armies in time of peace, the United States would be in the strangest situation ever seen—a nation that cannot prepare for its defense before it was actually invaded. The government couldn't begin drafting men until an enemy was physically within our borders. The nation couldn't prepare for a danger. Our property and liberty would be exposed to foreign invaders. They could capture us because we were afraid that rulers—elected by us and ruling according to our will—might endanger our liberty by abusing the power necessary to defend us.

Depending on the country's militia—armed citizens—to defend the nation nearly lost us our independence. And it cost our country millions that could have been saved. The militia can't be our only defense. We must have a regular, disciplined army to defend against other disciplined armies.

The militia's valor during the recent war erected eternal monuments to their fame. But the bravest of them know that they could not have established the liberty of their country alone. Like most things, war is a science that is perfected by diligence, perseverance, time, and practice.

Number 26 [6]

...Two States tried to restrict legislative authority over military establishments. A monarch's power must be feared. However, the over-reaction by these States extended this fear to the people's representatives. Some States didn't make this error but they have unnecessarily declared that standing armies are not to be kept up in peacetime WITHOUT THE CONSENT OF THE LEGISLATURE. There is a similar provision in the English Bill of Rights. But the States don't have the same reason for the provision. Under the State constitutions, only the legislatures have the power to raise armies. So, it was superfluous to declare that it should not be done without the consent of a body, which alone had the power of doing it...

Number 30 [8]

...[when] war breaks out. We can't depend on State requisitions. The federal government would have to take appropriated funds from their proper objects to defend the States...

Number 31 [1]

      ...There should be no limitation of a power meant to fulfill a purpose that can't be limited...

Number 41 [9-11, 16-17, 18]

      Is the power of raising armies and equipping fleets necessary? This is part of self-defense.

      But was an indefinte power of raising troops ... necessary? Should troops and fleets be maintained in peace? This is discussed in another place. The answer seems obvious. How can we limit the U.S. defensive force when the offensive force of other nations cannot be limited? If a federal Constitution could block the ambition of all other nations, then it might prudently limit its own government's defense.

      Limiting the term for military appropriations is a second precaution against the danger from standing armies. The Constitution has this precaution.

      Opponents of the Constitution say Great Britain requires an annual vote of the legislature for military appropriations and the American Constitution has lengthened this critical period to two years. [Article 1, Section 8] Is this a fair comparison? Does the British Constitution limit military appropriations to one year? Does the American require two-year Congressional appropriations? No. The British Constitution has no limit on military appropriations. And the American Constitution limits military appropriations to no more than two years.

      Although the British Constitution doesn't have a term limit for appropriating supplies to the army, in practice the parliament has limited it to one year...

      A bad cause seldom fails to betray itself. The opposition to the federal government is an example of this truth. And their most striking blunder is their attempt to enlist the support of people who have sincere concerns about a standing army.

      This is an important subject. The Constitution is the best guard against this danger. If the States disunite, each separate State or Confederacy will have a standing army. These armies will endanger properties and liberties more than the size of the military necessary under a united and efficient government. A strong Constitution will preserve the Union and support national defense.

Number 45 [11]

      ...The Articles of Confederation gives Congress the powers relating to war and peace, armies and fleets, treaties and finance. The proposed Constitution doesn't enlarge these powers. It substitutes a more effective way to administer them...

Number 69 [6]

      ...The British king has far more power. He can declare war, and he can raise and regulate fleets and armies. Under the proposed Constitution, Congress will have this authority...

Under Articles of Confederation

Number 22 [5-6]

      Under the Articles of Confederation, when the federal government needs to raise troops it must requisition quotas from the States. During the recent war, the requisition system made a vigorous and economical defense very difficult. To fill their quotas, States competed against each other, offering enormous rewards. Men who wanted to serve put off enlisting, hoping to get a larger bonus.

The result? During emergencies, enlistments were few, slow, short-term and very expensive. The constantly changing troops ruined discipline and the soldiers who had mustered out threatened public safety. The occasional forced enlistment only worked because of enthusiasm for liberty.

Using State quotas to raise troops doesn't work. The enlistment bonuses hurt the economy. And only some of the States filled their quotas. The States near the heart of the war, influenced by self-preservation, furnished the required number of men. Usually, the States that were not in immediate danger didn't fulfill their quotas. Of course, if a State falls behind paying their money quota, it can be made up. It's impossible to supply delinquent deficiencies of men. However, States probably won't pay for their monetary failures. Whether it is used to raise men or money, the quota system is unequal and unjust.

Number 23 [7-8]

...Congress can requisition (demand that each State send a specific amount) men and money and control the army and navy. Congressional requisitions are constitutionally binding on the States; the States have a legal duty to furnish the required supplies. The Articles of Confederation authorized the federal government to command all resources that are necessary for the "common defense and general welfare." The authors of the Articles assumed that the States would be aware of their best interests and duty to the Union and they would fill the federal requisitions.

However, this was a mistaken assumption. If we really want to give the Union energy and a long life, we must stop making laws that States are supposed to obey. Federal laws must extend to individual citizens. Quotas and requisitions are impractical and unjust. They must be discarded.

The Union should have the power and money to draft troops, support an army, and build and equip a navy in the same way as other governments.

Number 25 [4]

Separate State military forces are dangerous to the Union. Under the Articles of Confederation, Congress must approve State ships or troops. Both federal and State governments cannot have armies.

Military Appropriations

Number 24 [3-4]

Current newspaper articles give the impression that either the Constitution says that standing armies should be kept up in time of peace or it gives the PRESIDENT the whole power of raising troops without any legislative control.

However, neither provision is in the Constitution. The *legislature*, not the *president*, has the power to raise armies. And the legislature's power is limited. Money to support an army can only be appropriated for two years. This precaution becomes security against keeping troops when they are unnecessary.

Number 26 [9-10, 13]

      Some people want to ban all military during times of peace. The proposed Constitution limits military appropriations to a two-year period. A peacetime military ban tries to do too much and will not be obeyed; a two-year appropriation provides for emergencies and will be a powerful remedy.

      At least once in every two years the United States legislature will be *forced* to decide whether to keep a military force and declare their position by a formal, public vote. They cannot give the president unlimited funds for an army.

      A partisan spirit infects all political bodies. Funding a military force will always be a favorite topic to denounce. As often as the question arises, the opposition party will publicly argue about it. If the majority party wants to appropriate more money than seems proper to support the military for two years, the community will be warned and be able to take measures to guard against it.

      People will debate the issue. State legislatures will jealously guard the citizens' rights against encroachments from the federal government. If national rulers act improperly, they will sound the alarm. State legislatures will be the voice and, if necessary, the arm of the people's discontent.

      Some people say limiting military appropriations to the period of two years won't be safe. They say that once the president has a large enough military to force the people into submission, it would also be large enough to get supplies without help from the legislature.

      But what pretense could the President use to build a big military force in peacetime? If it was created in response to a domestic insurrection or foreign war, it can't be called a peacetime military buildup. Military forces should be raised to stop a rebellion or resist an invasion. If defense of the community makes it necessary to have an army large enough to threaten its liberty, this is one of those calamities that can't be prevented or cured. No form of government can provide against this. It might even happen in a simple league, if the allies need to form an army for common defense.

Number 30 [1]

      The federal government should have the ability to support the national army. This includes the expenses of recruiting troops, building and equipping fleets, and all other military expenses...

Number 34 [4, 6-7, 9]

      ... We must look into the remote future. A civil government's constitution tries to combine existing needs with probable future needs. We cannot infer from an estimate of immediate needs, the extent of power it is proper to give the national government. It is unsafe to limit the national government's capacity to provide for future emergencies. The federal government must provide the national defense. It must protect the nation against foreign war and domestic violence. We cannot predict the possibility of internal attacks. We must be able to defend our commerce. And we must be able to support a navy and pay for naval wars.

      What are the chief sources of expense in every government? Wars and rebellions. We must guard against these two mortal diseases of society.

The expenses for domestic police, the legislative, executive, and judicial branches of government, and the encouragement of agriculture and manufacturing (in other words, almost all State expenditures), are insignificant when compared with the expense for national defense.

In the kingdom of Great Britain, only 7% of the nation's annual expenses support the ostentatious monarchy. The other 93% goes to national defense...

... If the States are given sources of tax revenue that the Union is excluded from using, funding sources that are needed for national defense will be given to local governments that have no just or proper use for them.

Number 41 [6]

The powers within the *first* class [1. Security against foreign danger] are ... providing armies...

Number 43 [6]

The federal government must have authority over forts, military depots, arsenals, dockyards, etc. Public money will be spent on such places...

Number 72 [1]

... Government administration includes... asking for and spending public money as appropriated by the legislature,

To provide and maintain a Navy;

Number 4 [14]

The fleets of Britain have been praised. If we are wise, in time the fleets of America may also be praised. But if Britain's one national government hadn't regulated navigation, making it a place for seamen to learn—if one national government hadn't used national resources and materials to form fleets—their prowess and ability would not be praised.

Let England have its navigation and fleet—let Scotland have its navigation and fleet—let Wales have its navigation and fleet—let Ireland have its navigation and fleet—let the four parts of the British empire be under four independent governments and they would each dwindle into insignificance.

Number 8 [12]

Great Britain is seldom exposed to internal invasions. Since it is an island and has a powerful navy it doesn't need a large army within the kingdom. It only needs a force large enough to hold invaders at bay until the militia can be raised. Neither national policy nor public opinion has tolerated a lot of domestic troops. And it has been a long time since an internal war has produced a military state.

Britain being an island has helped preserve its liberty, in spite of corruption. If Britain was on the continent, she would need internal military establishments as big as other European powers. She, like them, would probably be a victim of a dictator.

The island might be enslaved from other causes, but not from the small army that is usually kept within Britain.

Navy Will Help Commerce

Number 11 [2, 5-end]

America's adventurous commercial spirit worries several naval powers in Europe. They worry that we will cut into their shipping trade, which supports their naval strength.

Some nations have colonies in North America. Those nations worry about our abilities. If we stay united and have the resources to create a powerful navy, we will be a threat to their American colonies.

Europe will encourage disagreements between States. This could deprive us of an active commerce in our own ships. Therefore, we could not interfere in European navigation; Europe would get the major profits from our trade and keep us from being a dangerously powerful nation. We would probably be able to trace Europe's policy of limiting our commerce to its governments.

A federal navy would influence European commerce. If the Union continues, it will create a navy. It might not be a great navy but it could change the outcome of a struggle if it allied with either side of a conflict, especially in the West Indies. A few ships, helping either side, could decide the fate of a campaign that had halted trade. We could bargain for commercial privileges and sell supplies. We could become the arbiter of Europe in America.

But if we disunite, the rivalries between us will produce a stalemate, frustrating our great natural advantages. Warring nations will meddle with our commerce. They'll plunder our property. Neutrality is respected only when defended by adequate power; a weak nation forfeits even the privilege of being neutral.

European alliances could restrain our growth. However, if we have a strong national government, they would be less successful. Europe would be less likely to make the alliances. We would create an active commerce, extensive navigation, and a flourishing navy.

If we disunite, European alliances might be successful. Nations with a powerful navy could dictate the conditions of our political existence.

They'd want to carry our products and prevent us from becoming their shipper. They'd probably form alliances, destroy our navigation, and confine us to passive commerce. We would have to accept the first price for our commodities. Our profits would be snatched from us to enrich our enemies and persecutors would get our profits. American merchants and navigators have an unequaled spirit of enterprise and an inexhaustible mine of national wealth. It would be stifled and lost. Poverty and disgrace would spread across a country that could have been the envy of the world.

Our Union has some very important trade rights, especially the fisheries and the navigation of Western lakes and the Mississippi. If the Union dissolved, the future of these rights would come into question. Spain's attitude towards the Mississippi needs no comment. France and Britain view our fisheries as important to their navigation. Since we can undersell those nations in their own markets, they would ban our dangerous competition.

Commerce will improve our navigation. This resource will help when we build a navy.

A navy. Staying united will support this great national objective. Every institu tion grows and flourishes in proportion to the amount of resources put towards its formation and support.

It will be easier for the United States to create a navy than any single State or small confederacy. Different areas of the country have different resources. The southern States have naval stores—tar, pitch, and turpentine. Their wood is more solid and lasting. Some southern and middle States have high quality iron. The northern States will supply most of the seamen.

Naval protection of our commerce is important; maritime commerce will help our navy.

Unrestrained commerce between the States will advance trade. The free circulation of commodities will replenish the veins of commerce. The States will have a diversity of products. When the staple of one State fails from a bad harvest, it can get the staple of another.

Both the variety and value of export products contribute to an active foreign commerce. Trade competitions and market fluctuations are a part of foreign commerce. Our commerce will be more profitable if we have a large variety of products of a given value than a small number of the same value. Some products may be in great demand at certain periods and unwanted at others. But if there were a variety of products, rarely would they all be unwanted.

Speculative traders understand that this analysis is valid. The total commerce of the United States would be better than that of 13 separate States or several small confederacies.

Some people may argue that whether the States are united or disunited, interstate commerce would achieve the same ends. But disunity would hurt commerce. Unified commercial and political interests can only be achieved through a unified government.

We should aim for a position of dominance in American affairs.

The world is politically and geographically divided into four parts. Each part has a distinct set of interests. Unhappily for the other three, Europe, using arms and negotiations, by force and fraud, has extended her dominion, to varying degrees, over them all. Africa, Asia and America have successively felt her domination. Europe's superiority has tempted her to crown herself Mistress of the World, considering the rest of mankind as created for her benefit.

Some philosophers say Europeans are physically superior. And they have gravely asserted that all animals, including humans, degenerate in America. They say that even dogs cease to bark after breathing our air for a while.

For too long, facts have supported these European pretensions. We must save the honor of the human race and teach Europe moderation. As a Union, we can do it. Disunion will add another victim to Europe's triumphants.

Let Americans refuse to be European pawns! Let the 13 States, as a Union, erect one great American system that controls all transatlantic force or influence, and dictate how the old and new world will be connected.

Number 23 [7, 8]

... [Under the Articles of Confederation] Congress can requisition (demand that each State send a specific amount) men and money and control the army and navy.

...The Union should have the power and money to draft troops, support an army, and build and equip a navy in the same way as other governments.

Number 24 [13]

We must form a navy. It is necessary for our commerce and safety along our Atlantic coast. We will need forts and soldiers to defend our dockyards and arsenals. A powerful navy can protect its dockyards without additional soldiers. Until our navy is fully established, moderate garrisons will be an indispensable security against destructive attacks on arsenals and dockyards, and sometimes the fleet itself.

Number 34 [4]

...we must be able to support a navy and pay for naval wars.

Number 41 [9-11, 19]

Is the power to raise armies and equip fleets necessary? This is part of self-defense.

But is an indefinite power of raising troops and fleets necessary? Should troops and fleets be maintained in peace? This is discussed in another place. The answer seems obvious. How can we limit the U.S. defensive force when the offensive force of other nations cannot be limited? If a federal Constitution could block the ambition of all other nations, then it might prudently limit its own government's defense.

A navy is necessary. As in Great Britain, a navy will be our primary security against danger from other countries. And, happily, while a navy will repel foreign invaders, usurpers in government can never turn it against our liberties.

Number 47 [19]

The South Carolina legislature appoints all State officers, including the chief executive, judges, justices of the peace, sheriffs, and captains in the army and navy of the State.

Number 69 [6]

The President is to be the "commander-in-chief of the army and navy of the United States...

Number 74 [1]

The President of the United States is to be "commander-in-chief of the army and navy of the United States...

To make Rules for the Government and Regulation of the land and naval Forces;

To provide for calling forth the Militia to execute the Laws of the Union, suppress Insurrections, and repel Invasions;

To provide for organizing, arming, and disciplining the Militia, and for governing such Part of them as may be employed in the Service of the United States, reserving to the States respectively, the Ap-

pointment of the Officers, and the Authority of training the Militia according to the discipline prescribed by Congress;

Number 4 [12, 17]

...The army will have one chain of command up to the President. One army is more efficient than thirteen, or three or four independent forces.

Whatever our situation—one national government or several confederacies—foreign nations will know and will act towards us accordingly. If they see an efficient national government with regulated trade, a disciplined army, well-managed resources, good credit, and a free and united people, they will want to be our friends rather than our enemies...

Number 8 [12]

Great Britain is seldom exposed to internal invasions. Since it is an island and has a powerful navy it doesn't need a large army within the kingdom. It only needs a force large enough to hold invaders at bay until the militia can be raised.

Number 24 [11]

Since before the Revolution, small military forts on our Western frontier have been necessary. They are indispensable, if only for protection against the plundering of the Indians. Occasionally, the forts must get more military personnel either militia or federal army soldiers.

Using militia members is impractical and dangerous. Citizens would eventually refuse to leave their jobs and families to perform the most disagreeable duty in times of peace. Even if they could be forced, frequently calling up the militia would be expensive. And losing the commercial and farm labor force would injure both the public and private citizens...

Number 25 [8]

Depending on the country's militia—armed citizens—to defend the nation nearly lost us our independence. And it cost our country millions that could have been saved. The militia can't be our only defense. We must have a regular, disciplined army to defend against other disciplined armies.

The militia's valor during the recent war erected eternal monuments to their fame. But the bravest of them know that they could not have established the liberty of their country alone. Like most things, war is a science that is perfected by diligence, perseverance, time, and practice.

Number 26 [14]

... It is hard to imagine dangers formidable enough to attack the whole nation, demanding a force large enough to place our liberties in jeopardy, especially when we remember that the militia should always be counted on as a valuable and powerful addition to the military...

Number 28 [2, 3, 4]

...A small revolt in part of a State can be suppressed by the militia from other parts of the State. And the militia would be ready to serve...

... Suppose New York decided to reestablish control over Vermont. Could she have been successful using the militia alone? She would have needed a regular army.

The States need a force other than the militia during severe problems.

... Whether we have one government for all the States or several governments, sometimes a force other than the militia may be necessary to keep the peace and maintain the lawful authority against revolts and rebellions.

Militia Not Threat to Liberty

Number 29 [all]

During an internal revolt or an invasion by a foreign nation, the militia helps keep peace and defends the Confederacy.

All members of the militia must have the same organization and discipline to get the best results. And uniformity requires national regulation of the militia. Therefore, the Constitution properly says that the Union will "provide for organizing, arming, and disciplining the militia, and for governing such part of them as may be employed in the service of the United States, *reserving to the States respectively the appointment of the officers, and the authority of training the militia according to the discipline prescribed by Congress.*"

Some opponents of the Constitution attack this provision. This wasn't expected. A disciplined militia is the natural defense of a free country. The federal government is responsible for guarding national security. Therefore, it should regulate the militia.

Standing armies can endanger liberty. The national government won't have any reason to keep a standing army if it controls the militia. If the federal government can command the militia during emergencies, it won't use the army. However, if it can't use the militia, it will have to use the army. If we don't want a permanent army, making it unnecessary works better than a thousand prohibitions on paper.

Opponents say the Constitution has no provision for calling out the posse comitatus to help the chief executive enforce the law, suggesting that military force will be the only alternative.

This shows how illogical the objections to the Constitution have been. Opponents first say the federal government's power will be despotic and unlimited and then say it doesn't even have the authority to call out the posse comitatus. Fortunately, neither statement is true.

The government can pass all laws *necessary and proper* to execute its powers. Therefore, it can require citizens to assist those officers who must enforce those laws. And even if the government is allowed to use the military when necessary, it is not the only way to enforce laws.

We are told to fear the militia, if the federal government regulates it. It is said that a young, eager corps may be formed and used by a tyrant. We don't know how the national government will regulate the militia. But I don't see it as dangerous. If the Constitution is ratified, my feelings about a militia would be as follows:

It would be impossible to train the entire militia of the United States. Becoming an expert in military movements requires time and practice. A day or a week isn't enough. Making citizens go through military exercises often enough to become a well-disciplined militia would be a hardship on the people and a serious public loss. Annually, the country would lose nearly as much productive labor as the whole expense of all the State governments.

Spending the time and money to train the entire militia would injure labor and industry. And if tried, it couldn't succeed. Citizens would refuse to do it. Instead, we can only attempt to arm and equip the general population. And to do this, they will need to assemble once or twice every year.

Disciplining the whole nation is impractical. However, we should adopt a well-formed plan to create a militia as soon as possible. The government should form a small army that is fit for service in case of need. With a clear plan, a trained militia will be ready whenever the defense of the States requires it. We will need fewer military forts and bases. And if circumstances ever force the government to form a large army, it will never be a big threat to the liberties of the people. There will be a large body of citizens who are members of the militia. They will be disciplined and trained in the use of arms. They will be ready to defend their own rights and those of their fellow citizens. This is the only substitute for a standing army. And it is the best security against a standing army, if it exists.

However, I don't know how the national legislature may reason on this subject.

The idea that the militia will endanger liberty is far-fetched. Where are our fears to end if we can't trust our sons, brothers, neighbors, and fellow citizens? We all share the same feelings, sentiments, habits, and interests.

The States have the *sole and exclusive power to appoint officers*. Since they appoint the militia's officers, the States will have the greatest influence over the militia. This should remove our fears about a militia under the federal government.

If a man who knows nothing about the proposed Constitution read the articles written against it, he might think he is reading a horror story. He might think that it will transform the government into a monster.

Exaggerations about the militia are examples: The articles make it sound like the New Hampshire militia will be marched to Georgia, the Georgia militia to New Hampshire, the New York militia to Kentucky, and the Kentucky militia to Lake Champlain. And that we plan to pay our debts to France and Holland with militiamen instead of money.

First they say a large army will ruin the liberties of the people. Then they say Virginia's militia will be dragged 500 or 600 miles to tame rebels in Massachusetts, and Massachusetts's militia will travel an equal distance to subdue aristocratic Virginians. Do the people who make these wild claims think that their eloquence can convince the people of America that any absurd statement is true?

If a tyrant were going to use the army to take over the country, why would he need a militia? If there was no army, he would try to use the militia, sending them great distances to enslave follow countrymen. But the militia would become irritated, march to the seat of the tyrant, and crush him.

Rulers do not usually start their career with evil acts of power that do not fulfill any goal and that draw universal hatred on themselves. Arguments that the army or militia will be used despotically are made by people who like to stir up trouble. Even if the national rulers were very ambitious, it is impossible to believe they would use such a preposterous way to accomplish their designs.

During an internal revolt or an invasion by a foreign nation, the militia can be marched into a neighboring State to defend against an invader or guard the republic against the violence of faction or sedition. This happened during the recent war. And this mutual security is an important goal of our political association. If direction of the militia was left to the States, one State could easily ignore an invasion or revolt in a neighboring State. The nation will be more secure if the Union directs the militia.

Number 41 [6, 21]

The powers within the *first* class (security against foreign danger) are ... regulating and using the militia,..

Regulating and calling forth the militia has already been discussed and justified.

Number 45 [8]

...State and local officials—State legislators, governors, judges, militia officers, county and city officers—will know all types of people. They will have more influence than the people employed by the federal government...

Number 46 [9]

Military force is the only other way that the federal government could usurp State power. And it would take a very large military force. The federal government would have to build up the military... Let's say an army devoted to the federal government was formed. The State governments—with the people on their side—could repel the danger. According to the best computations, the size of a country's standing army cannot exceed 1% of the total population or 4% of the number able to bear arms. In the United States, the army could be no bigger than 25,000 or 30,000 men. The militia with nearly half a million armed citizens and officers appointed by the States would oppose the federal army. The militia would fight for their common liberties. Local governments would lead the militia. And the militia would be loyal to the State governments.

Such a small federal army probably couldn't conquer the militia, just as we successfully resisted the British army. Americans, unlike the people of almost every other nation, have the advantage of being armed. And the people are attached to the State governments, which appoint the militia officers. This forms a barrier against federal ambition.

Several European kingdoms have large military establishments. Yet they are afraid to trust the people with arms. Citizen arms alone might not be powerful enough to defeat a monarchy. But if the people had the additional advantage of local elected governments, who could direct the national attacks and appoint militia officers, the throne of every tyranny in Europe would be speedily overturned in spite of the legions that surround it...

Number 53 [5]

... Trade, taxes, and the militia are the important subjects of federal legislation. Federal representatives need a lot of information on these and other subjects.

Number 56 [4, 8]

Commerce, taxation, and the militia are the areas of federal legislation that require local knowledge.

The comments on taxation apply to the militia. Although different States may have different rules of discipline, they are the same throughout each State.

Number 69 [6]

The President is to be the "commander-in-chief of the army and navy of the United States, and of the militia of the several States, when called into the actual service of the United States;... The President will only occasionally command the nation's militia. Congress must first call the militia into service.

Number 74 [1]

The President of the United States is to be "commander-in-chief of the army and navy of the United States, and the militia of the several States *when called into the actual service* of the United States."...

To exercise exclusive Legislation in all Cases whatsoever, over such District (not exceeding ten Miles square) as may, by Cession of particular States and the Acceptance of Congress, become the Seat of the Government of the United States,

Number 32 [2]

... State sovereignty is transferred to the Union in three cases: (1) where the Constitution expressly grants exclusive authority to the Union; The next-to-the-last clause of article one, section eight, says Congress will exercise "*exclusive legislation*" over the capital district. This answers the first case.

Number 43 [4-5]

"To exercise exclusive legislation in all cases whatsoever over such district (not exceeding ten miles square) as may, by cession of particular States and the acceptance of Congress, become the seat of the Government of the United States, and to exercise like authority over all places purchased by the consent of the legislature of the State in which the same shall be, for the erection of forts, magazines, arsenals, dockyards, and other needful buildings."

The seat of government must be independent. If it was located in a State, that State might influence national councils. Federal money will improve the capital. This public trust should not be left in the hands of a single State. And it would be nearly impossible to ever move the capital, which would further limit its independence.

The size of this federal district is limited. The State ceding the land for this use must consent. The State will make a compact with the federal government, assuring the rights of the citizens of the district. The inhabitants will have enough inducements to become willing parties to the cession. An elected municipal legislature will exercise authority over them. The legislature of the State and the people who live in the ceded part will agree to the cession and ratify the Constitution. Therefore, this seems to cover every objection.

Number 84 [13-15]

Objectors also say, "It is improper to give such large powers to the national government, because the capital will be too far away from many of the States. The citizens won't know the conduct of the representative body."

If this argument proves anything, it proves there should be no federal government. For the powers that everyone seems to agree should be vested in the Union cannot be safely entrusted to a body that is not under every requisite control.

But the objection is baseless. Most of the arguments about distance are imaginary.

How do people in Montgomery County, New York, receive the information they use to judge the conduct of their representatives in the State legislature? Not by personal observation. They must depend on information from men who they trust. And how do these men get their information? They get it from the type of public measures passed, from press reports, from correspondences with their representatives and with other persons who live in the state capital.

This applies to all the counties that are far from the seat of government.

The same sources will be used for information about the federal government.

The State governments will carefully watch it. This, alone, will overbalance the distance problem. The executive and legislative bodies of each State will watch every part of the national government. They will use a regular and effective system of intelligence. Therefore, they will know the behavior of national representatives. And they can easily communicate their knowledge to the people. They will tell the community about anything that may prejudice its interests, if only because of jealousy of a rival power.

The people may know more about the conduct of their national representatives than their State representatives.

The citizens who live in or near the capital will, in all questions that affect general liberty and prosperity, have the same interest with those who are at a distance. They will sound the alarm when necessary. And they will point out the actors in any harmful project.

Newspapers will quickly spread information to the most remote areas of the Union.

and to exercise like Authority over all Places purchased by the Consent of the Legislature of the State in which the Same shall be, for the Erection of Forts, Magazines, Arsenals, dockyards, and other needful Buildings;—

Number 8 [2]

...Fortifications also delay conquests. The nations of Europe are encircled by fortified places. Campaigns against armed forts waste invasion resources. Obstacles occur at every step. Their strength is exhausted. The invader's progress is delayed. Formerly, an invading army got to the heart of a country almost as quickly as news of its approach reached its rulers. Now, a small force of disciplined defensive troops block larger invasions...

Number 24 [12-13]

...If we don't want to be defenseless, we will need to increase our frontier garrisons as our Western settlements increase. Some military posts will serve large districts of territory. Some posts will also be important to trade with the Indian nations. Leaving them vulnerable to seizure by such powerful neighbors would be imprudent.

We must form a navy. It is necessary for our commerce and safety along our Atlantic coast. We will need forts and soldiers to defend our dockyards and arsenals. A powerful navy can protect its dockyards without additional soldiers. Until our navy is fully established, moderate garrisons will be an indispensable security against destructive attacks on arsenals and dockyards, and sometimes the fleet itself.

Number 43 [6]

The federal government must have authority over forts, military depots, arsenals, dockyards, etc., is evident. The public money spent on such places, and the property and equipment stored there, requires that they should be exempt from the authority of a State. Nor is it proper that the places so important to the security of the entire Union may depend, to any degree, on one State.

Objections are prevented by requiring the concurrence of the States concerned in every such establishment.

Number 45 [2]

Is the Union essential for the security of the American people?...Does it guard against...the poisoning effect of military bases?

Number 85 [3]

… By staying united, fewer military forts and bases will be needed…

And To make all Laws which shall be necessary and proper for carrying into Execution the foregoing Powers, and all other Powers vested by this Constitution in the Government of the United States, or in any Department or Officer thereof.

Number 22 [17]

Currently, Congress does not have the powers that the federal government needs…

Number 29 [4]

…Opponents [of the new Constitution] first say the federal government's power will be despotic and unlimited and then say it doesn't even have the authority to call out the posse comitatus. Fortunately, neither statement is true.

The government can pass all laws *necessary and proper* to execute its powers. Therefore, it can require citizens to assist those officers who must enforce those laws. And even if the government is allowed to use the military when necessary, it is not the only way to enforce laws.

Number 33 [1-6]

The "necessary and proper" clause of the Constitution is the last clause of Article 1, Section 8. It authorizes the national legislature "to make all laws which shall be ***necessary*** and ***proper*** for carrying into execution the foregoing *powers*, and all other powers vested by this Constitution in the government of the United States, or in any department or officer thereof."

Article 6 says that "the Constitution and the laws of the United States which shall be made *in pursuance thereof* and all treaties made, or which shall be made, under the authority of the United States, shall be the ***supreme law*** **of the land**; . . . anything in the constitution or laws of any State to the contrary notwithstanding."

These two clauses have been vehemently denounced. Using exaggeration and misrepresentation, opponents say these clauses will destroy both local governments and individual liberties. They are seen as monsters that will devour everyone.

However, they only declare a truth. The act of creating a federal government and giving it specific powers implies these clauses. The constitutional operation of the proposed government would be precisely the same if the clauses were removed or if they were repeated in every article.

The term "power" means having the ability to do something. "Legislative power" means that the legislature will have the power to make laws.

Article One, Section 8 says, "Congress shall have power to lay and collect taxes." Therefore, it is a legislative power. In other words, a power to make **necessary and proper** laws about taxes.

By following this simple reasoning, we can judge the true meaning of the controversial clause. The truth is obvious: the power to lay and collect taxes includes all laws *necessary* and *proper* to execute that power. The "necessary and proper" clause in the Constitution only restates this obvious conclusion. (This clause is sometimes called the "sweeping clause.")

I'm using the taxation example because taxation is our current subject and taxation is the government's most important authority. But the same reasoning applies to every power in the Constitution. The "necessary and proper" clause authorizes the national legislature to pass those laws that are necessary and proper to execute the powers listed in the Constitution.

Any objection must be to the specific powers, not the general declaration. The declaration may be redundant, but it is harmless.

But suspicious people may ask why the "necessary and proper" clause was added to the Constitution. It could have been put in the Constitution to guard against attempts to limit and evade the legitimate authorities of the Union. The greatest threat to our political welfare is the State governments sapping the foundations of the Union. Therefore, on this important point, perhaps the convention wanted to leave nothing to interpretation.

Who judges whether federal laws are necessary and proper?

First, if we removed the "necessary and proper" clause, we can still ask the question about the powers themselves. Second, the national government, the States and the citizens must judge the proper exercise of its powers.

If the federal government overreaches its authority and uses its power tyrannically, the people, who created it, must go to the Constitution. They must correct the injury done to the Constitution. To determine if a law is constitutional, we must look at whether the law is based on Constitutional powers.

Suppose the federal legislature attempts to change the law of descent in a State. Clearly, this is outside the federal government's jurisdiction and would trespass on the State's authority.

Or suppose that the federal government tries to abolish a State's property tax, saying it interferes with federal revenues. This would be an invasion of the concurrent tax jurisdiction.

"To make all laws which shall be necessary and proper for carrying into execution the foregoing powers, and all other powers vested by this Constitution in the Government of the United States, or in any department or officer thereof."

This clause has been vigorously attacked. Yet on objective investigation, no part appears more invulnerable. Without the *substance* of this power, the whole Constitution would be a dead letter. Therefore, people who object to it must mean that the *form* is improper. Is there a better way to phrase it?

The Constitution could have approached this subject four ways:

1) Copy Article Two of the Articles; prohibit any power not expressly mentioned.

2) Try to list every power that is "necessary and proper."

3) Try to list every power that is not "necessary and proper."

4) Remain silent on the subject; leave the definition of "necessary and proper" powers to interpretation and inference.

[Articles of Confederation, Article Two: "Each State retains its sovereignty, freedom, and independence, and every power, jurisdiction, and right, which is not by this Confederation expressly delegated to the United States in Congress assembled."]

If the convention had copied the Second Article of the Confederation, the new Congress would have the same problem as the current Congress. Should the term "*expressly*" be interpreted strictly or loosely? A strict interpretation would strip the federal government authority and Congress could betray the public interests by doing nothing. A loose interpretation would destroy the restriction: Congress could violate the Constitution by using powers that are necessary and proper but are not *expressly* granted.

If the convention had tried to list every necessary and proper power, it would have meant listing every law on every subject in the Constitution, including future laws.

Trying to list every power not necessary or proper to execute the general powers is also unrealistic. And would create another objection—every defect in the list would be the same as granting an authority. If they had listed only a few exceptions, the unnecessary and improper powers not included in the list would be less forcibly excepted than if no partial list existed.

What if the Constitution had no "necessary and proper" clause? The federal government would still have all the powers that are required to execute the general powers. It is an axiom of law and reason that whatever the goal, the means are authorized: Wherever a general power is authorized, the specific powers needed to reach the goal are included. Therefore, every current objection to the clause would remain. And it would create a real problem: The "necessary and proper" clause can be used on critical occasions to raise doubt about the essential powers of the Union.

What will happen if Congress misconstrues the "necessary and proper" clause and exercises powers not warranted by its true meaning? I answer, the same thing will happen as will occur if they misconstrue or enlarge any power vested in them. The same thing as if the State legislatures violated their respective constitutional authorities.

First, the power usurpation will only succeed if the executive and judiciary departments, which execute and interpret legislative acts, support it.

And in the last resort, the people will remedy the problem; they can elect more faithful representatives, who can annul the acts of the usurpers. This remedy may work better against the unconstitutional acts of the federal than the State legislatures, simply because every federal usurpation will invade the rights of a State. The States will notice deviations, sound the alarm, and use their influence to change federal representatives. There is no such intermediate body between the State legislatures and the people. Violations of the State constitutions are more likely to remain unnoticed and unredressed.

Number 83 [7]

The Constitution declares that the *national legislature's* power will extend to specific cases. This list of specific authorities excludes a general legislative authority. If a general authority was intended, a list of special powers would be absurd and useless.

ARTICLE 1 SECTION 9. The Migration or Importation of such Persons as any of the States now existing shall think proper to admit, shall not be prohibited by the Congress prior to the Year one thousand eight hundred and eight, but a tax or duty may be imposed on such Importation, not exceeding ten dollars for each Person.

Number 38 [9]

...Is the importation of slaves permitted by the new Constitution for 20 years? By the old (Articles of Confederation), it is permitted forever.

Number 42 [1, 7-8]

...The national government will... regulate foreign commerce including a power to prohibit, after 1808, the importation of slaves and, until then, lay a duty of ten dollars per head as a discouragement to such importations.

We wish that the Constitution banned the importation of slaves. Instead, the power to ban it is postponed until 1808.

For a long time, this traffic has been called barbarous. It is a great point in favor of humanity that in 20 years it might be banned forever within these States. During that period, the federal government will discourage it. The majority of the Union already prohibits it. And it can be totally abolished if the few States that allow the unnatural traffic agree to prohibit it. It would be happy for the unfortunate Africans if Europe also had a plan to prohibit it in twenty years!

Some opponents use this clause to object to the Constitution. One side says it is a criminal toleration of an illicit practice. The other says it was put in to prevent voluntary and beneficial emigrations from Europe to America. I mention these misconstructions only to show the manner and spirit of some people opposing the proposed government.

Number 43 [18]

... I have not mentioned the unhappy group of people in some of the States who are considered below the level of men. During times of civil violence, they may become men and give superior strength to the side they join.

Number 54 [4, 5]

...But the pretexts of laws, alone, have made Negroes property. And if laws restored the rights that have been taken away, the Negroes could not be refused an equal share of representation...

... Some people reproach the Southern States for the barbarous policy of considering part of their human brethren as property...

The privilege of the Writ of Habeas Corpus shall not be suspended, unless when in Cases of Rebellion or Invasion the public Safety may require it.

Number 83 [12]

...trial by jury in criminal cases, aided by *habeas-corpus*, is important. The Constitution provides for both.

Number 84 [4-5]

...Section 9, clause 2: "The privilege of the writ of *habeas corpus* shall not be suspended, unless when in cases of rebellion or invasion the public safety may require it."

...The proposed Constitution establishes the writ of *habeas corpus*,... Blackstone is worth quoting: "To bereave a man of life, (says he) or by violence to confiscate his estate, without accusation or trial, would be so gross and notorious an act of despotism, as must at once convey the alarm of tyranny throughout the whole nation; but confinement of the person, by secretly hurrying him to jail, where his sufferings are unknown or forgotten, is a less public, a less striking, and therefore *a more dangerous engine* of arbitrary government."[*]

To remedy this fatal evil, Blackstone praises the *habeas corpus* act. He calls it "the bulwark of the British Constitution."[**]

No Bill of Attainder or ex post facto Law shall be passed.

Number 44 [6]

Bills of attainder, *ex post facto* laws, and laws impairing the obligation of contracts contradict the social compact and every principle of sound legislation. Some State constitutions expressly prohibit bills of attainder and *ex post facto* laws; the spirit of the State constitutions prohibits them all.

However, experience teaches us to create additional barriers against these dangers. Therefore, the Constitution adds this protection of personal security and private rights. Fluctuating policy often directs public councils. Americans are angry with laws that affect personal rights and laws that profit speculators while snaring the less-informed citizens. One improper law is just the first link of a long chain of improper laws. Each one grows out of the effects of the preceding. Reform is needed. Speculations about public measures must end. General prudence and industry must be encouraged.

Number 78 [9]

In a limited Constitution, courts must be completely independent. A "limited" Constitution has specific exceptions to the legislative authority. For example, the legislature cannot pass bills of attainder or *ex post facto* laws. Courts of justice preserve these limitations. They declare all acts contrary to the meaning of the Constitution void. Without this, all Constitutional rights and privileges would mean nothing.

---

[*] *Vide* Blackstone's *Commentaries*, vol. 1., p. 136. –PUBLIUS

[**] *Vide* Blackston's *Commentaries*, vol. Iv., p. 438. –PUBLIUS

Number 84 [5]

...The proposed Constitution... prohibits ex-post-facto laws... a provision not in the New York constitution.

Tyrants love using *ex-post-facto* laws. These laws create crimes after someone has done something. In other words, men are punished for actions that, when they were done, broke no law. The tyrant can put anyone in prison by using this method.

No Capitation, or other direct, Tax shall be laid, unless in Proportion to the Census or Enumeration herein before directed to be taken.

(See Article 1 Section 8 taxation page 157)

No Tax or Duty shall be laid on Articles exported from any State.

Number 11 [12-13]

Unrestrained commerce between the States will advance trade. The free circulation of commodities will replenish the veins of commerce. The States will have a diversity of products. When the staple of one State fails from a bad harvest, it can get the staple of another...

Some people may argue that whether the States are united or disunited, interstate commerce would achieve the same ends. But disunity would hurt commerce. Unified commercial and political interests can only be achieved through a unified government.

Number 22 [4]

Contrary to the true spirit of the Union, some State regulations hurt the commerce in other States. Without national control, there will be more of these policies and anger between the States will grow, further damaging commerce.

The Encyclopaedia[*] ("Empire") describes Germany's commercial situation. Each German prince taxes the merchandise that travels through his state. The wide variety of taxes within Germany has put commerce in constant turmoil. And shippers have to stop and pay taxes so many times along the commercial routes that they don't even bother using Germany's navigable rivers.

This description may never completely apply to us. But as each State makes different commercial regulations, citizens of one State will treat citizens of other States no better than foreigners and aliens.

Number 32 [1, 2, 3]

... The States need an independent authority to raise revenues that the federal government can't control. With the sole exception of taxes on imports and exports, under the Constitution the States keep that authority...

...Another clause declares that no tax or duty shall be laid on articles exported from any State...

...the State ban on taxing imports and exports implies that the States have the power to tax...

---

[*] The article title is "Empire."

Number 33 [8]

...a federal law abolishing or preventing collection of State taxes (unless on imports and exports) would not be the supreme law of the land...The States will be able to raise revenue from any kind of taxation, except duties on imports and exports...

Number 42 [11]

...Some noncommercial States must import and export through other States. If they could, States would charge import and export taxes on merchandise and material passing through their State. This would create animosities and probably end in violence...

Number 44 [8]

...The States may charge a reasonable inspection fee but the federal government can block any abuse of this discretion...

Potential Reasons for Wars Between Disunited States

Number 7 [5-6]

Commerce is another source of controversy. Each State or separate confederacy would have a unique commercial policy with different taxes and product incentives. Commerce in this country has always been based on equal privileges. The change would make some States unhappy.

Injuries are caused by legitimate and justifiable acts of independent sovereignties with different interests.

America's enterprising businesses use every opportunity to improve. If trade regulations are made that only benefit one State, the other States probably won't obey them, which would lead to arguments, new regulations aimed at hurting the other States, then wars.

Some States would make commercial laws that make other States involuntarily subservient. The situation of New York, Connecticut, and New Jersey is an example.

New York put a tax on imports from Connecticut and New Jersey. Consumers in the two exporting States pay a large part of these taxes. New York will not voluntarily give up this advantage. How long would Connecticut and New Jersey pay taxes that only benefit New York? Would New York survive with the weight of Connecticut on one side and New Jersey on the other?

No Preference shall be given by any Regulation of Commerce or Revenue to the Ports of one State over those of another; nor shall Vessels, bound to, or from, one State, be obliged to enter, clear, or pay Duties in another.

No Money shall be drawn from the Treasury, but in Consequence of Appropriations made by Law; and a regular Statement and Account of the Receipts and Expenditures of all public Money shall be published from time to time.

Number 15 [3]

...But the Union has no troops, nor treasury, nor government to repel an aggressor. We can't even protest with dignity...

Number 41 [26]

...Article eight [in the Articles of Confederation] says: "All charges of war and all other expenses that shall be incurred for the common defense or general welfare, and allowed by the United States in Congress, shall be defrayed out of a common treasury," etc.

Number 72 [1]

...Government administration includes... asking for and spending public money as appropriated by the legislature,...

No Title of Nobility shall be granted by the United States;

Number 39 [6]

The Constitution prohibits titles of nobility...

Number 44 [6]

The prohibition against titles of nobility is copied from the Articles of Confederation and needs no comment.

Number 69 [9]

...The king of Great Britain is called the fountain of honors. He not only appoints to all offices, but can create offices. He can confer titles of nobility and give out an immense number of church honors. In this area, the President has less power than the British king.

Number 84 [6]

Prohibiting titles of nobility is important. This is the cornerstone of republican government. As long as titles are excluded, there can never be serious danger that the government will be any other than that of the people.

Number 85 [3]

If we adopt the Constitution... It will exclude all titles of nobility.

And no Person holding any Office of Profit or Trust under them, shall, without the Consent of the Congress, accept of any present, Emolument, Office, or Title, of any kind whatever, from any King, Prince, or foreign State.

ARTICLE 1 SECTION 10. No State shall...

State v. Federal Authority/Powers

Number 15 [5]

Our national system is defective. A remedy based on the only principles with a chance of success has been proposed. But adversaries of the federal system are very opposed to it. They admit the United States government has no energy, then fight against giving it the powers necessary to supply that energy.

They have disgusting and mutually exclusive goals. They want to increase federal authority without reducing State authority. They want a sovereign Union with completely independent members...

Number 37 [8]

Deciding the proper boundary between federal and State authorities was also a complicated task. Scientists and philosophers have tried to classify the abilities of the mind but no one has completed the task. The boundaries between the mental activities of sense, perception, judgment, desire, choice, memory, and imagination elude the subtlest investigations and are a source of controversy.

The boundaries between the various genuses and species in nature are another example of the same truth. Naturalists have not perfectly defined the line separating vegetable life from non-organic matter, or the line separating vegetable and animal life. There is an even greater obscurity between the objects in each category of nature.

Number 32 [2]

An entire consolidation of the States into one national sovereignty would imply an entire subordination of the parts; State powers would be completely dependent on the federal government. But the Constitution is only a partial union or consolidation. The States retain all the rights of sovereignty they had before except those that are not *exclusively* delegated to the United States by the Constitution. State sovereignty is transferred to the Union in three cases:

(1) where the Constitution expressly grants exclusive authority to the Union;

(2) where it grants a specific authority to the Union and prohibits the States from exercising the same authority;

(3) and where it grants an authority to the Union, to which similar authority in the States would be absolutely and totally *contradictory* and *repugnant*.

This last case is different from concurrent jurisdiction. When there is a concurrent jurisdiction, national and State *policies* may overlap occasionally, but there won't be any direct contradiction of constitutional authority.

The three cases of exclusive federal jurisdiction may be exemplified by the following:

(1) The next-to-the-last clause of article one, section eight, says Congress will exercise "*exclusive legislation*" over the capital district. This answers the first case.

(2) The first clause of article one, section eight empowers Congress "*to lay and collect taxes, duties, imposts, and excises*;" and the second clause of article one, section ten declares that, "*no State shall*, without the consent of Congress, *lay any imposts or duties on imports or exports*, except for the purpose of executing its inspection laws."

Therefore, the Union would have exclusive power to lay duties on imports and exports, with the specific exception mentioned. But this power is limited to *duties on imports*. Another clause declares that no tax or duty shall be laid on articles exported from any State. This answers the second case.

(3) The third is the clause that declares Congress will "establish a uniform rule of naturalization throughout the United States." This must be an exclusive power because if each State had power to prescribe a distinct rule, there could not be a uniform rule.

Number 80 [3]

...the Constitution limits State authority. The States are prohibited from doing several things. Some are incompatible with the interests of the Union. Others are incompatible with the principles of good government. There must be a way to enforce the restrictions.

For example, the States cannot tax imported articles. And(41) they cannot issue paper money. State prohibitions would not be obeyed if the federal government didn't have the power to stop or correct the infractions of them. The federal government needs either the power to veto State laws or an authority in the federal courts to overrule any violation of the Union's Constitution. The convention preferred the latter.

enter into any Treaty, Alliance, or Confederation; grant Letters of Marque and Reprisal;

Number 44 [3]

The Articles of Confederation also prohibits treaties, alliances, and confederations. Under the Articles, States could grant letters of marque after war is declared. In the new Constitution, they must be obtained from the federal government. Uniformity in foreign policy justifies this change. The States are responsible to the nation; the nation is responsible for the conduct of every State.

coin Money;

Number 44 [4]

The States cannot coin money. The federal government regulates the alloy and value of coins. Allowing States to manufacture coins has created two problems: many expensive mints and a diversity of shape, size, and weight of coins. State mints prevented the inconvenience of transporting gold and silver to the central mint. Establishing local mints under the national authority can solve this problem.

emit Bills of Credit; make any Thing but gold and silver Coin a Tender in Payment of Debts;

Number 38 [9]

...The present Congress... can emit bills of credit as long as it can pay for the paper.

Number 44 [5]

Prohibiting State bills of credit [paper money] is just and promotes public prosperity. Since the peace, paper money has eroded the confidence so necessary between man and man, in public councils, in industry, and in the republican government. It has become an enormous debt that the issuing States will not be able to pay off for a long time.

States are denied the power to regulate coin for good reasons. For the same reasons, they should not create paper money. If every State could regulate the value of its coin, every State could have a different currency, hurting interstate commerce. If a State retroactively changed the relative value of its money, it would injure the citizens of other States, kindling animosities among the States themselves. The citizens of foreign nations might also suffer, discrediting and embroiling the Union by the indiscretion of a single State could discredit the entire Union.

pass any Bill of Attainder, ex post facto Law, or Law impairing the Obligation of Contracts,

Number 44 [6]

Bills of attainder, *ex post facto* laws, and laws impairing the obligation of contracts contradict the social compact and every principle of sound legislation. Some State constitutions expressly prohibit bills of attainder and *ex post facto* laws; the spirit of the State constitutions prohibits them all.

However, experience teaches us to create additional barriers against these dangers. Therefore, the Constitution adds this protection of personal security and private rights. Fluctuating policy often directs public councils. Americans are angry with laws that affect personal rights and laws that profit speculators while snaring the less-informed citizens. One improper law is just the first link of a long chain of improper laws. Each one grows out of the effects of the preceding. Reform is needed. Speculations about public measures must end. General prudence and industry must be encouraged.

or grant any Title of Nobility.

Number 44 [6]

...The prohibition against titles of nobility is copied from the Articles of Confederation and needs no comment.

No State shall, without the Consent of Congress, lay any Imposts or Duties on Imports or Exports, except what may be absolutely necessary for executing its inspection Laws: and the net Produce of all Duties and Imposts, laid by any State on Imports or Exports, shall be for the Use of the Treasury of the United States; and all

such Laws shall be subject to the Revision and Controul of the Congress.

Number 7 [6]

Some States would make commercial laws that make other States involuntarily subservient…

Number 22 [4]

…some State regulations hurt the commerce in other States.

Number 32 [1-3]

…The States need an independent authority to raise revenues that the federal government can't control. With the sole exception of taxes on imports and exports, under the Constitution the States keep that authority.

State sovereignty is transferred to the Union in three cases: …(2) where it grants a specific authority to the Union and prohibits the States from exercising the same authority;…

The three cases of exclusive federal jurisdiction may be exemplified by the following: … (2) The first clause of article one, section eight empowers Congress "*to lay and collect taxes, duties, imposts, and excises*;" and the second clause of article one, section ten declares that, "*no State shall*, without the consent of Congress, *lay any imposts or duties on imports or exports*, except for the purpose of executing its inspection laws."

Therefore, the Union would have exclusive power to lay duties on imports and exports, with the specific exception mentioned. But this power is limited to *duties on imports*.

The federal government and the individual States have concurrent and coequal authority to impose taxes on all articles other than exports and imports.

The clause does not give the Union *exclusive* power. And no clause prohibits States from the power to tax. On the contrary, the State ban on taxing imports and exports implies that the States have the power to tax. And it also implies that State authority remains undiminished. In all cases not restricted, the States would have a concurrent power of taxation with the Union.

The clause that bans State import and export taxes is called a negative pregnant—that is, a *negation* of one thing and an *affirmation* of another. States **cannot** impose taxes on imports and exports and **can** impose them on all other articles. It is sophistry to argue that it excludes States *absolutely* from duties and allows them to lay other taxes *subject to the control* of the national legislature.

Number 33 [8]

…The States will be able to raise revenue from any kind of taxation, except duties on imports and exports…

Number 34 [1]

Under the proposed Constitution, the States and the Union will have coequal taxing authority, except duties on imports…

Number 36 [13]

There won't be double sets of officers in two cases: The first is when the Union has exclusive right to impose the tax, for instance, duties on imports...

Number 42 [11]

...Some noncommercial States must import and export through other States. If they could, States would charge import and export taxes on merchandise and material passing through their State. This would create animosities and probably end in violence...

Number 44 [8]

...The States may charge a reasonable inspection fee but the federal government can block any abuse of this discretion.

Number 80 [3]

...the States cannot tax imported articles...

No State shall, without the Consent of Congress, lay any duty of Tonnage, keep Troops, or Ships of War in time of Peace, enter into any Agreement or Compact with another State or with a foreign Power, or engage in War, unless actually invaded, or in such imminent Danger as will not admit of delay.

Number 25 [4]

Separate State military forces are dangerous to the Union. Under the Articles of Confederation, Congress must approve State ships or troops. Both federal and State governments cannot have armies.

ARTICLE 2 SECTION 1. The executive Power shall be vested in a President of the United States of America.

Federalist Papers 67-77 discuss the executive branch of the government. To me, the terms "legislative" and "judicial" are clear descriptions of those branches of government. "Executive" seemed less clear. I realized this was because the primary duties of the President--enforcing the laws of the nation and acting as commander-in-chief--is usually done out of the limelight.

When we see the President, he is performing his lesser duties: "from time to time give to Congress Information of the State of the Union, and recommend to their consideration such measures as he shall judge necessary and expedient." (Article 2 Section 3) I call these "lesser" because the first is simply a report to Congress and the second was expected to be limited.

When framing the Executive branch of the government, the first decision was whether to put the entire power of the branch in one person or a council. For reasons detailed below, the framers decided on one person. This led to the next dilemma: With all the power of the Executive combined in one person, would the position of President evolve into something that looks and acts like a monarch? The Founding Fathers were keenly aware that a title or name wasn't a block to monarchial behavior or a dictatorship.

Number 38 [7]

People who want an executive council can't agree on how it would be formed. Some people want a small council appointed by the House of Representatives. Others think the President should appoint a large council.

Plural Executives in States

Number 47 [13-15, 17]

New Jersey's constitution blends the powers of government even more. The legislature appoints the governor. The governor judges some cases, is one of the supreme court judges, and is president—with a casting vote—of one of the legislative houses. The same legislative house is the governor's executive council and, with him, they are the Court of Appeals...

In Pennsylvania, the legislature has the primary role in electing the chief executive. The chief executive and his council appoint judges and form an impeachment court for trial of officers, judiciary and executive. The legislature may remove supreme court judges and justices of the peace. The legislature has some power to pardon, normally an executive power. The members of the executive council are EX OFFICIO [automatically] justices of peace in the State.

In Delaware, the legislature elects the chief executive every year. The speakers of the two legislative houses are vice-presidents in the executive branch. The chief executive with three people appointed by each legislative house is the Supreme Court of Appeals. The chief executive joins with the legislature to appoint other judges.

In all the States, it appears that legislators may also be justices of the peace. In New York, the members of one house are justices of the peace, as are the members of the executive council. The legislature appoints most executive officers...

...the Virginia legislature appoints the chief executive and his council. Every three years, the legislature removes two members of the executive council.

Number 48 [15]

...Pennsylvania's executive council has more members than the other States, so it's similar to a legislative assembly...

Why a Plural Executive is Dangerous

Number 48 [15]

...a council doesn't feel the same restraint as an individual, who is personally responsible for his acts. Members get confidence from each other and are influenced by each other so that unauthorized measures are more easily tried than where the executive branch is administered by a single hand or a few hands.

Benefits of Unified Executive

Number 69 [2]

One person will hold most of the Executive authority, the President. This feature doesn't help us decide if the Executive authority, as defined in the Constitution, is appropriate. Because it is one person, it may look like the king of Great Britain. However, it also looks like the Grand Seignior, the Khan of Tartary, the Man of the Seven Mountains, and the governor of New York.

Number 70 [all]

Some people say that a republic cannot have an energetic Executive. People who understand and support this type government must hope that there is no foundation for this idea. If it were true, it would condemn their belief in the principles of good government.

The executive branch of government must have the powers to fulfill its duties. Energy in the executive is an important characteristic of good government.

The community must be protected against foreign attacks. Property must be protected against conspiracies that block justice. And liberty must be protected from the negative effects of ambition, faction, and anarchy.

The republic of Rome often had to give all executive power to a single man with the title of Dictator. He stopped internal conspiracies, led by ambitious and tyrannical people who threatened the government. And he blocked invasions by external enemies who tried to conquer and destroy Rome.

Feeble Executive Leads to Bad Government

A feeble executive implies a feeble execution of government. A feeble execution is another way to say a bad execution. And a badly executed government is a bad government.

Safe Republic, Energetic Executive

Therefore, let's agree that an energetic executive is necessary. What ingredients create this energy? How can they be combined with the ingredients that keep the republic safe from a dictator? And how well does the proposed Constitution combine an energetic executive with republican safety?

Qualities of Energetic Executive

To have energy, the executive needs:

(1) unity,
(2) duration,
(3) guaranteed compensation,
(4) and enough powers.

Qualities of Republican Safety

The ingredients that constitute safety, in the republican sense, are: (1) due dependence on the people, (2) due responsibility.

One Executive; Numerous Legislature

Respected statesmen say that there should be a single executive and a large legislature. They say that energy is the most important quality of the executive branch of government. And this is achieved when one person holds the executive power.

A large legislature is best for deliberation and wisdom. It will have the people's confidence and secure their privileges and interests.

Benefits of Unified Executive

Unity promotes energy. One man can be more decisive, keep secrets, and act faster than any greater number of people. And as the number of people increases, these qualities diminish.

Executive Unity Destroyed

Unity may be destroyed in two ways. Executive power can be given to two or more people with equal status and authority. Or it can be given ostensibly to one man who is subject, in whole or part, to the control and cooperation of other people who act as counselors to him.

The two consuls of Rome are an example of the first. We find examples of the second in several State constitutions. New York and New Jersey, I think, are the only States that give one man the entire executive authority.*

There are supporters of both ways of destroying the unity of the executive, but more people want an executive council. The two types of plural executive are different. However, objections to them are similar and can be examined together.

---

* New York only has a council for appointing to offices. New Jersey's governor may consult a council. But I don't think their resolutions bind him.—PUBLIUS

History: Plural Executives

History teaches us little about this topic. Looking at the experiences of other nations, we learn that a plural executive is not a good idea.

The Achaeans tried having two Praetors, but they were forced to get rid of one.

Roman history records the problems that arose from arguments between the Consuls and the military Tribunes, who were at times substituted for the Consuls.

But history gives us no examples of any real advantages of a plural executive. We might be surprised that disagreements between Consuls were not more frequent or more fatal, until we remember the Roman republic's almost constant situation. The government was divided between the Consuls, who were usually chosen from the aristocrats. The aristocrats constantly fought with the common people to keep their ancient authorities. The Consuls often united to defend the privileges of their class.

After the military increased the size of the republican empire, the Consuls divided the administration of the empire between themselves by lot. One Consul remained at Rome to govern the city and surrounding area. The other took command of the distant areas of the country. This probably prevented rivalries that might have threatened the peace of the republic.

Logic Rejects Plural Executive

If we leave the lessons of history and use only logic and good sense, we discover more reasons to reject the idea of a plural Executive of any kind.

Plural Executive: Animosity Inevitable

Wherever two or more persons are engaged in a common pursuit, there is always danger of differences of opinion. If it is a public trust or office, where they have equal rank and authority, there is a real danger of personal envy and even animosity. Envy and animosity often cause bitter disagreements. The people who disagree lose some respect and authority. And they distract from the plans and operations needed to attain the goal.

Let's say that two or more people must serve as the top executives of a country. During an emergency, envy and animosity could slow down or even block important government actions. And worse, they might split the community into violent and irreconcilable factions that support the different individuals who compose the executive.

Envy, Pride Motivate Opposition

Men often oppose a thing just because they had no part in planning it or because people they dislike may have planned it. But if they have been consulted and have disapproved, their opposition becomes an absolute duty of self-love. They feel bound in honor and personal infallibility to defeat a plan that is contrary to their beliefs.

This psychological reaction can lead men to take desperate actions. And men often have enough followers to sacrifice the interests of society to their vanity, conceit, and obstinacy.

Perhaps the consequences of the question now before the public may give us sad proofs of the effects of this despicable frailty, or detestable vice, in the human character.

Legislature Designed to Act Slowly

In a free government these inconveniences must be tolerated from the legislature. But it is unnecessary and unwise to introduce them into the executive branch. And they can be the most harmful in the executive.

In the legislature, fast decisions are more often evil than good. Although different opinions and party haggling can sometimes obstruct good plans, they often promote deliberation and careful analysis. They block excesses by the majority. Also, when a law is passed, the opposition must end. And breaking the law is punishable.

But there are no advantages to disagreements in the executive branch. There are only disadvantages. There is no point at which they cease to operate.

Disagreements about a specific plan would weaken the execution of the plan, from the first step to the end. Vigor and expedition are necessary executive qualities. Disagreements among the executives would block these without any counterbalancing good.

During war, when national security depends on a strong executive, everything would be feared from a plural executive.

Council Also Weakens Executive

These comments principally apply to the first case, a plural executive where each person has equal authority. Few people want this type of executive.

But if the ostensible executive needs the approval of an executive council before he can act, most of the same comments apply. An artful cabal in the council could distract and weaken the whole system of administration. If no such cabal existed, the diversity of views and opinions, alone, would make the executive feeble and slow to act.

Plurality Hides Faults, Individual Responsibility

But one of the strongest objections to both types of plural executive is that it tends to conceal faults and destroy responsibility.

There are two types of responsibility: moral and legal. Irresponsibility leads to censure and to punishment. Censure is the more important, especially in an elective office. An irresponsible man in public office will more often act in a way that makes him unworthy of trust than in a way that makes him subject to legal punishment.

But when more than one person holds the position of Executive, it is difficult to figure out who is morally or legally responsible. The people in the executive will accuse each other. It often becomes impossible to determine who to blame or punish for a harmful act. Blame is shifted from one to another with so much dexterity that the public doesn't know who made the decision.

The circumstances leading to any national misfortune can be extremely complicated. We could clearly see that there has been mismanagement. But if several people were involved in making the decision, it may be impossible to say who is truly responsible for the evil.

"I was overruled by my council."

"The council was so divided in their opinions that it was impossible to obtain any better resolution on the point."

These and similar pretexts are always available, whether true or false. And who will take the trouble or incur the odium of a strict scrutiny into the secret discussions of the council? If a zealous citizen wants to take on the task and if there is collusion between the parties involved, it would be easy to make each participant's part in the plan so ambiguous that no one could discover the precise conduct of each member of the council.

New York's Disastrous Experience

The governor of New York is coupled with a council for one duty, appointing to offices. And we have seen the mischiefs described: scandalous appointments to important offices. Some cases, indeed, have been so flagrant that everyone agrees they are improper. When asked about them, the governor has blamed the members of the council who blamed it on his nomination. Meanwhile, the people have no idea who picked such unqualified and improper people.

Accountability, Plural Executive

The people have two securities that public officials will use their delegated powers faithfully. A plural Executive tends to deprive the people of these securities.

First. The restraints of public opinion lose their effectiveness because it is difficult to divide censure among a number of people.

Second. It will be difficult to discover which public official is responsible for misconduct, so they can be removed from office or punished, if appropriate.

King Unaccountable, Perpetual Executive

In England, the king is the lifetime executive. For the sake of public peace, he is unaccountable for his administration and his person is sacred. Therefore, giving the king a constitutional council means that someone will be responsible to the nation for the advice they give. Without this, there would be no responsibility whatever in the executive branch—an idea inadmissible in a free government.

But the king is not bound by the resolutions of his council, though they are answerable for the advice they give. He is the absolute master of his own conduct as the nation's executive. He can use or disregard the advice given to him.

Council Would Damage U. S. Executive

But in a republic, every executive should be held personally responsible for his behavior in office. The reason for the British council doesn't apply. And an executive council might decrease the executive's perceived responsibility. In the American republic, a council would greatly diminish the responsibility of the Chief Executive himself.

The monarch of Great Britain, who is the chief executive, cannot be held responsible. To some degree, the monarch is a hostage to the national justice for his good behavior.

One Executive Safer

Many State constitutions include a council to the Executive. They have developed from the maxim of republican jealousy, which considers power as safer in the hands of a number of men than of a single man. In this case, I think the disadvantages outweigh this possible advantage.

But I do not think the maxim applies to the national executive power. I agree that to be "deep, solid, and ingenious, the executive power is more easily confined when it is one."[*] It is far safer for the people to watch one person. And a plural Executive is more dangerous than friendly to liberty.

Easier for Group to Usurp Power

The kind of security sought for in a plural EXECUTIVE is unattainable. The number has to be so great that conspiracy is difficult; otherwise conspiracies become a source of danger rather than security.

When power is placed in a small number of men, a talented leader can easily get them to agree to a common enterprise. A small group is easier to abuse and more dangerous when abused, than a single man. One man can be closely watched and more easily suspected.

The Decemvirs of Rome, whose name denotes their number,[**] could more easily usurp power than any one of them, alone.

No one would think of proposing an executive much larger than the Decemvirs. From six to a dozen have been suggested for the number of the council. The largest number isn't too great for an easy conspiracy. America would have more to fear from such a conspiracy than from the ambition of any single individual.

A council to an executive, who is responsible for what he does, clogs his good intentions, becomes accomplices of his bad deeds, and almost always is a cloak to his faults.

Plural Executive Expensive

I won't dwell on the subject of expense. However, a council, which is large enough to fulfill the goal aimed at by instituting it, would be very expensive.

Prior to the discussion about the proposed Constitution, nearly every intelligent man I met said that the unity of the New York executive is one of the best features of our State constitution.

Number 67 [2-5]

Framing the executive branch was probably the most difficult part of the Constitution. Yet the vehement criticism isn't based on sound judgment.

Critics Magnify President into Monarch

When they write about the executive branch, opponents of the Constitution have showed their talent for misrepresentation. The people hate and fear the monarchy. Building on this fear, opponents of the Constitution claim the President will be just another form of a monarchy. To prove this, they have even drawn arguments from fiction.

They claim he will have more dignity and splendor than a British king. He has been pictured with a sparkling crown, wearing imperial robes, sitting on a throne. We've seen images of murdering guards and a mysterious future palace.

---

[*] DeLolme.—PUBLIUS
[**] Ten.—PUBLIUS

The attempts to morph the president into a king make it necessary to look at its real nature and form.

Opponents use false arguments to pervert public opinion on the subject. They exceed the usual unjustified license of party artifice. It's difficult to treat them seriously. Opponents are deliberately using fraud and deception.

Number 69 [10-11]

President: Far Less Power than King

With the exception of the President's authority in making treaties, it is difficult to determine whether he would have more or less power than the governor of New York.

It is very clear that there is no reason for the parallel that some people have attempted to make between him and the king of Great Britain. But to highlight the difference, we will take a closer look at the dissimilarities.

President vs. Monarch's Authorities

The President of the United States would be elected every *four* years; the King of Great Britain is a perpetual and *hereditary* prince.

The one could face personal punishment and disgrace; the other is sacred and inviolable.

The one would have a *qualified* negative on the acts of the legislative body; the other has an *absolute* negative.

The one would have a right to command the military and naval forces of the nation; the other also has the authority to *declare* war, and *raise* and *regulate* fleets by his own authority.

The one would have a concurrent power with a branch of the legislature in the formation of treaties; the other is the *sole possessor* of the power to make treaties.

The one can confer no privileges whatever; the other can make citizens of aliens, noblemen of commoners, can erect corporations with all the rights of corporate bodies.

The one cannot regulate the commerce or currency of the nation; the other can regulate commerce, establish markets and fairs, regulate weights and measures, lay embargoes for a limited time, coin money, authorize or prohibit the circulation of foreign coin. The one has no religious jurisdiction; the other is the supreme head of the national church!

What should we say to people who try to tell us that things so dissimilar resemble each other? The same answer that should be given to people who tell us that a government, with the whole power in the hands of the elective and periodical servants of the people, is an aristocracy, a monarchy, and a despotism.

He shall hold his Office during the Term of four Years,

Number 39 [5]

The President's term in office is four years. And he is impeachable at any time during his time in office…

Number 69 [3]

    The President will be elected for *four* years. He is re-eligible as often as the people of the United States think him worth their confidence. [*This was changed with the presidential term limits amendment.*]

    This is totally different than a British king, who is a *hereditary* monarch. His crown is passed down to his heirs forever.

    However, the President and a New York governor are similar. The governor is elected for *three* years and is re-eligible without limitation. It would be quicker to establish a dangerous influence in a single State than establishing a similar influence throughout the nation. We must conclude that the President's *four*-year term is less dangerous than a *three*-year term for the governor in a single State.

Number 71 [all]

    The second requirement for energy in the Executive is duration in office. Duration includes:

    1) the executive's personal firmness in the employment of his constitutional powers

    2) and stable system of administration adopted under his sponsorship.

    First. The longer the time in office, the greater is the probability of getting this advantage. It is a principle of human nature that a man is interested in something he possesses in proportion to the firmness or precariousness by which he holds it. He will be less attached to something he holds for a short time. And he will be willing to risk more for something he firmly holds than for the something he precariously holds.

    This remark applies to a political office just as to any article of property. We can infer that a chief executive who knows he *must* leave his office may have little interest in it. He might not take the chance of censure or entanglement from the independent use of his powers. He won't act if he might encounter ill-humors from either a large part of society or a large faction in the legislative body.

    Instead, if he only *might* leave office unless reelected, and if he wants to be reelected, his wishes, conspiring with his fears, would tend still more powerfully to corrupt his integrity or debase his fortitude.

    In either case, the executive would become feeble and irresolute.

Leaders Ignore Bad Fads

    Some people think that a pliant Executive, who acts as the community or legislature seems to want, is good. But these people have crude ideas about the purpose of government and the true way to promote public happiness.

    The republican principle demands that the will of the community should govern the conduct of those people who are entrusted with management of their affairs. But it does not require absolute compliance to every sudden passion or impulse aroused within the people by clever men who flatter the community's prejudices to betray their interests.

    It is true that the people commonly *intend* the public good. This often applies even to their errors. But the people's good sense would hate the adulator who pretends that they always *reason right* about the *means* of promoting it.

    They know from experience that they sometimes err. It is amazing that they make so few mistakes. They are constantly bombarded by the wiles of parasites and sycophants, by the snares of the ambitious, the avaricious, the desperate, by the artifices of men who have more confidence than they deserve, and of those who seek to possess rather than to deserve it. When the interests of the people are different than what they may want, it is the government's duty to guard those interests, to withstand the temporary delusion and give them time for cooler, sedate reflection.

We can show examples of when leaders saved the people from fatal consequences of their own mistakes. The people are thankful to the leaders who had courage to serve them at the peril of their displeasure.

Executive Should Act Independently

But even if we insist that the Executive always comply with the will of the people, we can not argue that the legislature must comply in the same way. Sometimes the legislature may oppose the executive. At other times, the people may be neutral. In either case, it is certainly desirable that the Executive should act on his own opinion with vigor and decision.

Separation Avoids Legislative Dominance

Separation of power between the branches of power is very important. Each branch should be independent of the others. Why separate the executive or the judiciary from the legislative, if the legislative can void the acts of both the executive and the judiciary? Such a separation would be in name only. And it couldn't produce the result for which it was established.

Being subordinate to the laws is different from being dependent on the legislative body. The first agrees with and the last violates the fundamental principles of good government. And despite the Constitution, it unites all power in the same hands.

As shown in earlier papers, the legislative branch tends to absorb every other branch. In a republic, this tendency is almost irresistible. The representatives of the people sometimes seem to believe that they are the people themselves. They become impatient when the executive or judiciary exercise their rights. They act like it is a breach of legislative privilege and an outrage to the representatives' dignity.

The legislature often seems to want imperial control over the other branches. And since they commonly have the people on their side, they act with a force that makes it very difficult for the other branches of the government to keep the constitutional balance.

Term Effects Executive Independence

How can a short term in office affect the independence of the Executive on the legislature, unless the one has the power of appointing or displacing the other?

One answer comes from the principle already mentioned. A man is apt to have less interest in an office he holds for a short term. And he will have little reason to expose himself to inconvenience or hazard. Another answer is that the legislature influences voters. Their influence might be used to prevent the re-election of a man who, by resisting a sinister legislative project, makes himself the target of its resentment.

Is four years the proper term in office? If not, should it be a shorter period because it provides a greater security against ambitious designs. Or a longer period that is too short to inspire the desired firmness and independence of the executive.

4-Year Term Seems Best

We don't know for sure that four years is the correct period of time. But it would influence the spirit and character of the government. Between the beginning and end of a four-year term, there would be a long time before the thought of having to get reelected would have an improper effect on the conduct of a man with enough fortitude. He could promise himself that there was enough time to make the community aware that the measures he wishes to pursue are proper.

As reelection approaches, his confidence might decline. But it will increase if he has established himself in the esteem and good will of his constituents during his time in office. So he might take a chance, if he has proven his wisdom and integrity, and become respected by his fellow citizens.

A four-year term contributes to the firmness of the Executive. But it is not long enough to justify any alarm for the public liberty.

The British House of Commons has *the small power to agree or disagree to new taxes*. Using this one power, from its beginning the House of Commons has been able to reduce the monarch's choices and the nobility's privileges. They have set limits to each that they feel are compatible with the principles of a free government. At the same time, the House of Commons has raised itself to the rank of co-equal branch of the legislature. In one instance, they abolished both the royalty and the aristocracy, and overturned all the ancient establishments, in the Church as well as the State...

Therefore, what would be feared from an elected executive with a four-year term and the limited authorities of a President of the United States? What but that he might be unequal to the task assigned him by the Constitution?

I will only add that if a term of four years leaves a doubt of his firmness, that doubt is inconsistent with the worry about his encroachments.

Number 79 [2]

The President is elected for no more than four years.

Presidential Term Limits

The absence of term limits has been mentioned in the above Papers. The subject is more thoroughly discuss in the following Papers. The drafters of the new Constitution did not expect it to be perfect. Paper Number 37 [5] reminds us: The Convention could only avoid the errors made by our Confederation and other countries, and provide an amendment process to correct the convention's errors, as future experience exposes them.

The authors of the Federalist Papers had given themselves the task of recommending the new Constitution for ratification, even if there was something in the Constitution that they might not agree with. In the argument against term limits, I feel a bit of a strain by the author, as if he is not in full agreement. He even hedges his own psychological arguments about ambitious men, saying that "might" do this or "probably" would do that. And he ignores their ability to sway large groups of people.

Number 71 [1]

The second requirement for energy in the Executive is duration in office. Duration includes:

1) the executive's personal firmness in the employment of his constitutional powers

2) and stable system of administration adopted under his sponsorship.

First. The longer the time in office, the greater is the probability of getting this advantage. It is a principle of human nature that a man is interested in something he possesses in proportion to the firmness or precariousness by which he holds it. He will be less attached to something he holds for a short time. And he will be willing to risk more for something he firmly holds than for the something he precariously holds.

This remark applies to a political office just as to any article of property. We can infer that a chief executive who knows he *must* leave his office may have little interest in it. He might not take the chance of censure or entanglement from the independent use of his powers. He won't act if he might encounter ill-humors from either a large part of society or a large faction in the legislative body.

Instead, if he only *might* leave office unless reelected, and if he wants to be reelected, his wishes, conspiring with his fears, would tend still more powerfully to corrupt his integrity or debase his fortitude.

In either case, the executive would become feeble and irresolute.

Number 72 [all]

In its largest sense, the administration of government includes all government operations. But in its most precise definition, it is limited to executive duties.

Government administration includes conducting foreign negotiations, preparing financial plans, asking for and spending public money as appropriated by the legislature, directing the army, navy and operations of war, and other similar duties. Therefore, the people who manage these areas should be considered assistants or deputies of the chief executive. The President should appoint them or, at least, nominate and supervise them. This suggests the close connection between the President's term in office and a stable administration.

To prove his worth, a new office-holder often reverses his predecessor's actions. When the change is because of an election, the new person can assume that his predecessor lost the election because people disliked his measures.* And the less he acts like his predecessor, the more his constituents will like him. For these reasons and the influence of friends, every new President will probably change the men filling offices. For these reasons, the government's administration can become dangerously mutable.

Reelection of Good Administrator

The President will serve for four years and will be eligible to be reelected. The four-year term gives the president the desire to do a good job. And it gives the community time to see his measures and form an opinion of their merits. Without term limits, the

---

* Assuming the previous President wasn't blocked from re-election by term limits. --Webster

people may reelect him. He can continue using his talents and virtues. The government will have the advantage of continuing a wise system of administration.

Presidential Term Limit Bad Idea

Some respected people want presidential term limits. It appears like a good idea. But close inspection shows that it is not a good idea. Term limits mean that a president continues in office for a certain period of time and then is excluded from that office either for a limited period or forever.

Whether temporary or forever, excluding a man from running for President would have almost the same effects. And these effects would be more harmful than beneficial.

Possible Reelection Effects Behavior

One bad effect: Term limits would reduce the reasons for good behavior. Most men feel less zeal to perform a duty when they know that the advantages connected with their office must be given up at a predetermined time. They have more zeal when there is a hope of *obtaining*, by *meriting*, a continuance in office.

The desire for a reward motivates human conduct. And the best security for fidelity is to make a man's interest coincide with his duty.

The love of fame is the strongest passion of the noblest minds. A man might undertake difficult tasks for the public benefit that require a long time to finish if he feels he might be reelected and be able to finish what he started. However, the desire for fame would stop him from starting the project if he knows he must leave before finishing the work. He wouldn't want to give the project and his reputation to a successor who might be unequal or unfriendly to the task. The most we can expect of men who cannot be reelected is the negative merit of doing no harm, instead of the positive merit of doing good.

Effect on Avaricious Office Holder

Second bad effect: The man would be tempted to evil thoughts, embezzlement, and usurpation. An avaricious man, who knows when he must give up the benefits of his office, would be tempted to make the best use of his limited opportunity. He might use corrupt methods to make his harvest as large as it was transitory.

If the same man felt he might be reelected, he might be content with the regular benefits of his office. He might not want to risk the consequences of abusing his opportunities. His avarice might be a guard on his avarice.

Perhaps he is vain or ambitious, as well as avaricious. And if he expected to be reelected if he behaved properly, he might hesitate to sacrifice his desire to be reelected to his desire for gain. But if he is forced to leave office, his avarice would probably win over his caution, his vanity, or his ambition.

Effect on Ambitious Office Holder

Also, let's say an ambitious man held his country's highest position of honor. If term limits were going to force him to descend from the exalted eminence forever and if he knows that no merit on his part could save him, he would be tempted to find a way to prolong his power. He will risk every personal hazard to maintain his position.

Effect of Living Ex-Presidents

Would the community be more peaceful or the government more stable if a half-dozen former presidents were wandering among the people like discontented ghosts, sighing for a place they are destined never more to possess?

Experience Parent of Wisdom

Third bad effect: The community could not use the experience gained by a president.

Experience is the parent of wisdom. Experience is the most desirable and essential quality in the head of a nation. Is it wise to constitutionally ban this desirable and essential quality? This is what term limits would do.

Effect of Changing During Crisis

Fourth bad effect: Men who might be needed during emergencies could not be President. Every nation has needed, at one time or another, the services of specific men in specific situations, perhaps even to save the nation. Therefore, term limits prohibit a nation from using its own citizens during emergencies!

Even if a man weren't essential, changing Presidents as a war breaks out or during any similar crisis, even for a man of equal merit, would always be detrimental to the community. It would substitute inexperience for experience. And it would tend to unhinge and set afloat the already settled administration.

Effect of Policy Changes

Fifth bad effect: Term limits would create a constitutional ban on a stable administration. By *requiring* a change of President, it would guarantee mutable measures. When the man holding an office changes, policies will also change. And we need not worry about too much stability when there is the option of changing. We should not prohibit citizens from reelecting someone they trust when they may prevent the inconveniences of changing councils and policy.

Partial/Perpetual Term Limits

These are some of the disadvantages of term limits, especially lifetime exclusion. And a partial exclusion would make reelecting a former President a remote possibility. Therefore they apply nearly as fully to both cases.

Advantages of Term Limits

What are the promised advantages of term limits? They are (1) greater independence in the executive and (2) greater security to the people.

The first advantage can only be inferred if the exclusion is permanent. Couldn't he sacrifice his presidential independence to a future objective? Won't he have friends for whom he may sacrifice it? Might he be less willing to take decisive actions that could make personal enemies when he knows that very soon he will be just a citizen? And he will be exposed to their resentments on an equal, even an inferior, footing?

It is hard to say whether he would be more or less independent in such a situation.

Term Limits: People's Security

There is a greater reason to doubt the second supposed advantage.

Let's say a man was excluded from the office for the rest of his life. A man of irregular ambition would reluctantly leave the office forever, an office where he had acquired a passion for power and pre-eminence. If he had been fortunate or adroit enough to become a favorite of the people, he might get them to reconsider the effects of term limits. He could show that term limits are an odious and unjustifiable restraint on the people because it takes away their right to give a fresh proof of their attachment to a favorite.

We can imagine the people becoming disgusted because they can't reelect a favorite man. Liberty could be in more danger than could be feared from the possibility of continuing in office by the voluntary votes of the community.

Disadvantages Outweigh Advantages

The idea of stopping the people from voting to continue in office men who they admire is too much refinement. The advantages are at best speculative and equivocal. And they are overbalanced by certain and decisive disadvantages.

Number 85 [2]

The proposed Constitution resembles New York's constitution. The New York constitution has many of the same imagined defects, as well as the real excellences.

Among the imagined defects are:

> no term limits for the Executive,
>
> no executive council,

…New York's constitution doesn't have these provisions. And it doesn't have several others. If a man bitterly complains about the proposed Constitution but easily excuses the New York constitution, he isn't consistent.

Some people who admire the New York state government have furiously attacked the new Constitution for provisions that are also in New York's constitution. This proves that their attacks on the Constitution are insincere.

and together with the Vice President, chosen for the same Term, be elected as follows:

Each State shall appoint, in such Manner as the Legislature thereof may direct, a Number of Electors, equal to the whole Number of Senators and Representatives to which the State may be entitled in Congress: but no Senator or Representative, or Person holding an Office of Trust or Profit under the United States, shall be appointed as Elector.

[The Electors shall meet in their respective States, and vote by Ballot for two Persons, of whom one at least shall not be an Inhabitant of the same State with themselves. And they shall make a List of all Persons voted for, and of the Number of Votes for each; which List they shall sign and certify, and transmit sealed to the Government of the United States. Directed to the President of the

Senate. The President of the Senate shall, in the Presence of the Senate and House of Representatives, open all the Certificates, and the Votes shall then be counted. The Person having the greatest Number of Votes shall be the President, if such Number be a Majority of the whole Number of Electors appointed; and if there be more than one who have such Majority, and have an equal Number of Votes, then the House of Representatives shall immediately chuse by Ballot one of them for President; and if no person have a Majority, then from the five highest on the List the said House shall in like manner chuse the President. But in chusing the President, the Votes shall be taken by States, the Representation from each State having one Vote; a quorum for this Purpose shall consist of a Member or Members from two-thirds of the States, and a Majority of all the States shall be necessary to a Choice. In every Case, after the Choice of the President, the Person having the greatest Number of Votes of the Electors shall be the Vice President. But if there should remain two or more who have equal Votes, the Senate shall chuse from them by Ballot the Vice President.]

changed by Amendment 12

The Electors shall meet in their respective states, and vote by ballot for President, and Vice President, one of whom, at least, shall not be an inhabitant of the same State with themselves; they shall name in their ballots the person voted for as President, and in distinct ballots the person voted for as Vice-President, and they shall make distinct lists of all persons voted for as President, and of all persons voted for as Vice-President, and of the number of votes for each, which lists they shall sign and certify, and transmit sealed to the seat of the government of the United States, directed to the President of the Senate;--The President of the Senate shall, in the presence of the Senate and House of Representatives, open all the certificates and the votes shall then be counted; The person having the greatest number of votes for President, shall be the President, if such number be a majority of the whole number of Electors appointed; and if no person have such majority, then from the persons having the highest numbers not exceeding three on the list of those voted for as President, the House of Representatives shall choose immediately, by ballot, the President. But in choosing the President, the votes shall be taken by states, the representation from each State having one vote; a quorum for this purpose shall consist of a member or members from two-thirds of the states, and a majority of all the states shall be necessary to a choice. [And if the House of Representatives shall not choose a President whenever the right of choice shall devolve upon them, before the fourth day of March next following, then the Vice-President shall act as President, as in the case of the death or other constitutional disability of the President---]* The person having the greatest number of votes as Vice-President, shall be the Vice-President, if such number be a majority of the whole number of Electors appointed, and if no person have a majority, then from the two highest numbers an the list, the Senate shall choose the Vice-President; a quorum for the purpose shall consist of two-thirds of the whale number of Senators, and a majority of the whale number shall be necessary to a choice, But no person constitutionally ineligible to the office of President shall be eligible to that of Vice-President of the United States.

* Superseded by section 3 of 20th Amendment.

Section 3. If, at the time fixed for the beginning of the term of the President, the President elect shall have died, the Vice-President elect shall become President. If a President shall not have been chosen before the time fixed for the beginning of his term, or if the President elect shall have failed to qualify, then the Vice-President elect shall act as President until a President shall have qualified; and the Congress may by law provide for the case wherein neither a President elect nor a Vice-President elect shall have qualified, declaring who shall then act as President, or the manner in which one who is to act shall be selected, and such person shall act accordingly until a President or Vice-President shall have qualified.

Number 68 [all]

Method of Electing President

Opponents of the Constitution have slightly approved the method of appointing the chief Executive of the United States. If the method isn't perfect, it is at least excellent. It clearly unites all the advantages wished for.

Electing Presidential Electors

The President will hold an important trust. The will of the people should be included in the choice. To achieve this objective, the people will choose the men [electors] who make the decision. The electors will be chosen at the appropriate time for this specific purpose, rather than having any pre-established body make the decision.

Small Group, Higher Qualifications

The men electing the President will study the important qualities. They should make a thoughtful decision. Reason should govern their choice. A small number of

255

people, selected by their fellow citizens, will probably have the information and the judgment needed for a thorough investigation.

Electors Vote in Home State

The President of the United States will administer the government. When electing an executive to such an important job, tumult and discord are feared evils. But the Constitution has security against these evils.

The people will choose *several* men to form a group of electors. By choosing several, riots within the community are less likely to happen than if only *one* person was elected.

The electors are to assemble and vote in the State that chose them. This detached, divided situation will expose them to less heat and turmoil than if they were all to be convened at one time in one place.

Foreign Influence, Presidential Elections

Every practical block to conspiracies and corruption must be erected. These are deadly adversaries of republican government. They can come from several places. But they will most likely come from foreign powers that want an improper influence in our government. The best way to influence our government is to promote a person they want as President of the Union.

But the convention carefully guarded against all danger. The appointment of the President doesn't depend on a pre-existing group of men who might be tampered with beforehand to sell their votes.

Instead, the people of America will choose electors for the temporary and sole purpose of making the appointment. Any people who are too devoted to the President in office are not eligible to be electors. No Senator, Representative, or other person holding a place of trust or profit under the United States can be an elector. Thus, without corrupting all citizens, the presidential electors will at least begin the task free from any sinister bias. Because of their brief existence and detached situation, they should be unbiased. To corrupt such a large number of people requires time and funds.

And it would not be easy to suddenly start a corrupt conspiracy. The spread of electors over thirteen States is another protection. Between the appointment of electors and their election of the President, it won't be easy for them to conspire for motives that might not be corrupt, but might mislead them from their duty.

President Elected by People

There is another goal. The President should depend on the people, alone, for reelection. Otherwise, he might be tempted to sacrifice his duty to ingratiate himself with people whose favor was necessary to stay in office. His reelection will depend on electors, picked for the single purpose of electing the President.

Constitution Includes All Safeguards

The Constitution combines all these advantages. The people of each State will choose a number of electors, equal to the number of senators and representatives of each State in the national government. The electors will assemble within the State and vote for some fit person as President. Their votes will be sent to the seat of the national government. The person with a majority of the whole number of votes will be the President.

One man might not receive a majority of the votes. And it might be unsafe to permit less than a majority to be conclusive. Therefore, the Constitution says that, if this happens, the House of Representatives will select the man they feel is best qualified for the office from the five candidates with the highest numbers of votes.

Election Method Assures Highest Quality

This method of electing the President makes sure that no man who doesn't have the qualifications will hold the office of President.

A man who is talented in low intrigues and who is popular and charming may be able to become a State governor. But he will need other talents and a different kind of merit to get the esteem and confidence of the whole Union. He'll need enough talents and merits to become a successful candidate for the distinguished office of President of the United States. We can say that men known for their ability and virtue will fill the office.

This will highly recommend the Constitution to people who understand that the executive in every government is largely responsible for its good or ill administration. We cannot agree in the political heresy that says:

For forms of government let fools contest—
That which is best administered is best—

But we can say that the true test of a good government is its aptitude and tendency to produce a good administration.

Vice President Chosen Same Way

The Vice President is to be chosen in the same manner with the President, with one difference. The Senate is to do, in respect to the former, what is to be done by the House of Representatives, in respect to the latter.

V-P Senate's President, May Be President

The appointment of a second person as Vice President has been objected to as superfluous, if not mischievous. Some people have suggested that the Senate elect a Senator to fill the office.

But two reasons seem to justify the convention's decision. First, so that the Senate will never have a tie vote, the President of the Senate should have only a casting vote. If a Senator from any State was taken from his seat and made President of the Senate, his home State would lose a vote in the Senate.

Second, the Vice President may occasionally become President. So, all the reasons that recommend the way the President is elected, apply to the election of the Vice President.

This objection could be made against the constitution of New York. We have a Lieutenant-Governor, who is chosen by the people at large. He presides in the senate. And New York's Lieutenant-Governor becomes Governor under the same circumstances that would authorize the Vice President to exercise the authorities and discharge the duties of the President.

Direct Presidential Elections

Number 64 [3-4]

...In the Constitution, electors, selected by the people for that purpose, will choose the President... This system has a great advantage over direct elections by the people. Party zeal has a great influence in direct elections. It can take advantage of indifference, ignorance, and the hopes and fears of the unwary and uninterested people. And men are often elected by a small proportion of the electors.

Electors will choose the President...They will usually be enlightened and respectable citizens. We can presume that they will vote for able and virtuous men, who have the people's confidence. The Constitution supports this objective. The President must be at least 35.... The people will have time to judge the candidates. Sometimes a candidate can briefly appear brilliant and patriotic, misleading and dazzling the public. But the electors and legislators will not be deceived.

The electors will have extensive and accurate information about men and their characters. Their appointments should be made with discretion and discernment.

We can infer that the President..., so chosen, will understand our national interests, whether as related to the States or foreign nations. They will promote those interests. They will have reputation for integrity that inspires confidence...

Number 39 [5, 12]

The Constitution follows the republican form... The people indirectly elect the President.

The executive power will come from a compound source. The States, as political units, will elect the President. The number of votes each State gets is based on a compound ratio. Each State has the same number of votes as their number of members in the US Congress: an equal number (two Senators) and a proportional number (number of Representatives). If no one wins that election, the national House of Representatives will pick the President; each State will have one vote, making the States distinct, equal political bodies.

Number 44 [26]

...State officials will be essential agents of the federal Constitution. The election of the President and Senate will depend on the State legislatures...

Number 45 [7]

...The State legislatures are an essential part of the presidential election...

Number 77 [11]

Remember, the President is elected every four years by persons immediately chosen by the people for that purpose.

Number 66 [7]

Sometimes, no presidential candidate will get a majority of electors. The House will decide those elections.

The Congress may determine the Time of chusing the Electors, and the Day on which they shall give their Votes; which Day shall be the same throughout the United States.

No person except a natural born Citizen, or a Citizen of the United States at the time of the Adoption of this Constitution, shall be eligible to the Office of President; neither shall any Person be eligible to that Office who shall not have attained to the Age of thirty-five Years, and been fourteen Years a Resident within the United States.

Number 64 [4, 15]

The President must be at least 35 and Senators 30 years old. The people will have time to judge the candidates. Sometimes a candidate can briefly appear brilliant and patriotic, misleading and dazzling the public. But the electors and legislators will not be deceived.

The electors will have extensive and accurate information about men and their characters. Their appointments should be made with discretion and discernment.

Integrity, Fear Guarantee Responsibility

It is difficult to imagine how their responsibility could be increased. The influences of honor, oaths, reputations, conscience, love of country, and family affections and attachments afford security for their fidelity. The Constitution has been careful that they shall be men of talents and integrity...And so far as the fear of punishment and disgrace can operate, the motive for good behavior is supplied by the article on the subject of impeachments.

Number 68 [8]

A man who is talented in low intrigues and who is popular and charming may be able to become a State governor. But he will need other talents and a different kind of merit to get the esteem and confidence of the whole Union. He'll need enough talents and merits to become a successful candidate for the distinguished office of President of the United States. We can say that men known for their ability and virtue will fill the office.

Number 75 [4]

...anyone who has seriously studied how the President will be elected knows that men of wisdom and integrity will fill the office...

Number 76 [4]

Because of the method for electing the President, he will probably be a man of abilities, at least respectable...

[In Case of the Removal of the President from Office, or of his Death, Resignation, or Inability to discharge the Powers and Duties of the said Office, the same shall devolve on the Vice President, and the Congress may by Law provide for the Case of Removal, Death, Resignation, or Inability, both of the President and Vice Presi-

dent, declaring what Officer shall then act as President, and such Officer shall act accordingly until the Disability be removed, or a President shall be elected.]

changed by Amendment 25

Section 1. In case of the removal of the President from office or of his death or resignation, the Vice President shall become President.

Section 2. Whenever there is a vacancy in the office of the Vice President, the President shall nominate a Vice President who shall take office upon confirmation by a majority vote of both Houses of Congress.

Section 3. Whenever the President transmits to the President pro tempore of the Senate and the Speaker of the House of Representatives his written declaration that he is unable to discharge the powers and duties of his office, and until he transmits to them a written declaration to the contrary, such powers and duties shall be discharged by the Vice President as Acting President.

Section 4. Whenever the Vice President and a majority of either the principal officers of the executive departments or of such other body as Congress may by law provide, transmit to the President pro tempore of the Senate and the Speaker of the House of Representatives their written declaration that the President is unable to discharge the powers and duties of his office, the Vice President shall immediately assume the powers and duties of the office as Acting President.

Thereafter, when the President transmits to the President pro tempore of the Senate and the Speaker of the House of Representatives his written declaration that no inability exists, he shall resume the powers and duties of his office unless the Vice President and a majority of either the principal officers of the executive department or of such other body as Congress may by law provide, transmit within four days to the President pro temp ore of the Senate and the Speaker of the House of Representatives their written declaration that the President is unable to discharge the powers and duties of his office. Thereupon Congress shall decide the issue, assembling within forty-eight hours for that purpose if not in session. If the Congress, within twenty-one days after receipt of the latter written declaration, or, if Congress is not in session, within twenty-one days after Congress is required to assemble, determines by two-thirds vote of both Houses that the

President is unable to discharge the powers and duties of his office, the Vice President shall continue to discharge the same as Acting President; otherwise, the President shall resume the powers and duties of his office.

The President shall, at stated Times, receive for his Services, a Compensation, which shall neither be increased nor diminished during the Period for which he shall have been elected,

Number 34 [7]

Our frugal republic will have a modest executive branch.

Number 51 [3]

If executive and judicial branches depend on the legislature for their pay, they would not be independent. Therefore, members of each branch should depend—as little as possible—on other branches for their pay.

Number 70 [4]

To have energy, the executive needs:

> (1) unity,
> (2) duration,
> (3) guaranteed compensation,
> (4) and enough powers.

Number 73 [1-2]

The third ingredient for an energetic President is the provision for its support. Without this, there really would be no separation between the executive and the legislative branch.

If the legislature could change the salary and benefits of the Chief Executive, he would have to do what the legislature wanted him to do. They might pay him nothing or tempt him with a lot of money. There are men who would never sacrifice their duty for money. But this stern virtue is rare. Generally, power over a man's support is power over his will.

There are plenty of examples that confirm this truth, even in this country. Executives have been either intimidated or seduced by the legislature that is paying their salary.

Presidential Compensation Unalterable

Therefore, the proposed Constitution pays close attention to this subject. It provides that "The President of the United States shall, at stated times, receive for his service a compensation *which shall neither be increased nor diminished during the period for which he shall have been elected; and he shall not receive within that period any other emolument* from the United States, or any of them."

This is an appropriate provision. When a President is elected, the legislature will state the compensation for his services during his term in office. Once done, they cannot change his salary. It will not increase or decrease until the next presidential election.

They cannot refuse to pay the President, which could weaken his courage. And they cannot bribe him and corrupt his integrity with more money. Neither the Union nor any State can give him more money. And he cannot accept any other benefits. He can have no monetary reason to not be independent.

Number 79 [1-2]

> *...a power over a man's subsistence amounts to a power over his will...*

This is the best provision possible. The value of money and the payment rate for jobs changes. Therefore, the Constitution couldn't state a fixed salary. An amount that might be extravagant today could be totally inadequate in half a century. Therefore, the legislature must be able to change the salary as circumstances change...

The convention set up the compensation for the President and for judges differently. The President's pay cannot be increased or decreased... The President is elected for no more than four years. Therefore, an adequate salary, fixed at the time he enters office, will almost always be adequate until the end of the four years.

Number 84 [21]

> ...The expenses of the President of the United States may not be much more than the current president of Congress...

and he shall not receive within that Period any other Emolument from the United States, or any of them.

Before he enter on the execution of his Office, he shall take the following Oath or Affirmation:—

"I do solemnly swear (or affirm) that I will faithfully execute the Office of President of the United States, and will to the best of my Ability preserve, protect, and defend the Constitution of the United States."

ARTICLE 2 SECTION 2. The President shall be Commander in Chief of the Army and Navy of the United States, and of the Militia of the several States, when called into the actual Service of the United States;

Number 4 [12]

...when one part of the nation is attacked, it can use the resources and power of the whole to defend that part. The army will have one chain of command up to the President...

Number 26 [13]

Some people say limiting military appropriations to the period of two years won't be safe. They say that once the president has a large enough military to force the people into submission, it would also be large enough to get supplies without help from the legislature.

But what pretense could the President use to build a big military force in peacetime? If it was created in response to a domestic insurrection or foreign war, it can't be called a peacetime military buildup. Military forces should be raised to stop a rebellion or resist an invasion. If defense of the community makes it necessary to have an army large enough to threaten its liberty, this is one of those calamities that can't be prevented or cured. No form of government can provide against this. It might even happen in a simple league, if the allies need to form an army for common defense.

Number 69 [6, 11]

...The President will only occasionally command the nation's militia. Congress must first call the militia into service.

The king of Great Britain and the governor of New York are always in command of all the militia within their jurisdictions. In this authority, the power of the President is inferior to that of either the monarch or the governor.

The President is to be commander-in-chief of the army and navy of the United States.

Both the President and the British king have the title "commander-in-chief." But the President's authority is far more limited than the king's. The President is only the supreme commander of the military and naval forces. He is first general and admiral of the Union.

The British king has far more power. He can *declare* war, and he can *raise* and *regulate* fleets and armies. Under the proposed Constitution, Congress will have this authority.

The governor of New York can only command the militia and navy. The constitutions of several other States expressly declare their governors can also be commander-in-chief of the army. New Hampshire and Massachusetts, in this respect, may give their governors more power than a President of the United States...

...The President would have a right to command the military and naval forces of the nation; the British monarch also has the authority to *declare* war, and *raise* and *regulate* fleets by his own authority.

Number 74 [1]

The President of the United States is to be "commander-in-chief of the army and navy of the United States, and the militia of the several States *when called into the actual service* of the United States."

This provision is proper and consistent with the State constitutions. Little need be said to explain or enforce it. Most of the people, who want an executive council in other areas of power, agree that the President, alone, should have the military authority.

The direction of war is a governmental concern that demands that one person have the power. The direction of war implies the direction of the common strength. And the power of directing the common strength is an essential part of the executive authority.

Number 78 [7]

The executive...holds the community's sword.

he may require the Opinion, in writing, of the principal Officer in each of the executive Departments, upon any subject relating to the Duties of their respective Offices,

and he shall have Power to Grant Reprieves and Pardons for Offenses against the United States, except in Cases of Impeachment.

Number 20 [5]

The chief executive of the United Netherlands... has the power of pardon...

Number 69 [6]

...The power of the President, in respect to pardons, would extend to all cases *except impeachment.*

The governor of New York can pardon even impeachment, except for treason and murder. Isn't the power of the governor, as far as political clout in this area, greater than that of the President? A group of people could conspire against the State government. If their plot is discovered before they take treasonous actions, the governor can pardon them. They won't be punished. If a governor of New York led a conspiracy, until the hostilities actually started, he could insure his accomplices entire impunity.

On the other hand, the President of the United States can pardon treason when prosecuted in the ordinary course of law. But he could not shelter an offender from the effects of impeachment and conviction.

If the governor of New York led a conspiracy against public liberty and if the plan was discovered before it was carried out, New York's governor could pardon his coconspirators, something the President could not do. If the plan was carried out, the President might be able to pardon his coconspirators. However, if the coconspirators realized that the President might be impeached and convicted, they would also realize that he would be unable to pardon them during any stage of planning or execution of the plan. There would be a greater temptation to continue a conspiracy with the governor of New York than the President.

The proposed Constitution limits the offense of treason "to levying war upon the United States, and adhering to their enemies, giving them aid and comfort." The laws of New York have a similar definition...

Humanity and good policy dictate that the pardoning power should be available. Every country's criminal code is very severe. Without the power to pardon cases of unfortunate guilt, justice would be too cruel.

Feelings of responsibility are stronger as fewer people are involved. Therefore, we may infer that a single man would most carefully study the motives that might plead for a mitigation of the rigor of the law. And one man is less likely to shelter a proper target of its vengeance. When the fate of a person depended on his *sole fiat,* he would be scrupulous and cautious. Equal caution, though of a different kind, would come from the dread of being accused of weakness or connivance.

On the other hand, men generally derive confidence from a group. A group of men with this power might often encourage each other's inflexibility. A group might be less attuned to suspicious apprehensions or censure for an injudicious or affected clemency. For these reasons, one man is a better dispenser of the government's mercy than a group.

Pardons for Treason

The Presidential power of pardoning has only been questioned in relation to the crime of treason. It has been urged that pardons for treason should depend on one or both houses of the legislature agreeing.

There are strong reasons for requiring this concurrence. Treason is a crime against the society. When an offender has been found guilty, it seems like the legislature should decide if he should be pardoned. And the Chief Executive ought not to be entirely excluded.

But there are also strong objections to such a plan. A single man of prudence and good sense is better fitted to balance the motives that may plead for and against a pardon, than any group of people.

It is important to remember that treason will often be connected with seditious acts by a group of people in the community, as recently happened in Massachusetts. In these cases, the people's representatives may feel the same spirit that motivated the offense. And when parties are equally matched, the secret sympathy of friends of the condemned person might bestow impunity where the terror of an example was necessary.

Expedited pardons

On the other hand, when the causes of the sedition inflame the resentments of the majority party, they might be obstinate and inexorable when policy demands clemency.

But the principal argument for giving the power of pardoning in this case to the Chief Executive is this: during times of insurrection or rebellion, there are often critical moments when a well-timed offer of pardon to the insurgents or rebels may restore the tranquility of the nation. And if the time passed with no action, it may never be possible afterwards to recall. It takes time to convene the legislature or one of its houses. The golden opportunity could be lost. The loss of a week, a day, or an hour may sometimes be fatal.

It may be suggested that the President could be given the power to pardon in such a situation. There are two problems with this suggestion. First, in a limited Constitution, the power could probably not be delegated by law. Second, it would be unwise to take any step before hand that might hold out the possibility of impunity. Giving the President this power, out of the usual course, could be seen as timidity or weakness. And it would have a tendency to embolden guilt.

He shall have Power, by and with the Advice and Consent of the Senate, to make Treaties, provided two-thirds of the Senators present concur;

Number 64 [3-8, 10-15]

The power to make treaties is important. It relates to war, peace, and commerce. Qualified men should make treaties, in the manner most conducive to the public good...

We can infer that the President and Senators...will understand our national interests, whether as related to the States or foreign nations. They will promote those interests. They will have reputation for integrity that inspires confidence. The power of making treaties may be given to such men.

...Some people want the House of Representatives to make treaties. However, House membership changes too quickly. Two years is not long enough for Representatives to study all the issues required to make treaties. Therefore, the convention wisely gave the Senate the power to make treaties.

Senators will have six-year terms. Able and honest Senators will be in office long enough to understand national concerns and create a system to manage them. While in office, they can increase their political information. Their total experience will benefit their country.

The Constitution has another good feature. If the entire Senate was elected every six years, all great affairs could be totally transferred to new men. By leaving a lot of the members in place, uniformity and order and the succession of official information will be preserved.

Trade and navigation regulations should be cautiously formed and steadily pursued. Both treaties and laws should support trade and navigation. Conformity should be carefully maintained. This is supported by making the Senate agree to both treaties and laws.

Treaties Drafted Secretly, Quickly

Frequently, treaties must be negotiated in *secrecy* and require immediate *execution*. Sometimes the most useful intelligence can be obtained if the people who have it can be free from the fear of discovery. This fear effects people whether they have mercenary or friendly motives. Many people with either mercenary or friendly motives would rely on the secrecy of the President. Yet they wouldn't want to talk to the Senate, let alone the larger House of Representatives.

The convention has divided the power to make treaties so that the President can manage intelligence as prudence suggests. Then he will form the treaties with the advice and consent of the Senate.

There are cycles in the affairs of men. The cycles are very irregular in their duration, strength, and direction. And they seldom run twice exactly in the same manner or measure.

People who preside over national affairs must understand and profit by these cycles. Experienced men say that there are times when days, or even hours, are precious. The loss of a battle, the death of a prince, the removal of a minister, or other events changes the posture and appearance of affairs. Sometimes they turn the most favorable cycle into a negative one.

As in the field, so in the cabinet. There are moments to seize as they pass. And people presiding in either should have the capacity to improve them.

Until now, we have not had secrecy and speed. The Constitution needed to address those objectives. Secrecy and speed are needed to facilitate attaining the objectives of the negotiation. The President will be able to provide these. And if anything occurs that requires the advice and consent of the Senate, he may at any time convene them.

The Constitution provides treaty negotiations with the advantages of talents, information, integrity, and deliberate investigations on the one hand. On the other hand, it provides for secrecy and dispatch.

Treaties as Law

Some people object because ratified treaties will have the force of laws. They say that only the legislature should make treaties.

The legislature has the power to make laws. However, other acts also have the force of laws. Judgments from our courts and constitutional commissions given by our governor are as valid and binding as the laws passed by our legislature. All constitutional acts of power are as legally valid as those from the legislature. Therefore, the power of making treaties may be given to the executive or judicial branch.

It doesn't follow that just because the power of making laws is given to the legislature that, therefore, they must have every sovereign power by which the citizens are bound and affected.

Objection: Treaty is Supreme Law

Other critics are averse to treaties being the *supreme* laws of the land. They insist, and say they believe that treaties, like legislative acts, should be repealable at pleasure. This idea seems to be new and specific to this country. But new errors, as well as new truths, often appear.

Remember that a treaty is only another name for a contract. And no nation would make any contract with us that would be binding on them *absolutely*, but on us only so long and as far as we may think.

People who make laws may, without doubt, amend or repeal them. And people who make treaties may alter or cancel them. But let us not forget that two contracting parties make treaties. Consequently, since the consent of both was essential to their formation, both must agree to alter or cancel them.

The proposed Constitution, therefore, hasn't extended the authority of treaties. They are currently binding and beyond the lawful reach of the legislature. They will be the same in the future, under any form of government.

Fear: Treaties Bad for Some States

Jealousy is useful in republics, just like bile is useful in the human body. But when too much jealousy infects politics, people are easily deceived by delusional appearances. This causes some people to fear that the President and Senate may make treaties without an equal eye to the interests of all the States.

Others suspect two thirds of the Senate will oppress the remaining third. They ask whether those gentlemen are made sufficiently responsible for their conduct. Whether, if they act corruptly, they can be punished. And if they make disadvantageous treaties, how are we to get rid of those treaties?

Promote Good of Whole Nation

All the States are equally represented in the Senate. Senators will promote the interests of their constituents. They will have an equal degree of influence, especially while the proper people are carefully appointed and their punctual attendance is demanded.

As the United States assumes a national form and character, the good of the whole will get more attention. If the national government forgets that the good of the whole can only be promoted by advancing the good of each of the parts, it will be very weak.

Neither the President nor the Senate will have the power to make treaties by which they and their families and estates will not be equally bound and affected with the rest of the community. And having no private interests distinct from those of the nation, they will be under no temptations to neglect the latter.

Corruption Voids Treaty

The problem of corruption is not imaginable. Anyone who thinks that the President and two-thirds of the Senate will ever be capable of such unworthy conduct, must either have been very unfortunate in his interactions with the world or has a heart very susceptible to such impressions. The idea is too gross and too invidious to be entertained. But if it should ever happen, the treaty so obtained from us would, like all other fraudulent contracts, be null and void by the law of nations.

Integrity, Fear Guarantee Responsibility

It is difficult to imagine how their responsibility could be increased. The influences of honor, oaths, reputations, conscience, love of country, and family affections and attachments afford security for their fidelity. The Constitution has been careful that they shall be men of talents and integrity. We believe that the treaties they make will be as advantageous as could be made, all circumstances considered.

And so far as the fear of punishment and disgrace can operate, the motive for good behavior is supplied by the article on the subject of impeachments.

Number 66[4, 10-12]

…The Senate will have concurrent authority with the Executive in forming treaties and appointing to offices…

Objection to Senate as Impeachment Court: Senate Ratifies Treaties

An objection comes from the Senate's union with the Executive in making treaties. The objectors say that when a corrupt or perfidious treaty is made, the Senators would have to judge themselves. If they conspired with the Executive to betray the interests of the nation in a ruinous treaty, would they get the punishment they deserved if they were the impeachment court? Would they find themselves guilty of the accusation brought against them for the treachery?

This is the most earnest and reasonable objection against this part of the Constitution. But it rests on an erroneous foundation.

The Constitution provides security against corruption and treachery when forming treaties. This security comes from the numbers and characters of the people who are to make them. Both the President and two-thirds of the Senate, a body carefully selected by each State legislature, must approve treaties. This assures fidelity in forming treaties.

When writing the Constitution, the convention might have included a punishment for the President if he doesn't follow the Senate's instructions or doesn't act with integrity during treaty negotiations. They might also have suggested how a few of the leading individuals in the Senate might be punished, if they used their influence in the Senate for foreign corruption. But the convention could not suggest impeaching and punishing two-thirds of the Senate, if the Senate agreed to an improper treaty...

Number 69[7, 11]

The President will, with the advice and consent of the Senate, make treaties, provided two-thirds of the senators present concur.

The king of Great Britain is the only representative of the nation in all foreign transactions. On his own, he can make treaties of peace, commerce, alliances, and of every other description. Some people have said that his treaties with foreign powers are subject to the revision and ratification of Parliament. But I believe this doctrine was never heard of until it was broached on the present occasion. Every jurist[*] in Britain and every man acquainted with its constitution knows that the monarch makes all treaties. And they are legal and valid.

Sometimes Parliament changes existing laws so that they conform to a new treaty. This may be where the idea that Parliament needs to approve treaties came from. But this parliamentary action comes from a different cause—the need to adjust an artificial, intricate system of revenue and commercial laws to conform to the treaty.

In the making of treaties, there is no comparison between the limited presidential power and the actual power of the British sovereign. The British king can do alone what the President can only do with the concurrence of a branch of the legislature.

In this area, the President's power exceeds that of any State executive. But this arises naturally from the sovereign power relating to treaties. The question of whether governors have this important power would only come up if the Confederacy was dissolved.

...The President would have a concurrent power with a branch of the legislature in the formation of treaties; the King of Great Britain is the *sole possessor* of the power to make treaties...

---

[*] *Vide* Blackstone's *Commentaries*, vol. I. p.257. –PUBLIUS

Number 75 [all]

The President will have the power, "by and with consent of the Senate, to make treaties, provided two thirds of the senators present concur." This provision has been strongly attacked. However, it is one of the most unexceptional parts of the Constitution.

One objection says it mixes powers. Some people say the President alone should make treaties. Others, the Senate. Others object to the small number of people who can make a treaty. Some want the House of Representatives involved. Others think that two thirds of *all* Senators should have to agree rather than two thirds of the members *present*. An earlier Paper covered this subject. I will make a few more remarks.

Treaty Roles, Separation Rule

Other Papers explained the separation of powers rule. The union of the President with the Senate when forming treaties does not break that rule. And because of the nature of treaties, the union is particularly proper.

Several people say making treaties is an executive authority. However, this is an arbitrary classification. If we look at how treaties operate, they have more legislative than executive characteristics. But they don't fall strictly within the definition of either.

The legislature makes laws. It makes the rules that regulate society. The executive enforces laws and employs the common strength.

The power to make treaties is not one or the other. Treaties don't enforce existing laws or make new ones. And they don't have anything to do with using the common strength.

Treaties are contracts with foreign nations. They have the force of law, but they are enforced through good faith. They are not laws prescribed by the sovereign to the subjects, but agreements between sovereign governments. Therefore, this power forms a separate category; it is neither a legislative nor executive power.

The qualities needed for foreign negotiations are listed in another Paper. They show that the Executive is the best agent in those transactions. But treaties are an important trust and operate like laws. The legislative body should have some role in making them.

Foreign Influence if President Acted Alone

It may be proper and safe to give a monarch, who is chief executive, the entire power to make treaties. But it would be improper and unsafe to give that power to an elected President with a four-year term.

A monarch often oppresses his people. But he has personally too much stake in the government to be in any danger of being corrupted by foreign powers.

But a private citizen will become President, with a moderate or small fortune. And in a short time he will be a private citizen again. He will be tempted to sacrifice his duty to his personal interest. He would need great virtue to not give in to the temptation. An avaricious man might betray the nation to acquire wealth. A foreign power might help an ambitious man make his own aggrandizement the price of his treachery to his constituents.

The nation's dealings with the rest of the world are delicate and very important. If the President was solely responsible for foreign negotiations, he would have to be very virtuous. And the history of human conduct doesn't justify the opinion that people have that much virtue.

Advantages of President's Involvement

If the Senate, alone, made treaties, the benefits of the President's participation in foreign negotiations would be lost. The Senate could employ a person to do the negotiations. But the Senate would have the option of not doing this. Animosity or cabal might cause them to do the latter rather than the former.

Besides this, if the Senate employed a person to negotiate, he would not get the same respect from foreign nation as the President. And he would not have the same influence or efficacy. The Union would lose an important advantage in foreign negotiations. And the people would lose the additional security from the President's involvement.

It would not be wise to give such an important trust to the Executive, alone. But his participation would add to society's safety.

The President and Senate will have the joint power to make treaties. This provides more security than if either of them have the whole power. Also, anyone who has seriously studied how the President will be elected knows that men of wisdom and integrity will fill the office. The President's participation in forming treaties will be very desirable.

House Too Inexperienced, Large

An earlier Paper showed why the House of Representatives shouldn't have a role in making treaties. House membership will change frequently. And the House will grow very big. Therefore, we can't expect it to have the qualities essential to properly execute such a trust.

The people involved in treaty negotiations need several characteristics: knowledge of foreign politics, stable views of the national character, decisiveness, *secrecy*, and speed. House membership changes too often and is too large to have these characteristics.

Needing so many different people to agree is an objection. Also, the House would need more and longer sessions to agree to each new part of the treaty. This would be inconvenient and expensive, and should condemn the idea.

Two-Thirds Ratification, Minority Rule

The last objection is to require two thirds of all Senators to agree, rather than two thirds of the members *present*.

When more than the majority is required to pass resolutions, it hurts governmental operations. And the will of the majority is subject to the minority. This is important. The convention has secured the advantage of numbers in the formation of treaties. And it will support the majority will of the community.

If two thirds of all Senators were required, some Senators could simply not attend the session. To pass, every Senator present might need to agree to the treaty. The history of every political body using this principle is a history of impotence, perplexity, and disorder. Proof comes from the examples of the Roman Tribune, the Polish Diet, and the Netherlands' States-General. However, an example at home makes other examples unnecessary.

Proposed Senate, Current Congress

What if a fixed proportion of the whole Senate was required to approve treaties? This would probably not add to the advantage of requiring two thirds of the attending members.

When a specific number of votes are needed to pass every resolution, there is less reason for members to attend the sessions. But when a resolution can be passed based on a proportion of the members who are present, it has the opposite effect. The absence or presence of a single member can be very important. This promotes punctuality. And the members tend to show up. As many members will probably decide Senate resolutions as if two thirds of all members were required, with fewer reasons for delay.

Under the existing Confederation two members *may*, and usually *do*, represent a State. Consequently, Congress, which holds *all the powers* of the Union, rarely has more members than the proposed Senate. Members vote by States. When only one member from a State is present, a State vote is lost. In the proposed Senate, members will vote individually. There will rarely be fewer active members than in the existing Congress.

When we include the President of the Senate, we will have more security against an improper use of the power to make treaties under the new Constitution than under the Confederation. And the Senate will get larger as new States are added. There will be enough members to entrust the power. A body larger than the Senate will become would not be fit for the proper discharge of the trust.

Number 77[10]

…The Senate has a role with the Executive in making treaties. It might be necessary to convene the Senate…

Number 84[22]

…the President will handle much of the business that now keeps Congress sitting through the year. Even the management of foreign negotiations will devolve on him, cooperating with the Senate and subject to their final agreement…

and shall nominate, and, by and with the Advice and Consent of the Senate,

Number 38 [7]

One [opponent of the Constitution] says the Senate should not have to approve presidential appointments. Another says that House of Representatives should also approve appointments.

Number 65 [1]

The Senate participates with the executive in the appointment to offices.

Number 66 [4-5, 8-9]

… The Senate will have concurrent authority with the Executive in forming treaties and appointing to offices…

A *third* objection to the Senate as an impeachment court is based on the Senate's role in the appointments to office. Since the Senate participates in an appointment, it is imagined that the Senate would be too indulgent when judging the office holder's conduct.

This objection would condemn a practice seen in all the State governments, if not in all governments. I'm talking about the practice of making people who hold offices during pleasure dependent on the pleasure of those who appoint them. The objectors seem to be saying that when political appointees misbehave, the people who appointed them will protect them from punishment.

However, the people who make appointments will feel responsible for the fitness and ability of the people they appoint. They will want a respectable administration of affairs. And they will want to remove anyone whose conduct proves them unworthy of the trust. This is a basically sound presumption.

The Senate only approves executive choices. This will not blind them to such extraordinary evidence of guilt that the Representatives of the nation accuse him.

The President will *nominate* and, with the advice and consent of the Senate, *appoint*. Of course, the Senate will have no part in the *choice*. The Senate may defeat one person that the President has chosen, but they cannot *choose*. The Senate can only ratify or reject the choice of the President.

The Senate might prefer someone else, but confirm the appointment because it has no grounds to oppose him. And what if the Senate didn't approve the nomination? It would have no way of knowing who the next nominee would be. It might not even be a person who—in their estimation—was more meritorious than the one rejected.

Number 76 [2-end]

Paper #68 said, "The true test of a good government is its aptitude and tendency to produce a good administration." If true, the method of appointing the national officers is very good. It will promote a judicious choice of men. And the character of government administration depends on having good men in national offices.

Of course, having the public make appointments is impractical. If nothing else, they would have little time to do anything else. Therefore, appointments can be made in one of three ways: by a one man, by a moderate sized group of people, or by a single man with the approval of a moderate sized, select group.

People are spread out across the nation. If the people made the appointments, they could not be coerced by cabals and intrigue. The fear of coercion is the main objection to giving the power to a smaller group of men.

Because of the method for electing the President, he will probably be a man of abilities, at least respectable. Based on this, I'll state this rule: One man of discernment does a better job analyzing the qualities needed for specific offices than a group of men of equal, or even superior, discernment.

Reasons Group Decision Bad

One man will feel the full responsibility and a sense of duty. He will feel obligated to investigate the qualities required to fill the offices. And he will impartially prefer the persons who have the most qualifications.

He will have *fewer* personal attachments than a group of men, who each may have an equal number. He will be less likely to be misled by friendship. A group's decision can be warped by diverse views, feelings, and interests. A single, well-directed man does not have as many distractions.

People become very passionate when they have to choose a person. Deep personal feelings can influence the choice. When a group of men appoint people to offices, all private and party friendships and animosities felt by the people in the group effects the choice. The choice will be a victory of one party over the other or a compromise between parties. The candidate's merit will often not be considered.

The ability to unite the party's votes will be more important than the person's job qualifications. The choice will often be a compromise: "Give us the man we wish for this office and you can have the one you wish for that." This will usually be the bargain. Public good will rarely be the primary objective of either party victories or party negotiations.

Nominate vs. No Approval Needed

The intelligent people who don't like this provision know this is true. They say the President, alone, should appoint federal officers. But the power of *nomination* will have nearly all the same advantages. And several disadvantages will be avoided.

The President will use his judgment when he nominates a candidate. With the Senate's approval, the man he nominates will fill an office. Therefore, the President will be responsible for the choice. In this respect, there is no difference between nominating and appointing. The same motives will influence the choice. No man could be appointed without being nominated, so every man appointed will be the President's choice.

His nomination might be overruled. But he will make the next nomination. The person ultimately appointed will be his choice, though perhaps not his first. And his nomination will probably not be overruled very often.

The Senate might prefer a different person. But they won't be tempted to reject the nomination because they couldn't be sure that the person they wanted would be the second or any other nomination. A future nomination might not be a more acceptable candidate. And since their rejection might stigmatize the nominee and reflect badly on the President's judgment, they will rarely reject a nominee except when there are strong reasons.

Senate Restraint on President

Why require the Senate's approval? Needing their approval will have a powerful, though often silent, operation. It will be a check on presidential favoritism. And it will tend to prevent the appointment of unfit people from State prejudice, family connection, personal attachment, or from a desire to be popular. It will also make the administration more stable.

When a man has the sole power to appoint people to offices, his private desires and interests will often guide his choice. When a house of the legislature must agree, he will be more careful. The possibility of rejection is a strong motive to be careful when nominating.

The Senate will study the choice. And the Senate's opinion influences public opinion. He will not want to show favoritism or pursue popularity because the Senate's reaction could hurt his reputation or political life. Federal offices are distinguished and lucrative. He would be afraid to nominate candidates with no other merit than coming from the same State, or being a personal ally, or being so pliant that they will always agree with him.

Executive Influence on Senate

Some people say that the President's nomination power will influence the Senate to approve the nomination. Assuming that human nature is universally weak is as wrong as assuming universal integrity. Delegated power implies that some people have virtue and honor. And experience justifies the theory. Virtue and honor exists even during the most corrupt periods of the most corrupt governments.

The British House of Commons has long been accused of accepting bribes. And many members have been bribed. But many members are independent, public-spirited men who influence the nation's councils. Even during the present reign, it often controls the monarch both with regard to men and to measures.

The President may influence some Senators. But he probably could not buy the integrity of the entire Senate. A man with a realistic view of human nature, who doesn't exaggerate its virtues or vices, will be confident of the Senate's integrity. Corrupting and seducing a majority of the Senate would be impractical. And he will need the Senate's approval. This will restrain the President's conduct.

We don't have to rely on the Senate's integrity, alone. The Constitution has important guards against the danger of executive influence on the legislative body. The Constitution says it that "no senator or representative shall, during the time *for which he was elected*, be appointed to any civil office under the United States which shall have been created, or the emoluments whereof shall have been increased, during such time; and no person, holding any office under the United States, shall be a member of either house during his continuance in office."

Number 77 [1-8]

The Senate's role in appointments will help create a stable government. The Senate must consent to displacing as well as appointing. When a new President is elected, fewer government officers will change than if he, alone, appointed officers. When a man is doing a good job, a new President will be less likely to replace him with his choice. He will worry that the Senate might block the attempt, bringing some discredit on himself.

People who believe a steady administration is important will like this provision. It connects government officers with the approval or disapproval of the Senate, which will probably be the most stable part of the government.

Balanced Plan

The Senate and the President will each have a role in appointments. Some people say the President has too much influence over the Senate. Others say it will have an opposite effect—a strong proof that neither suggestion is true.

The first argument says the President will improperly *influence* the Senate because the Senate will have the power to *restrain* him.

This is absurd. If the President had the entire power of appointment, he might establish a dangerous empire over the Senate. But he only has the power of nomination, subject to the Senate's control.

The opposite idea is that "the Senate will influence the Executive."

This objection is imprecise. And there is no precise answer. How will the Senate influence the President?

As used here, the power to influence a person implies a power of giving him a benefit. How could the Senate benefit the President? It can only reject his nomination. Sometimes the Senate might agree to the President's choice when public opinion disagrees with it. However, the President will be too rarely interested in the result to be materially affected by the Senate's decision.

The person or group with the power to *originate* the disposition of honors and salary is more likely to attract than be attracted to the power that can only block them.

If "influencing" the President means *restraining* him, this is the intention. The restraint will have a good effect. But it will not destroy the advantages of the President making the appointments. Nomination produces all the good of an appointment and avoids most of its evils.

Public Evaluates Appointments

We can compare the plan for appointing officers in the Constitution with New York's constitution. The United States Constitution is better. In New York, the Executive has the total power of nomination.

The US Constitution makes it necessary to submit each nomination to the judgment of an entire house of the legislature. Because of this, the appointment process becomes a public issue. And the public can determine what part was performed by the different actors. The President will be blamed for a bad nomination. The Senate will probably be blamed for rejecting a good nomination. If a bad appointment is made, the Executive, for nominating, and the Senate, for approving, will share the blame.

New York Appointments Veiled in Secrecy

The reverse of all this characterizes the manner of appointment in New York. The appointment council has three to five people, including the governor. This small group makes appointments in secret.

The governor claims the right of nomination based on some ambiguous clauses in the constitution. But no one knows when he actually nominates someone or when he is contradicted or opposed.

Each person's role is uncertain. The censure of a bad appointment is neither strong nor long lasting. And when there is an open opportunity of conspiracy, all responsibility is lost. The public only knows that the governor claims the right of nomination. *Two* out of the small number of *four* men can too often be influenced without much difficulty. If some of the members of the council don't want to go along with the plan, the council can meet at times when it is inconvenient for them to attend. Whatever the cause, a great number of very improper appointments are made.

Does a governor of New York use his power in this important part of the administration? Or does he appoint people whose chief merit is their devotion to his will? This would support a despicable and dangerous system of personal influence. Unfortunately, we can only speculate about the answers to these questions.

Appointment Counsel

No matter how it is put together, every appointment council will support cabal and intrigue. Without an unacceptable increased expense, it cannot be large enough to exclude easy conspiracy.

Each member would have a bank and connections to provide for. Members of the council would scandalously barter for votes. The private attachments of one man might easily be satisfied. But to satisfy the private attachments of a dozen, or of twenty men, a few families might end up holding a monopoly of government offices. This would lead directly to an aristocracy or an oligarchy.

To avoid this problem, the council members could change frequently. However, this would create all the problems of a mutable administration.

An appointment council would be more likely to influence the executive than the Senate. It would be smaller than the Senate and its actions would get less public scrutiny. A council would be expensive. It would multiply the evils of favoritism and intrigue in giving out public honors. The government would be less stable and diminish the security against an improper influence of the Executive. And yet some people want an amendment to the proposed Constitution, creating such a council.

House: No Part in Appointments

A few people have said that the House of Representatives should have a role in appointments. I can't imagine that many people think this is a good idea. The House is large and frequently changes membership. It can never be deemed proper for the exercise of that power. Remember that in only fifty years it may have three or four hundred members. All the advantages of stability, both of the Executive and of the Senate, would be defeated by including the House of Representatives. And infinite delays and embarrassments would happen. The example of most of the States encourages us to reject the idea.

shall appoint Ambassadors, other public Ministers and Consuls, Judges of the supreme Court, and all other Officers of the United States, whose Appointments are not herein otherwise provided for, and which shall be established by Law; but the Congress may by Law vest the Appointment of such inferior Officers, as they think proper, in the President alone, in the Courts of Law, or in the Heads of Departments.

Number 69 [9]

The President is to nominate and, *with the advise and consent of the Senate,* appoint ambassadors and other public ministers, Supreme Court judges, and all officers of the United States established by law and whose appointments are not otherwise provided for by the Constitution.

Number 72 [1]

In its largest sense, the administration of government includes all government operations. But in its most precise definition, it is limited to executive duties.

Government administration includes conducting foreign negotiations, preparing financial plans, asking for and spending public money as appropriated by the legislature, directing the army, navy and operations of war, and other similar duties. Therefore, the people who manage these areas should be considered assistants or deputies of the chief executive. The President should appoint them or, at least, nominate and supervise them.

This suggests the close connection between the President's term in office and a stable administration.

To prove his worth, a new office-holder often reverses his predecessor's actions. When the change is because of an election, the new person can assume that his predecessor lost the election because people disliked his measures. And the less he acts like his predecessor, the more his constituents will like him. For these reasons and the influence of friends, every new President will probably change the men filling offices...

The President shall have Power to fill up all Vacancies that may happen during the Recess of the Senate, by granting Commissions which shall expire at the end of their next Session.

Number 67 [5-end]

Opponents use false arguments to pervert public opinion on the subject [of the executive]. They exceed the usual unjustified license of party artifice. It's difficult to treat them seriously. Opponents are deliberately using fraud and deception.

President and Senate Vacancies

For example, they have had the nerve to say that the President of the United States will have a power that the proposed Constitution *expressly* gives to the State Executives. I'm talking about the power to fill Senate vacancies.

False Conclusion Built on False Premise

This has been argued by a writer who (whatever may be his real merit) has often been applauded by his party. He has built a series of observations. Each is based on this false, unfounded suggestion. Let him now see the evidence. And let him, if he is able, justify the shameful outrage he has offered to the dictates of truth and the rule of fair dealing.

Constitution: Executive Appointments

Article 2, section 2, clause 2 gives the President of the United States the power "to nominate, and by and with the advice and consent of the Senate, to appoint ambassadors, other public ministers, and consuls, judges of the Supreme Court, and all other *officers* of the United States whose appointments are *not* in the Constitution *otherwise provided for,* and *which shall be established by law.*"

Opponents use the next sentence to say the President has a power that the Constitution does not give him. It says, "The President shall have power to fill up all *vacancies,* that may happen *during the recess of the Senate,* by granting commissions which shall *expire at the end of their next session.*"

The obvious meaning of the clauses shows that the deduction is not even plausible.

President Appoints Non-Constitutional Officers

The first clause provides a way to appoint officers, "whose appointments are *not otherwise provided for* in the Constitution, and which *shall be established by law.*" Based on this clause, the President cannot appoint senators. The appointment of Senators is *oth-*

erwise provided for in this Constitution and are established by the Constitution. The ap-pointment of Senators is a Constitutional power and cannot be changed by law.

President Never Appoints Senators

Clearly, the second clause does not include the power to fill vacancies in the Senate, for the following reasons.

First. The relationship of the clauses shows that the second clause is only a supplement to the first clause. Since the President and Senate *jointly* make appointments, without the second clause, appointments could only be made while the Senate is in session. However, vacancies might happen *in their recess.* These offices may need to be filled without delay. The second clause authorizes the President, *by himself,* to make temporary appointments "during the recess of the Senate, by granting commissions which shall expire at the end of their next session."

Second. The *vacancies* mentioned in the second clause refer to the "officers" described in the preceding clause. This excludes members of the Senate.

Third. The power is to operate "during the recess of the Senate" and the ap-pointments will last until "to the end of the next session." These phrases further clarify the provision. If it included senators, the clause would have referred to the State legislatures, not the national Senate. The State legislatures appoint Senators. If the clause referred to Senate vacancies, it would mention the recess of State legislatures. And the temporary senators would stay in office until the next session of the State legislature, instead of mak-ing it expire at the end of the next session of the national Senate. The clause mentions only the national Senate. Therefore, the clause must be talking about vacancies in offices to which the President and Senate, jointly, make permanent appointments.

Lastly. Article 1, section 3, clauses 1 and 2 destroys all doubt and misconcep-tions. The former provides that "the Senate of the United States shall be composed of two Senators from each State, chosen *by the legislature thereof* for six years." And the latter directs that "if vacancies in that body should happen by resignation or otherwise, *during the recess of the legislature of* any state, the Executive thereof may make temporary ap-pointments until the *next meeting of the legislature,* which shall then fill such vacancies."

The State Executives will fill vacancies in the Senate by temporary appointments. The President will not have the power to fill vacancies in the national Senate. This proves that the opponents' arguments are deceptive. The deception is obvious. And it is too atrocious to be excused by hypocrisy.

Example Proof of Misrepresentations by Opponents of Constitution

This misrepresentation proves the inexcusable cunning used by opponents of the Constitution. They want to prevent a fair, impartial judgment based on the real merits of the Constitution. I ask any honest opponent of the new Constitution: Does language give us severe enough denouncements for this shameless attempt to defraud the citizens of America?

Number 76 [1]

... The President shall have the power to fill up *all vacancies* which may happen *during the recess of the Senate,* by granting commissions which shall *expire* at the end of their next session."

ARTICLE 2 SECTION 3. He shall from time to time give to the Congress Information of the State of the Union,

Number 77 [9]

The remaining powers of the Executive include... giving information to Congress on the state of the Union

and recommend to their Consideration such Measures as he shall judge necessary and expedient;

Number 71 [3]

But even if we insist that the Executive always comply with the will of the people, we can not argue that the legislature must comply in the same way. Sometimes the legislature may oppose the executive. At other times, the people may be neutral. In either case, it is certainly desirable that the Executive should act on his own opinion with vigor and decision.

Number 77 [9]

The...remaining powers of the Executive include: recommending to their consideration measures he thinks expedient,...

he may, on extraordinary Occasions, convene both Houses, or either of them, and in Case of Disagreement between them, with Respect to the Time of Adjournment, he may adjourn them to such Time as he shall think proper;

Number 69 [6]

... The President can only adjourn Congress in the single case of disagreement about the time of adjournment...

Number 77 [9]

... powers of the Executive include:... adjourning [both houses of Congress] when they cannot themselves agree on the time of adjournment...

he shall receive Ambassadors and other public Ministers;

Number 42 [3-4]

The federal government needs the powers to make treaties, send and receive ambassadors. Both are in the Articles of Confederation, with two differences. States cannot block treaties. And the Articles only mentions "ambassadors," the highest rank of public ministers; but Congress has used lower levels of ministers, including sending and receiving consuls.

…under the Articles, admitting foreign consuls into the United States may be part of the power of making commercial treaties. When no commercial treaties exist, putting American consuls in foreign countries *may* be covered under the authority of article nine of the Confederation "to appoint…such…civil officers necessary for managing the general affairs of the United States."

However, the Articles of Confederation do not mention admitting consuls into the United States, when no treaty mentions them. The new Constitution corrects this omission. It is a small change. However, the tiniest provisions become important when they prevent the need or pretext for gradual, unobserved usurpations of power.

Defects in the Articles have forced Congress to violate its authorities. The new Constitution corrects both small and large defects in the Articles of Confederation.

Number 69 [8]

The President will also receive ambassadors and other public ministers. Many speeches have been given on this topic. But this is more a matter of dignity than of authority. It will have no effect on the administration of the government. And this will be far easier than if the legislature or one of its houses had to meet every time a foreign minister arrived, even though he was only replacing a departing minister.

he shall take Care that the Laws be faithfully executed,

Number 75 [4]

…The executive enforces laws and employs the common strength….

and shall Commission all the Officers of the United States.

Number 77 [9]

The remaining powers of the Executive include… commissioning all the officers of the United States.

ARTICLE 2 SECTION 4. The President, Vice President and all civil Officers of the United States. Shall be removed from Office on Impeachment for, and Conviction of, Treason, Bribery, or other high Crimes and Misdemeanors.

Number 39 [5]

The President's term in office is four years. And he is impeachable at any time during his time in office.

Number 69 [4]

The President can be impeached, tried, and if convicted of treason, bribery, or other high crimes or misdemeanors, removed from office. Afterwards he can be prosecuted and punished in the ordinary course of law.

The king of Great Britain is sacred and inviolable. He is not accountable to any constitutional tribunal. And a national revolution is the only way he can be punished.

In the delicate and important area of personal responsibility, the President of the United States will be like the governor of New York. And he will have more personal liability than the governors of Massachusetts and Delaware.

ARTICLE 3 SECTION 1. The judicial Power of the United States, shall be vested in one supreme Court, and in such inferior Courts as the Congress may from time to time ordain and establish.

Since I am not a history scholar, as I was reading the Federalist Papers for the first time, some of the arguments were difficult to follow because I didn't have an understanding of how the federal government was structured under the Articles of Confederation. I didn't understand federal legislation for States and was surprised to learn there was no federal judiciary.

Legislation for States

Number 15 [6-7, 12-end]

The basic defect of the Confederation is the principle of legislation for states in their collective capacities rather than for the individuals living in the States.

This principle doesn't apply to all the federal government's powers. However, it is such an important part of our current system that it leaves the Union virtually powerless. For example, the United States can requisition men and money, but it has no authority to directly raise either from individual citizens. In theory, federal resolutions are constitutionally binding on the States; but in practice, they are merely recommendations that the States observe or disregard.

Legislation for States Ruined Confederation

This shows how fickle people are. Some men object to the new Constitution because it doesn't include the principle [legislation for States] that ruined the old, a principle that can only be enforced with the violence of the sword. Courts and judges will do the enforcement under the new Constitution.

We were told that States wouldn't violate federal regulations. Some people said that States would comply because of our common interests. Today, this sounds ludicrous. It betrayed an ignorance of psychology and contradicted the original reason for establishing civil power...

Sovereignties Hate Outside Control

By its very nature, sovereign power hates control and it hates any external attempt to restrain or direct its operations. Because of this, when a group of small sovereign states unites in a league or alliance, the smaller units tend to fly off from the common center. The origin of this tendency is the love of power. Power controlled or restrained is almost always the enemy of that power doing the controlling. Administrators of individual states in an alliance will not be always ready to execute the decrees of the general authority. So predicts the psychology of human nature.

Therefore, if the alliance's resolutions can only be enforced by each member state, they probably won't be implemented at all. The rulers of the member states, whether they have a constitutional right to do it or not, will try to judge each resolution. They will consider whether the resolution is important to their immediate interests. They will then decide if enforcing the resolution will be inconvenient. These judgments will be made without knowing the national situation or the reasons for the resolution, both essential information.

And local plans and objectives will also influence the decision. Every member of the alliance will repeat this process. Some states will comply and others won't, depending on the information, lack of information and prejudiced opinions of each state. The distant legislatures of the states that make up the alliance will discuss the resolution at different times. Each will have different views on the subject and they can't be forced to cooperate.

States Not Supporting Confederation

Under the current Confederation, the thirteen sovereign States must agree to enforce every important resolution and law proposed by the Union. What happened was expected. The measures have not been executed. State delinquencies have grown, stopping the wheels of the national government.   Congress is barely able to keep some kind of administration until the States can agree on a functioning replacement for the present shadow of a federal government.

Our current awful situation didn't happen overnight. At first, a few States didn't fulfill the Union's requisitions. When they didn't pay, the least delinquent States were tempted not to pay, feeling that they shouldn't pay proportionately more than other States in the Union. Why should they pay more than their share of the common burden? Each State has successively withdrawn its support. Now the frail and tottering national confederation seems ready to fall on our heads and crush us beneath its ruins.

Number 16 [1-6]

Legislation for States or communities hurts all confederate governments. It has hurt our government. Historically, the negative effects of legislation for States increase as it is used in more areas of the government.

State Noncompliance Leads to Civil War

Legislation for states is the parent of anarchy. It is very easy for States to not fulfill their requisitions. Some States are delinquent. When States are delinquent, the only constitutional remedy is force. The national government must send troops to the State to fulfill its requisitions. The consequence of using force is a civil war.

Our government might not even be able to enforce the legislation. If the national government doesn't have a standing army, it can't use force. And if it could use force, violations by the States would start wars between different parts of the Confederacy. The strongest force would prevail, whether it supported or defied the national authority.

A delinquency would rarely be confined to a single State. If more than one neglected their duty, they probably would unite for common defense.

If a large, influential State were delinquent, some non-delinquent States would support its cause. The delinquent State would create excuses for their delinquencies. They would use specious arguments like warning of the danger to liberty.

Excuses for deficiencies would be invented to increase fears, inflame passions, and win over the good will of some non-delinquent States. For example, the ambitious rulers of a large state might not want the federal government to control them. They would not pay their requisitions to advance their plans for personal aggrandizement. They probably would encourage the leaders of adjacent States to join them. If other States didn't become allies, they would ask a foreign nation for aid. Foreign powers would promote disagreements within the Confederacy because if it is firmly united, they will have much to fear.

Once the sword is drawn, men's passions rule over their objectivity. If the Union used force against delinquent States, resentment and wounded pride would push those States to avenge the insult to avoid the disgrace of submission. The first war of this kind would probably dissolve the Union.

More States will be Delinquent

The Confederacy could die violently. Currently, we are close to a more natural death. We must quickly and substantially renovate the federal system.

Our history suggests that complying States would rarely support the Union's authority by going to war against non-complying States. Instead, they would identify with the delinquent states and imitate their example. Their common guilt would become their common security. Our experience has shown this.

In fact, it would be difficult to decide when to use force. A State might not send funds because they didn't want to pay. Or it might not be able to pay, an excuse they could always use. And the deception must be obvious to justify forced compulsion. Every delinquency would produce factious views, partiality, and oppression by the majority in the national congress.

Military Coercion Never Works

The States shouldn't want a national Constitution that needs a standing army to enforce ordinary laws. Yet this must happen if the Constitution doesn't extend to individuals. If practical at all, it would instantly degenerate into a military tyranny.

But it is, in every way, impractical. The Union won't be able to afford to create and maintain an army capable of forcing the larger States to do their duty.

Even in confederacies with members smaller than our States, the principle of legislation for sovereign states, enforced by the military, has never worked. It has only been enforced against the weaker states. And it usually produced bloody civil wars.

Federal Authority over Individuals

Number 15 [10-11]

…Union authority must extend to the citizens—the only proper objects of government.

A government has the power to make laws. A law needs a sanction—a punishment or penalty for disobedience. If no penalty is tied to disobedience, resolutions that pretend to be laws are nothing more than advice or recommendations.

A penalty can be only inflicted in two ways: by the courts or by military force—by coercion of the judiciary or by coercion of arms. The first can apply only to individual people; the last must be employed against politic groups, communities, or states.

Of course, courts have no way to directly enforce laws. Sentences may be pronounced against violators. But sentences can only be executed by the sword. If the authority is based on an alliance, every breach of the law must involve a state of war—punishment by the military. Such a situation doesn't deserve to be called a government. And no prudent man would depend on it for his happiness.

Number 16 [7-end]

If a federal government is supposed to regulate common concerns and preserve tranquility, it must have authority over the citizens. It must not need approval from the State legislatures. The judiciary must have the authority to enforce its resolutions. The federal government, like each State, must be able to focus on the hopes and fears of individuals and attract support from the strong passions of the human heart. In short, it must have the ability and the right to execute its powers as the State governments do.

Non-Compliance vs. Active Resistance

An objection to this reasoning could be raised. If any State becomes disloyal to the Union's authority, it could still use force to obstruct the execution of the Union's laws.

However, there is an important difference between NON-COMPLIANCE, and DIRECT and ACTIVE RESISTANCE. If every federal law must be approved by each State legislature, if a State just doesn't ACT (NON-COMPLIANCE) they defeat the law. A State could make up an excuse for neglecting its duty. State leaders might even create a temporary convenience, exemption, or advantage. It would be easy to convince the people that they were not defying the federal Constitution or ignoring a federal law.

But how could a State block a national law that applies directly to citizens? The State government would have to use violent, unconstitutional power to block them. Ignoring the law would not be enough. They would be forced to act. Everyone could see the encroachment on national rights. With a constitution able to defend itself, this action would be hazardous. Enlightened citizens would know the difference between legal authority and illegal usurpation of authority.

Blocking a national law would require a factious majority in the State legislature, the courts, and the citizens. If judges didn't conspire with the legislature, they would rule that the State law was contrary to the supreme law of the land, unconstitutional, and void. The people are the natural guardians of the Constitution. If they didn't agree with the State legislature, they would support the national government. Because of the danger to them, State leaders would not lightly or rashly attempt this, except when the federal government uses its authority tyrannically.

National and Local Laws Enforced Same Way

If rebellious individuals opposed national laws, the judiciary would guard the laws from illegal or immoral behavior. The federal government could suppress a faction within a single State.

Deadly feuds sometimes spread violence through a whole nation or a large part of it. Discontent with the government would spread the violent feuds. We can't estimate how far the violent feuds would spread. When they happen, they usually become revolutions that dismember an empire. No form of government can always either avoid or con-

~~fool them. It is impossible to guard against events that are impossible to predict. It is stu~~
pid to object to a government because it could not perform impossibilities

Federal Judiciary

Number 22 [14-15]

The Confederation's worst defect is the lack of a judiciary power. Laws are pointless without courts to interpret and define their true meaning and operation.

Treaties must be considered as part of the law of the land. Their effect on individuals must, like all laws, be defined by judicial decisions. To have uniform decisions, as a last resort they should be submitted to one SUPREME TRIBUNAL that is created under the same authority that signs the treaties.

If each State has a court of final jurisdiction, there may be as many different final decisions on an issue as there are courts. Men hold a limitless variety of opinions. We often see not only different courts, but also judges of the same court, differing from each other. Contradictory decisions create confusion. To avoid this, all nations have established one court of last resort, authorized to settle a uniform rule of civil justice.

State Courts Will Not Always Agree

This is more important when the laws of the whole country are in danger of being contradicted by the laws of the States or regions. If State or regional courts have the final opinions, a bias based on local views and local regulations would produce contradictions. People might prefer a local law over a federal law. Men in office naturally yield to the authority to which they owe their job.

Currently, thirteen different legislatures and thirteen different supreme courts can interpret or misinterpret every treaty signed by the United States. Therefore, the reputation and peace of the whole country are at the mercy of the prejudices, passions, and interests of each State. Can foreign nations either respect or trust such a government? How long will Americans entrust their honor, happiness, and safety to this unstable foundation?

Number 81 [1. 3-end}

The judicial authority will be divided between different courts.

There should be one supreme court of final jurisdiction. I stated the reasons for this in another place. They don't need to be repeated.

One question has been asked: Should the Supreme Court be a separate body or one house of the legislature?

Some men object to the Senate acting as the impeachment court, saying it improperly mixes powers. Now the same men seem to want to give the ultimate decision of all causes, in the whole or in a part, to the Senate.

Supreme Court as Legislative Body

This seems to be their argument:

"The proposed Supreme Court will be a separate, independent body. The Supreme Court will interpret laws, according to the *spirit* of the Constitution. It will be able to mold laws into any shape it thinks proper. Therefore, its authority will be superior to the legislature because the legislature cannot correct its decisions. This is unprecedented and dangerous.

"In Britain, the House of Lords, part of the legislature (Parliament), has the judicial power of last resort. The State constitutions imitate this. Both Parliament and the State legislatures can correct, by law, court decisions they object to. But there will be no way to correct the errors and usurpations of the Supreme Court of the United States."

On examination, this will be found to be false reasoning based on misconceived fact.

Judging Constitutionality of Laws

Nothing in the new Constitution *directly* give the national courts the power to interpret laws according to the spirit of the Constitution. In this respect, it has no more power than the courts of every State.

The Constitution should be the standard for the construction of laws. When laws conflict with the Constitution, the Constitution takes precedence over the laws. But this doctrine is not in the proposed Constitution. It comes from the general theory of a limited constitution. And, as far as this doctrine is true, it also applies to the State governments.

Therefore, this objection could be made against local courts. And it will not help to condemn every constitution that tries to limit legislative actions.

Legislators, Judges: Different Talents

But perhaps the objection is to the specific organization of the Supreme Court.

The Supreme Court will be a separate body of judges. It will not be one of the legislative houses as in Great Britain and New York.

If the authors of the objection insist that the Supreme Court must be part of the legislature, they must renounce the meaning of the separation of powers maxim.

These Papers explain the separation of powers maxim. It is not violated by giving the ultimate power of judging to *part* of the legislature. But it is close to violating it. And the structure in the Constitution fulfills the maxim better than making the federal judiciary part of the legislature.

Even if the legislature was only partly responsible for passing bad laws, the same branch would rarely want to change them. The same spirit that made the laws would probably interpret them. The same legislators, who infringed on the Constitution when they made the laws, would not feel like repairing the breach when they act as judges.

Nor is this all. There are good reasons for judges to have a lifetime tenure, during good behavior. The same reasons argue against giving the judiciary power, in the last resort, in a body of men, who serve for a limited period. Federal judges with lifetime tenure would hear the cause first. Then the final appeal would be heard by judges who are temporarily in office. This would be absurd.

The lower-court federal judges will be selected for their knowledge of the laws, learned through long and laborious study. Then the final appeal would be made to legislators who don't have the same knowledge. It is even more absurd. Legislators will rarely be chosen because they have the qualifications of a judge. We could expect all the bad consequences that come from not having the right information.

Legislatures naturally divide by party. Therefore, faction may poison the fountains of justice. Out of habit, Senators are on the opposites sides of issues. The voices of law and equity will probably not be heard.

Separate Supreme Court, Legislature

In some States, the judicial court of last appeals is an independent body of men, separate from the legislature. This is wise.

In this respect, the Constitution copies the constitutions of New Hampshire, Massachusetts, Pennsylvania, Delaware, Maryland, Virginia, North Carolina, South Carolina, and Georgia. We applaud following those models.

Changing Supreme Court's Ruling

There is another point. The future United States Congress can overrule objectionable decisions just like the Parliament of Great Britain and the State legislatures. This theory authorizes the legislature to revise the judicial ruling by passing a new law. It is not forbidden in the proposed Constitution. The impropriety of the thing, on the general principles of law and reason, is the only obstacle.

A legislature, without exceeding its authority, cannot reverse a determination once made in a specific case. But it can make a new rule for future cases. This is the principle. It applies to the State governments. And it applies to the national government under consideration. Not the least difference can be pointed out in any view of the subject.

Legislature can Impeach Judges

Lastly, the danger of judiciary encroachments on the legislative authority is often mentioned. This will not happen. Now and then, specific laws may be misconstrued. Or, occasionally the will of the legislature may be blocked. But they can never be extensive enough to inconvenience or change the political system.

This is inferred from several things: the nature of judicial power, its objects, the way it is exercised, its weakness, and its inability to support its usurpations by force.

This conclusion is strengthened by the important constitutional check on the judiciary. One part of the legislative body can impeach judges and the other tries them.

This is complete security. Judges will not want to usurp the legislature's authority while the legislature has the power to punish them and remove them from office.

This should remove all worries on the subject. It also is a good argument for making the Senate the court for the trial of impeachments.

Inferior Federal Courts

I trust that these points have removed the objections to an independent Supreme Court. I will now show that the power of creating inferior courts is proper.* And I will show the relationship between these and the Supreme Court.

With inferior federal courts, every case of federal jurisdiction will not need to go to the Supreme Court. The national government can *authorize* inferior courts in each State or district. Those courts can decide matters of national jurisdiction within their limits.

---

* Some people claim this power abolishes all the county courts in the States, which are often called inferior courts. But the Constitution says: to constitute "tribunals INFERIOR TO THE SUPREME COURT." This means that local courts, subordinate to the Supreme Court, can be created either in States or larger districts. It is ridiculous to say it abolishes county courts. –PUBLIUS

State Courts Hearing Federal Cases

Could State courts fill this role? This has several answers.

Even if the State courts are competent to handle federal cases, this constitutional power is necessary. Before the State courts could try federal cases, the national legislature would have to give them jurisdiction over causes arising out of the national Constitution. Congress might give the State courts the power to decide federal cases. That action would perhaps fulfill the requirement "to constitute tribunals."

But should the Constitution say that State courts should be used? There are good reasons why it shouldn't.

Local attitudes and opinions may disqualify local courts from hearing federal cases.

And the structures of some of the State judiciary systems are improper channels of the Union's judicial authority.

Some State judges hold their offices during pleasure or from year to year. They will not be independent enough to objectively execute national laws. If the United States Constitution said that State courts must be the first court to hear federal cases, the door for appeals would need to be as wide as possible. Appeals should be easy or difficult in proportion to the grounds of confidence in or distrust of the subordinate tribunals. I believe the appellate jurisdiction, as defined by the Constitution, is proper. However, anything that allows *unlimited* appeals is a source of inconvenience.

Federal Court Districts

The United States might be divided into four, five or six districts. Each district could have a federal court instead of putting one in every State. The district court judges, with the help of State judges, may hold circuits to try cases in their district. Justice can be administered with ease and dispatch. And appeals may be safely limited.

This plan appears to me the best that could be adopted. The power of creating inferior courts should be in the Constitution.

Inferior Federal Courts Imperative

The Constitution gives Congress the power to create inferior federal courts. Without this power, the Constitution would be defective.

Let us examine how the judicial authority will be divided between the Supreme and the inferior courts of the Union.

Ambassadors, Consuls, States

The Supreme Court will have original jurisdiction only "in cases affecting ambassadors, other public ministers, and consuls, and those in which a State shall be a party."

Public ministers are representatives of their sovereigns. All cases involving them are directly connected with the public peace. To keep the public peace and out of respect to the countries they represent, the highest court in the nation should hear their cases.

Consuls are not strictly diplomatic, but they are the public agents of their nations. So the same observation applies to them.

Cases that involve a State shouldn't be turned over to an inferior tribunal.

Citizens Suing State for Debt

Although it is not part of the subject of this paper, I will mention a mistaken idea that has alarmed some people.

Some people say that if public securities of one State are assigned to citizens of another State, the citizens could sue the State in the federal courts for the amount of those securities. This assumption has no foundation.

A sovereign nation or state cannot be sued by an individual *without its consent.* Every State has this exemption. Therefore, unless the Constitution gives up this immunity, the States will keep it.

And the danger intimated must be merely ideal. The circumstances needed to remove State sovereignty were discussed when taxation was discussed. They need not be repeated here. By adopting the Constitution, the State governments would not lose the privilege of paying their own debts in their own way. Their only constraint will be the obligations of good faith.

The contracts between a nation and individuals are only binding on the conscience of the sovereign. A nation cannot be forced to comply. They confer no right of action independent of the sovereign will.

What would be the purpose of authorizing suits against States for the debts they owe? How could recoveries be enforced? Clearly, it couldn't be done by waging war against the State. And to give federal courts the ability to destroy a pre-existing right of the State governments would not be justified.

Supreme Court Hears 2 Types of Causes

Let us resume studying the subject of this paper.

The Supreme Court will have original jurisdiction in only two classes of causes. And they rarely happen.

All other federal cases will be heard by the inferior courts. The Supreme Court will have only appellate jurisdiction "with such *exceptions* and under such *regulations* as the Congress shall make."

Appeals Based on Law, Facts

The propriety of this appellate jurisdiction has been rarely questioned. But the clamors have been loud against it as applied to matters of fact.

Some well-intentioned men in New York have gotten ideas from the language and forms that apply to New York courts. They believe that "appellate jurisdiction" implies that trial by jury will be replaced by the civil-law mode of trial that is used in the New York courts of admiralty, probate, and chancery. New York State uses a technical meaning to the term "appellate." It often refers to appeals in the course of civil law.

However, I don't believe any part of New England would give it the same meaning. In New England, an appeal from one jury to another is familiar. It is a matter of course until there have been two verdicts on one side.

Therefore, the word "appellate" will not have the same meaning in New England as in New York. This shows it is improper to use a technical interpretation from the jurisprudence of only one State.

The expression means that one tribunal reviews the proceedings of another, either as to the law or fact, or both. The method used for appeals depends on ancient customs or legislative provision. (In a new government it must depend on the latter.) And the appeals court may or may not use juries.

Therefore, if the proposed Constitution allows the reexamination of a fact once determined by a jury, it may be regulated to be heard by a second jury. It could be remanded to the court below for a second trial of the fact or directed immediately out of the Supreme Court.

Reexamination of Facts Not Imperative

But it does not mean that the reexamination of a fact, once determined by a jury, will be permitted in the Supreme Court.

When a writ of error is brought from an inferior to a superior court of law in New York, does the latter have jurisdiction of the fact as well as the law? It cannot start a new inquiry concerning the fact. But it takes jurisdiction of it as it appears on the record. And it pronounces the law arising on it.* This is jurisdiction of both fact and law.

They cannot be separated. Juries in the common-law courts of New York State determine disputed facts. They have jurisdiction of both fact and law. When the facts are agreed in the pleadings, there is no need for a jury and they proceed at once to judgment. Therefore, the expression, "appellate jurisdiction, both as to law and fact," does not necessarily mean that the Supreme Court will reexamine facts decided by juries in the inferior courts.

Appellate Court May Review Facts

The following ideas could have influenced the convention in relation to this provision.

The appellate jurisdiction of the Supreme Court (they may have argued) will extend to causes determined in different modes. Some may be determined in the course of the common law and others in the course of the civil law. In the former, the proper role of the Supreme Court will be the revision of the law. In the latter, the reexamination of the fact is agreeable to usage. And in some cases (prize causes, for example), determining the fact might be essential to preserve the public peace. The appellate jurisdiction should sometimes extend in the broadest sense to matters of fact.

Cases originally tried by jury cannot be completely excluded because in some States *all causes* are tried by jury.** And matters of fact could not be reviewed, when proper.

The Supreme Court will have appellate jurisdiction both as to law and *fact*. And this jurisdiction will be subject to *exceptions* and regulations written by the national legislature. The government can modify it so it serves public justice and security.

---

* This word is composed of JUS and DICTO, *juris, dictio,* or a speaking or pronouncing of the law.—PUBLIUS

** I believe States will have concurrent jurisdiction with the inferior federal courts in many cases of federal jurisdiction. This is explained in my next paper. –PUBLIUS

Trial by Jury Not Abolished

Some people have said this provision *abolishes* trial by jury. This is fallacious and untrue. The United States Congress will have full power to say that in appeals to the Supreme Court facts cannot be reexamined if juries tried the original causes. This would be an authorized exception. But if it is thought too extensive, it might be limited to causes determined at common law by jury trials.

Summary: Judicial Branch

These are the observations made about the authority of the judicial branch:
- It is restricted to causes that are proper for the national judicature.
- The authority is divided. A small part of original jurisdiction is given to the Supreme Court. The rest is given to the inferior tribunals.
- The Supreme Court will have an appellate jurisdiction both as to law and fact in all the cases referred to them, both subject to any *exceptions* and *regulations* that may be thought advisable.
- This appellate jurisdiction does not *abolish* the trial by jury.
- And an ordinary degree of prudence and integrity in the national councils will insure that we have the advantages of the proposed judiciary without exposing us to the inconveniences that have been predicted.

Judicial Independence

Number 47 [7-9]

Montesquieu said, "There can be no liberty where the legislative and executive powers are united in the same person, or body of magistrates," and "if the power of judging be not separated from the legislative and executive powers."… The judges have no executive power, though the executive chooses them. And judges don't make laws, although they can advise legislative councils.

"Were the power of judging joined with the legislative, the life and liberty of the subject would be exposed to arbitrary control, for *the judge* would then be *the legislator*. Were it joined to the executive power, *the judge* might behave with all the violence of *an oppressor*."

Number 71 [4]

Separation of power between the branches of power is very important. Each branch should be independent of the others. Why separate the executive or the judiciary from the legislative, if the legislative can void the acts of both the executive and the judiciary? Such a separation would be in name only. And it couldn't produce the result for which it was established.

Number 73 [15]

Judges cannot be too separate from every other avocation than that of expounding the laws. It is very dangerous to place them in a situation where they could be either corrupted or influenced by the Executive.

Number 78 (5-end] , see next section

The Judges, both of the supreme and inferior Courts, shall hold their Offices during good Behaviour,

Number 9 [3]

Judges need lifetime appointments and can only be removed for bad behavior.

Number 39 [5]

Judges have a lifetime appointment and can be impeached and removed from office.

Number 51 [2]

...since judges are appointed for life, they will not feel obligated or dependent on the people who appoint them.

Number 78 [5-end]

The tenure of judges concerns how long they stay in office, how they will be paid, and precautions for their responsibility.

All federal judges will hold their offices *during good behavior*. This conforms to the most approved State constitutions, including New York's. Adversaries of the Constitution question whether this is proper. This criticism shows us that opponents of the Constitution are so determined to find objections that their judgment is impaired. Lifetime judicial appointments, during good behavior, are a great improvement in government.

In a monarchy, it is a barrier to a king's tyranny. In a republic, it helps block encroachments and oppressions by the legislature. In any government, it is the best way to secure an impartial administration of the laws.

When the government's powers are separated into three branches, the judiciary is the least dangerous to constitutional rights. It will be least able to injure them.

The executive decides who will have government jobs and holds the community's sword. The legislature commands the purse and creates the laws that regulate every citizen.

The judiciary, however, doesn't have a sword or a purse. It can take no actions. The judiciary has neither force nor will, merely judgment. It even depends on the executive to enforce its judgments.

Permanency in Office: Independence

The judiciary is the weakest of the three branches of power.[*] It can never successfully attack the other two. And it must be able to defend itself against their attacks.

The courts of justice might oppress a single person. However, if the judiciary is separate from the legislature and the executive branches, it will not be dangerous to the

---

[*] Montesquieu says: "Of the three powers above mentioned, the judiciary is next to nothing." *Spirit of Laws,* Vol. I, page 186.—PUBLIUS

general liberty of the people. "There is no liberty if the power of judging is not separated from the legislative and executive powers."[**]

Liberty has nothing to fear from the judiciary alone. But if the judiciary unites with either of the other branches, liberty will be in danger. If the judiciary had to depend on the other branches, we would see the negative effects.

The judiciary is weak. It is always in danger of being overpowered or influenced by the legislature or executive. A lifetime appointment makes it more firm and independent. Therefore, it is indispensable. And it is important to public justice and public security.

In a limited Constitution, courts must be completely independent. A "limited" Constitution has specific exceptions to the legislative authority. For example, the legislature cannot pass bills of attainder or *ex post facto* laws. Courts of justice preserve these limitations. They declare all acts contrary to the meaning of the Constitution void. Without this, all Constitutional rights and privileges would mean nothing.

Power to Void Unconstitutional Laws

If laws are contrary to the Constitution, the courts will declare them void. Some people argue that since judges can declare laws void, the judicial power must be superior to the legislature's power.

This is an important doctrine in all the American constitutions. A brief discussion of it is appropriate.

The Constitution defines the legislature's authorities. No legislative act contrary to the Constitution is valid. Denying this would mean that the representatives of the people are superior to the people themselves. Or that a man may do both what he has the authority to do and what he is forbidden from doing.

Authority: Constitution vs. Legislature

It may be argued that the legislature decides what its constitutional powers are. And the other branches have to accept the legislature's interpretation. But this is not a logical conclusion from any part of the Constitution.

The Constitution does not say that the people's representatives can substitute their *will* for the people's will. The courts stand between the people and the legislature. Among other things, the courts keep the legislature within their constitutional limits.

Courts interpret law. A constitution is a fundamental law. Therefore, the courts determine its meaning, as well as the meaning of legislative acts. If the two conflict, the superior one should be preferred.

Therefore, the Constitution is preferred over the statute; the intention of the people is preferred to the intention of their agents.

This doesn't mean that judicial power is superior to the legislative power. It only means that the power of the people is superior to both.

When the will of the legislature, as seen in the laws it passes, opposes the will of the people, as declared in the Constitution, judges should be governed by the Constitution. Their decision should be based on fundamental laws.

[**] *Idem*, page 181.

Decide Validity of Contradictory Laws

When two laws contradict each other and neither has a repealing clause, the courts decide which is superior. The courts have the authority and duty to clarify the laws' meaning and operation. When this is impractical, one law takes effect and the other law does not.

The courts usually decide that the most recent law is the more valid law. But no law created this "rule." It just seems logical. The courts don't have to follow this rule, but it seems proper that it should direct their conduct as interpreters of the law. It seems reasonable that between conflicting acts of an *equal* authority, the last indication of its will should have preference.

Constitution Superior to Laws

The legislature is a lower authority. It was created by the people's Constitution. The Constitution is the superior, original authority. When the legislature passes a law that conflicts with the Constitution, the opposite of the "rule" must be followed. The earlier act of a superior authority, the Constitution, is preferred to the later act of a lower authority.

Therefore, when a law contradicts the Constitution, judicial courts must follow the Constitution and disregard the law.

Courts Negating Legislative Will

Some people argue that if the courts find a law repugnant, they may substitute their own will for the constitutional intentions of the legislature. This could happen when two laws contradict each other or during the adjudication of a single law.

This argument carries no weight. The courts must declare the meaning of the law. And if they exercise their will instead of judgment, their will would be substituted for the will of the legislative body.

Courts of justice guard a limited Constitution against encroachments by the legislature. This duty is a strong argument for the lifetime tenure. Judges will feel independent. Independence is essential to do this difficult duty.

Independent Judges Protect Liberty

Independent judges guard both the Constitution and the rights of individuals. People need protection from bad ideas. Bad ideas can come from designing men. Or they can simply spread through the community. As the people get better information, bad ideas quickly go away. However, before they do, the government can make dangerous changes and seriously oppress the minority in the community.

The people can alter or abolish the constitution if it is not consistent with their happiness. This is the fundamental principle of republican government. Friends of the proposed Constitution will never agree with its enemies[*] and question that fundamental principle.

---

[*] *Vide* "Protest of the Minority of the Convention of Pennsylvania," Martin's Speech, etc.—
    PUBLIUS

But let's say a majority of the people don't like a provision in the existing consti tution. They tell their representatives. Then the representatives pass an unconstitutional law based on the people's wishes. The courts could not uphold the unconstitutional law. Until the people have changed or abolished the Constitution, through an authoritative act, it is binding on them collectively and individually. No presumption or knowledge of the people's wishes gives representatives the authority to depart from the Constitution. Judges need great fortitude. They must faithfully guard the Constitution after legislative invasions of it are started by the majority voice of the community.

Restraint on Bad Legislation

Independent judges are an essential safeguard against bad laws, not just Constitutional infractions. Sometimes these involve an injury to the rights of specific citizens by unjust laws.

The lifetime appointment of judges lessens the severity of such laws. It both moderates the problems caused by laws that have been passed and it operates as a check on the legislative body in passing them. The legislature will realize that the courts will block their unjust actions. And it will be more careful about the laws it passes.

This restraint on bad legislation will influence the character of our governments. Several States have already felt the benefits of an honest and moderate judiciary. The courts may displease people with sinister motives. But virtuous people praise them.

Everyone should prize whatever will tend to create or fortify that temper in the courts. No man can be sure that he may not be tomorrow the victim of a spirit of injustice by which he gains today. Injustice saps the foundations of public and private confidence, replacing it with distrust and distress.

Owe Allegiance Only to Constitution

Courts of justice must strictly enforce Constitutional and individual rights. But judges with a temporary tenure cannot be expected to have this strength.

Temporary appointments would be fatal to judicial independence. If the president or legislature appointed judges, judges might give in to the branch making the appointment.

If the president and legislature jointly made the appointment, judges would not want to displease either. If the people appointed judges or if a special council appointed judges, popularity would be more important than knowledge of the Constitution and the laws.

Limited Number of Qualified People

There is another, more important reason for the permanency of judges. It comes from the qualifications they need.

A huge number of laws is a necessary inconvenience of a free government. To avoid arbitrary decisions, the courts should follow strict rules and precedents that define their duty in every case that comes before them. A variety of controversies grow out of the folly and wickedness of mankind. Therefore, precedents will swell to a very large bulk. Long and laborious study will be needed to acquire a competent knowledge of them. Hence, only a few men in the society will have enough knowledge of laws to qualify them for the office of judge.

Some people will be disqualified for the ordinary depravity of human nature. The number of people with both the integrity and knowledge to become judges is still smaller.

The government has limited choices between people of fit character. A temporary time in office would discourage qualified people from quitting a lucrative practice to accept a seat on the bench. Temporary tenure would tend to throw the administration of justice into hands less able and less well qualified. Temporary tenure would have great disadvantages.

Good Behavior Important Inclusion

The convention acted wisely in copying from the constitutions that have established *good behavior* as the tenure for judges.

Rather than being blamed for including this, their plan would have been inexcusably defective if it didn't include this important feature of good government. The experience of Great Britain illustrates the excellence of the institution.

Judicial Corruption and Impeachment

Number 83 [17]

The importance of trial by jury in civil cases depends on circumstances other than the preservation of liberty. Security against corruption is the strongest argument in its favor.

There is more time to tamper with a judge than with a jury summoned for one trial. Perhaps a judge could more easily be corrupted than a jury. This argument is, however, diminished by other considerations.

The sheriff summons ordinary juries. The clerks of courts nominate special juries. Both are standing officers. It might be easier to corrupt them than judges. Those officers could select corrupt jurors.

It might be easier to corrupt jurors, who are randomly chosen, than to corrupt judges, who are chosen for their good character.

Despite these considerations, trial by jury is a valuable check on corruption.

Currently, both the judge and the jury would have to be corrupted. When the jury is clearly wrong, the judge will generally grant a new trial. In most cases, it would be useless to corrupt the jury unless the judge is also corrupted. This is a double security.

Judges will be less tempted when it is necessary to also corrupt the jury than if they exclusively determined all causes.

Number 79 [4]

To assure that judges will act responsibly, they can be impeached by the House of Representatives and tried by the Senate. If convicted, a judge may be dismissed from office and disqualified for holding any other. This is the only provision that could be made that is consistent with judicial independence. It is also in the New York State constitution.

Number 81 [9]

Lastly, the danger of judiciary encroachments on the legislative authority is often mentioned. This will not happen. Now and then, specific laws may be misconstrued. Or, accordingly the will of the legislature may be blocked. But they can never be extensive enough to inconvenience or change the political system.

This is inferred from several things: the nature of judicial power, its objects, the way it is exercised, its weakness, and its inability to support its usurpations by force.

This conclusion is strengthened by the important constitutional check on the judiciary. One part of the legislative body can impeach judges and the other tries them. This is complete security. Judges will not want to usurp the legislature's authority while the legislature has the power to punish them and remove them from office.

This should remove all worries on the subject. It also is a good argument for making the Senate the court for the trial of impeachments.

and shall, at stated Times, receive for their Services, a Compensation, which shall not be diminished during their Continuance in Office.

Number 79 [1-4]

After permanency in office, nothing assures independent judges more than a fixed provision for their support. The comment made about the President applies equally here: *a power over a man's subsistence amounts to a power over his will.*

The complete separation of the judicial from the legislative power will never happen if judges depend on the legislature for their pay.

Some State constitutions don't have instructions about paying judges. And friends of good government lament this omission. Some State constitutions say that *permanent** salaries should be established for judges. But, in practice, the wording is not precise and legislatures can evade paying judges.

An unambiguous provision is required. Therefore, the Constitution provides that the judges of the United States "shall at *stated times* receive for their services a compensation which shall not be *diminished* during their continuance in office."

This is the best provision possible. The value of money and the payment rate for jobs changes. Therefore, the Constitution couldn't state a fixed salary. An amount that might be extravagant today could be totally inadequate in half a century. Therefore, the legislature must be able to change the salary as circumstances change. However, the legislature cannot lower a judge's pay. A judge cannot be deterred from his duty by fears that his salary will be diminished.

The clause has two advantages. When necessary, the salaries of judicial officers may be changed. But the pay of a specific judge can never be lower than when he was appointed.

The convention set up the compensation for the President and for judges differently. The President's pay cannot be increased or decreased. Judges' pay can only not be decreased. This difference probably arose from the difference in the terms in office. The President is elected for no more than four years. Therefore, an adequate salary, fixed at the time he enters office, will almost always be adequate until the end of the four years.

---

* Vide *Constitution of Massachusetts,* chapter 2, section 1, article 13. —PUBLIUS

Judges, if they behave properly, will have a lifetime job. It may happen, especially in the early years of the government, that a salary that is enough when they are appointed will become too small over the time they serve.

Judicial Independence

This provision for the support of the judges is wise and effective. Together with lifetime tenure, it makes federal judges more independent than any of the State judges.

To assure that judges will act responsibly, they can be impeached by the House of Representatives and tried by the Senate. If convicted, a judge may be dismissed from office and disqualified for holding any other. This is the only provision that could be made that is consistent with judicial independence. It is also in the New York State constitution.

Number 84 [21]

...The support of the judges will be an extra expense. The amount will depend on the specific plan adopted. But in no reasonable plan can it amount to a huge sum.

ARTICLE 3 SECTION 2. The judicial Power shall extend to all Cases, in Law and Equity, arising under this Constitution, the Laws of the United States, and Treaties made, or which shall be made, under their authority;

Number 78 see previous section

Number 37 [10]

Brilliant legislators and jurists have tried to define the objectives and limits of different laws and courts of justice. This subject has been extensively studied in Great Britain. But the line between the different types of laws—common law, statute law, maritime law, ecclesiastical law, corporate law, and local laws and customs—still isn't clearly defined. The jurisdiction of Great Britain's different courts is frequently discussed, but it still isn't perfectly clear.

New laws are written with the greatest technical skill and passed after long deliberations. Yet they are considered as more or less obscure and equivocal until their meaning is ascertained by a series of discussions and adjudications.

Obscurity comes from (1) the complexity of the subjects, (2) human imperfections, and (3) the medium [i.e. words, sentences] used to convey men's ideas.

Humans use words to express ideas. Clear expression requires well-formed ideas and the appropriate words. But no language has words and phrases for every complex idea. And many words have several meanings. Therefore, the definition of even a precise subject can be inaccurate because words are inaccurate. This unavoidable inaccuracy grows worse as the subject becomes more complex or novel.

When God himself talks to mankind in our language, his meaning—brilliant as it must be—is made dim and doubtful by the cloudy medium through which it is communicated.

Number 39 [14]

A *national* government has authority over individual citizens with an indefinite supremacy over all persons, things, and issues that can be objects of lawful government. A *federal* government vests some supremacy in the united body and some in the local legislatures.

A *national* legislature can control, direct, or abolish local authority at any time. In a *federal* system, local governments have areas of supreme power. The areas of local authority are no more subject to the federal authority than the federal authority is subject to State and local governments.

In the extent of its powers, the proposed government is not *national*. Federal jurisdiction extends to specific objectives only. The States will have a total sovereignty over all other issues.

The Supreme Court will ultimately decide boundary disputes between two jurisdictions. The federal government will establish the Supreme Court. But this doesn't change the principle. Such a tribunal is essential to prevent armed conflict between States and dissolution of the Union. Few people would argue against the national government creating the Supreme Court.

Number 44 [17]

What will happen if Congress misconstrues the "necessary and proper" clause and exercises powers not warranted by its true meaning? I answer, the same thing will happen as will occur if they misconstrue or enlarge any power vested in them. The same thing as if the State legislatures violated their respective constitutional authorities.

First, the power usurpation will only succeed if the executive and judiciary departments, which execute and interpret legislative acts, support it…

Number 81 [5]

Nothing in the new Constitution directly give the national courts the power to interpret laws according to the spirit of the Constitution… The Constitution should be the standard for the construction of laws. When laws conflict with the Constitution, the Constitution takes precedence over the laws. But this doctrine is not in the proposed Constitution. It comes from the general theory of a limited constitution…

Number 80 [2-4, 13-14]

The judicial authority of the Union should extend to several types of cases:

1. Cases that concern the execution of the provisions in the Constitution.
2. Cases that come from the laws of the United States passed through the constitutional power of legislation…

1. Constitutional Provisions

The first seems obvious. There should be a way to enforce constitutional provisions.

For example, the Constitution limits State authority. The States are prohibited from doing several things. Some are incompatible with the interests of the Union. Others are incompatible with the principles of good government. There must be a way to enforce the restrictions.

For example, the States cannot tax imported articles. And they cannot issue paper money. State prohibitions would not be obeyed if the federal government didn't have the power to stop or correct the infractions of them. The federal government needs either the power to veto State laws or an authority in the federal courts to overrule any violation of the Union's Constitution. The convention preferred the latter.

2. Federal Legislation

The government's judicial power should be as extensive as its legislative power.

National laws must be interpreted uniformly. If each State had an independent court of final jurisdiction over the same cases, arising out of the same laws, it would create a hydra in government. The State courts would contradict each other and their decisions would be confusing.

The federal judiciary decides all cases in law and equity *arising under the Constitution* and *the laws of the United States*. This corresponds with the two types of cases, discussed above. And it is proper jurisdictions of the United States.

How are "cases arising under the Constitution," different from cases "arising under the laws of the United States"?

The difference has been already explained. For example, the Constitution restricts the authority of the State legislatures. They are not to emit paper money. This restriction comes from the Constitution. It is not connected with any law of the United States. If paper money is emitted, the controversies concerning it would be cases arising under the Constitution and not the laws of the United States.

"Equitable" Jurisdiction

It has been asked why the word "equity" is needed. What equitable causes can grow out of the Constitution and laws of the United States?

Almost every subject of litigation that doesn't involve *fraud, accident, trust,* or *hardship* could be an object of equitable rather than legal jurisdiction as the distinction is known and established in the States.

For example, it is the duty of an equity court to relieve against what are called hard bargains. These contracts may not involve direct fraud or deceit sufficient to invalidate them in a court of law. But it may take advantage of the needs or misfortunes of one of the parties that a court of equity would not tolerate. When foreigners are concerned on either side of such cases, it would be impossible for the federal courts to do justice without equitable as well as legal jurisdiction.

Agreements to convey lands claimed under the grants of different States are another example of the need for an equitable jurisdiction in the federal courts. This reasoning may not be as obvious in the States where the formal and technical distinction between law and equity is not maintained, unlike in New York where it is used every day.

—to all Cases affecting Ambassadors, other public Ministers and Consuls;—to all Cases of admiralty and maritime Jurisdiction;—to Controversies to which the United States shall be a Party;—to Controversies between two or more States;—[between a State and Citizens of another State;—]* between Citizens of different States;—between Citizens of the same State claiming Lands under Grants of different States, [and between a State, or the Citizens thereof, and foreign States, Citizens, of Subjects.]

changed by Amendment 11

The judicial power of the United States shall not be construed to extend to any suit in law or equity, commenced or prosecuted against one of the United States by Citizens of another State, or by Citizens or Subjects of any Foreign State.

Number 80 [1-2, 5-11, 15-21]

The judicial authority of the Union should extend to several [other] types of cases:

    3. Cases in which the United States is a party.

    4. Cases involving the peace of the confederacy, whether they relate to the relationship between the United States and foreign nations or between the States themselves.

5. Cases that originate on the high seas and are of admiralty or maritime jurisdiction.

6. Cases in which the State courts cannot be expected to be impartial and unbiased.

3. Nation vs. States or Citizens

Even less needs to be said about the third type. Only national courts can decide controversies between the nation and its States or citizens. Any other plan would be contrary to reason, precedent, and decorum.

4. U.S. vs. Foreign Nations, Citizens

The fourth type rests on the idea that the peace of the whole should never depend on a part. The Union will answer to foreign powers for the conduct of its States. And the responsibility for an injury should always be accompanied with the ability to prevent it.

If a citizen of another country is denied justice or is wrongfully convicted, it can become a just cause for war. Therefore, the federal judiciary should have jurisdiction in all cases concerning the citizens of other countries. This is essential to both public faith and tranquility.

Treaties and the laws of nations may seem different than municipal laws. Treaties and the laws of nations may seem proper for federal jurisdiction and municipal laws for State jurisdiction. However, let's say a foreign citizen gets an unjust sentence solely because of the location in our country where he is tried. If the unjust sentence is not corrected, his native country could see it as an aggression. It could also be seen as a violation of a treaty stipulation or the general laws of nations.

And it would be very difficult, if not impossible, to decide if a case falls under federal or municipal jurisdiction. Many cases in which foreigners are parties involve national questions. It is safer and faster to refer them to national courts.

Between States, Citizens of Different States

To keep the Union peaceful, the federal government must have the power to determine causes between two States, between one State and the citizens of another, and between the citizens of different States.

Wars between Germanic states devastated Germany before Maximilian created the Imperial Chamber in the 15th century. This court made the final decision in differences among the Germanic states. And it created peace in the empire.

Territorial Disputes

Until now, the federal government has been able to decide territorial disputes between the States. But there are many other sources of bickering and anger between States, besides territorial claims.

We have seen some already. I am talking about the fraudulent laws that have been passed in many of the States. The proposed Constitution establishes specific guards against repeating those cases. But we should worry that the same spirit that produced them will assume a new shape, which cannot be foreseen nor specifically provided against.

It is proper for the federal government to control things that disturb the harmony between the States.

Interstate Citizenship

It is the foundation of the Union that "the citizens of each State shall be entitled to all the privileges and immunities of citizens of the several States." Every government *should have the ability to execute its own provisions by its own authority.* Therefore, to keep the equality of privileges and immunities, the national judiciary should preside in all cases where one State or its citizens are opposed by another State or its citizens.

This fundamental provision can be effective only in a court that has no local attachments. The court will probably be impartial between the different States and their citizens because it is a federal court. Therefore, its only bias will probably be towards the principles on which it is founded.

5. Maritime Jurisdiction

There will be little criticism of the fifth type. Even the most bigoted idolizers of State authority say the national courts have jurisdiction of maritime causes. These are often based on the laws of nations and often affect the rights of foreigners. They relate to the public peace. Under the present Confederation, the federal courts determine the most important cases.

6. When State Courts Can't Be Impartial

The national courts should decide cases where the State courts cannot be impartial.

No man should be a judge in his own cause or in any cause in which he has an interest or bias. The federal courts are the proper tribunals for determining controversies between different States and their citizens. And it should have the same operation in regard to some cases between citizens of the same State.

Claims to land under grants of different States are of this description. The courts of neither State could be expected to be unbiased. The laws may have even prejudged the question. The courts may be forced to rule in favor to the grants of the State to which they belong. And even where this had not been done, it would be natural that the judges, as men, would feel partial to the claims of their own government.

Treaties, Ambassadors

To treaties made, or which shall be made, under the authority of the United States, and to all cases affecting ambassadors, other public ministers, and consuls. These belong to the fourth class of cases; they have a clear connection with the preservation of the national peace.

Admiralty, Maritime

Admiralty and maritime cases are the fifth class of causes proper for national jurisdiction.

United States a Party

To controversies to which the United States shall be a party. These constitute the third class.

Between States

To controversies between two or more States; between a State and citizens of another State; between citizens of different States. These belong to the fourth class and partake, in some measure, of the nature of the last.

Land Disputes, Citizens of the Same State

To cases between the citizens of the same State, claiming lands under grants of different States. These fall within the last class. And they are the only instances in which the proposed Constitution directly contemplates the jurisdiction of disputes between the citizens of the same State.

State, Citizen vs. Foreign Country, Citizen

To cases between a State and the citizens thereof and foreign countries, citizens or subjects. These belong to the fourth class. They are the proper subject of the national judicature.

In all Cases affecting Ambassadors, other public Ministers and Consuls, and those in which a State shall be a Party, the supreme Court shall have original Jurisdiction. In all the other Cases before mentioned, the supreme Court shall have appellate Jurisdiction, both as to Law and Fact, with such Exceptions, and under such Regulations as the Congress shall make.

Number 80 [22]

The specific powers of the federal judiciary, as stated in the Constitution, seem to conform to the principles that govern the structure of the judiciary. And they are necessary. If some seem inconvenient, the national legislature will have the authority to make *exceptions*. Congress can make any regulations that are needed to prevent or remove these inconveniences.

There is a possibility of specific mischiefs. However, this is not a solid objection. The principle avoids most problems and produces many advantages.

Number 81 [23]

These are the observations made about the authority of the judicial branch:
- It is restricted to causes that are proper for the national judicature.
- The authority is divided. A small part of original jurisdiction is given to the Supreme Court. The rest is given to the inferior tribunals.
- The Supreme Court will have an appellate jurisdiction both as to law and fact in all the cases referred to them, both subject to any *exceptions* and *regulations* that may be thought advisable.
- This appellate jurisdiction does not *abolish* the trial by jury.
- And an ordinary degree of prudence and integrity in the national councils will insure that we have the advantages of the proposed judiciary without exposing us to the inconveniences that have been predicted.

Number 81 [11]

The Constitution lists the cases within federal jurisdiction. Federal courts can't extend their jurisdiction beyond these limits. A more extensive authority is excluded.

Federal v. State Judiciary

Number 82 [2-end]

There have been questions about the proposed Constitution, especially the judiciary branch. What is the role of State courts in causes that fall under federal jurisdiction? Is the federal jurisdiction to be exclusive? Or will the State courts have a concurrent jurisdiction? If the latter, what will be their relationship to national courts?

Wise men ask these questions. And they certainly deserve attention.

Federal Authorities Defined

An earlier Paper explained that the States will keep all *preexisting* authorities not exclusively given to the federal government. There are three types of exclusive federal authority:

1) where the Constitution says that the federal government will have exclusive authority,

2) where the Constitution gives the federal government a specific authority and the States are prohibited from having a similar authority,

3) or where the Constitution gives the federal government an authority and a similar authority in the States would be incompatible.

These principles apply to both judiciary and legislative power. Therefore, the State courts will *keep* the jurisdiction they now have, unless one of the three ways takes it away.

Concurrent State/Federal Jurisdiction

One statement in the Constitution confines the causes of federal jurisdiction to the federal courts: "The JUDICIAL POWER of the United States *shall be vested* in one Supreme Court and in *such* inferior courts as the Congress shall from time to time ordain and establish."

This might be interpreted in two ways. It could mean that the supreme and inferior courts of the Union should have all the power to decide federal causes. Or it could mean that the national judiciary should be one Supreme Court and as many lower courts as Congress appoints. In other words, the United States should exercise its judicial power through one supreme tribunal and a number of inferior ones.

The first excludes, the last includes, the concurrent jurisdiction of the State tribunals. The first would alienate State power by implication. But the last appears to be the most natural and the most defensible interpretation.

Limited Concurrent Jurisdiction

Concurrent jurisdiction applies only to cases where the State courts have jurisdiction before adopting the Constitution. It does not apply to cases that are *specific* to the Constitution. Not allowing State jurisdiction in these cases would not limit preexisting authority.

The United States Congress may pass legislation that gives the decision of cases arising from a specific law to the federal courts alone, if it seems expedient. But State courts will not lose any of their original jurisdictions further than an appeal. When States are not expressly excluded by the future acts of the national legislature, they will take jurisdiction of the cases to which those acts may give birth.

I infer this from the nature of judicial power. The judicial power of every government looks beyond local or municipal laws. And in civil cases, it looks at all subjects of litigation between parties within its jurisdiction, even if the disputes deal with laws in the most distant part of the globe. Those of Japan, not less than of New York, may furnish the objects of legal discussion in our courts.

The State and national governments are parts of ONE WHOLE. The State courts have a concurrent jurisdiction in all cases arising under the Union's laws when not prohibited.

Final Appeal to Supreme Court

Another question arises. What relationship would exist between the national and State courts in cases with concurrent jurisdiction?

An appeal could be made to the Supreme Court of the United States. The Constitution gives the Supreme Court appellate jurisdiction in all the cases of federal jurisdiction where it doesn't have original jurisdiction. It doesn't confine its operation to the inferior federal courts.

The objects of appeal, not the courts from which it is made, are alone considered. Therefore, it extends to State courts. Either this is true or the local courts must be excluded from a concurrent jurisdiction in matters of national concern. If this was not true, the judicial authority of the Union could be avoided by every plaintiff or prosecutor. Neither of these consequences should be involved without clear necessity. The latter would be entirely wrong because it would defeat some of the most important purposes of the proposed government and would embarrass its measures. Nor do I see any foundation for such an assumption.

The national and State systems are to be regarded as ONE WHOLE. The State courts will be natural auxiliaries to the execution of the laws of the Union. And an appeal from State courts will naturally be to the federal judiciary. The federal judiciary will unite and assimilate the principles of national justice.

The Constitution lists specific causes that will receive their original or final determination in the federal courts. There are important public reasons for this.

If the appellate jurisdiction of the Supreme Court were confined to appeals from inferior federal courts instead of allowing their extension to the State courts, it would abridge the latitude of the terms in subversion of the intent, contrary to every sound rule of interpretation.

Appeal to Lower Federal Courts

Could an appeal be made from the State courts to an inferior federal court? This question is more difficult than the former. The following considerations suggest an affirmative answer.

First, the Constitution authorizes the national legislature "to constitute tribunals inferior to the Supreme Court."*

Next, it says, "the JUDICIAL POWER of the United States *shall be vested* in one Supreme Court, and in such inferior courts as Congress shall ordain and establish." It then lists the cases to which this judicial power extends. Afterwards, it divides the jurisdiction of the Supreme Court into original and appellate. But it doesn't define the jurisdiction of the subordinate courts. They are only described as "inferior to the Supreme Court." And they won't exceed the limits of the federal judiciary.

Whether the lower courts' authority is original or appellate or both is not defined. This seems left to the discretion of the legislature. I can see no reason why there can't be an appeal from the State courts to the inferior national courts. And there could be many advantages. There would be fewer reasons to have multiple federal courts. The State courts could hear federal cases and most appeals. And appeals to State court decisions could be made to district federal courts.

The Trial of all Crimes, except in Cases of Impeachment, shall be by Jury; and such Trial shall be held in the State where the said Crimes shall have been committed; but when not committed within any State, the Trial shall be at such Place or Places as the Congress may by Law have directed.

Number 48 [11]

[In Pennsylvania] the constitutional trial by jury has been violated and powers not delegated by the constitution have been assumed.

Number 81[21-23]

The Supreme Court will have appellate jurisdiction both as to law and *fact*. And this jurisdiction will be subject to *exceptions* and regulations written by the national legislature. The government can modify it so it serves public justice and security.

Some people have said this provision *abolishes* trial by jury. This is fallacious and untrue. The United States Congress will have full power to say that in appeals to the Supreme Court facts cannot be reexamined if juries tried the original causes. This would be an authorized exception. But if it is thought too extensive, it might be limited to causes determined at common law by jury trials…This appellate jurisdiction does not *abolish* the trial by jury…

Number 83 [all]

Paper Number 83 is the longest and most difficult Paper for me to "translate." You can almost feel the author's frustration. Specious arguments on a subject are always frustrating to logical thinkers.

Some people object to the Constitution because it doesn't have a *constitutional provision* for the trial by jury in civil causes. This objection is disingenuous.

---

* Section 8, article 1. –PUBLIUS

The proposed Constitution says nothing about *civil causes.* Opponents claim this means that trial by jury is being abolished. They say that trials by jury are being abolished in all civil and *criminal causes.* To argue that trial by jury is being abolished in criminal cases is vain and fruitless.

Silence Doesn't Imply Prohibition

Regarding civil causes, opponents argue that since trial by jury *isn't mentioned*, it is *abolished.* However, there is a big difference between *silence* and *abolition.* The inventors of this fallacy try to support it by perverting the true meaning of *legal maxims* of law interpretation. Therefore, let's look at their arguments.

They base their arguments on maxims like this: "A specification of particulars is an exclusion of generals;" or "The expression of one thing is the exclusion of another."

They say, the Constitution establishes trial by jury in criminal cases and is silent about civil cases. Therefore, this silence is an implied prohibition of trial by jury in civil cases.

The rules of legal interpretation are rules of *common sense* adopted by the courts in the interpretation of the laws. Therefore, the true interpretation is whether it conforms to the source from which it is derived.

If a provision says that criminal cases must be tried by juries, does that mean that the legislature cannot permit trial by jury in other cases? Is this common sense? It isn't rational to say that requiring trial by jury in certain cases is a ban of it in others.

Create Courts → Determine Trial Mode

The legislature has the power to create courts, which includes the power to impose the mode of trial. Therefore, if the Constitution said nothing about juries, the legislature could either adopt trial by jury or not.

The Constitution says all criminal cases must be tried by jury but it doesn't mention civil cases. There is no obligation to use juries in civil cases. But the legislature has the power to decide the proper mode of trial. Therefore, to say the national legislature could not require that federal civil cases be heard by juries is a lie. Trial by jury in civil cases would not be abolished. And using the maxims in this way is contrary to reason and common sense.

Even if these maxims were being used correctly in this case, which they are not, they never apply to a government's constitution. Constitutional provisions are to be interpreted using their obvious meaning, not technical rules.

I will show how the maxims are used properly by examples.

The Constitution declares that the *national legislature's* power will extend to specific cases. This list of specific authorities excludes a general legislative authority. If a general authority was intended, a list of special powers would be absurd and useless.

The Constitution lists the cases within federal jurisdiction. Federal courts can't extend their jurisdiction beyond these limits. A more extensive authority is excluded.

These examples show how the maxims should be used. Here is another example.

Suppose a New York law says that a married woman cannot convey her property. So the legislature makes a law that says she can dispose of her property by deed executed in the presence of a judge. In this case, the specific rule excludes all other methods because the woman had no previous power to dispose of her property.

Now let us say that later in the same law it says that no woman can dispose of property of a **specific value** without the consent of three of her nearest relatives and they must sign the deed. Could we infer from this regulation that a married woman could not get the approval of her relatives when conveying property of inferior value? This is absurd. Yet this is the reasoning of people who say that trial by jury in civil cases is abolished because it is required in criminal cases.

Civil Causes: State Jurisdiction

Clearly, the Constitution doesn't abolish trial by jury.

And in civil cases between individuals, trial by jury will be the same as provided in the State constitutions. It will not change by the adoption of the Constitution. The national judiciary will not have jurisdiction. They will continue to be heard in State courts, according to the State constitutions and laws.

All land causes, except those involving claims from different States, will belong to the jurisdiction of State courts. And all other controversies between the citizens of the same State, unless they involve violations of the US Constitution by acts of the State legislatures, will also be under State court jurisdiction.

Admiralty cases and most equity cases are decided by our government without a jury.

State jurisdiction of civil cases will not be greatly affected by the proposed change in our system of government.

Trial by Jury Valuable

Friends and adversaries of the Constitution agree that trial by jury is valuable. But there may be a small difference between them. Friends of the Constitution regard it as a valuable safeguard to liberty. Adversaries represent it as the only safeguard.

I hold trial by jury in high esteem. It is essential in a representative republic. It is even more important as a defense against the oppression of a hereditary monarch. Trial by jury is useful and friendly towards liberty. But I cannot see the inseparable connection between the existence of liberty and the trial by jury in civil cases.

Judicial despotism comes from arbitrary impeachments, arbitrary methods of prosecuting pretended offenses, and arbitrary punishments on arbitrary convictions. These all relate to criminal trials. Therefore, trial by jury in criminal cases, aided by *habeas-corpus*, is important. The Constitution provides for both.

Safeguard Against Oppressive Taxes

It is said that trial by jury is a safeguard against oppressive taxation. This idea deserves to be studied.

Trial by jury cannot influence the legislature, which decides the *amount* of taxes, the *objects* of taxation, and the tax apportionment *rule*. Therefore, trial by jury can only influence how taxes are collected and the conduct of the revenue officers.

In New York, trial by jury is rarely used for tax collection. Taxes are usually levied by the summary proceeding of distress and sale. And everyone agrees that this is essential to the efficacy of the revenue laws. The delay of a trial to recover the taxes imposed on individuals would not fulfill public needs. And it would often cost more than the original tax.

Revenue officers who abuse public authority or extort citizens commit criminal offenses against the government. Trial by jury in criminal cases will give complete security. Officers can be indicted and punished.

Corrupting Officers of the Court

The importance of trial by jury in civil cases depends on circumstances other than the preservation of liberty. Security against corruption is the strongest argument in its favor.

There is more time to tamper with a judge than with a jury summoned for one trial. Perhaps a judge could more easily be corrupted than a jury. This argument is, however, diminished by other considerations.

The sheriff summons ordinary juries. The clerks of courts nominate special juries. Both are standing officers. It might be easier to corrupt them than judges. Those officers could select corrupt jurors.

It might be easier to corrupt jurors, who are randomly chosen, than to corrupt judges, who are chosen for their good character.

Despite these considerations, trial by jury is a valuable check on corruption.

Currently, both the judge and the jury would have to be corrupted. When the jury is clearly wrong, the judge will generally grant a new trial. In most cases, it would be useless to corrupt the jury unless the judge is also corrupted. This is a double security.

Judges will be less tempted when it is necessary to also corrupt the jury than if they exclusively determined all causes.

Constitutional Definition Difficult

I doubt that trial by jury in civil cases is essential to liberty. However, it is an excellent way to determine property questions. Because of this alone it would be entitled to a constitutional provision if it were possible to define the limits within which it should be used. However, this is difficult. In a federal government that is composed of societies whose ideas and institutions vary from each other that difficulty increases. I believe that real obstacles prevented including this subject in the Constitution.

Judiciary in State Constitutions

Within the States, the use of the jury trial varies widely. An explanation of the differences is necessary before we make a judgment about its omission from the Constitution.

The New York judicial system resembles Great Britain's. New York has courts of common law, courts of probates (similar to the spiritual courts in England), a court of admiralty, and a court of chancery. The trial by jury prevails only in the courts of common law and there are exceptions. In all the others, a single judge presides without a jury, following either canon or civil law.*

---

* It has been erroneously said that the Chancery Court tries disputed facts by a jury. The truth is, juries in that court are rare and not necessary except where the validity of a devise of land comes into question.—PUBLIUS

In New Jersey, a court of chancery is like New York's. But it doesn't have courts of admiralty nor of probates, like the New York courts. The New Jersey courts of common law have the jurisdiction in cases that in New York are determined in the courts of admiralty and of probates. And the jury trial is more extensive in New Jersey than in New York.

Pennsylvania doesn't have a court of chancery, and its common-law courts have equity jurisdiction. It has a court of admiralty, but none of probates, at least like New York's.

Delaware is like Pennsylvania. Maryland and Virginia are like New York, except that Virginia has many chancellors. North Carolina is most like Pennsylvania; South Carolina is like Virginia. I believe, however, that some States with admiralty courts use jury trials for those cases.

Georgia has only common-law courts. An appeal, of course, lies from the verdict of one jury to another, called a special jury, which has a specific mode of appointment.

In Connecticut, they have no separate courts of chancery or admiralty. Their probate courts have no jurisdiction of causes. Their common-law courts have admiralty and some equity jurisdiction. In important cases, their General Assembly is the only court of chancery. In Connecticut, therefore, the trial by jury extends in *practice* further than in any other State yet mentioned.

The situation in Rhode Island is, I believe, much the same as Connecticut. Massachusetts and New Hampshire, in regard to the blending of law, equity, and admiralty jurisdictions, are similar. In the four Eastern States, trial by jury has a broader foundation than in the other States. And they have a function that is not seen in the other States. There is an appeal from one jury to another, until there have been two verdicts out of three on one side.

State Standard Couldn't Be Used

The use of trial by jury in civil cases in the States is diverse. From this fact we see that:

First, the convention couldn't make a general rule that corresponded with the use of trial by jury in civil cases in all the States.

Second, the convention might have adopted the rule of one State. But that would have caused more problems than omitting any provision and leaving the matter, as has been done, to legislative regulation.

Federal Judiciary New Institution

People have suggested how to correct the omission. However, the suggestions illustrate the problem, they don't correct it. The minority of Pennsylvania proposed that "Trial by jury shall be as heretofore." This would be senseless and worthless.

All provisions in the proposed Constitution refer to the United States, in their united or collective capacity. Although each State uses jury trials, in the United States, *as such*, it is unknown. The present federal government has no judiciary power. Therefore, there is nothing to which the term *heretofore* could relate. It has no meaning. It is too uncertain to be used. On the one hand, this provision would not fulfill the intent of the people proposing it. On the other, it would be inexpedient.

I presume that what they mean to say is this: Inferior federal courts will be located in the States. And these inferior federal courts should use the same mode of trial as the States in which they sit. Therefore, if a State where the federal court is located uses trial by jury in a specific type of case, then the federal court should use trial by jury. For example, admiralty cases should be tried by a jury in Connecticut, but without one in New York.

Using different modes of trial for similar cases under the same government is capricious. Cases would be tried with or without a jury, depending on the accidental situation of where the court and the parties to the case are located. This is a really bad idea.

Technical Knowledge Important

But this is not the greatest objection. I believe that trial by jury is not appropriate for all cases. This is particularly true in cases that concern the public peace with foreign nations. Those cases usually involve the laws of nations.

All prize causes are this type of case. Juries would need a thorough knowledge of laws and usages of nations. We can't assume that juries will have this knowledge. And they will sometimes be influenced by considerations other than public policy. The rights of other nations might be infringed by their decisions, giving reasons for reprisal and war.

Although juries are supposed to determine matters of fact, in most cases, legal consequences are complicated with fact. It may be impossible to separate the two.

Treaties Often Specify Trial Types

Also, treaties often state the method of determining prize causes. By treaty, in Great Britain the king, in his privy council, determines them. The fact and the law are reexamined.

This shows why putting a provision in the Constitution, making the State systems a standard for the national government is a bad idea. And it shows why it is dangerous to put provisions in the Constitution that are not absolutely proper.

Separating Equity, Law Jurisdictions

Separating equity from law jurisdiction has advantages. It is improper to give juries cases that belong in equity courts.

The primary use of equity courts is to give relief *in extraordinary cases*, which are *exceptions** to general rules. If the jurisdiction of such cases was united with the ordinary jurisdiction, every case would need a *special* determination. Separating them has the opposite effect. One will be a sentinel over the other. And each stays within its limits.

Equity cases are often very complicated. They often require long and deliberate investigation. Therefore, they are incompatible with jury trials. It would be impractical to call men from their jobs and force them to decide the case before they could return to their jobs.

---

* The principles governing that relief are now reduced to a regular system. But it is no less true that they are usually applicable to SPECIAL circumstances that form exceptions to general rules.—P

Trial by jury requires that the matter to be decided should be reduced to a single, obvious point. Chancery trials often include many tiny and independent facts.

The separation of the equity from the legal jurisdiction is unique to the English system of justice. Several States follow this model.

But trial by jury has not been used in cases where they are united. The separation is essential. It preserves trial by jury.

An equity court can easily extend its jurisdiction to matters of law. But extending the jurisdiction of the courts of law to equity causes will change the nature of the courts of law. It will undermine trial by jury by introducing questions too complicated for a decision in that mode.

For these reasons, the national judiciary should not use the system proposed by the Pennsylvania minority.

Massachusetts Suggests Tiny Change

Let's examine the suggestion from Massachusetts. It says: "In civil actions between citizens of different States, every issue of fact, arising in *actions at common law, may be tried by a jury if the parties, or either of them, request it."

This defines one type of cause. We can infer one of two things. Either they thought it is the only class of federal causes proper for trial by jury. Or they may have wanted a more extensive provision, but they found it impractical to devise one. If the first, the omission of such a minor point is not a material imperfection in the Constitution. If the last, it corroborates the extreme difficulty of the thing.

What cases entitled to jury trial?

But this is not all. Let's look at the State courts again and their different powers. Some have vague descriptions of when trial by jury is allowed.

In New York, the line between common law and equitable jurisdiction follow the rules in England. In many of the other States, the boundaries are less precise.

In some, every cause is tried in a court of common law. Every action may be considered an action at common law to be determined by a jury, if any of the involved parties choose it. Therefore, this would create the same confusion that I mentioned as resulting from the regulation proposed by Pennsylvania. In one State, a cause would be determined by a jury, if any of the parties requested it. But in another, the same cause must be decided without a jury, because the State judicatories vary as to common-law jurisdiction.

Before the Massachusetts suggestion can be used, all the States must adopt one plan that sets the limits of common-law and equitable jurisdictions. This is a difficult task. It might even be impossible to create a regulation acceptable to all the States or that would perfectly conform to the State institutions.

Choosing One State System Won't Work

Why couldn't the constitution of New York be used as a standard for the United States? Other States probably don't have the same opinion of our institutions as we do. They probably like their own systems more.

If the convention used one State as a model, its adoption would be difficult. Each representative would favor his own government. And it is uncertain which State would have been the model. It has been shown that many of them would be improper ones.

If the convention had selected one State's system, the other States might be jealous. And the enemies of the Constitution would have many pretexts for raising prejudices against it that might endanger its ratification.

Defining which cases should be tried by juries would be difficult. To avoid these problems, men have suggested a constitutional provision establishing it in all cases. I don't believe any State has a precedent for this. And the establishment of the trial by jury in *all* cases would have been an unforgivable error in the plan.

In short, any provision would say too much or too little. Or it might have opened other sources of opposition to the essential objective of introducing a firm national government.

Conclusions of This Discussion

The different views of the subject in this paper will remove most worries on the point. They have shown the following:

- Trial by jury in criminal cases, alone, is necessary to secure liberty. This is provided for in the Constitution.
- Most civil cases will use trial by jury. This is established in the State constitutions, untouched and unaffected by the Constitution.
- Trial by jury is not abolished* by the Constitution.
- And there are great, if not insurmountable, difficulties to making a proper provision for it in a Constitution for the United States.

Trial by Jury May Be Overused

Wise people will not want a constitutional provision for jury trials in civil cases. They know that society continually changes. In many cases, a different method to determine property cases is preferred.

I believe it could be extended to some cases in New York to which it does not currently apply. And it might be limited in others.

All reasonable men agree that it should not be used in all cases. The examples in these States as well as in Great Britain show that it should be limited. Future experience may discover that other exceptions may be proper and useful. I suspect it is impossible, because of its nature, to fix the exact point where the operation of the institution should stop. This is a strong argument for leaving the matter to the discretion of the legislature.

Constitution: General Principles

This is now the case in Great Britain and Connecticut.

More encroachments have been made on the trial by jury in New York since the Revolution than in Connecticut and Great Britain. The men who make these encroachments often tell the people that they are great defenders of liberty. Then they ignore any constitutional obstacles to their career.

---

* *Vide* Number 81 refutes the idea that it is abolished by the appellate jurisdiction in matters of fact being vested in the Supreme Court.—PUBLIUS

Truthfully, only the general genius of a government can be relied on for permanent effects. Specific provisions, although not useless, have less virtue than commonly ascribed to them.

It is both harsh and extraordinary to say that there is no security for liberty in a Constitution that establishes the trial by jury in criminal cases, because it does not do it in civil also. Connecticut, which is always regarded as the most popular State in the Union, has no constitutional provision for either.

Judge Influences Jury

Number 65 [8]

But judges frequently influence juries. Juries are sometimes encouraged to find verdicts that the judge wants.

Article 3 SECTION 3. Treason against the United States, shall consist only in levying War against them, or in adhering to their enemies, giving them Aid and Comfort. No Person shall be convicted of Treason unless on the Testimony of two Witnesses to the same overt Act, or on Confession in open Court.

The Congress shall have power to declare the Punishment of Treason, but no Attainder of Treason shall work Corruption of Blood, or Forfeiture except during the Life of the Person attained.

Number 43[8]

Since treason may be committed against the United States, the United States should have the authority to punish it. However, some people have created new, artificial treasons, and used them as an excuse for malicious vengeance. The Constitution erects a barrier against this danger. It defines treason. It states the proof necessary for conviction. And Congress may not extend the punishment beyond the guilty person.

Number 74[4]

...Treason is a crime against the society... It is important to remember that treason will often be connected with seditious acts by a group of people in the community, as recently happened in Massachusetts.

Number 69[6]

...the President of the United States can pardon treason when prosecuted in the ordinary course of law...

Number 74[4]

The Presidential power of pardoning has only been questioned in relation to the crime of treason.

ARTICLE 4 SECTION 1. Full Faith and Credit shall be given in each State to the public Acts, Records, and judicial Proceedings of every other State. And the Congress may by general Laws prescribe the Manner in which such Acts, Records and Proceedings shall be proved, and the effect thereof.

Number 42 [19]

The federal power to determine how public acts, records, and judicial proceedings of each State will be proved, and the effect they will have in other States, is clearly a valuable improvement on the Articles of Confederation. This Constitutional power will be most beneficial on the borders of contiguous States where the effects liable to justice may be suddenly and secretly changed, in any stage of the process, within a foreign jurisdiction.

ARTICLE 4 SECTION 2. The Citizens of each State shall be entitled to all Privileges and Immunities of Citizens in the several States.

Number 42 [17]

Our current naturalization rules are confusing. The fourth Article of the Confederacy declares "that the *free inhabitants* of each of these States, paupers, vagabonds, and fugitives from justice excepted, shall be entitled to all privileges and immunities of *free citizens* in the several States; and *the people* of each State shall, in every other, enjoy all the privileges of trade and commerce," etc.

Why were the terms *free inhabitants* used in one part, *free citizens* in another, and *people* in another? And the meaning of the phrase "all the privileges of trade and commerce" is not clear.

It also seems to say that when people defined as *free inhabitants* of one State—but who are not citizens of that State—travel to a different State, they have all the privileges of *free citizens*. In other words, they may have greater privileges than in their home State. If the term "inhabitants" was changed to "citizens," the difficulty would only be diminished, not removed. Each State would retain the very improper power to naturalize aliens in every other State.

For example, let's say that in one State a short-term resident has all criteria for citizenship but another State requires more qualifications. An alien, therefore, only has to first reside in the former to elude the greater qualifications in the latter. Thus, preposterously, the law of the first State is dominant to the law of the second, within the jurisdiction of the second State.

We have escaped embarrassment on this subject only by good luck. Several States prohibit resident aliens from both the rights of citizenship and the privileges of residence. What would have happened if such persons had become citizens under the laws of another State, then demanded their rights to both residency and citizenship within the State that prohibit it? The consequences would probably have been very serious.

The new Constitution corrects this problem. The federal government will establish a uniform rule of naturalization throughout the United States.

A Person charged in any State with Treason, Felony, or other Crime, who shall flee from Justice, and be found in another State, shall on Demand of the executive Authority of the State from which he fled, be delivered up, to be removed to the State having Jurisdiction of the Crime.

[No Person held to Service or Labour in one State, under the Laws thereof, escaping into another, shall, in Consequence of any Law or Regulation therein, be discharged from such Service or Labour,

but shall be delivered up on Claim of the Party to whom such Service or Labour may be due.]

changed by Amendment 13

Section 1 . Neither slavery nor involuntary servitude, except as a punishment for crime whereof the party shall have been duly convicted, shall exist within the United States, or any place subject to their jurisdiction.

Section 2. Congress shall have power to enforce this article by appropriate legislation.

ARTICLE 4 SECTION 3. New States may be admitted by the Congress into this Union; but no new State shall be formed or erected within the Jurisdiction of any other State; nor any State be formed by the Junction of two or more States, or parts of States, without the Consent of the Legislatures of the States concerned as well as of the Congress.

Number 14 [9]

...the immediate goal of the federal Constitution is to secure the union of the thirteen original States and adding new States. But how will the territory on our northwestern frontier be handled? This is best left to people whose experience, at the time, will make them equal to the task.

Number 43[10]

The Articles of Confederation doesn't mention the formation of new States. Canada was to be admitted. And other *colonies*, which probably means other British colonies, could be admitted at the discretion of nine States. This omission had been inconvenient. And it has led Congress into an assumption of power. The new system corrects the defect.

The federal authority and the States concerned must approve the formation of new States. This is an appropriate precaution. New States may not be formed by dividing a State without its consent; this quiets the jealousy of the larger States. There is a similar precaution against joining States without their consent.

The Congress shall have Power to dispose of and make all needful Rules and Regulations respecting the Territory or other Property belonging to the United States; and nothing in this Constitution shall be so construed as to Prejudice any Claims of the United States, or of any particular State.

Number 43 [12]

This provision is probably necessary because of jealousies and questions about the Western territory.

Number 80 [8]

Until now, the federal government has been able to decide territorial disputes between the States...

ARTICLE 4 SECTION 4. The United States shall guarantee to every State in this Union a Republican Form of Government, and shall protect each of them against Invasion; and on Application of the Legislature, or of the Executive (when the Legislature cannot be convened) against domestic Violence.

Number 9 [13]

Since the government is composed of small republics, it has internal happiness.

Number 21 [3-5]

The Articles say nothing about a mutual guaranty of the State governments. A guaranty would be useful and we might suggest that it exists, but it would flagrantly violate the States' rights clause. Although not having a guaranty may endanger the Union, it isn't as dangerous as the federal government not having the constitutional power to enforce federal laws.

Without a guaranty, the Union cannot help fight domestic threats to State constitutions. Usurpations could trample State liberties and the national government could legally do nothing but watch in anger and sorrow. A successful faction could erect a tyranny within a State and the Union could not constitutionally help supporters of the State's constitutional government.

Massachusetts barely survived the recent turmoil. What if someone like Caesar or Cromwell had led the malcontents? If despotism had been established in Massachusetts, how would it have changed liberty in New Hampshire, Rhode Island, Connecticut, or New York?

Some people object to a federal government guaranty. They say that the federal government should not interfere in internal State issues. But they misunderstand the provision. And they want to deprive us of advantages expected from union. A majority of the people could still legally and peacefully reform a State's constitution. The guaranty could only operate when violence was used to force changes.

The people hold the whole power of the government. When disagreements appear, the people will have fewer excuses to use violence. In a representative government, the natural cure for poor administration is changing men. A national guaranty would be used against both tyrannical rulers and community factions.

Number 39 [6]

The Constitution prohibits titles of nobility and guarantees the republican form of government.

Number 43 [14]

In a republican confederacy, the federal government needs the authority to defend against aristocrats, monarchs or dictators taking over any part of it. The Union has the right to insist that a republican government be *substantially* maintained.

A federal coalition of States is more successful if the State governments are founded on the same principles. Montesquieu says that "the confederate republic of Germany" has both "free cities and petty states, subject to different princes…" He says Germany is "more imperfect than Holland and Switzerland . . . Greece was undone," he adds, "as soon as the king of Macedon obtained a seat among the Amphictyons." In the latter case, a large army and the king of the new confederacy influenced events.

Is this precaution needed? If the federal government's intervention isn't needed, this Constitutional provision will be superfluous. But who can say what the States might try doing, or how ambitious State leaders or foreign powers may influence them?

Can the federal government change the State governments without the States agreeing? The national government only *guarantees* the republican form of government; this assumes a preexisting republican form. Therefore, the existing republican forms are guaranteed by the federal Constitution. If the States choose to substitute a different republican form, they have the right to do so and to claim the federal guarantee. The only restriction is that they shall not exchange a republican for an anti-republican Constitution.

Number 85 [3]

If we adopt the Constitution, our republic, our liberty, and our property will be more secure… It will guarantee a republican form of government in each State.

ARTICLE 5. The Congress, whenever two-thirds of both Houses shall deem it necessary, shall propose Amendments to this Constitution, or, on the Application of the Legislatures of two thirds of the several States, shall call a Convention for proposing Amendments, which, in either Case, shall be valid to all Intents and Purposes, as Part of this Constitution, when ratified by the Legislatures of three-fourths of the several States, or by Conventions in three fourths thereof, as the one or the other Mode of Ratification may be proposed by the Congress; provided that no Amendment which may be made prior to the Year One thousand eight hundred and eight shall in any manner affect the first and fourth Clauses in the Ninth Section of the first Article; and that no State, without its Consent, shall be deprived of its equal Suffrage in the Senate.

Number 39 [15]

The Constitution's amendment process is neither totally *national* nor totally *federal*.

If it was totally *national*, a *majority* of the people of the Union could vote to ratify the Constitution. And a majority of people could alter or abolish the Union's government at any time.

On the other hand, if it were totally *federal*, every State in the Union would have to agree to constitutional amendments.

The amendment process in the Constitution doesn't follow either principle. By requiring more than a majority of *States*, not *citizens*, it has a ***federal*** character. By requiring less than the total number of States agree, it is less *federal* and more ***national***.

Number 43 [25-26]

Article Five says that three fourths of the States are needed to ratify amendments with two exceptions only.

Experience will suggest how the Constitution should be altered. An extremely easy amendment process would make the Constitution too mutable. An extremely difficult process would preserve the faults discovered within it. Either the federal or the State governments can originate the amendment process.

One exception, referring to equality in the Senate, is probably a safeguard to the remaining sovereignty of the States, which have equal representation in one branch of the legislature. The States that worried about equality probably insisted on it.

The other exception must have been admitted on the same considerations that produced the privilege defended by it.

Number 85 [9-10, 12-13]

…one view of amendments hasn't been discussed. I will discuss it now.

The Constitution can be amended after it is ratified. This will be much easier than doing it before the ratification process is finished. Why do I say this?

If the Constitution is altered before it is ratified, it immediately becomes a new constitution. And it must be ratified again in each State. All thirteen States would have to agree to the new constitution.

However, if all the States ratify the Constitution, nine States can change it at any time. The chances are as thirteen to nine* in favor of an amendment after ratification over adoption of an entire governmental system.

Once the Constitution is established, each amendment would be brought forward separately. Compromises on other points would not be necessary. The will of the required number would decide the issue. Whenever ten States want an amendment, that amendment will become part of the Constitution.

Opponents argue that it may be impossible to amend the Constitution after it is ratified. They argue that the people administrating the national government will not want to give up any of their authority once they have it.

When people carefully consider an amendment and decide that it should pass, I believe it will deal with the organization of the government, not to the extent of its powers. For this reason alone, people serving in the national government will not oppose it.

Also, governing thirteen States will be difficult. I believe national rulers will need to fulfill the reasonable expectations of their constituents.

But there is another consideration that proves the observation is wrong. It is this: the national rulers, whenever nine States concur, will have no option on the subject. By the fifth article of the Constitution, the Congress will be *obliged* "on the application of the legislatures of two thirds of the States (currently, nine), to call a convention for proposing amendments, which *shall be valid*, to all intents and purposes, as part of the Constitution, when ratified by the legislatures of three fourths of the States, or by conventions in three fourths thereof."

The words of this article are peremptory. The Congress "*shall* call a convention." Nothing is left to the discretion of Congress. Consequently, all the arguments about the disinclination to a change vanish.

It may be difficult to unite two thirds or three fourths of the States in amendments that affect local interests. However, such a difficulty cannot be feared on issues that effect the general liberty or security of the people. The State legislatures will block encroachments by the national government.

---

* It is actually TEN. Two thirds may propose the measure, but three fourths must ratify.—PUBLIUS

ARTICLE 6. All Debts contracted and Engagements entered into, before the Adoption of this Constitution, shall be as valid against the United States under this Constitution, as under the Confederation.

This Constitution, and the Laws of the United States which shall be made in Pursuance thereof; and all Treaties made, or which shall be made, under the Authority of the United States, shall be the supreme Law of the Land; and the Judges in every State shall be bound thereby, any Thing in the Constitution or Laws of any State to the Contrary notwithstanding.

Number 64 [11]

Objection: Treaty is Supreme Law

Some critics are averse to treaties being the *supreme* laws of the land. They insist, and say they believe that treaties, like legislative acts, should be repealable at pleasure. This idea seems to be new and specific to this country. But new errors, as well as new truths, often appear.

Remember that a treaty is only another name for a contract. And no nation would make any contract with us that would be binding on them *absolutely*, but on us only so long and as far as we may think.

People who make laws may, without doubt, amend or repeal them. And people who make treaties may alter or cancel them. But let us not forget that two contracting parties make treaties. Consequently, since the consent of both was essential to their formation, both must agree to alter or cancel them.

The proposed Constitution, therefore, hasn't extended the authority of treaties. They are currently binding and beyond the lawful reach of the legislature. They will be the same in the future, under any form of government.

Number 16 [10]

But how could a State block a national law that applies directly to citizens? The State government would have to use violent, unconstitutional power to block them. Ignoring the law would not be enough. They would be forced to act. Everyone could see the encroachment on national rights. With a constitution able to defend itself, this action would be hazardous. Enlightened citizens would know the difference between legal authority and illegal usurpation of authority.

Blocking a national law would require a factious majority in the State legislature, the courts, and the citizens. If judges didn't conspire with the legislature, they would rule that the State law was contrary to the supreme law of the land, unconstitutional, and void. The people are the natural guardians of the Constitution. If they didn't agree with the State legislature, they would support the national government. Because of the danger to them, State leaders would not lightly or rashly attempt this, except when the federal government uses its authority tyrannically.

Number 27 [6]

The new Constitution extends federal authority to the citizens of the States. It allows the government to use State courts to execute its laws. The federal government will use the same methods to secure obedience as the State governments. In addition, States can call on the whole Union for assistance and support, which will influence public opinion.

The Constitution lists the Union's jurisdiction. A *legitimate* Union law will become the supreme law of the land. All State officers—legislative, executive, and judicial—will be bound by an oath. Thus the State legislatures, courts, and executives will be part of the national government *as far as its just and constitutional authority extends* and will help enforce its laws. If the Union is administered prudently, the Union laws will be peacefully obeyed...

Number 33 [7-8]

The laws of the Union are to be the *supreme law* of the land. What does this mean?

What if federal laws were not supreme? Clearly, they would amount to nothing. A law, by definition, includes supremacy. A law is a rule that those to whom it applies are bound to observe.

If individuals form a governed society, the laws of that society must be the supreme regulator of their conduct. If a number of political societies combine into a larger political society, the laws enacted by the larger society, if they are within its constitutional powers, must be supreme over the small societies and the individuals in them. Otherwise it would be a mere treaty—a treaty is dependent on the good faith of the parties—and not a government, which is only another word for political power and supremacy.

But this doctrine does not mean that acts of the larger society that are *not among* its constitutional powers, acts that invade the authority of smaller societies, will become the supreme law of the land. These will be acts of usurpation and deserve to be treated as such.

Hence, the clause that declares the supremacy of Union laws only repeats a truth. When a federal government is instituted, its laws are supreme. But it *expressly* confines this supremacy to laws made *pursuant to the Constitution*. This is an example of caution by the convention; the limitation would have been understood even if it had not been expressed.

Therefore, a United States tax law would be supreme in its nature and couldn't be legally opposed or controlled. However, a federal law abolishing or preventing collection of State taxes (unless on imports and exports) would not be the supreme law of the land. It would be a usurpation of power not granted by the Constitution.

If the State and federal governments taxed the same object and collection became difficult, this would be inconvenient for both. Neither has superior power. The federal government, the State government, or both using their power in a disadvantageous way would cause the problem. Presumably, the federal and State governments would cooperate and change their tax policies until they were more convenient.

The States will be able to raise revenue from any kind of taxation, except duties on imports and exports. The federal government will not have the authority to control States' taxes...

Number 44 [19-23]

Adversaries of the Constitution attack this provision. But without it, the Constitution would have been very defective. What would happen if the federal Constitution confirmed the supremacy of the State constitutions by a saving clause in their favor?

First. Any authorities contained in the proposed Constitution that exceed those listed in the Articles of Confederation would be annulled. The new Congress would be as impotent as its predecessors.

Second. Some of the State constitutions do not expressly recognize the Confederacy's existing powers. A statement in the Constitution of the States' supremacy could create challenges of every power in the proposed Constitution.

Third. The State constitutions differ from each other. A treaty or national law important to all the States might contradict some State constitutions. Consequently, it would be valid in some States and have no effect in others.

In the end, the world would have seen a system of government founded on an inversion of the fundamental principles of all government. The authority of the whole Union would have been subordinate to the States, like a monster whose individual parts with different goals directing its head.

Number 53 [2]

...Americans understand that the people create a Constitution. And it is the supreme power. The government cannot alter the Constitution. On the other hand, the government makes laws and the government can change them. Other countries don't seem to understand this distinction.

When the legislature has supreme power, the legislature can change government's structure. British citizens discuss political liberties, civil liberties, and constitutional rights. But Parliament's authority is supreme. Several times, Parliament has passed laws that fundamentally change the government, specifically, the election period...

Number 78 [10-15]

...If laws are contrary to the Constitution, the courts will declare them void...

The Constitution defines the legislature's authorities. No legislative act contrary to the Constitution is valid. Denying this would mean that the representatives of the people are superior to the people themselves. Or that a man may do both what he has the authority to do and what he is forbidden from doing.

It may be argued that the legislature decides what its constitutional powers are. And the other branches have to accept the legislature's interpretation. But this is not a logical conclusion from any part of the Constitution.

The Constitution does not say that the people's representatives can substitute their *will* for the people's will. The courts stand between the people and the legislature. Among other things, the courts keep the legislature within their constitutional limits. Courts interpret law. A constitution is a fundamental law. Therefore, the courts determine its meaning, as well as the meaning of legislative acts. If the two conflict, the superior one should be preferred.

Therefore, the Constitution is preferred over the statute; the intention of the people is preferred to the intention of their agents. This doesn't mean that judicial power is superior to the legislative power. It only means that the power of the people is superior to both.

When the will of the legislature, as seen in the laws it passes, opposes the will of the people, as declared in the Constitution, judges should be governed by the Constitution. Their decision should be based on fundamental laws.

Number 81 [5]

...The Constitution should be the standard for the construction of laws. When laws conflict with the Constitution, the Constitution takes precedence over the laws. But this doctrine is not in the proposed Constitution. It comes from the general theory of a limited constitution...

The Senators and Representatives before mentioned, and the Members of the several State Legislatures, and all executive and judicial Officers, both of the United States and of the several States, shall be bound by Oath or Affirmation, to support this Constitution;

Number 44 [25-26]

Why must State officials support the federal Constitution? Officers of the United States don't take a similar oath in favor of the State constitutions.

There are several reasons. I'll give one. Federal officials will not be agents of State constitutions. However, State officials will be essential agents of the federal Constitution. The election of the President and Senate will depend on the State legislatures. State officers will probably conduct the election of the House of Representatives, according to the laws of the States.

but no religious Test shall ever be required as a Qualification to any Office or public Trust under the United States.

Number 52 [3]

Good people of every description may become Representatives, whether native or adoptive, young or old, and without regard to poverty, wealth, or religion.

Number 57 [6]

Who will be elected? The candidate will be a citizen whose merit recommends him to the esteem and confidence of his country. There are no qualifications of wealth, birth, religious faith, or civil profession.

ARTICLE 7. The Ratification of the Conventions of nine States, shall be sufficient for the Establishment of this Constitution between the States so ratifying the Same.

Number 1 [8]

The alternative to adoption of the new Constitution is dismemberment of the Union.

Number 22 [17]

If the new Constitution is not adopted, the country will either fall apart or Congress will be given tyrannical powers. A weak federal government and the schemes of ambitious men who expect to increase their personal power will push the Union towards dissolution. If the country doesn't fall apart, a single "congress" will accumulate all the sovereign powers, creating the tyranny that adversaries of the new Constitution say they don't want.

Number 38 [5]

Writing a new Constitution is complicated and difficult. In areas with little historical experience, there will be errors even if the subject is carefully researched. And the errors will not be found until actual trial points them out.

Both logical reasoning and our experience with the Articles of Confederation suggest this. During the ratification of the Articles of Confederation, many objections were made and amendments were suggested. But no one mentioned the great error that actual trial uncovered. Although the objections proved immaterial, some States would have clung to them with dangerous inflexibility if their zeal for their opinions and interests had not been stifled by the more powerful sentiment of self-preservation. Although the enemy was within our country, one State refused to ratify the Articles for several years. She finally complied out of fear of being charged with protracting the public calamities and endangering the outcome of the war.

Number 39 [10-11]

The Constitution's **foundation** refers to the ratification process. It could have been set up several ways. If ratification required that a *majority* of the people of the entire nation accept the Constitution, then ratification would be a *national* act. However, this is not how the Constitution will be ratified. Nor will a *majority* of the States make the decision.

Instead, the people of each State will vote to ratify the Constitution. They will be acting as citizens of independent States, not as citizens of one nation. And the States must *unanimously* ratify the Constitution. The people—not the legislature—must accept the Constitution.

As they vote to ratify the Constitution, each State is a sovereign body. Each State will act independently and be bound only by its own voluntary act. In its **foundation**, the new government will be *federal*, not *national*.

Number 40 [13,19]

In one area, the convention departed from their specific commission. *Nine States* need to ratify the Constitution, instead of *all the States*. Although this could be an objection to the Constitution, it is rarely mentioned. This is probably because it would be absurd to subject the fate of twelve States to the perverseness or corruption of the thirteenth. Therefore, it has received little criticism. I dismiss it without further comment.

Opponents of the proposed Constitution say that the convention exceeded its power. The only change was the ratification process, which is rarely mentioned by the objectors. Otherwise, the charge has no foundation.

And if they did exceed their powers, they were not only justified but also required. They were servants of their country, who used their liberty to fulfill their mission.

And finally, even if they violated both their powers and their duty in proposing a Constitution, it should be ratified, if it seems to meet the goals and promote the happiness of the people of America. We are investigating whether this describes the Constitution.

Number 43 [28-31]

Only the people can validate the Constitution. If all thirteen States had to ratify the Constitution, the essential interests of the entire Union would be exposed to the caprice or corruption of a single State.

Two questions present themselves:

1. What is the principle that allows the new Constitution to replace the Articles of Confederation without the consent of all thirteen States?

2. What relationship will exist between the nine or more States ratifying the Constitution and the remaining few who do not ratify it?

The first question is answered by saying that it is absolutely necessary. Self-preservation is a primary law of nature and God. All political institutions are created to keep people safe and able to pursue happiness. When a political system fails to fulfill those goals, it must be sacrificed.

We may also find an answer within the compact itself. In many of the States, only the legislature ratified the Articles. This is one of its defects. Reciprocity requires that its obligation on the other States should be reduced to the same standard.

When a legislature makes a compact with another sovereign state, the agreement has no more validity than a treaty between the parties. Treaties are only mutual conditions of each other. A breach of any one article in a treaty is a breach of the whole treaty. A breach committed by either party releases the others. They may pronounce the compact violated and void. And the Articles of Confederation have been violated in many ways.

The second question is also delicate. We hope that all States ratify the Constitution.

No political relationship will continue to exist between the assenting and dissenting States.

But the moral relationships will remain. Claims of justice on both sides must be fulfilled. The rights of humanity must always be duly and mutually respected. Hopefully, considerations of a common interest and, above all, the remembrance of the endearing scenes past, will urge moderation on one side and prudence on the other.

Number 83 [32]

If the convention had selected one State's system, the other States might be jealous. And the enemies of the Constitution would have many pretexts for raising prejudices against it that might endanger its ratification.

Number 85 [all]

In Conclusion, Ratify Now, Amend Later

I listed the subjects to be discussed in the first paper. Two points remain: "A comparison of the proposed Constitution to the New York constitution," and "How the Constitution will preserve liberty, property and the republican form of government."

However, these topics have been discussed in these Papers. Now I can only repeat, in a diluted form, what has been already said.

Same "Defects" in NY Constitution

The proposed Constitution resembles New York's constitution. The New York constitution has many of the same imagined defects, as well as the real excellences.

Among the imagined defects are:
- no term limits for the Executive,
- no executive council,
- no formal bill of rights, and
- no provision for the liberty of the press.

New York's constitution doesn't have these provisions. And it doesn't have several others. If a man bitterly complains about the proposed Constitution but easily excuses the New York constitution, he isn't consistent.

Some people who admire the New York state government have furiously attacked the new Constitution for provisions that are also in New York's constitution. This proves that their attacks on the Constitution are insincere.

New Constitutional Securities

If we adopt the Constitution, our republic, our liberty, and our property will be more secure.

Keeping the Union will restrain local factions and insurrections. And it will restrain the ambition of powerful people in single States who could become despots.

Breaking up the Confederacy would invite foreign intrigue. Keeping the Union will limit foreign influence.

If the States disunited, they would find reasons to fight each other. By staying united, fewer military forts and bases will be needed.

It will guarantee a republican form of government in each State.

It will exclude all titles of nobility.

And it will guard against the States repeating acts that have hurt property and credit, planted mutual distrust between citizens, and caused an almost universal decrease of morals.

Presented Rational Arguments

I have finished the task I assigned to myself. With what success, your ratification vote must determine.

I hope, at least, that I have addressed myself purely to your judgments. And I hope I avoided the harshness that often disgraces political disputes and has been seen in the language and conduct of the opponents of the Constitution.

Supporters of the new Constitution have been indiscriminately charged with conspiracy against liberty. This charge is wanton and malignant. Everyone who knows it is a lie is angry. The lies keep citizens from hearing the truth. All honest men must demand reprobation. Because of these circumstances, I may have used some intemperate expressions that I did not intend. I often struggled between emotional responses and moderation. If the former sometimes prevailed, my excuse is that it has not been often or much.

Every Man Must Now Decide

Have these Papers vindicated the Constitution from the aspersions thrown on it? Is the Constitution worthy of approval? And is the Constitution necessary for public safety and prosperity?

Every man must answer these questions, according to his conscience and understanding. And he must vote as his judgment demands. This is a duty without dispensation. As a member of society, he is obligated to vote sincerely and honestly. No special interests, temporary passions or prejudices, or partial motives should sway his vote. They will not justify to himself, to his country, or to his posterity, an improper vote.

Every man must beware of stubbornly voting the way his party wants him to vote. He must remember that his vote to ratify the Constitution will effect more than just his community. It will determine the very existence of the nation. And let him remember that a majority of America has already ratified the plan that he is to approve or reject.

Constitution Best Solution for Us

I am confident of the arguments that recommend the Constitution to your adoption. And I believe that the opposing arguments are not persuasive. I believe it is the best for our political situation, habits, and opinions. And the Constitution is superior to any plan that the revolution has produced.

Constitution Admittedly Imperfect

The friends of the new Constitution have said that it isn't absolutely perfect. Its enemies see this as a small triumph. They ask, "Why should we adopt an imperfect plan? Why not amend it and make it perfect before it is irrevocably established?"

This may be plausible, but it is only plausible. In the first place, they have exaggerated the concessions. They are stated as if they are an admission that the Constitution is very defective. And that it needs some big changes before the rights and the interests of the community can be safely confided to it.

Although the Constitution may not be perfect, it is a good plan. It is the best that the present views and circumstances of the country will permit. And it promises every type of security that a reasonable people can desire.

Group Decisions Never Perfect

It is unwise to prolong the dangerous state of our national affairs. We should not expose the Union to the jeopardy of more experiments in the effort to find a perfect plan.

Imperfect men can never create a perfect plan. Group discussions always include errors and prejudices, as well as good sense and wisdom, just like the people in the groups. The agreement that will make thirteen States into a union must be a compromise of many different interests. How can a perfect plan come from such materials?

New Convention Not Good Idea

An excellent pamphlet was recently published in New York City.[*] It gives the reasons why a new convention probably couldn't be assembled under circumstances as favorable to producing a good constitution as those in which the late convention met, deliberated, and concluded. I will not repeat the arguments. I assume a lot of people have seen it. Every friend to his country should read it.

However, one view of amendments hasn't been discussed. I will discuss it now.

Amend After Ratification

The Constitution can be amended after it is ratified. This will be much easier than doing it before the ratification process is finished. Why do I say this?

If the Constitution is altered before it is ratified, it immediately becomes a new constitution. And it must be ratified again in each State. All thirteen States would have to agree to the new constitution.

However, if all the States ratify the Constitution, nine States can change it at any time. The chances are as thirteen to nine[**] in favor of an amendment after ratification over adoption of an entire governmental system.

Issues, States Multiply Difficulty

This is not all. Every Constitution for the United States must include the interests of thirteen independent States. In any group given the duty to write it, we will see different people agreeing on different points. People in the majority on one question may become the minority on a second. And a different group may be the majority on a third.

The document must be written to satisfy all the States. Therefore, the difficulties of getting every State to agree multiply. And the multiplication must be a ratio of the number of issues and the number of States.

Amendment: One Issue Each

However, once the Constitution is established, each amendment would be brought forward separately. Compromises on other points would not be necessary. The will of the required number would decide the issue. Whenever ten States want an amendment, that amendment will become part of the Constitution.

---

[*] Entitled "An Address to the People of the State of New York."—PUBLIUS

[**] It is actually TEN. Two thirds may propose the measure, but three fourths must ratify.—PUBLIUS

Therefore, there is no comparison between the ease of adding an amendment and of establishing a complete Constitution.

National Rulers Must Allow Amendments

Opponents argue that it may be impossible to amend the Constitution after it is ratified. They argue that the people administrating the national government will not want to give up any of their authority once they have it.

When people carefully consider an amendment and decide that it should pass, I believe it will deal with the organization of the government, not to the extent of its powers. For this reason alone, people serving in the national government will not oppose it.

Also, governing thirteen States will be difficult. I believe national rulers will need to fulfill the reasonable expectations of their constituents.

But there is another consideration that proves the observation is wrong. It is this: the national rulers, whenever nine States concur, will have no option on the subject. By the fifth article of the Constitution, the Congress will be *obliged* "on the application of the legislatures of two thirds of the States (currently, nine), to call a convention for proposing amendments, which *shall be valid*, to all intents and purposes, as part of the Constitution, when ratified by the legislatures of three fourths of the States, or by conventions in three fourths thereof."

The words of this article are peremptory. The Congress "*shall* call a convention." Nothing is left to the discretion of Congress. Consequently, all the arguments about the disinclination to a change vanish.

It may be difficult to unite two thirds or three fourths of the States in amendments that affect local interests. However, such a difficulty cannot be feared on issues that effect the general liberty or security of the people. The State legislatures will block encroachments by the national government.

Ratification Before Amending

If the forgoing argument is a fallacy, then I am deceived by it. It is one of those rare cases where a political truth can be mathematically tested. People who zealously want amendments must agree that the Constitution must be ratified first.

Delicate Balance of Creating Constitution

The people who want to amend the Constitution before it is established must stop if they agree with the following observations of a writer equally solid and ingenious.[*]

"To balance a large state or society (says he), whether monarchical or republican, on general laws, is a work of so great difficulty, that no human genius, however comprehensive, is able, by using only reason and reflection, to do it. The judgments of many must unite in the work; Experience must guide their labor; Time must bring it to perfection, and the feeling of inconveniences must correct the mistakes which *inevitably* are seen during their first trials and experiments."

These wise thoughts contain a lesson of moderation to all the sincere lovers of the Union. They should guard against hazarding anarchy, civil war, a perpetual alienation

---

[*] Hume's *Essays*, vol. I, page 128: "The Rise of Arts and Sciences."—PUBLIUS

of the States from each other, and perhaps the military despotism of a victorious demagogue, while they pursue what they can only learn from time and experience. I may lack political fortitude, but I believe that it is dangerous to continue in our present situation.

A nation without a national government is an awful spectacle. The establishment of a Constitution, during peacetime, by the voluntary consent of a whole people, is an extraordinary accomplishment. I look forward to its completion with trembling anxiety.

I can think of no reason to let go of the hold we now have on this arduous an enterprise. Seven out of the thirteen States have ratified the Constitution. There is no reason to start over again. I dread the consequences of new attempts because I know that powerful individuals, in this and in other States, are enemies of any national government.

Done in Convention by the unanimous Consent of the States present the Seventeenth day of September in the Year of our Lord one thousand seven hundred and Eighty seven and of the Independence of the United States of American the Twelfth In Witness whereof We have hereunto subscribed our Names,

338

```
12,15]     5
[6,12,15] 170
[10-11]   285
[12]        1
[12]        3
[6-7, 12-end] 283


Number 16
[1-6]     284
[7]        52
[10]       27
[10]      327
[10]       84
[11]       19
 [7-end]  286


Number 17
[1]       192
[2]        83
[2]        84


Number 18
[14]      205
[9-10, 18] 64


Number 19
[4, 16]   205
[7,10-11] 171
[14]       54
[16]      210


Number 20
[4,14-16,
   22]    171
[4]       210
[5]       264
[18]       69


Number 21
[1-9]       6
[3-5]     323
[4]        83
[5]        27
[6-11]    171
[6-7]     192
[11]      110


Number 22
```

```
[13]      103
[1-4]     194
[14-15]   287
[1-7,14-18] 8
[17]      225
[17]      331
[17]       97
[2, 4]    202
[2]       193
[2-3]     199
[4]       231
[4]       237
[5-6]     212
[7-13]    110
[7-9]      97


Number 23
[3]         1
[3]       193
[3]       200
[3]       202
[4]       210
[6-8]     173
[7, 8]    217
[7]       187
[7-8]     213
[9]       189
[11]       27
[all]      54


Number 24
[3-4]     213
[11]      219
[12]      204
[12-13]   224
[13]      218
[all]     180


Number 25
[1]        56
[2,5]      57
[3]        83
[4]       213
[4]       238
[5-8]     210
[7]        78
[8]       219
[9]        78
[all]     182
```

```
Number 26
[11]       74
[13]      263
[14]      219
[2, 11]    28
[2, 4-6, 13]  78
[2]        56
[2]        67
[2-end]   185
[6]       211
[9-10, 13]214


Number 27
[2]       125
[2]       131
[6]       328


Number 28
[2, 3, 4]  219
[4]        52
[7]        28
[8]        71


Number 29
[3,7,9,11] 79
[4]       225
[7]        71
[11]      178
[all]     220


Number 30
[1,6,8,10]178
[1]       214
 [1-2, 5-6,
   8,10]  160
[3-5,
   7-8]   173
[6, 7]    177
[8]       211
[10]      189


Number 31
[1]       212
[10]      166
[12]       28
[5-8]     160
[6]        56
```

Number 32
[1, 2, 3]   231
[1, 3-4]   166
[1-3]   237
[2]   204
[2]   223
[2]   234
[5]   84

Number 33
[1-6]   225
[3, 4, 8]   167
[6]   28
[7-8]   328
[8]   232
[8]   237

Number 34
[1]   237
[4, 5]   56
[4,6-7,9]   214
[4]   190
[4]   218
[7]   261
[8]   179
[all]   167

Number 35
[1-4]   161
[2-4]   177
[5]   115
[6-11]   105

Number 36
[1-2]   107
[3-16]   162
[6, 9]   112
[9]   114
[9]   188
[10]   174
[13]   178
[13]   238

Number 37
[1-2]   14
[2-end]   20
[6]   28

[10]   301

Number 38
[4]   80
[5]   331
[5-9]   22
[7]   112
[7]   123
[7]   132
[7]   140
[7]   164
[7]   239
[7]   272
[7]   81
[9]   73
[9]   189
[9]   229
[9]   236
[9-10]   174
[9,10]   179
[11]   69

Number 39
[4]   28
[5, 12]   103
[5, 12]   258
[5]   125
[5]   126
[5]   246
[5]   282
[5]   294
[6]   233
[6]   323
[10-11]   331
[12]   123
[14]   301
[15]   325
[all]   90

Number 40
[11]   205
[13,19]   332
[15]   84
[16]   11
[16]   57
[all]   15

Number 41

[5]   1
[5-12]   65
[6, 21]   222
[6]   179
[6]   215
[9-11, 16-17,18]   212
[9-11,19]   218
[6, 8]   210
[13-14. 18]   80
[14-15, 18,26]   44
[15]   70
[17]   99
[22]   178
[22]   189
[22]   200
[22-23]   164
[23-end]   188
[26]   67
[26]   233

Number 42
[1, 5]   208
[1, 7-8]   229
[1]   200
[3-4]   280
[9-12, 18, 20]   202
[10, 13]   204
[10, 14-15, 16]   205
[10, 15]   206
[10, 17]   204
[10, 18]   205
[10, 20]   207
[11]   193
[11]   232
[11]   238
[11-13]   194
[17]   320
[19]   319

Number 43
[2-3]   207
[4-5]   223
[6]   215
[6]   225

[8]	318
[10]	322
[12]	322
[14]	323
[18]	229
[22-24]	179
[25-26]	325
[26]	123
[28-31]	332
[30]	58

Number 44
[2, 4-5]	206
[2, 3]	210
[3]	235
[4]	235
[5]	236
[6]	230
[6]	233
[6]	236
[6]	236
[8]	203
[8]	232
[8]	238
[10-17]	227
[17]	302
[19-23]	329
[25-26]	330
[26]	103
[26]	125
[26]	258

Number 45
[2]	45
[2]	52
[2]	58
[2]	70
[2]	188
[2]	225
[7]	103
[7]	125
[7]	258
[8]	222
[9]	201
[10]	56
[11]	175
[11]	188
[11]	193
[11]	212

Number 46
[1 ,6]	28
[9]	222

Number 47
[2]	81
[2-8]	81
[3]	71
[3]	97
[6-7]	117
[7]	132
[7-9]	293
[13-15,17]	239
[19]	218

Number 48
[2,4-13,15,16]	95
[4]	73
[4-5]	76
[5]	74
[6]	165
[11]	309
[15]	240
[15]	240

Number 49
[3]	29

Number 50
[2, 3, 8]	97
[10]	71

Number 51
[1, 6]	97
[2, 10]	71
[2]	294
[2]	82
[3]	150
[3]	261
[4, 9, 10]	29
[4]	1
[4]	4
[4]	84
[6]	151
[6]	155
[10]	47

Number 52
[2]	103
[3]	105
[3]	330
[4-5, 8-9]	99
[5]	74

Number 53
[2]	29
[2]	329
[2]	84
[4, 5, 9]	107
[5, 6]	203
[5]	165
[5]	201
[5]	222
[7]	209
[10]	148
[all]	100

Number 54
[1-10]	112
[4, 5]	229
[4]	82
[7, 9]	104
[8]	58
[11]	109

Number 55
[1-3]	109
[4, 7]	102
[6]	114
[7]	75
[9]	150
[9]	74

Number 56
[4, 8]	222
[4-6]	203
[6]	178

Number 57
[1-4]	108
[3, 6-10]	107
[5, 14-17]	104
[6]	330
[11]	102
[12-13, 21]	75

Number 58
[1-14]   115
[4]   114
[6]   123
[8, 12] 151
[14]   147
[15]   148

Number 59
[6]   125
[7]   25
[8]   123
[8]   126
[8]   128
[8]   148
[10]   46
[all]   140

Number 60
[3, 11] 104
[3,4,8] 125
[3]   108
[7]   203
[9]   193
[11]   105
[11]   130
[all]   142

Number 61
[1, 3]   72
[all]   145

Number 62
[10]   108
[11]   67
[12, 15] 75
[12,14,15,
17,18]   126
[16-17] 193
[2]   105
[3]   126
[4-6]   123
[7-10,
12-end] 119
[2]   130

Number 63
[17]   71
[1-9,12, 15-17,
21]   120
63 [3-6] 127
63 [7]   75

Number 64
[3]   196
[3-4,14-15]131
[3-4]   126
[3-4]   258
[3-8,
10-15]   266
[4, 15] 259
[4]   131
[5]   128
[5]   128
[6]   194
[11]   327
[14]   209

Number 65
[1]   272
[11]   25
[5]   118
[7,8]   138
[8]   317
[9]   138
[all]   132

Number 66
[2, 7]   118
[2]   138
[2]   152
[2]   155
[4-5, 8-9]272
[4, 10-12]268
[7]   151
[7]   258
[12]   126
[all]   135

Number 67
[2-5]   245
[5-end] 278
[6-11]   129
[10]   126

Number 68
[0]   259
[10]   132
[all]   255

Number 69
[2]   240
[3]   247
[4]   138
[4]   282
[5]   152
[6, 11] 210
[6, 11] 263
[6]   149
[6]   212
[6]   218
[6]   223
[6]   264
[6]   280
[6]   318
[7]   201
[7, 11] 269
[8]   281
[9]   233
[9]   277
[10-11] 246
[11]   197
[11]   206

Number 70
[1]   47
[1-2,
21-22]   76
[4]   261
[15]   138
[all]   240

Number 71
[1]   250
[3]   280
[4]   293
[7]   77
[all]   247

Number 72
[1]   215
[1]   233
[1]   277
[13]   80

[all]   250

Number 73
[1-2]   261
[4]   155
[4-end]   152
[15]   293

Number 74
[1]   218
[1]   223
[1]   264
[3-5]   265
[4]   318
[4]   318

Number 75
[4]   259
[4]   281
[7]   128
[7]   132
[all]   270

Number 76
[1]   279
[2-end]   273
[4]   259

Number 77
[1-8]   275
[9]   149
[9]   280
[9]   280
[9]   280
[9]   281
[10]   272
[11]   258

Number 78
[5-end]   294
[6]   76
[7]   264

[8]   82
[9]   230
[10-15]   329
[13]   29
[18]   11
[18]   47

Number 79
[1-2]   262
[1-4]   299
[2]   249
[4]   118
[4]   137
[4]   298

Number 80
[1-2,5-11,
  15-21] 303
[2-4,
13-14]   302
[2, 6, 10] 209
[3, 13]   206
[3]   235
[3]   238
[8]   322
[22]   306

Number 81
[1. 3-end]287
[3, 9]   138
[5]   302
[5]   330
[9]   298
[10-14]   207
[21-23]   309
[23]   306

Number 82
[1]   25
[2-end]   307

Number 83
[7]   228
[8]   307
[12]   230
[13-16]   165
[14]   112
[17]   298
[23]   209
[32]   333
[all]   309

Number 84
[4-5]   230
[5]   233
[5]   73
[6]   233
[8, 10]   29
[8]   27
[10-11]   72
[13-15]   223
[18]   46
[21]   262
[21]   300
[22]   272
[22-23]   98
[23]   175
[footnote 3]166

Number 85
[2]   253
[3]   66
[3]   46
[3]   48
[3]   225
[3]   233
[3]   324
[4]   72
[5]   58
[7-8,15]   25
[9-10,
  12-13] 325
[all]   333

8410101R0

Made in the USA
Lexington, KY
03 February 2011